The Theological Education of the Ministry

The Theological Education of the Ministry

Soundings in the British Reformed and Dissenting Traditions

ALAN P. F. SELL

☙PICKWICK *Publications* • Eugene, Oregon

THE THEOLOGICAL EDUCATION OF THE MINISTRY
Soundings in the British Reformed and Dissenting Traditions

Copyright © 2013 Alan P. F. Sell. All rights reserved. Except for brief quotations in critical publications or reviews, no part of this book may be reproduced in any manner without prior written permission from the publisher. Write: Permissions, Wipf and Stock Publishers, 199 W. 8th Ave., Suite 3, Eugene, OR 97401.

Pickwick Publications
An Imprint of Wipf and Stock Publishers
199 W. 8th Ave., Suite 3
Eugene, OR 97401

www.wipfandstock.com

ISBN 13: 978-1-62032-593-3

Cataloguing-in-Publication data:

Sell, Alan P. F.

The theological education of the ministry : soundings in the British reformed and dissenting traditions / Alan P. F. Sell.

xiv + 314 pp. ; 23 cm. Includes bibliographical references and indexes.

ISBN 13: 978-1-62032-593-3

1. Theology—Study and teaching—Great Britain. 2. Religious education—Great Britain. 3. Dissenters, Religious—Great Britain. 4. Reformed Church—Great Britain. I. Title.

BV4020 S4 2013

Manufactured in the USA

The cover illustration is of Lancashire Independent College, Manchester (1843–1958). © Mr. Mike Widdas. Source English Heritage.

In Memoriam

George William Curry (1900–1991)

Dales Minister *extraordinaire*

εἰς ἔργον διακονίας (Ephesians 4:12)
—The motto of Lancashire Independent College,
Manchester (1843–1958)

"It is too often forgotten that the ideal ministerial education is not to send a man out with some knowledge of every subject he will afterwards find useful. It is to send him out with a mind that can tackle with success any subject as the need arises."

—Robert Sleightholme Franks (1871–1964),
Principal of Western (Congregational) College, Bristol

Contents

Preface   ix

1   Introduction   1

2   Caleb Ashworth of Daventry: His Church, Academy and Students   5

3   Scottish Religious Philosophy, 1850–1900   57

4   Living in the Half Lights: John Oman in Context   84

5   Clarity, Precision, and on towards Comprehension: The Intellectual Legacy of N. H. G. Robinson (1912–1978)   154

6   Geoffrey Nuttall in Conversation   177

7   Is Geoffrey also among the Theologians?   211

8   A Valued Inheritance of New Testament Scholarship   265

Bibliographical Appendix   291

Index of Persons   295

Index of Educational Establishments   307

Index of Subjects   311

Preface

I HAVE LONG HAD a general interest in education and, more particularly, in theological education and the preparation of ministers. As the Introduction following will make clear, in this book I have gathered together some of my studies of the varied institutions in which British Reformed and Dissenting ministers were theologically educated, and of some of the principals, professors and lecturers who devoted themselves to that task. For the present I wish first to thank those who have given permission to reprint papers that have been published in widely scattered places. I have updated references where necessary, and I leave to textual critics the challenge of discovering which chapter contains a substantial quotation which did not appear in the original published version because I was in danger of exceeding the permitted number of words. Secondly, I shall thank those involved in the publication of this book. Thirdly, I shall pay brief tribute to George Curry, to whose memory the book is dedicated.

An abbreviated version of Chapter 2, on Caleb Ashworth, was delivered at the Summer Event of the Friends of the Congregational Library held at Dr. Williams's Library, London, on 12 June 2010. I am grateful to the Friends' committee for their kind invitation. The paper is published here for the first time.

The provenance of chapters 3 to 8 is as follows. "Scottish Religious Philosophy," written at the invitation of Dr. William Mander of Harris Manchester College Oxford as a contribution to the *Oxford Handbook of British Philosophy in the Nineteenth Century* (2013), appears here by kind permission of Oxford University Press. Chapter 4, on John Oman, is in Adam Hood, ed., *John Oman: New Perspectives*, Milton Keynes, UK: Paternoster, 2012. I thank Dr. Hood for inviting me to present an abbreviated version of this paper at an Oman colloquium at Westminster College, Cambridge, in September 2009, and Dr. Michael Parsons of Paternoster, for permission to reprint it in full.

Chapter 5, on N. H. G. Robinson, first appeared in a *Festschrift* for my friend and colleague of Calgary days, Dr. Irving Hexham: Ulrich van

Preface

der Heyden and Andreas Feldtkeller, eds, *Border Crossings: Explorations of an Interdisciplinary Historian. Festschrift for Irving Hexham*, Stuttgart: Franz Steiner Verlag, 2008. Permission to reprint has been granted by the publisher. Chapters 6 and 7, on Geoffrey Nuttall, first appeared (the latter in two parts) in *The Journal of the United Reformed Church History Society*, 8 (November 2009), 8 (November 2011), 8 (May 2012), whose editor, Professor Clyde Binfield, has kindly consented to their being reprinted here. I was honoured to be invited to contribute my recollections of my teachers of New Testament to the *Festschrift* of Professor Zsolt Geréb of the Protestant Theological Institute, Cluj/Kolosvár, Romania. It appears in the celebratory issue of *Studia Doctorum Theologia Protestantis*, 1, Kolosvár: Protestant Theological Institute, 2011, and is reprinted, as chapter 8, by kind permission of Dezső Kállay.

A bibliography follows every chapter, and a Bibliographical Appendix follows chapter 8. In the latter I have supplied the names of all the English and Welsh Dissenting and Nonconformist theological teachers on whom I have written, and in a footnote I have referred to some Anglicans, Scots and one Irishman who have not escaped my net.

Far from being a mere formality, it is a great pleasure to thank Dr. K. C. Hanson, Dr. Robin Parry, Christian Amondson, and their colleagues at Wipf and Stock for once again serving me so well with their prompt attention and professional expertise. Nor is it a mere formality to thank my wife, Dr. Karen Sell, who features regularly in my prefatory expressions of thanks because she is such a constant encourager of the several aspects of my work.

I dedicate this book to the memory of the Reverend George William Curry (1900–1991). A larger than life character, his enthusiasm for the gospel was infectious, his preaching was gripping, and his pastoral care was exemplary. Following an engineering apprenticeship in Sunderland, his ministry began in 1920 among the Methodists as a horse-back circuit rider in Saskatchewan, from which rigorous pursuit he returned to the gentler Isle of Wight, removing thence to Mount Tabor Church, Sunderland. Having become persuaded of the Congregational Way, he trained for the ministry at Yorkshire United College, Bradford, and was ordained in 1937. There followed ministries in Newport Pagnell, Bolton, and Newcastle-upon-Tyne. By the time my wife and I met him he was the Dales Minister. This post gave him a roving commission as a resource to churches scattered over wide area of rural Yorkshire, which territory he traversed, at hair-raising speed, in a Mini, the boot of which was weighed down with sizeable rocks during winter snow and ice by way of aiding traction. It was through him that we came to our first pastorate at Sedbergh and Dent. I could have had no better companion in ministry. George never interfered, but was always available. He was as happy photographing birds on the Isle of Skye as he was photographing three babies on their successive arrival in our manse. His final pastorate was in the Dales, at Grassington. He was "an all round good egg" (not that, as a down-to-earth north-easterner, he would have countenanced such a high falutin' Wodehousian expression). He gave me two pieces of advice. The first was spoken with such a twinkle in his eye that I knew that he did not follow it, and that he did not expect me to follow it either: "Do thorough exegesis for all your sermons in your first pastorate, and you'll never have to bother with exegesis again!" The second was more to the point: "Know when it matters! If you turn every trifling bugbear into a question of high principle, the church members will never know when you really think that something significant is at stake." Thanks be to God for one whose like we shall not see again.

Alan P. F. Sell
University of Wales Trinity Saint David, U.K.

Abbreviations

BTL	*Better Than Life: The Lovingkindness of God*
CC	*Christ and Conscience*
CCPD	*Calendar of the Correspondence of Philip Doddridge, DD, (1702–1751)*
CHST	*Congregational Historical Society Transactions*
CM	*The Claim of Morality*
CPH	*Christian Pacifism in History*
CQ	*The Congregational Quarterly*
CYB	*The Congregational Year Book*
DECBP	*Dictionary of Eighteenth-Century British Philosophers*
DMBI	*A Dictionary of Methodism in Britain and Ireland*
DNCBP	*Dictionary of Nineteenth-Century British Philosophers*
DSCHT	*Dictionary of Scottish Church History and Theology*
DTCBP	*Dictionary of Twentieth-Century British Philosophers*
DVURC	Daventry United Reformed Church (records at NRO)
FD	*Faith and Duty*
GCE	*The Groundwork of Christian Ethics*
HMSO	Her Majesty's Stationery Office
HSO	*The Holy Spirit and Ourselves*
HSPFE	*The Holy Spirit in Puritan Faith and Experience*
JURCHS	*Journal of The United Reformed Church History Society*
NCL.MSS	New College London Manuscripts
NRO.MSS	Northamptonshire Record Office Manuscripts
ODNB	*Oxford Dictionary of National Biography*
PS	*The Puritan Spirit*
RB	*Richard Baxter*
RH	*The Reality of Heaven*
URCYB	*The United Reformed Church Year Book*

Abbreviations

VS	*Visible Saints*
WTW	*Who They Were*
WWW	*Who Was Who*

1

Introduction

WHEN PURITANS THOUGHT OF a learned ministry, they characteristically thought of one learned in the things of God. This by no means precluded a concern for the education of ministerial candidates in relevant disciplines. When, between 1660 and 1662 (the Great Ejectment) some 2,000 ministers resigned, or were dismissed from, their livings because of their conscientious inability to give their "unfeigned assent and consent" to the *Book of Common Prayer*, and to use it only in worship, the question arose, How may we provide a higher education for our young men who will not submit to the religious tests imposed by the Universities of Oxford and Cambridge? They answered by establishing Dissenting academies, which were open both to those destined for the Dissenting ministry, and to those whose career aspirations led them in other directions. The earliest tutors had themselves been schooled at Oxford or Cambridge. For example, John Woodhouse (c. 1627–1700), who conducted a significant academy at Sheriffhales from 1676 to 1697, was an alumnus of Trinity College, Cambridge, while Matthew Warren (1642?–1706), of St. John's College Oxford, was in charge of the Taunton Academy from 1687 until his death. None, however, lived more dangerously than Richard Frankland (1630–1698), who had studied at Christ's College Cambridge. His academy, begun at Rathmell in 1670 was, owing to authorities intent upon persecution, forced into a peripatetic existence. He removed with his academy on four occasions until 1689 when, with the arrival of the Toleration Act on the statute book, he returned to Rathmell. Despite the difficulties under which he worked he educated no fewer that 304 students, many of whom became the mainstay of the Dissenting ministry in the north of England, while some made a name for themselves as far afield as London.

The Theological Education of the Ministry

It might be thought that with the passing of the Toleration Act in 1689 the way ahead for Dissent would be eased, and to a certain extent it was. Orthodox Protestant Dissenters could now worship according to their consciences, build meeting houses, and establish academies. But they were still second-class citizens, barred from the professions. Moreover, throughout the eighteenth century there were those who wished to turn back the clock of toleration, not least where the work of the Dissenting academies was concerned. In this context Caleb Ashworth conducted his significant Daventry Academy—the successor to that of Philip Doddridge at Northampton. Chapter 2 comprises the first full account of Ashworth's work and influence, and it may represent the continuance into the eighteenth century of the Dissenting academies after the original pattern—albeit Doddridge had introduced teaching through the medium of English rather than Latin, and Ashworth followed suit.

In chapter 3 we proceed to the nineteenth century and cross the border to Scotland, with its strong philosophical tradition in which many ministerial candidates were schooled. In the absence of some acquaintance with this intellectual background it is harder to appreciate the context in which John Oman (chapter 4) and N. H. G. Robinson (chapter 5) learned their trade. Oman taught at the college of the Presbyterian Church of England—a theological college as distinct from a Dissenting academy—which, on its removal to Cambridge took the name Westminster College, and became closely related to the University. Norman Robinson was professor in the Faculty of Divinity at Scotland's senior university, St. Andrews, at a time when such faculties educated a high proportion of ministers for Scotland and further afield, and did so within the university, rather than the seminary, context.

Returning to England, we come to two chapters on Geoffrey Nuttall, the most distinguished and meticulous historian of Puritanism and Dissent of the twentieth century. He spent his teaching career at New College, London, the Congregational College which resulted from the amalgamation in 1850 of Coward, Highbury and Homerton Colleges. It came to be associated with the University of London; students read for London degrees, and the full-time tutors were members of the Faculty of Theology. The College closed in 1976. Charles Duthie was its last Principal, and the distinguished alumnus from the days of P. T. Forsyth's principalship, H. F. Lovell Cocks, preached the closing sermon.[1]

---

1. For Duthie and Lovell Cocks see the Bibliographical Appendix below.

Introduction

For the final chapter we head north to Manchester, where Lancashire Independent College was established in 1843, in succession to Blackburn Independent Academy, which had been founded in 1816. In December 1903 the University of Manchester resolved to inaugurate a Faculty of Theology, the first academic session of which began in 1904. This was "the first entirely free faculty in the kingdom in which theological instruction formed a part of the regular curriculum of the University itself."[2] Religious tests were eschewed, from the outset provision was made for women to take theological degrees, and the Faculty pioneered the study of comparative religion and, later, Christian ethics. The eight theological colleges in the city in 1904 were involved in the Faculty's work. The University appointed its own scholars, A. S. Peake among them, and also drew upon such distinguished theological college colleagues as J. T. Marshall (Baptist), W. H. Bennett, W. F. Adeney and Robert Mackintosh (Congregationalists), J. H. Moulton (Methodist) and Alexander Gordon (Unitarian).[3] The New Testament scholars recalled in this chapter epitomize the easy relationship between the University and the theological colleges at the middle of the twentieth century; for while T. W. Manson held the Rylands Chair of Biblical Criticism and Exegesis, W. Gordon Robinson, Owen Evans and Eric Hull all taught both in the theological colleges of their denominations and in the University. Of these, Evans, the Methodist, is the sole non-Reformed/Dissenting scholar to figure significantly in this book.

The soundings taken here indicate the variety of ways in which British Reformed and Dissenting Christians sought, in significantly different socio-political contexts, to educate a confessing ministry: from the early academies offering a general higher education to young men, through the free-standing theological colleges, to the various permutations of college-university relations. In such places a learned ministry was sought and frequently achieved.[4] But while, in what follows, appropriate reference will be made to a significant academy, and to some colleges and universities, this is not primarily a history of institutions. Rather, the emphasis is upon a selection of those whose vocation[5] it was to educate ministerial

2. Parsons, "The Commemoration of the Twenty-fifth Anniversary," 53.

3. For Bennett, Adeney and Mackintosh see the Bibliographical Appendix below. The scholars discussed in this book will also be found therein.

4. I do not overlook the fact that some Nonconformist denominations provided non-collegiate routes into the ministry. In my experience some of those recruited in this way were gifted preachers and devoted pastors. To the best of my knowledge, this is a field which remains to be tilled by scholars.

5. Note to those who have ears to hear: it was not a "job," still less a stage within, or the culminaton of, a personally-devised, progressive, "ministerial career plan"!

candidates in these diverse contexts; and it will be noted that the scholars on whom I have concentrated: Ashworth, Oman, Norman Robinson, Nuttall, Manson, Gordon Robinson, Owen Evans and Eric Hull, between them represent what I continue to regard as the core disciplines where the theological education of the ministry is concerned: biblical studies, ecclesiastical history, philosophy, doctrine and systematic theology.

BIBLIOGRAPHY

Parsons, R. G. "The Commemoration of the Twenty-fifth Anniversary of the Establishment of the Theological Faculty in the University of Manchester with Some Reference to Its Origins and History." *Bulletin of the John Rylands Library* 14 (1930) 53–58.

2

Caleb Ashworth of Daventry
His Academy, Church, and Students

IF THE ETERNAL DESTINATION of parents is to any degree conditional upon the adoption by their offspring of correct doctrinal views then Richard and Mrs. Ashworth had some of the most prominent bases covered; for their son Thomas became a Particular Baptist minister, John a General Baptist minister, and Caleb a Congregational or Independent minister. Richard himself is said by Alexander Gordon and W. N. Terry[1] to have been a Particular Baptist lay preacher, and, no doubt, they are reliant upon Caleb Ashworth's student, Samuel Palmer, who uses that phrase;[2] but the relevant records refer to him as pastor and minister. He was born in 1667, and on a document of 11 February 1705 that records Robert Litchford's donation of a building in Clough Fold to the Baptists, he is listed among the trustees as Richard Ashworth of Tunstead.[3] He subsequently lived at Carr House, near Rawtenstall, Lancashire, about a mile and a half from Clough Fold in Rossendale. In 1699 Richard had assumed a position of leadership in what was known as "the Church of Christ in Rossendale."[4] This was a group of scattered Particular Baptist causes which included Clough Fold, Bacup and Tottlebank in Lancashire, and extended into the Yorkshire towns of Bradford, Rawdon and Keighley. By 1705 Richard

---

1. See "Caleb Ashworth," in *The Oxford Dictionary of National Biography* (hereinafter ODNB).
2. Palmer, "Memoir of Dr. Caleb Ashworth," 693.
3. For the document see Parry, *History of the Cloughfold Baptist Church*, 145. Hardman draws on this book in his article, "Caleb Ashworth of Cloughfold and Daventry."
4. See Overend, *History of the Ebenezer Baptist Church, Bacup*, 111, 112.

Ashworth was listed among the trustees of the group. In 1715, by which time he was designated pastor of the Rossendale church and addressed as 'the Reverend', he and others conveyed to a meeting at Rawdon the names of members who wished to be dismissed from the Rossendale roll with a view to forming a new church at Rawdon and Heaton, where they lived. On 28 August in the same year he and others signed a document dismissing further Rossendale members with a view to constituting a further church at Gildersome, Yorkshire.[5]

A glimpse of the worship at Clough Fold was recounted to Palmer by Caleb Ashworth in the following terms: the congregation, "carrying the matter of extemporaneous devotion to such a length as not to allow of singing pre-composed hymns, required [Richard Ashworth] to deliver extempore ones, line by line, with which requisition he continued to comply for some years: in what manner [Palmer drily adds], and with what success, I presume not to say, and leave your readers to judge."[6]

The Clough Fold church had been inaugurated in 1675, and from 1695 the Baptist causes in Rossendale had been in fellowship with one another. But in 1718 Richard Ashworth, who is described as "a man of considerable ability,"[7] was instrumental in organizing an Association, which first met at Rawdon in May 1719. Messengers from seven churches were present and on this occasion, and at three subsequent meetings, Ashworth was elected Moderator, Association Preacher, and Letter Writer. A Calvinistic confession of faith was adopted, and such topics as closed communion, hymn singing and the place of women in decision-making were discussed. Following the first meeting there was circulated *The Letter to the Churches of the Lancashire and Yorkshire Association, 1719. Drawn up by the hand of Richard Ashworth*. Replete with biblical quotations and references, pastors and people are exhorted to be faithful in their duties and, not least, "to spend one day weekly in prayer and supplication, as everyone's convenience may allow, by meeting together or retiring into our closets, or with our families, or in the frame and temper of our mind—which last especially may be done by all, without exception . . ."[8]

---

5. For the churches planted from Clough Fold see Parry, *History of the Cloughfold Baptist Church*, ch. 9.

6. Palmer, "Memoir of Dr. Caleb Ashworth," 693.

7. Wylie, *The Baptist Churches of Accrington and District*, 2.

8. Quoted by Parry, *A History of the Cloughfold Baptist Church*, 90. The letter is reproduced in its entirety, ibid., 86–90.

Caleb Ashworth of Daventry

We may suppose that the confession of faith adopted was the Particular Baptist *Second London Confession* of 1677/1689, and that moderate Calvinism was the order of the day at Clough Fold. This would seem to be confirmed by the fact that, as we shall see, the evangelical moderate Calvinist, Alvery Jackson of Barnoldswick, had good relations with Richard Ashworth; and above all by the fact that in the 1719 *Letter to the Churches* Ashworth included such a tellingly anti-antinomian charge to the ministers as the following: "Let ministers and all gifted brethren 'declare the whole counsel of God', and compel sinners to come in by proclaiming salvation and the terms of it. A minister thus moulded cannot miscarry in his work. He will certainly succeed to some comfortable degree . . . [and] shall have his crown and reward of his labour."[9]

The Association gathered for it third session at Bacup on 7–8 June 1721, and Ashworth is designated minister of that church. At the previous meeting he had been charged with preparing a statement addressing the question of "the propriety of administering the Lord's Supper to a dying person unbaptized."[10] Ashworth read his carefully-argued and biblically-based paper to the messengers at Bacup, concluding that "whatever countenance soever our answer, rightly considered, gives to such a practice, it is rather intended as a harbour for the humble broken soul after shipwreck than a port for the presumptuous."[11] He delivered a sermon on Malachi 3:14; 1:13; and Job 21:17 at the Sutton meeting of the Association, in 1724, and following that gathering records cease.[12] The Association gradually weakened, and ceased *circa* 1738. By that year Richard Ashworth, who now had the help of his son Thomas, was losing his sight.[13] Formal gatherings of Baptists in the area were not resumed until 1787, when the Yorkshire and Lancashire Association was constituted. At its third meeting, held at Clough Fold in 1789, the writer of the Circular Letter was Thomas Ashworth.

The Baptist cause at Bacup gave one of its sons to the metropolis, for on 19 August 1716 Thomas Dewhurst, became a member of the Turners' Hall Particular Baptist Church, London, and on the 29th of the same

---

9. Ibid., 88; cf. ibid., 112–13.

10. Ibid., 91.

11. Ibid.,97.

12. So Parry, ibid. But Whitley had in his possession a copy of the 1738 circular letter. See his *Baptists of North-West England*, 101.

13. See Overend, *History of the Ebenezer Baptist Church, Bacup*, 126–27; Sellers, *Our Heritage*, 12–13.

month he was ordained to the ministry there. On that occasion the charge to the church was delivered by the High Calvinist John Skepp; and further evidence of Dewhurst's doctrinal inclinations are seen when, in 1719, he joined the list of subscribers to the statement devised at the Salters' Hall conference.[14] The conference participants differed over whether doctrine of the Trinity, which had by then been under discussion for some decades, should be formally subscribed to or not.[15]

In 1724 the Baptist work in Rossendale was divided, when David Crosley became pastor at Bacup, while Ashworth remained at Clough Fold.[16] In March 1745 an appeal was launched for a new meeting house at Bacup, and to this fund Richard Ashworth contributed £5/0/0. Such was the success of the appeal that building work began four months later, in July. Richard Ashworth died on 28 May 1751, in his seventy-fourth year. Alvery Jackson delivered the funeral sermon, and the burial took place in the garden of Carr House.

Thomas the Particular Baptist was the eldest of Richard Ashworth's ministerial sons. Having assisted his father at Clough Fold he succeeded him there and remained until 1755. On 26 June of that year he was ordained at Gildersome. He is said to have been "a man of great piety and an amiable temper. He continued a Baptist, and was many years the pastor of a Calvinistical congregation, at Heckmondwick [sic], in Yorkshire. Though he possessed no great share of learning, and was remarkably plain in his manner and appearance, he was a very useful preacher, and his prayers were peculiarly excellent."[17]

---

14. See Wilson, *The History and Antiquities of Dissenting Churches*, I, 144–45. John Butterworth (1727–1803) of Goodshaw was greatly impressed by John Wesley's preaching in Rossendale in 1745, and by that of other Methodist preachers but, being a Calvinist, he was baptized by Richard Ashworth. He was called to the pastorate of Jordan Well Baptist Church, Coventry, where he remained until his death. He compiled a Bible concordance, and in 1793 a larger chapel was built for his congregation in Cow Lane. See Sibree and Caston, *Independency in Warwickshire*, 114–15. George Burder wrote a memoir of Butterworth in *Evangelical Magazine* (1804) 243–49. John and his three brothers were pupils of the school at Tatop Farm, near Goodshaw, conducted by David Crosley, the "Northern Baptist Apostle." James ministered at Bromsgrove, Lawrence at Bengeworth, Evesham, and Henry at Bridgnorth. Lawrence preached sermons on John 1:47 and Luke 2:29 on the Sunday following his brother's interment on 6 May 1803. See Langley, *Birmingham Baptists*, 28; Binfield, *Pastors and People*, 24–28.

15. See Sell, *Dissenting Thought*, ch. 5. ODNB, again relying upon Palmer, describes John Ashworth as a "colleague" of Foster's. He was, clearly, a friend, but as far as I can discover they were not at any time pastoral colleagues in the same church.

16. See Overend, *History of Ebenezer Baptist Church, Bacup*. 129, 252.

17. Palmer, "Memoir of Dr. Caleb Ashworth." 693.

Caleb Ashworth of Daventry

When the youngest ministerial son, John, then pastor of White's Alley General Baptist Church, London, died in 1742, James Foster delivered a funeral sermon in that church on the text, "All flesh is grass, and all the goodliness thereof is as the flower of the field" (Isaiah 40:6).[18] Foster had begun as a Presbyterian who sided with the non-subscribers at the Salters' Hall conference. In succession to John Gale, whose treatise against paedobaptism had persuaded Foster to turn believer Baptist, he became co-pastor of the General Baptist Church in Paul's Alley, Barbican, London; and, finally, he succeeded Jeremiah Hunt as minister of the Independent church at Pinners' Hall.[19] Of Foster it was said that he was "far gone in the Socinian scheme, and laid but little stress upon the peculiar doctrines of revelation."[20] It is almost unthinkable that John Ashworth would not have been in broad sympathy with his views, but there is no reference to doctrinally neuralgic matters in Foster's sermon. We are, however, informed by one who spoke from first-hand knowledge that with Ashworth's passing

> The *world* has lost a person of most diffusive, flowing, uncontroulable benevolence of nature . . . who was a bright example of *every* kind and friendly disposition, and of *all* the social virtues . . . a composer of unhappy differences and animosities among Christians . . . *Religion* has lost an able defender . . . and the cause

---

18. See Foster, *A Sermon Preached at White's-Alley, on Sunday, October 31, 1742. On Occasion of the Death of the Reverend Mr. John Ashworth*. A certain caution is required when reading about Rossendalian John Ashworths. In addition to Richard's son, Caleb's brother, there was a John Ashworth of Newchurch in Rossendale who, following the death of Joseph Cooke, became the leader of the Methodist Unitarians of north-east Lancashire. Chapels were built for Cooke (who in 1806 had been expelled from the Wesleyan Conference on doctrinal grounds) and Ashworth in Newchurch, Todmorden, and Rochdale (Providence). The Methodist Unitarians had close associations with the cooperative movement, the home of which was Rochdale, and this Ashworth was proud to say that "Unitarianism is *adapted to the poor.*" See McLachlan, *The Unitarian Home Missionary College*, 12; McLachlan, *Essays and Addresses*, ch. 13; Wilkinson, "The rise of other Methodist traditions," being ch. 7 of Davies, George and Rupp, *A History of the Methodist Church in Great Britain*, II, especially 326–29; Evans, *Vestiges of Protestant Dissent*, 185, 213; Herford and Evans, *Historical Sketch of the North and East Lancashire Unitarian Mission*, 105–8, 131; Anon., *The Unitarian Heritage*, 90. Another John Ashworth's mother was a founder member of the Baptist church at Lumb in Rossendale, where John was born. He was an "out and out Christian," who removed first to the church at Clough Fold, and thence to Accrington. "He died on November 18, 1917, aged 77, after an honourable record as Sunday school teacher for 55 years, and at the time of his death was one of the oldest deacons at Cannon-street Church." Wylie, *The Baptist Churches of Accrington and District*, 291.

19. For Foster (1697–1753) Gale (1680–1721) and Hunt (1678–1744) see ODNB.

20. Wilson, *The History and Antiquities of Dissenting Churches*, II, 279.

of *virtue* a warm and zealous advocate... *This church* has lost an affectionate and vigilant pastor, of serious piety, but unaffected and free from ostentation... a judicious preacher... who was indefatigable in his work, and *watched for the souls* of those that were under his care, as one who knew he must *give an account* ...[21]

If, as seems likely, John Ashworth and James Foster were likeminded, is certain that Philip Doddridge disagreed strongly with them. Indeed, this generally hospitable man refused to allow Foster into his pulpit;[22] and it was to Doddridge that the third of Richard Ashworth's ministerial sons, Caleb, was sent for his higher education, his father having been greatly impressed by Doddridge's book, *The Rise and Progress of Religion in the Soul* (1745).[23]

I

We have no firm date of birth for Caleb Ashworth, though we know that it took place at Clough Fold, near Rawtenstall, in Rossendale. We also know that on 25 September 1732 he was baptized at the age of twelve in the open-air baptistery near Carr House, the service being conducted by Alvery Jackson of Barnoldswick.[24] It is further clear that he died on 18 July 1775, and in a note in his funeral sermon for Ashworth, Samuel Palmer laments that at the time of his death Ashworth was "but fifty-three years of age."[25] To this the inscription on Ashworth's tomb in the Daventry churchyard adds a further year,[26] while the year of birth recorded by Coleman, 1719, would have made him fifty-five or fifty-six.[27] We are on safer ground in saying that in 1739 Caleb enrolled at Doddridge's academy in Northampton. The authors of Caleb's entry in *The Oxford Dictionary of*

---

21. Foster, *A Sermon Preached at White's Alley*, 25–27.

22. See his letter of 27 December 1737 to Samuel Clark of St. Albans, and Clark's reply of 6 January 1737/8. Clark said that he would refuse Foster only if he thought that his coming would distress the congregation. See Nuttall, *Calendar of the Correspondence of Philip Doddridge, DD* (hereinafter CCPD), nos. 479, 480.

23. See New College, London MSS (hereinafter NCL.MSS), L54/3/44.

24. A quotation from Alvery Jackson's diary confirms this date. The diary entry is quoted by Parry, *History of Clough Fold Baptist Church*, 98.

25. Palmer, *The Want of Labourers in the Gospel Harvest*, 2 n.

26. As does Thomas Taylor in his notes on the early history of Daventry Independent Church. See Northamptonshire Record Office (hereinafter NRO) DVURC 24, 1.

27. Coleman, *Memorials of the Independent Churches in Northamptonshire*. 195.

National Biography surmize that he "was probably not in sympathy with his father's religious views." I can find no evidence of this prior to his departure for Northampton, though it is "presumed" by Samuel Palmer that "he became a convert to Paedobaptism"[28] during his student days. The Baptist historian W. T. Whitley is bolder and less disinterested in informing us that Ashworth, who was baptized in 1732, was sent to study under Doddridge at Northampton, where "he inhaled too much of the atmosphere, and quitted the denomination."[29] Palmer adds that "I have in my possession several letters of [Ashworth's] relation to [the baptism] controversy, which he wrote to me on my application to him, when, in the early part of my ministry, I had some difficulties on that subject; and they were of considerable use in determining my judgment and practice."[30]

Doddridge had himself been educated under John Jennings at his academy at Kibworth.[31] In a letter to Samuel Clark of St. Albans of September 1722, Doddridge wrote, "Mr. Jennings encourages the greatest freedom of inquiry, and always inculcates it as a law, that the scriptures are the only genuine standard of faith . . . [he] does not follow the doctrines or phrases of any particular party; but is sometimes a Calvinist, sometimes an Arminian, and sometimes a Baxterian, as truth and evidence determine him."[32] This non-doctrinaire openness of mind which to the high Calvinist Abraham Taylor, for example, would surely have been denounced as ungodly wavering,[33] was carried forward by Doddridge into his teaching at his academy, which opened in Market Harborough in 1729, and removed with Doddridge to Northampton when he accepted the Pastorate of Castle Hill Congregational Church on 24 December in the same year. In 1732 Doddridge let it be known that he contemplated a seminary for ministerial candidates only, but David Jennings, John's brother, dissuaded him from

28. Palmer, "Memoir of Dr. Caleb Ashworth," 694. In Farrer and Brownbill, eds. *A History of the County of Lancaster* VI, Caleb Ashworth is wrongly described as a "Baptist divine," and DNB is cited. See 437–41 and n. 13.

29. Whitley, *Baptists of North-West England*, 143.

30. S. Palmer, "Memoir of Dr. Caleb Ashworth," 694.

31. For Jennings (d. 1723) see ODNB; H. McLachlan. *English Education under the Test Acts*. Manchester: Manchester University Press, 1931; Sell, *Philosophy, Dissent and Nonconformity*, 49–50. He had been educated under Timothy Jollie at Attercliffe. His daughter, Jane, married Doddridge's first student, John Aikin, later of Warrington Academy. John and David (for whom see below) Jennings were sons of John Jennings (1634–1701), who was ejected from Hartley Westpall, Hampshire, in 1662. See Matthews, *Calamy Revised*, 297; Gordon, *Freedom After Ejection*, 292.

32. Nuttall, CCPD, no. 35.

33. For Taylor (fl. 1721–1740) see Sell, *Hinterland Theology*, ch. 3, and *passim*.

this course on grounds financial and educational (in that order): "The support of our Interest," he wrote on 9 December, "comes from the Layity, and they will not be obliged to bring up all their Sons ministers or Dunces . . . Make your Rules of Discipline as strict as you please; . . . but make no Rules to exclude any that will submit to your orders."[34] He went on to say that unless this course were followed, students intending to become physicians or lawyers, or to live as gentlemen would either be sent to Oxford or Cambridge, or would become "rakes in the foreign universities."[35] It was thus that a general higher education became the firm objective at Doddridge's academy, and this tradition, as well as the open-minded approach to learning, was maintained by Caleb Ashworth at Daventry.

When Ashworth entered Northampton Academy the subjects on the curriculum ranged from Logic and Metaphysics through Algebra, Trigonometry and Conic Sections, to Anatomy, Jewish Antiquities, English History and Divinity.[36] In addition, Hebrew, Greek and Latin were taught in evening tutorials, and all was done through the medium of English, not Latin—a departure on Doddridge's part from established practice, and another matter on which Ashworth later followed his teacher at Daventry.

His studies completed, Ashworth removed in the summer of 1746 to Daventry as assistant to the minister, James Floyd, and by the end of the year he had become co-pastor. Of Floyd it is written that he was "not possessed of very acceptable talents as a preacher, (though very eminent in prayer)" and that "upon marrying a lady of considerable fortune, [he] gave up the pastoral charge, to which Mr. Ashworth was then chosen, and he had a flourishing congregation, which after some years required a new gallery to be erected."[37] During his student days Ashworth had met a Miss Hemmings of Northampton; they were married, and in due course had three sons and three daughters. Unlike Mrs. Floyd, Miss Hemmings brought Caleb "but a slender fortune; so that having a growing family, he found himself in those straits which many of his brethren have experienced; a circumstance which occasioned him to give his pupils some prudential

---

34. Nuttall, CCPD, no. 382.

35. For David Jennings (1691–1762) see ODNB. He was educated under Isaac Chauncy, Thomas Ridgley and John Eames at Moorfields academy. For these see Sell, *Philosophy, Dissent and Nonconformity*, passim., and for Ridgley see Sell, *Hinterland Theology*, ch. 2.

36. For a fuller list of subjects see McLachlan, *English Education under the Test Acts*, 147.

37. Palmer, "Memoir of Dr. Caleb Ashworth," 694.

hints with respect to matrimonial connexions."[38] He was especially distressed at being unable to purchase books, and this prompted Doddridge to approach Isaac Watts who, in a postscript to a letter to Doddridge of 18 October 1746, writes, "I rejoice to hear so well of Mr. Ashworth. I hope my lady [Lady Abney] and I have set him up with commentaries, for which he has given us both thanks."[39]

In 1751 Doddridge died in Portugal, whither he had gone on health grounds. In the meantime the assistant tutor, Samuel Clark, the son of Doddridge's St. Albans friend of the same name, had held the fort, and did so until he and the students removed to Daventry in November 1752.[40] That Ashworth should take charge of the academy was in accordance with the recommendation in Doddridge's will that, since his "friend and associate" Job Orton had, to Doddridge's great distress,[41] left Northampton for Shrewsbury in 1741,[42] Ashworth was "a proper person to succeed him in the care of [the academy] and (as he there expressed it) to perpetuate those schemes which I had formed for the publick service, the success of which is far dearer to me than life."[43] Doddridge had given his decision legal status in 1749 by deleting the name of Orton in his will, and substituting that of Ashworth.[44] Years later Ashworth "expressed undiminished surprise at the Doctor's nomination and his own compliance."[45] Doddridge had hoped that Ashworth would follow him in both the academy and the Castle Hill pastorate. In his will he wrote, "if it should so happen, as I think it very probably may, that the [Castle Hill] congregation should desire to put themselves under his ministerial care, I do hereby make my dying request to him that he would accept the united charge."[46] Two explanations have

---

38. Ibid.

39. Ibid. Palmer quotes from the letter to which reference is made in Nuttall, CCPD, no. 1201.

40. For Clark (1728–1769) see Evans, *Midland Churches*, (beware confused dates); McLachlan, *English Education under the Test Acts*, where his surname is incorrectly spelled on p. 303 (an 'e' is added), while in the Index Dr. Samuel Clarke is deprived of his 'e'.

41. See Nuttall, CCPD, letters of Doddridge to Mercy Doddridge of 16 and 18 July 1741, nos. 691, 692.

42. For Orton (1717–1783) see ODNB. He published *Memoirs of the late Reverend Dr. Philip Doddridge*.

43. NCL.MSS, Joshua Wilson's "Memorandum," L54/3/43.

44. Arnold and Cooper, *History of the Church of Doddridge*, 146.

45. Thomas, "Supplementary hints," 11.

46. Coleman, *Memorials of the Independent Churches in Northamptonshire*, 196.

been offered as to why this did not occur. The first is that Ashworth did not wish to leave Daventry;[47] the second is that, "contrary to Doddridge's assumption, [Ashworth] failed to be invited to succeed him as minister to the congregation in Northampton."[48] The clearest extant evidence is in favour of the former explanation. With reference to Samuel Clark's interim duties at the Academy and the Castle Hill Church, we learn that

> Though the Doctor's congregation highly respected Mr. Clark, and thought themselves greatly obliged to him for his services during their pastor's absence, he was not sufficiently popular and Calvinistical fully to satisfy the generality of them, so as to be chosen assistant to the Doctor's successor in the ministerial part of his office, which, it is well known, was the principal reason of the removal of the academy from Northampton to Daventry, where Mr Caleb Ashworth was then minister, whom Dr. Doddridge had warmly recommended to succeed him, both in the academy and the congregation, and who would himself have been acceptable at least to the majority of the people. But he knew too well the value of Mr. Clark as an assistant tutor to part with him, and therefore determined to remain at Daventry, where Mr. Clark was used to preach once in a month, with the consent of the people, who highly venerated his character, though his strain and manner were not quite to their taste.[49]

It is also known that in March 1752 attempts were made by Castle Hill representatives to persuade Orton to leave Shrewsbury for them, but to no avail.[50]

Since Ashworth himself had no personal fortune, and since many of his students were poor, the question arises, How was the academy maintained? Indeed, a prior question is, How was it to be accommodated? Enter Caleb Ashworth in the role of developer and disposer of property. First, he superintended the construction of the academy adjoining the manse in Sheaf Street. This entailed the purchase and demolition of two cottages. In

---

47. Ibid. This view is endorsed by Arnold and Cooper, *History of the Church of Doddridge*, 146. I am grateful to the Revd Malcolm Deacon for supplying the reference to this book.

48. Thompson, *History of the Coward Trust*, 18. Similarly, Alan C. Clifford writes, "Since Ashworth was not called to succeed Dr. Doddridge as the minister of Castle Hill Church, the Academy moved to Daventry . . ." See *The Good Doctor*, 104. This might be taken as implying that Ashworth candidated for the vacancy but was not called. The balance of the evidence is that he did no such thing.

49. "Brief memoirs of the Rev. Mr. Samuel Clark," 618.

50. See "Job Orton." ODNB.

the Abstract of Title to two messuages in Sheaf Street to Caleb Ashworth in 1752 it is recorded that "the said two Mess/es Cottages or Tenements thereby granted & released were pulled down & one large Mess/e or Tenement which had been ever since then was used as an Academy for the education of Ministers of the Gospel was erected upon the Site or Ground whereon the said two Mess/es Cottages or Tenements stood."[51] The Coward Trust, named after the Congregational benefactor William Coward and composed of Congregational ministers and laymen,[52] from which Doddridge's students, among others, had benefited, advanced £100/0/0 towards the cost of the academy building. Further funds accrued from the lease in June 1752 of two cottages in Sheaf Street to John Guyse of Heatherstone Street, Bunhill Fields, London, for "the sum of five shillings of lawful money."[53] At the same time, on 24 June, Ashworth and Guyse entered into a "Deed of Covenant to levy a ffine with Declaration of the Use" of the properties, which led in turn to a final agreement between them, dated All Souls Day 1752, under which Guyse paid Ashworth £100/0/0. John Guyse (baptized in 1677) was now minister at New Broad Street Congregational Church, London, and a Coward Trustee. He was thoroughly committed to the gospel, and equally thoroughly convinced that too many ministers were not proclaiming it faithfully—notably "Arians" such as Samuel Chandler. He sallied forth against the Arians in his Coward Lectures of 1728, Samuel Chandler rebutted him, and a lively controversy preceded eventual personal, but not doctrinal, reconciliation.[54] Following Guyse's death in 1761, the two Daventry properties were released to Ashworth on 29 June 1762. The conveyance was managed by Edward Webber of Leadenhall Street, London, and the agreement was between himself and his wife, Joanna, granddaughter of Guyse, and Caleb Ashworth. Under this agreement Ashworth received £307/0/0.[55] For a final reference to property, we may note that on 22 June 1764 Ashworth and William Bazlee, as trustees of the meeting house, entered into an agreement concerning alterations to that 1722 building, which included the provision of a gallery at the south-west end.[56]

51. NRO MS.NPL 1125.

52. For Coward (1647/8-1738) see ODNB; Thompson, *A History of the Coward Trust*.

53. NRO, MSS NPL 1332, 651.

54. See Sell, *Hinterland Theology*, 110–13.

55. NRO, MS NPL 656.

56. NRO, MS NPL 655. Side galleries were added c. 1820. So Stell, *An Inventory of Nonconformist Chapels and Meeting-Houses in Central England*, 138.

Samuel Palmer sums up the results of Ashworth's property dealings as far as they affected his personal finances thus: "The academical building which he himself erected, with the assistance of friends and of the trustees, became his own property, and by means of great prudence and economy (which however were accompanied with great liberality) he was enabled to acquire some pecuniary remuneration for his labour, and in a course of years his circumstances were so much improved that he not only brought up his family with reputation, but left those who survived him a decent competency."[57]

II

In addition to its assistance towards the cost of the Academy building, the Coward Trust was important to Daventry students as a grant-awarding body. One hundred and fifty-eight students passed through the Academy during Ashworth's twenty-three year tenure as principal tutor. Of these 131 were destined for the ministry, and most of them were Coward exhibitioners. As a further sign of their confidence in Ashworth, in 1758 the Coward Trustees chose Daventry as one of the places in which they would lodge younger teenagers, each of whom received £4/0/0 *per annum* from the Trust. The objective was that these young scholars would study the classics under the tutelage of a clergyman resident in the town. They were required to attend evening prayers at the Academy, and Ashworth was responsible for their overall care and progress. Between 1754 and 1789, when the Academy returned to Northampton, 44 Daventry students received support from the Presbyterian Fund Board, founded in 1689, of which Ashworth was a member from 1754 until his death in 1775.[58]

The Academy opened with ten founding students, including Joseph Priestley, the first to enrol, who has left us a detailed shorthand account of his three years under Ashworth.[59] To these students, were added eleven others who, together with the tutor, Samuel Clark, migrated from Northampton to Daventry Academy on 9 November 1752. In the following year four students were transferred from the Kendal Academy, which had ceased on the death of its tutor, Dr. Caleb Rotheram.[60] Among them

---

57. Palmer, "Memoir of Dr. Caleb Ashworth," 695.

58. Jeremy, *The Presbyterian Fund and Dr. Williams's Trust*, 50–51.

59. See "Joseph Priestley's Journal while at Daventry Academy, 1754, transcribed from the original shorthand by Rail and Thomas."

60. For Rotheram (1694–1752) see ODNB; Nicholson and Axon, *The Older*

was Rotheram's son, also Caleb. The Presbyterian Fund Board resolved that he and his three fellow students should receive grants of £10/0/0 on their removal to Daventry, whereas they had received only £8/0/0 whilst at Kendal.[61]

I have already observed that the Daventry Academy, like its Northampton predecessor, was of the open-minded sort, and this was famously confirmed by Priestley. He refers to the London academy over which John Conder presided from 1754 to 1781: "My Aunt, and all my relations, being strict Calvinists, it was their intention to send me to the academy at *Mile-end*, then under the care of Dr. Cander [sic]. But, being at that time an Arminian, I resolutely opposed it, especially upon finding that if I went thither, besides giving an *experience*, I must subscribe my assent to ten printed articles of the strictest Calvinistic faith, and repeat it every six months."[62] It would seem that here we have a case of false memory, for Priestley entered Daventry Academy in 1752, whereas Conder was appointed to the Mile End Academy in 1754, on the death of Zephaniah Marryatt of Moorfields Academy, and he assumed his duties in 1755, having moved to London from Cambridge. Moorfields Academy was under the auspices of the Calvinistic King's Head Society. The Society was founded in 1730 by a group of Congregational laymen who had become suspicious of Moorfields because the Arminian, John Eames, was a tutor there, and because, in their opinion, insufficient attention was paid to the students' spiritual development. They therefore inaugurated the Mile End Academy. Marryatt's students did not pass to Mile End, but to David Jennings at Wapping, and the books and apparatus of the learned John Eames also found a home there. It is safe to say that Priestley's conscience would have been troubled as much by Moorfields as by Mile End.[63]

Priestley was very appreciative of Daventry Academy, and he further informs us that

---

Nonconformity in Kendal, ch. 25; Sell, *Church Planting: A Study of Westmorland Nonconformity*, 39–41 and *passim*.

61. See Nicholson and Axon, *The Older Nonconformity in Kendal*, 321. On this page three students only are named as leaving Kendal for Daventry, namely, Caleb Rotheram, Isaac Smithson and Thomas Whitehead; but on p. 632 Joseph Threlkeld is correctly said to have proceeded to Daventry.

62. Priestley, "Memoirs of Dr. Priestley," in Rutt, *The Theological and Miscellaneous Works of Joseph Priestley*, I pt. 1, 21.

63. For Conder (1714–1781) and Eames (1686–1744) see ODNB. For Marryatt (c.1684–1754) see Wilson, *The History and Antiquities of Dissenting Churches and Meeting-houses*, IV, 199–203. For the King's Head Society see Sell, *Hinterland Theology*, 47–48, 52–53, 54, 57, 111.

> In my time, the academy was in a state peculiarly favourable to the serious pursuit of truth, as the students were about equally divided upon every question of much importance, such as liberty and necessity, the sleep of the soul, and all the articles of theological orthodoxy and heresy; in consequence of which, all these topics were the subject of continual discussion. Our tutors also were of different opinions; Dr. Ashworth taking the orthodox side of every question, and Mr. Clark, the sub-tutor, that of heresy, though always with the greatest modesty . . .
>
> The general plan of our studies, which may be seen in Dr. Doddridge's published lectures, was exceedingly favourable to free enquiry, as we were referred to authors on both sides of every question, and were even required to give an account of them . . . In this situation, I saw reason to embrace what is generally called the heterodox side of almost every question . . . though Dr. Ashworth was earnestly desirous to make me as orthodox as possible . . . Notwithstanding the great freedom of our speculations and debates, the extreme of heresy among us was Arianism; and all of us, I believe, left the academy with a belief, more or less qualified, of the doctrine of *atonement*.[64]

According to Alexander Gordon, "At Northampton Doddridge always kept an absolutely free hand. At Daventry the appointments were made and the management was regulated under the supervision of the Coward Trustees."[65] We recall, however, that Ashworth was to all intents and purposes appointed by Doddridge, and it must not be supposed that the Trustees meddled with the curriculum as prescribed by the tutors. They did not impose doctrinal tests upon students, though under the terms of the Trust they could withdraw funds from their grantees, and have them removed on disciplinary grounds. They had recourse to this provision only once during Ashworth's tenure.

As to the curriculum, it largely followed Doddridge's scheme, and his lectures were used, though Ashworth reworked those on Jewish Antiquities, a subject especially close to his heart. These shorthand lectures were transcribed by William Parry and used by him at Wymondley Academy.[66] The academies at Hoxton and Rotherham also used them.[67]

64. Palmer, "Memoirs of Dr. Priestley," 23–25.

65. Gordon, *Addresses Biographical and Historical*, 220.

66. See McLachlan, *English Education under the Test Acts*, 171, 277, 292. For Parry (1754–1819) see ODNB. The three volumes of shorthand notes are among NCL MSS, L. 213.

67. See McLachlan, *Essays and Addresses*, 186, 189.

In 1763 Ashworth compiled *The Principal Rules of Hebrew Grammar* from a selection of competent sources, and 1768 he published a *Treatise on Trigonometry*. For the latter the Coward Trustees provided a subvention of £14/0/0 to cover the printing costs, on condition that Ashworth retained one hundred copies which they might distribute to students at their other academies.[68] Among other extant shorthand lecture notebooks, largely derived from Doddridge, are those on Mathematics, with discourses on topics such as addition, fractions and logarithms; Civil Government with references to Locke, Pufendorf, Hoadly and Hobbes; the Old Testament and the Apocrypha, in which a diverse range of authorities is cited—Witsius, Whitby, Cyprian, Doddridge, Chandler and Chillingworth among them; with references to specific works by Watts, Clarke, Calamy, Emlyn, Cudworth, Calvin and Butler; Church Order and the Sabbath, in which the names of Boyle, Barclay, Dodwell, Hooker, Gale, Towgood, Bunyan, Scougal, Tillotson, Warburton, Grotius, Pliny, Lowman, Worthington, Jennings and Owen appear together with others; Divinity incorporating a study of miracles—here the names include Butler, Locke, Chandler, Tindal, Leland, Plato, Lucian, Eusebius, Clement of Rome, Justin Martyr, Lardner, Whiston, Baxter, Stillingfleet and Gill.[69] Also extant is Ashworth's signed shorthand notebook of Philip Doddridge's *Lectures on the Evidences and Doctrines of the Gospel*,[70] and notebooks containing devotional addresses and sermons given at Northampton by a variety of divines including Job Orton and David Jennings.[71] Among the themes treated in one of the notebooks are "The heathen rejection of miracles," "The influence of good example," "The advantages of civil community," "The propriety of the time of Christ's appearance in the world," sermons by a number of preachers including Thomas Belsham, and, perhaps of particular local relevance, an address on "The pleasures of a studious life."[72] All this, and compulsory shorthand too.

This brief glimpse of the range of topics discussed and persons referred to bears out Priestley's judgment that a wide variety of opinions was set before the students. The following timetable, devised by Ashworth, would seem at first sight to justify another of Priestley's remarks: "there

68. See McLachlan, *English Education under the Test Acts*, 307, 308.
69. See NCL MSS, L. 237, L. 214. L. 177, L. 178, L. 180, L. 184.
70. NCL MSS, L. 218.
71. See NCL MSS, L. 215, 217.
72. NCL MSS, L.12.1.

was ... no provision made for teaching the learned languages. We had even no compositions or orations in Latin. Our course of lectures was also defective in containing no lectures on the Scriptures, or on ecclesiastical history...."[73]

General Scheme of Business[74]

	Monday	Tuesday	Wednesday	Thursday	Friday	Saturday
I. Messrs Moore Blake Gellibrand Cutler Boulton	Evid. of Christianity (10) CA	Schemes (10) CA	Evidences of Christianity (10) CA	Analys: or Homil: (10) CA	Evid. of Christianity (10) CA	Jewish Antiquit (10) CA
II. Messrs White Mercer Robins Scholefield Jackson	Philosophy (10) Mr. Clark	Ethicks (10) Mr. Clark	Philosophy (10) Mr. Clark	Orations Theses (10) Once in a Fortnight	Ethicks (10) Mr. Clark	Jewish Antiquit. (10) CA
III. Messrs Holland Alexander Bunyan Priestly Rollestone	Algebra (11)	Pneumat (11)	Algebra (11)	11 Orations 1 in a Fortnight reading	Pneumat (11) reading	Reading

Languages and the Bible do indeed appear to be absent from this scheme. Yet, as we have seen, Ashworth compiled a Hebrew grammar, and he taught the language in a class attended by Thomas Thomas, to whose recollections I shall shortly refer. As to Priestley's remark concerning the absence of study of the Scriptures, in a letter of 27 January 1773 Job Orton declares that Ashworth takes particular pains with the Epistles, presumably because he thinks them "as very important though difficult parts of the New Testament."[75]

73. "Memoirs of Dr. Priestley," 26.

74. NCL MSS, L57.10.

75. See Palmer, Orton's *Letters to Dissenting Ministers and to Students for the Ministry*, I, 134.

To learn something of Ashworth's deportment as head tutor and manner as lecturer we must turn to some of his students. From Palmer we glean the information that Ashworth was a strict disciplinarian where the students were concerned. It would thus seem that he had taken the advice given to him by Job Orton, whose judgment he respected, and to whom he applied for advice on entering his new sphere of work. In a letter to Ashworth, Orton obliged, cautioning his friend to beware of some of Doddridge's foibles, among them the neglect of discipline, the habit of speaking well of everyone, and allowing family prayers to go on for too long.[76] But if Ashworth expected a disciplined student body, he was also a hard taskmaster to himself. Indeed, "his intense application to study, and the want of exercise sufficient for a man of his corpulence, injured his constitution, naturally strong."[77] "To the love of order he was a slave," declares Thomas Thomas: "With him everything was reduced to system. His prayers as well as his sermons were copious and comprehensive in a degree almost unexampled. His prayers on some interesting occasions have been remembered and spoken of with pleasure for years, by young and old . . . His piety partook of his characteristic qualities. It was solid, not assuming."[78]

As to Ashworth's manner: "He did not aspire after being 'the life and soul of the party', but his company was pleasant and instructive to the mechanic, the manufacturer, the scholar and the divine. Though destitute of the polish of the world, he discovered the urbanity of the gentleman, and he would have been respectable in any class of society and on any signal occasion. . . To decorum of conduct he was minutely attentive . . . In little things, as they are commonly esteemed, he was not negligent."[79]

In the classroom,

> A lecture was a serious business . . . The subject of delivery on one day, was the subject of examination on another. . . . Occasional as well as frequent inadvertence was marked . . . Sharp attacks of gout did not long suspend his labours. Often have his pupils been under the painful necessity of going through (perhaps rather going over) long demonstrations amid his extorted moans, which sadly disturbed and confused mathematical harmonies. When crowded by the demands

---

76. Ibid., I. 1.
77. S. Palmer, "Memoir of Dr. Ashworth," 696.
78. Thomas, "Supplementary hints," 12, 80.
79. Ibid., 11, 80.

of his correspondents, he has attempted to write letters while conducting a Hebrew lecture, which would admit absence of regular thought better than the discussion of abstruse science: but the doctor did not appear to possess the capacity of dictating to three amanuenses on distinct subjects, at the same instant. He frequently tore and burned what he then wrote. He did not impose his peculiar sentiments on his pupils . . . Freedom of inquiry was left unrestrained. Truth was considered as having the sole right to control . . . He did not excel in the happy art of giving charm to a subject . . . Taste, as a distinct faculty and habit, he did not much cultivate. The rhetoric of Mr. Burke did not meet his fancy. For him, there was too little thought, too much flourish . . . Paul and Demosthenes were his favourite orators . . . Though not always alive to beauty, no genius ever more quickly discerned defects. A mixed metaphor quite distressed him . . . He could shew others what to avoid, not always exemplifying what was graceful . . . Under Dr. Doddridge, there was a more popular exterior: under Dr. Ashworth, a more disciplined interior.[80]

Samuel Palmer may be taken as speaking for many: "I am not insensible to his failings; but such were his excellencies, that to this day, after the lapse of above half a century, I often reflect with pleasure on the years I spent under his tuition as some of the happiest of my life."[81]

III

Unlike some academy tutors Ashworth did not flood the press with books and pamphlets. Thomas Thomas judged that while Ashworth's attainments "considered as qualifying for and actually applied to the useful sphere in which he moved . . . were very eminent," they "may not be allowed to be brilliant, considered only in a literary and philosophical point of view."[82] For his part, Palmer surmised that "had it not been for his great diffidence and his backwardness to appear as an author, he might have acquired much literary fame."[83] Thomas's further remark that "Of no individual science was [Ashworth] particularly enamoured"[84] is suggestive of

80. Ibid., 78, 79.
81. Palmer, "Memoir of Dr. Caleb Ashworth," 696.
82. Thomas, "Supplementary hints," 11.
83. Palmer, "Memoir of Dr. Caleb Ashworth," 695.
84. Thomas, "Supplementary hints," 11.

the generalist, the journeyman—roles which are not to be despised, least of all when an extensive curriculum is to be provided by too few people. The upshot is that apart from his text books and his guidance for choirs, to which I shall turn shortly, Ashworth has left us just three published sermons. From these, however, we may glean something of his style and thought processes.

One Sunday, following the afternoon service, Ashworth noticed a newspaper report of the death of his benefactor, Isaac Watts. He immediately composed a sermon entitled *Reflections on the Fall of a Great Man*, and delivered it that evening. A London friend of Watts requested a copy of the sermon and urged Ashworth to publish it which, with considerable reluctance, he did.[85] His text was 2 Samuel 3:38, "And the king said unto his servants, Know ye not that there is a prince and a great man fallen this day in Israel?" He first observes that in general terms the fall of any great man is a loss to the public, and that we may learn useful lessons from such losses. But now

> An event has happened in the church of God, which, from us Christians, demands deeper concern, than the fall of the most able Politician, the truest Patriot, or the bravest and most successful Warrior; those pillars, and bulwarks of a State. I mean the death of *Dr. Watts*: Whose writings have been of such remarkable service, to so great a part of the Christian world; have been perused by us, with so much pleasure; and will I doubt not be yet dear to us, and to our children after us, in many succeeding generations.[86]

The fall of a great man, he continues, "proclaims aloud the vanity of human greatness" by teaching us that "Death is not afraid to attack those, who are dignified with the highest titles."[87] The fall of Watts, however, "should engage us to bless God who made him great," and it "is a loud and affecting call to exert ourselves with greater diligence, in pursuit of the noblest purposes of life."[88] We can learn from Watts, who was eminent in prayer, and also from the fact that he maintained "a truly Catholick disposition to all about him. How much soever they differed from him, or how unkindly soever they treated him, if he could discern anything in their temper and conduct, that bespoke the real Christian, they were sure to be the objects

---

85. So Palmer, "Memoir of Dr. Caleb Ashworth," 695
86. Ashworth. *Reflections on the Fall of a Great Man*, 6.
87. Ibid., 14, 16.
88. Ibid., 19, 21.

of his charity."[89] Watts "laboured with uncommon diligence in the service of Religion and immortal Souls."[90] He left works which edify the young, instruct adults, and enhance public worship. He defended the Gospel, and stood up for divine revelation against those who unduly magnified human reason. He underscored the truth that Jesus Christ is our redeemer and sanctifier, and he laid great emphasis upon practical religion. In addition,

> He was a true Friend of Liberty, though he would never give up the cause of Truth, or sacrifice any part of the Gospel, to make a comprehension with Infidels. He knew how to *contend earnestly* [Jude 3], and yet in the Spirit of Peace, for the *Faith once delivered to the Saints*: and has explained and defended what appeared to him, according to Scripture standard, to be *Orthodoxy*, at the same time presenting it in the closest connection with *Charity*.[91]

At this point I interrupt the flow of the sermon to point out that Ashworth clearly sides with those who upheld Watts as in intention a doctrinally orthodox divine. It is well known that some, in his own time and since, have sought to annex Watts to the Unitarian cause: indeed a chapter is devoted to him in Robert Spears's book of 1876, *A Record of Unitarian Worthies*. My own view is that, undeniably, Watts never repudiated the doctrine of the Trinity in print, but that to the end of his days he wrestled with the problem of stating it clearly, and was never satisfied with his efforts in this regard. I now return to Ashworth's sermon.

In his opinion, over and above all of Watts's publications, "his *Heart and Life* were a fair Book, in which the several characters of a true Christian were plainly delineated."[92] As he works towards his conclusion Ashworth argues that "The fall of a great man . . . teacheth us that Death is not an absolute evil," for "God has a way of changing the aspect of Death, and making it a passage to life."[93] In this case it teaches us to "wean our hearts from the world they have left": "When we recollect the pleasure, we have sometimes felt in singing his *divine Hymns*, let our Souls say whether there is any Joy in our World, worthy to keep us from the heavenly melody . . ."[94] Finally, "the fall of a great man should teach us to prize and seek an

---

89. Ibid., 25–26.
90. Ibid., 26.
91. Ibid., 32–33.
92. Ibid., 33.
93. Ibid., 35, 36.
94. Ibid., 37, 39.

interest in the blessed Lord."[95] The Church will not die because great men are taken from it:

> One useful Minister after another may finish his Course, and be called home from his Labours, *but the children of his servants shall continue, and their seed be established before him* [Psalm 102:28]. God has, and will have, at least, a little Church in the world; and is able, and has engaged, to preserve and defend it, by whomsoever it is deserted and forsaken; and though many pious and venerable Fathers and Ministers are dead and dying, *the Lord liveth, and blessed be our Rock, and let the God of our salvation be exalted* . . . [W]hile we are mourning that a great man is fallen, and an illustrious Prophet has left us, let our eyes be on him who conferred this greatness upon him: and instead of the plaintive strain, *Our fathers where are they? And the Prophets do they live for ever?* Let our language be like that of *Elisha*, when his eye could no longer trace his ascending Master, *Where is the* LORD GOD *of Elijah!*[96]

Samuel Palmer did not exaggerate when he said that this sermon "affords proof of a wonderful facility in composition, and is at least equal to any other discourse published on the same occasion, although at that time he [Ashworth] could be but about 28 years of age: it soon came to a second edition."[97]

On 29 July 1759 Ashworth preached on the occasion of the death of his former senior colleague in the Daventry pastorate, James Floyd, who died in 21 July 1759, aged fifty-five. The text is 1 Thessalonians 4:13: "I would not have you ignorant, Brethren, concerning them which are asleep, that ye sorrow not even as others which have no Hope." Ashworth observes that death is inevitable, and mourning for pious friends is entirely proper, though "No Tears, which the Christian Hope can restrain, should drop on the present Occasion."[98] He proceeds to explain that the pious departed sleep in Jesus, but they shall rise, and meet Christ, and be with him for ever; and all of this because of the death and resurrection of Christ. We are not forbidden to mourn, but we are not to sorrow as those who have no hope. We are especially exhorted to *"remember those who have had the Rule over us, who have spoken to us the Word of God"*

---

95. Ibid., 40.
96. Ibid., 41, 42.
97. Palmer, "Memoir of Dr. Caleb Ashworth," 695.
98. Ashworth, *Hope, The Christian Mourner's Relief*, 8.

(Hebrews 13:7), "Who had a rational Regard for divine Revelation, and were zealous to promote and secure its peculiar Honours, without a mean Attachment to party Names, or Disposition to censure on Account of lesser Differences."[99] Indeed, "Must not any Society lament the Loss of an honourable and worthy Member? Shall it not drop a Tear over the Grave of a Person of a candid, catholic and peaceable Disposition; who studies to avoid every Occasion of giving, or taking Offence, whose Prudence gave Wisdom, whose Steadiness gave Firmness, whose Reputation gave Credit, and whose ready and zealous Concurrence gave Vigor to all their Measures for the public Good?"[100] There follow words especially addressed to the members of Floyd's family: to the nearest relatives, to the child, and to the "faithful Consort." As to the last, "May it not be allowed to her to mourn, who finds herself left to pursue and finish the Journey of Life alone, and to struggle with the Tempests of Adversity in the broken Bark of a delicate, infeebled Constitution?"[101] As he approaches his conclusion Ashworth reiterates the point that "We must mourn and smart under such a Stroke of divine Providence. But shall we—shall even those of us who are most intimately concerned, abandon ourselves to Grief or Despair? . . . God forbid!"[102] Rather, let us contemplate our own dissolution with peace and joy in our hearts, and "break forth in the triumphant Language of the Apostle, *O Death, where is thy sting! O Grave, where is thy Victory! Thanks be to God who giveth us the Victory, through our Lord Jesus Christ. Amen!*"[103]

A further ten years on we find Ashworth preaching on the occasion of the death of his former assistant tutor, Samuel Clark, who died, aged forty-two, on 6 December 1769, as a result of being flung from his horse in Birmingham three days earlier, as he was on his way to preach at Oldbury. Ashworth was clearly deeply moved on this occasion. Before announcing his text he gave a prologue in which he said,

> I am distressed for you; I am distressed for myself: you have lost a most able, faithful, wise, and tender Pastor; I, a sincere affectionate and faithful friend. Let me intreat you to exercise candour towards me; and in pity to me, and in kindness to yourselves, to join in a fervent prayer to Almighty God, that he

99. Ibid., 32.
100. Ibid., 33.
101. Ibid., 35.
102. Ibid., 37.
103. Ibid., 48.

> would assist me in the difficult service assigned me; would direct me to speak a word in season, and enable me to act the part of a skilful interpreter of that dark and distressing passage of his providence, which we are now to consider.[104]

The text is, "*Remember them which have the rule over you, who have spoken unto you the word of God: whose faith follow, considering the end of their conversation*" (Hebrews 13:7). He sallies forth in professorial mode by immediately saying that "the passage would have been still more suitable to the occasion, if our translation had been exact. The general air of the sentence . . . [is] that the persons recommended to the regards of the Hebrew Christians were no longer with them . . . It should therefore have been rendered, *Remember them who have had the rule over you . . .*"[105] He proceeds to speak first of the office of the Christian minister; then of the regard in which ministers are to be held; and, thirdly, of the motive for highly regarding them. They rule the Church, but not as those who have magisterial authority; they do not dictate even in matters of religion; they are guides, shepherds who lead the flock, officers who train and marshal the soldiers of Christ. He cautions his hearers that "since with our utmost care and pains we dare not be confident that all we say is right, we desire you to examine for yourselves, being never better pleased than when you search the scriptures daily. For we do not pretend to bring you a new revelation; or to be infallible interpreters of that already given."[106] Of those ministers who have gone before he writes,

> You know that they maintained the word of God to be the supreme and only infallible rule of faith and manners, in comparison with which the opinions of the wisest, the most learned, and the best of men, and the creeds and decisions of the most venerable councils are of no authority: that it was their great concern in the whole of their ministrations, to lead you to form a scriptural religion . . . Call to mind the affection with which they spake of the mercy of God, and the grace of our Lord Jesus Christ, as subjects which melted and delighted their hearts, gave a spring to every active principle of their souls, and inspired them with heavenly hopes.[107]

---

104. Ashworth, *The Regards a Christian Congregation Owe to Their deceased Ministers*, 1–2.

105. Ibid. 3.

106. Ibid., 7.

107. Ibid., 12, 14–15.

There follows an account of Samuel Clark himself. Ashworth traces his lineage from Samuel Clark the church historian, Samuel Clark of Aylesbury, author of *The Holy Bible . . . with Annotations and Parallel Scriptures* (1690), to his father, Dr. Samuel Clark of St. Albans. He trained under Doddridge, and when the latter's health broke down he assumed charge of the academy and church in Northampton. Then "When the academy was removed to *Daventry*, he kindly continued as assistant in it for five years; and I take pleasure in acknowledging in this publick manner, that his friendship, his abilities, and his prudent counsels were of essential service, and mainly contributed to the reputation and success, whatever they have been, with which that institution has been conducted."[108] Clark was a faithful preacher, an excellent pastor, who had a special concern for the sick and the poor, though he "was courted by the learned and polite."[109] He was modest and humble, and was "cut off in the prime of his life and usefulness."[110]

> This was occasioned by an accident. But are we, therefore, to think it the work of chance? Did it fall without the approbation and appointment of God? Was it an oversight in the great Governor of the world, and was he inattentive when it happened?— What notions can we then have of providence, or what trust can we place in it, if accidents like this are not within its plan, and under the direction of an allwise and gracious God? And if they are, let us hold our peace and submit . . . [A]s the great Mr. *Howe* observes, if God be pleased, and the glorified creature pleased, who are we that we should be displeased?[111]

Finally, Ashworth exhorts the congregation to proceed with coolness, deliberation and unanimity in seeking a successor to Mr. Clark: "Nothing would have grieved your late pastor more than the apprehension of discord in the choice of a successor."[112] He encourages them to remember that "the consolations of God are not small,"[113] and that Christ, "who employed and furnished and blessed the ministers we lament, can raise up others with equal talents; or, with inferior abilities, can render them equally useful . . . [O]n him let us rely . . . and ascribe to him, as the most wise and

108. Ibid., 33.
109. Ibid., 34.
110. Ibid., 37.
111. Ibid., 38, 39.
112. Ibid., 40.
113. Ibid.

gracious head of the church, blessing and honour, and glory, and power, for ever and ever. Amen!"[114]

This glimpse of Ashworth in the pulpit, and especially his remarks on the duties of ministers, prompt us to enquire into his own work at the church in Daventry.

IV

Unfortunately, at this point our resources are tantalisingly slight. From two account books[115] we can glean information concerning the church's income and expenditure. It appears that pew rents were collected quarterly in April, Midsummer, St. Thomas, and Lady Day, and defaulters were pursued by Joseph Bull. The quarterly income fluctuated between £12/0/0 and £15/0/0. Expenditure includes the following items:

Gave the Men that watched the Meeting house	00 – 00 – 6
Pd. John Coles for making the 6 Window Curtains	00 – 1 – 6
Pd. Mary Rawlins for Coals & Candles	00 – 00 – 6½
Paid for a Pare of Bellows & a Shovel	00 – 1 – 11

From time to time more significant expenditure was required. Thus a formal document of 19 September 1760 states that under Mrs. Floyd's will the £50/0/0 left by her husband and the £20/0/0 left by herself should be released to the church provided that the congregation add to it £30/0/0 towards the cost of rebuilding the parsonage. Caleb Ashworth contributed £5/5/0 to the resulting successful appeal, and the house was rebuilt.[116]

On 24 November 1760 forty-six male members of the church signed a letter addressed to their minister. It would seem that Ashworth had declared that unless the burden of sermon preparation were reduced he would have to leave Daventry. The members' reply makes abundantly clear the esteem in which they held their minister, and their willingness to do all they could to prevent his departure. The text is as follows:

> We whose names are hereunto subscribed, Members of the Congregation of protestant Dissenters at Daventry, having duly considered the Declaration which Mr. Ashworth our Pastor has made to us, and which we heard with great surprise and concern,

---

114. Ibid., 41.

115. NRO MSS,DVURC 25(a), February 1747 to May 1760; 25(b), May 1760 to April 1769.

116. NRO MSS, DVURC 24, 2.

desirous of promoting the comfort and ease of our Minister and the peace and well-being of religious Society, do make it our unanimous Request that Mr. Ashworth will continue his Labours amongst us. That he will according to his proposal give us a new Sermon every Sabbath afternoon. And as we apprehend our Morning Service to be of considerable Importance to our Selves and our Familys, our further request is that he will assist us every other Sabbath in the Morning. And whenever Mr. Ashworth's Duty as a Tutor or a Pastor shall prevent his having time to compose a new Sermon for the Morning, we will be content with a Repetition or Exposition which he pleases. We hope Mr. Taylor will continue his acceptable Services as usual which we suppose will be one Morning in the Month. [At other services the members will accept supplies procured by Ashworth]. We apprehend the above Proposals which we cannot but think considerate and Candid will fully relieve all those Grievances which Mr. Ashworth has laid before us and, as we cannot make any other, we beg his final Answer to these as soon as he is determined, and it is our prayer that his Mind may be influenced in that manner that will most contribute to his own Comforts and the peace and prosperity of this Religious Society.[117]

Ashworth was evidently sufficiently moved by this gracious letter to remain at Daventry—as it happened, for the rest of his days.[118]

Shortly before Ashworth died the aforementioned single gallery was erected at the end of the chapel. This is shown on the "Plan of the meeting house & the rate of the several seats as fixed at a meeting of Trustees May 23, 2775, to be paid quarterly."[119] The rates are from 10/- to 1/-. A further plan follows on which the names of seatholders are given. The singers, who do not pay pew rent, sit towards the rear of the congregation in pews 22 and 32 which span the centre of the chapel and are separated by aisles from shorter side pews. Behind the singers are four free pews. Maidservants sit at the rear of the gallery, rent free, while students occupy pews 15 and 30 on the ground floor at no charge.[120] It would seem that, his musical interests notwithstanding, Ashworth did not, or could not, have

117. NRO MSS, DVURC 24, 3. The letter is quoted by [Thornton], 1672–1972. I am grateful to Mrs. Betty Thornton for supplying me with a copy of this pamphlet *via* her friend, Pam Smith.

118. There is a suggestion that he was invited to take the pastorate of Crosby Square church, London. See Palmer, "Memoir of Dr. Caleb Ashworth," 694.

119. NRO MSS, DVURC 24, 4.

120. NRO MSS, DVURC 24, 5.

the singers moved into the gallery, as was so frequently happening in rural churches from the later eighteenth century onwards.[121]

Among other scraps of information are the following: in 1743 Doddridge reported his arrival at Daventry "wet to the Skin almost from my Shoulders to my Toes," and "poor Mr. Ashworth bestowed much labour that Night & the next Morning in drying my Breeches Stockings Wastcoat Boots, Hatt Coats &c."[122] On his forty-eight birthday, 26 June 1750, Doddridge wrote to his former student, Benjamin Fawcett, then minister of Old Meeting, Kidderminster, proposing Ashworth as editor of David Brainerd's *Journal*, but nothing came of this.[123] From Walter Wilson we learn that Ashworth, "when lecturing one day [in London] on the influence of the passions on the human frame, and on the mind in particular, spoke of fear, when raised to dread and terror, especially on a sudden, as sometimes causing partial insanity, which continued through life."[124] Ashworth illustrated his point by reference to Simon Browne, who was said to have become mentally unstable following an encounter with a highwayman. However, Wilson observes that another version of the tale has another man dealing with the rogue. But Ashworth's general point was not incorrect, and Simon Browne was subject to delusions. In 1766 Ashworth preached on behalf of the Charity School in St. Albans, on which occasion £19/19/1 was raised for the cause;[125] and 13 November 1767 he was awarded the unsolicited Honorary D.D. of Marischal College, Aberdeen.[126]

The most substantial extant items relating to Ashworth's church work concern the music of the sanctuary, as we shall see. But first it is instructive to return to Rossendale, where, from the 1740s to the 1860s there was a lively attachment to music of various kinds, much of it written and played by amateur composers, singers and instrumentalists. The inhabitants of the valley of Dean were so noted for their music that they were known as the Larks of Dean. It is particularly interesting to note that this music was kept alive more in the Baptist chapels than anywhere else, and even

---

121. See Guppy, programme notes to the CD, *Repeat their Sounding Joy*, performed by The Gladly Solemn Sound; Drage and Holman, programme notes to the CD, *While Shepherds Watched*, 6. The former observes that since by 1800 10% only of rural churches had organs, singers and instrumentalists came into their own from the late eighteenth century onwards.

122. Letter to Mercy Doddridge of 12 July 1743, Nuttall, CCPD, no. 904.

123. Ibid., no. 1630. For Fawcett (1715–1780) see ODNB.

124. Wilson, *The History and Antiquities of Dissenting Churches*, II, 345.

125. Urwick, *Nonconformity in Herts*, 206.

126. Palmer incorrectly gives the date as 1759. See his "Memoir," 695.

more interesting to learn that among the composers and performers of both sacred and secular music was one Robert Ashworth, a local preacher and subject of legends. It is said that he would announce a psalm from the pulpit, take his place in the band with his cello, and then return to the pulpit to deliver the sermon. His son, James, was also involved in the music.[127] Were these relatives of Caleb Ashworth? It is quite conceivable that they were Baptists. Either way, Ashworth with his musical predilections could hardly have been unaware of this musical tradition in his native area. Indeed, we learn that "The Cloughfold Chapel choir, like all the Rossendale religious choirs, had its full complement of instruments, and was, tradition tells us, accustomed to make most vigorous use of them."[128] What is undeniable is that Ashworth had a concern for the quality of the music in worship, and that he was both a hymn writer and a composer.[129]

Circa 1760 Ashworth published *A Collection of Tunes, Suited to the several Metres commonly used in publick Worship, set in Four Parts, and on the most easy Keys; With an Introduction to the Art of Singing and Plain Composition*. A second edition of this work appeared in 1765, by which time it was designated Part I, because in 1763 Part II had appeared, *A Collection of Tunes . . . Containing Anthems and Other Tunes, More proper to Entertain and Improve those who have made some Proficiency in the Art of Singing, than to be introduced into public Worship*.

In his "Advertisement" to the original edition and to Part I, Ashworth states his objectives thus:

---

127. For the information thus far in this paragraph I am indebted to Seymour, "The musicians of Rossendale." Her article first appeared in *West Gallery* 6 (Spring 1994), and is reproduced in an amended version at http://www.wgma.org.uk/Articles/Larks/article.htm. I refer to pp. 1 and 7 as on the internet. Seymour is the conductor of the continuing Larks of Dean Quire. See also Drage, "The Larks of Dean: Amateur musicians in Northern England." In Cowgill and Holman, *Music in the British Provinces*, ch. 10.

128. Parry, *History of Cloughfold Baptist Church*, 154. This activity evidently superseded Richard Ashworth's lining out of hymns, to which Samuel Palmer referred. Parry's history, 149–54, makes it clear that what are sometimes called "worship wars" are not unique to our own time. As elsewhere, the advent of an organ was among the catalysts.

129. There is a brief notice of Ashworth in Davidson, *Choirs, Bands and Organs*, 237. Unfortunately it is stated that his Academy served Baptist and Independent or Congregational students (no reference to Presbyterians), and that it existed for the training of ministers for those denominations, whereas its purpose was to provide a higher education to Dissenting young men whether or not they were destined for the ministry. On p. 238 Ashworth's tune, "Northampton," is printed, with the words, "O render thanks and bless the Lord, Invoke his sacred name."

Caleb Ashworth of Daventry

> *This collection is made to encourage persons to form a little acquaintance with the Art of Singing, and to furnish a convenient Book of Tunes for a place of worship. To answer these ends the Editor has given the plainest instructions he was able, the tunes are set on the most easy keys, and the price is fixed as low as possible; the compiler being determined not to get anything by it. The Tunes in each metre are placed alphabetically, (1.) short metre, (2.) common metre, (3.) long metre, (4.) common metre double, (5.) long metre double, (6.) peculiar measures. To render it more extensively useful, the tunes are collected from very different parts of the kingdom, and several pages with blank lines are added at the end, on which any others, that are peculiar to each place, may be written down.*

The tunes are preceded by an Introduction of five chapters. The first four concern basic music theory, time, pitch and composition, while the last "*Contains miscellaneous Advices in regard to Singing.*" This chapter is especially revealing as to Ashworth's *desiderata*, and by reading between the lines we may readily infer what he was eager to correct:

> 1. Let not the learner covet to run on too fast . . .
>
> 2. Let the learner's first care be to sing true, and to give the just sound of the note . . .
>
> 3. Let every person take the part to which his voice is adapted. If one whose organs are best suited to the bass will sing tenor, he hangs as a weight on the others, is sure to sink the tune, and his voice must be rough and forced.
>
> 4. A person should never exert all the strength of his voice, as if he aimed to sing as loud as he was able. This destroys the music of the voice, and makes it impossible to pass on with sufficient swiftness, where the notes are short . . .
>
> 6. Some persons insensibly contract an awkward distortion of face, or attitude of body. This will scarce ever be cured, unless an observer frequently, and in an obliging manner, acquaint them with it; and they are willing to receive the hint kindly, and make an early reformation.
>
> 7. Many good singers have an unhappy way of pronouncing the words . . .
>
> 9. It cannot be thought amiss to conclude an essay intended to assist persons in learning to sing with a view to conduct this exercise with more propriety on sacred occasions, by reminding the reader that singing is an act of religious worship . . . Happy

will it be if this hint is attended to, whatever else in this essay is overlooked or forgotten.[130]

I select by way of illustration examples of Ashworth's hymn and tune writing which may be heard to this day. "A Christmas Carol," for which Ashworth wrote the words and arranged the tune, is described by Sally Drage and Peter Holman as "A beautiful example of early Nonconformist psalmody." They further explain that, as in this case, "Nonconformist composers usually wrote in three parts rather than four, but expected both the upper ones to be doubled at the octave, so five parts were produced from three."[131] Homan elsewhere adds that "When an early composer such as Caleb Ashworth . . . hits the nail on the head, as with his delightful 'Let an anthem of praise,' . . . part of the attraction is the unorthodox part-writing, with consecutive fifths and unprepared sevenths."[132]

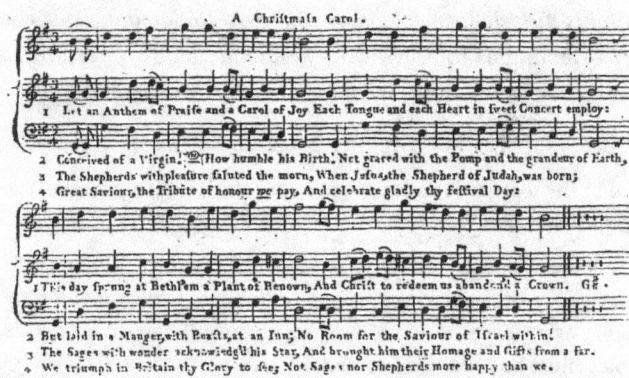

"A Christmas Carol" appears in Part II of Ashworth's work, together with settings of Watts's verse, a "Song in the Oratorio of Saul," a "Meditation over the corpse of a good man," and anthems on words from Psalms, Isaiah, Revelation, and the Burial Office.

For an example of one of Ashworth's hymn tunes from Part I of his collection I turn to his setting of Watts' metrical version of Psalm 49:1 33:

130. Ashworth, *A Collection of Tunes*, Part I, 22–23.

131. Drage and Holman, CD notes, 6.

132. Holman, "Performing psalmody," 92. The carol may be heard on track 2 of *While Shepherds Watched*.

Caleb Ashworth of Daventry

133

V

What of the Daventry alumni? The best known of them, Joseph Priestley, has already been mentioned, but a brief review of some of the others will prove instructive and even, in some cases, entertaining.[134] As we proceed we shall do well to remember that these students were being educated in a period of intense doctrinal debate when, a person could be born into Calvinism, become an Arminian, proceed to Arianism and end a Unitarian. We should also be aware of the fact that in the eighteenth century the term "Arian" signified the belief that Jesus Christ the Son of God was divine, but subordinate to the Father; it did not necessarily entail detailed, or, indeed, any knowledge of the third century heretic, Arius. Some of the eighteenth-century "Arians" denied all knowledge of him, and all of them, appealing to the doctrine of the sufficiency of Scripture, deduced their doctrinal position from the Bible. We may also note that some Arians, like Micaijah Towgood, thought it appropriate to offer worship to Christ, whereas others, Richard Price among them, did not.[135] Finally, we must remove from our minds the concept of the denominations with their central

---

133. Verses 6, 8, 12 and 14 may be heard on track 19 of the CD, *Repeat their Sounding Joy*. I am grateful to The British Library for permission to reproduce the texts and music of the hymns.

134. The basis for this survey is Belsham. "A list of students educated at the academy at Daventry," 163–64, 195–98, 284–87. References to students who entered under Ashworth cease with his death, 198.

135. I here seriously curtail a story as intriguing as it is complicated. See Sell, *Dissenting Thought*, chs. 2, 5, 7.

offices, committees and the like, as we have known them: these were creatures of the nineteenth century. Prior to that the term represented parties, or tendencies, and in fluidly doctrinal times it was not impossible for a minister to proceed from Independent, through Presbyterian or General Baptist, to Unitarian pastorates.

I begin these brief snapshots of a selection of Daventry alumni by referring to some who did not complete their course. John Haywood, who was enrolled in 1761, suffered death by drowning, possibly as a result of the epileptic fits he suffered. Philip Ashworth, Caleb's son, began his studies in 1769, but he died as a result of a spinal injury. He is described as "an amiable youth," and we have a letter from him which reveals both his politeness and Mercy Doddridge's continuing interest in the Ashworth family. He writes, on 14 January 1769 to thank her for the gift of Philip Doddridge's Hebrew Bible. He says that he will read it with particular pleasure when he begins to learn the language, "considering it as a volume which was once read and studied by the Great Doctor Doddridge and . . . that is was presented to me by his Lady."[136]

Secondly, I turn to some who were educated at Daventry but were not destined for the ministry. Philip Doddridge's son, Philip, was one of these. Born on 6 August 1735, he entered the Academy in 1753, became a solicitor in Tewkesbury, where he died on 13 March 1785.[137] John Ashworth, Caleb's son, entered in 1760, became a grazier and thereafter kept the Wheat Sheaf Inn at Daventry. James Johnstone (1753–1783) entered the Academy in 1767, subsequently graduated MD of Edinburgh University, became a physician, and died of typhus following a visit to prisoners in Worcester gaol.[138] His brother Edward (1757–1851) followed him to the Academy in 1773. He caught typhus during the epidemic of 1774, but recovered, and later took the disease as his subject for the Edinburgh MD. He became a well-known physician in Edgbaston, Birmingham,[139] while Thomas Lee, who enrolled as a student in 1774, became a solicitor in the same town.[140] William Tattersall, another MD, who also enrolled at Daventry in 1774, practised first in Liverpool and then in London. He

---

136. NCL MSS L.1.4.34.

137. See Deacon, *Philip Doddridge of Northampton*, 69.

138. See ODNB, Johnstone, James of Galabank (his father). In this article Ashworth is wrongly named Atwood.

139. See ODNB. This article does not mention his time at Daventry. His thesis of 1779 is entitled, *De febre puerperali*.

140. Birmingham was not granted city status until 1889.

published a paper entitled, *A Brief View of the Anatomical Arguments for the Doctrine of Materialism; Occasioned by Dr. Ferriar's Argument against it* (1794).[141]

Thirdly, I briefly note three students who conformed to the Church of England. According to the list of students in *The Monthly Repository*, a student named Mather entered the Academy in 1753 and settled at Stamford prior to conforming. According to Surman's Index[142] a minister named Matthew served at Stamford from 1757 to 1758. Since the dates are credible, we may perhaps assume that this was one and the same person. William Denny, who went to Daventry in 1760 conformed and became curate there, while Samuel Henley (1740-1815/16),[143] "a man of elegant accomplishments," who entered the Academy two years later, served as pastor at Green Street, Cambridge from 1762 to 1769, and then became Professor of Moral Philosophy at The College of William and Mary, Williamsburg, Virginia. He conformed, returned to be Vicar of Rendlesham, Suffolk, and from 1805 to 1815 was Principal of the East India Company's College at Hertford.

Fourthly, I refer to a few students who entered the ministry, but left it for other pursuits. Among these was Francis Webb (1735-1815), who began his studies at Daventry in 1753.[144] An Arian, he served General Baptist pastorates at Honiton and Paul's Alley, London, and resigned in 1766 to devote himself to literary and diplomatic activities. He was a radical Whig, and acted as secretary to the delegation which secured the peace of Amiens in 1802. He was a staunch upholder of civil and religious liberties, and ended as "a decided Unitarian." Joseph Dawson (1740-1813), who also studied at Glasgow University but did not graduate, entered the Academy in 1761. From 1765 to 1790 he ministered at Idle, Bradford. During that time he kept a school, kept hens in the churchyard and cattle fodder in part of the chapel, and opened one or two coal mines nearby. On his resignation from the pastorate he devoted himself full-time to mineralogy, and became proprietor of Low Moor iron works near Bradford. He was founding President of the Yorkshire and Derbyshire Ironmasters Association (1799), to whom he delivered their first lecture on "The effects of air

141. For John Ferriar (1761-1815), a prominent Manchester physician, see ODNB.

142. At Dr. Williams's Library, London, and online.

143. Belsham records him as William.

144. Though Wilson says that he began under Doddridge in Northampton, see *The History and Antiquities of Dissenting Churches*, III, (1810), 259. See also ODNB; Murch, *A History of the Presbyterian and General Baptist Churches in the West of England*, 325-27.

and moisture on blast furnaces." Originally an Arian, he became Unitarian in his views, and was a friend of Priestley, some of whose scientific apparatus came into his possession. He preached occasionally in the Unitarian chapel in Bradford, but was not a member there. J. H. Turner, who brands Dawson "no credit to Nonconformity" because, his mind being elsewhere, he allowed the congregation to dwindle, does concede he "was a man of great liberality and kindness."[145] *The Monthly Repository* list of Daventry alumni declares that Dawson "always maintained an exemplary character," while John James lauds him as "a learned and truly good man."[146]

Fifthly, I come to those who remained in pastoral charge of Dissenting churches throughout their careers. Radcliffe Scholefield (1733–1803) entered Northampton Academy in 1750, and removed from there to Daventry in 1752. His first pastorate was at Whitehaven, and in 1772 he succeeded Samuel Clark at Old Meeting, Birmingham.[147] Five years later John Reynell (1736–1800) enrolled. He ministered at the Presbyterian Church, Plymouth from 1762 to 1784, when he inherited an estate at Thorverton, near Exeter, where he supplied the small Presbyterian church. We learn that "He was unfriendly to controversy, and seldom dwelt on speculative points of theology. His heart overflowed with kindness, and he was ardently desirous of promoting a friendly disposition among Christians of all denominations. He was kind to the poor, and loved his books and rural pursuits and recreations."[148] William Buckley (1731–1797), who entered in 1756 and ministered at Atherstone and Dukinfield, forms a nice contrast with John Atchison (1743–1813),[149] who came to the Academy three years later, and was pastor at Gorton. Whereas the flamboyant Buckley was "not only an Arian, but also a clerical dandy" who was rebuked by a member of the congregation at Dukinfield who said "Where silk gowns and powdered wigs come, there cometh no gospel'—which led to a secession inspired, unusually, by sartorial considerations,[150] Atchison retired in 1778 because of "extraordinary diffidence" which rendered him unable to make "that public exhibition of himself which was required by the duties of his office

---

145. Turner, *Nonconformity in Idle*, 46.

146. James, *The History and Topography of Bradford*, 227. See also Musson and Robinson. *Science and Technology in the Industrial Revolution*, 158–59.

147. See Evans, *Midland Churches*, 50.

148. See Murch, *A History of the Presbyterian and General Baptist Churches of the West of England*, 508, 515–17.

149. The Daventry alumni list has "Atchinson."

150. See Nightingale, *Lancashire Nonconformity*, I, 293–94.

as a Christian minister."[151] A ministerial student who arrived at the Academy in 1758 was described as "a man of very superior talents'—and he had a very superior name to match: Ottiwell Heginbotham (1744–1768). He was ordained at Friar Street church, Sudbury, Suffolk in 1765, and died there three years later. Some of his hymns appear in *The Protestant Dissenter's Magazine*.[152]

Without question one of the most substantial pastoral alumni of Daventry was Samuel Palmer (1741–1813), Ashworth's memorialist. His studies at Daventry began in 1756, and he became the afternoon preacher at the Congregational church at Mare Street, Hackney, in 1762. He also preached at the Weigh House Chapel, and eventually succeeded William Hunt at Mare Street. He removed with the congregation to St. Thomas's Square, Hackney in 1771, and remained there until his death. He ran a day school, and pioneered a Sunday School in the church. He published a number of works, of which the most significant are *The Protestant Dissenter's Catechism* (1772), which went through many editions and was translated into Welsh, and *The Nonconformist's Memorial*, which appeared first in ten parts, and then in a revised, two-volume, edition in 1777 and 1778. He was a great friend of Job Orton, and a staunch upholder of the principles of Dissent.[153] John Hodgkinson (1744–1812) was enrolled at Daventry in 1763. Following service in Bolton, he was called to the Presbyterian (by now Unitarian) Church, Hindley, in 1779, where he remained until his death. On arrival, his stipend for the year was £29/19/4. He kept a boarding school, collected funds for a manse, and was greatly respected in the church and community: "His mild, frank, and unassuming manners endeared him to the society of his family and friends, and he discharged the duties of a Christian brother with unaffected seriousness, simplicity, and candour."[154]

By contrast with Hodgkinson's ministry, that of Hugh Worthington (1752–1813), who entered the Academy in 1768, was that of a metropolitan homiletic crowd-puller. An able student, it is written that "his habits of industry, regularity, and almost incessant diligence, in the pursuit of knowledge were singularly exemplary."[155] He was also a great reader of ser-

---

151. Ibid., 57.

152. Browne, *History of Congregationalism and Memorials of the Churches in Norfolk and Suffolk*, 447–48, reproduced word for word by Hosken, *History of Congregationalism and Memorials of the Churches of Our Order in Suffolk*, 184–85.

153. See Sell, *Dissenting Thought*, 637–38.

154. Nightingale, *Lancashire Nonconformity*, II (ii), 10.

155. Anon., "Memoir of the late Rev. Hugh Worthington," 562. See also ODNB; Wilson, *The History and Antiquities of Dissenting Churches*, II, 61.

mons—not least those which did not endorse his consistently-held Arian views. It is not surprising that he should have been chosen to continue at Daventry as the classical tutor, but it was not to be. During the interval between the completion of his studies and the beginning of term he went to London at the invitation of friends, assisted some of them in the pulpit, and was invited to become assistant to Francis Spilsbury at Salters' Hall.[156] Worthington "had, from his first appearance in the pulpit, that kind of eloquence which arrested the attention, and which effectually prevented the listlessness and languor that are too frequently observed in afternoon congregations. The popularity which he acquired at the outset of life, never once deserted him."[157] He published a number of sermons, and as for his doctrine, "Few men ever changed their opinions less than he. He began life as an Arian, with regard to the person of Christ; and was from his first entrance to the pulpit avowedly inimical to the gloomy doctrines of Calvinism. That he was not in the least careful to conceal these opinions all his stated hearers can testify."[158] Worthington was not, however, prepared to countenance the transition from Arianism to Unitarianism, and in 1789 he attended a meeting the objective of which was to arrest what was regarded (wrongly) as a Socinian drift. Among those present was Benjamin Carpenter, of whom more shortly. It was decided that dissertations would be written on "The person of Christ," "The personality of the Holy Spirit," and "The atonement," but "Unfortunately, the subject of INSPIRATION was started and it was found, that the reverend divines, who were about to crush [the Unitarians] Priestley, Belsham and others, could not agree among themselves on this, which was regarded as the fundamental point from which they were to set out. After three days debate the meeting was dissolved, and the several individuals, it is believed, separated from one another, very much dissatisfied with their performance."[159]

Another Daventry student who ran the gamut from evangelical *via* Arian to Unitarian sentiments was Samuel Fawcett (d. 1816). He was the son of Benjamin Fawcett, minister of Old Meeting, Kidderminster, in which there were Calvinists, Arminians and Arians.[160] Of the father it was said that "he managed so far to conceal his opinions as to be very

---

156. For the Spilsbury ministerial dynasty see Wilson, *The History and Antiquities of Dissenting Churches*, II, 55–60.

157. "Memoir of the late Rev. Hugh Worthington," 563.

158. Ibid., 571.

159. Ibid., 571 n.

160. For Benjamin Fawcett (1715–1780) see ODNB;

popular with his hearers, and these were very numerous."[161] In this he differed from Hugh Worthington, for example; but we should not jump to the conclusion that Fawcett was all things to all people, or that he had an eye to maintaining the size of his congregations in the interests of his stipend. The fact is that a significant number of heterodox ministers did not believe that the pulpit was the place for doctrinal controversy. They were in the mould of Micaijah Towgood, of whom it was said that "He led not his flock for nourishment, to the dry and barren hills of cold and unedifying speculation."[162] Returning to Samuel Fawcett, we find that he ministered at Beaminster from 1776 to 1790, when he was forced to resign on doctrinal grounds. He removed to Bridport and became a banker, and finally, from 1801 to 1816 he was pastor of the Unitarian church in Yeovil. It instructive to place side by side the comments on Fawcett, first of the Congregationalists William Densham and Joseph Ogle, and then of the Unitarian, Jerom Murch. The former write of his ministry at Beaminster, the latter takes a longer, and kinder, view of his ministry:

> Mr. Fawcett gradually abandoned evangelical sentiments, adopting first Arian, and then Socinian, or Unitarian opinions. His position at length became untenable. The influence of the great Evangelical Revival was felt at Beaminster, at that time one of the most progressive little towns in the kingdom. He resigned his now unpleasant position . . .[163]

> [Fawcett] was for some time a fellow-student of the late Mr. Belsham, like whom he was originally of Calvinistic sentiments. More than fourscore winters have now passed over his head; he retains as firm a conviction as ever of the truth of his principles, and feels as powerfully as ever their inestimable value.[164]

For a final example of one who began, and remained, in pastoral charge I turn to Joseph Bealey (1756–1813). He arrived at Daventry Academy in 1774. He was minister first at Narborough (1779–1781), then at Cockey Moor, Ainsworth (1781–1786). From 1786 to 1791 he was at Warrington and in the latter year he returned to Cockey Moor, where

---

161. Hunsworth. *Memorials of the Old Meeting House, Kidderminster*, 41, though Hunsworth queries the assertion.

162. Manning, *A Sketch of the Life and Writings of the Rev. Micaijah Towgood*, 92–93.

163. Densham and Ogle, *The Story of the Congregational Churches of Dorset*, 11.

164. J. Murch, *A History of the Presbyterian and General Baptist Churches in the West of England*, 218.

he remained until his death. He was a great friend of Thomas Barnes,[165] the prominent Manchester Unitarian, and having been a high Arian for most of his life, he publicly proclaimed himself a Unitarian in a sermon preached on 4 April 1813. This caused great dissention in the church, and a number of members seceded to Mawdsley Street church, Bolton. On 9 August 1813 Bealey died.[166]

The final category of alumni comprises those of Ashworth's students who became academy tutors. There were eleven of these in all, of whom eight taught at Daventry and three elsewhere. Thomas Tayler (1735–1831) began his studies under Doddridge in 1750, and proceeded to Daventry in 1752. His course completed, he followed Samuel Clark as tutor from 1756 to *circa* 1760. He then became chaplain to Elizabeth Abney of Stoke Newington, and was known to many as "the second Dr. Watts," for Watts had likewise served, and lived with, the Abney family. Tayler removed to Carter Lane, London as assistant in 1766, and became pastor there in 1788. He resigned in 1811. It had been the practice for the Carter Lane congregation to recite the Apostle's Creed every Sunday following the Bible reading. Tayler discontinued this practice. He was a Coward Trustee, and a member of both the Presbyterian and Congregational Fund Boards. In the churchyard of St. George's, Lisbon,[167] a large monument may be seen, which is thus inscribed:

---

165. For Barnes (1747–1810) see ODNB. Sell, *Philosophy, Dissent and Nonconformity*, 11–12 and *passim*. He ministered at Cross Street Chapel, Manchester, and in 1786 he became the first principal of the Manchester Academy founded in that year. Unable to maintain discipline, he resigned two years later.

166. For Bealey see Allard, *A Memoir of Joseph Bealey*; Nightingale, *Lancashire Nonconformity*, II (i), 124–25.

167. See Wilson, *The History and Antiquities of Dissenting* Churches, II, 160–63; McLachlan. *English Education under the Test Acts*, 154. There is no reference to Doddridge in the text of Hampton, with revisions by Staines, *History of the Lisbon Chaplaincy*.

> Philip Doddridge. DD
> Died 26th October 1752 aged 50
>
> ---
>
> With high respect for his
> Character & writings, this
> Monument was erected in June 1828
> At the expense of Thomas
> Tayler. Of all his numerous
> Pupils the only one then living.

Thomas Halliday, who entered the Academy in 1761, continued as classical tutor from 1765 to 1769, after which date his biography becomes confused with that of another Thomas Halliday. Meanwhile Noah Hill (1739–1815), whose early schooling had been under Noah Jones of Cradley,[168] had arrived as a student in Daventry in 1756, and followed Tayler as tutor from 1760 to 1770. At first he was responsible for mathematics, geography, philosophy, logic, natural theology and civil government. When Halliday left, Ashworth relieved Hill of some of these subjects so that Hill could cover classical studies. Two *prima facie* contradictory opinions of Hill's efforts have come down to us. Thomas Belsham, who studied under Hill, declared that "of Logic and Mathematics [Hill] knew but little, and was not at all ambitious of improving himself or his pupils, or of doing anything more than go over the same routine continually."[169] On the other hand, we learn that Hill's lectures were very interesting, and that "he possessed great felicity and copiousness in illustration . . . In his mathematical lectures he was particularly clear." But when this memorialist adds that the clarity of Hill's mathematical lectures "made many of his pupils wish that he had carried them a little further than the elements of that beautiful and attractive science"[170] one cannot suppress the thought that this may be tactful, restrained, "obituary-speak" for the kind of dissatisfaction that Belsham more bluntly expressed. Noah Hill was called to Old Gravel Lane Independent Church, London, where he happily remained until ill health prompted his resignation in 1808.

Thomas Robins (1732–1810) began his studies at Kibworth under John Aikin, then entered Doddridge's Academy in 1750, and transferred to Daventry in 1852. Following pastorates at Stretton-under-Fosse and West

---

168. For Noah Jones (1725–1785) see Sell, *Dissenting Thought*, ch. 12.
169. Williams, *Memoirs of the late Reverend Thomas* Belsham, 78.
170. Anon., "Memoir of the late Rev. Noah Hill," 186.

Bromwich, he succeeded Ashworth as head of the Daventry Academy in 1775. Ashworth had intimated to the Coward Trustees that he would like Robins to succeed him at both the Academy and the Daventry church, and Ashworth's wish, together with the Trustees' endorsement of the idea, was communicated to the church by Philip Furneaux of Clapham in a letter of 28 July 1775.[171] Robins removed to Daventry, but "very much to the regret of his congregation, his pupils and his Friends in general,"[172] he was obliged to resign in 1781 owing to the loss of his voice. He had served "with great reputation, acceptance, and success."[173] He was remembered as a person of fine sentiments and elegant prose. He published an abridgement of Matthew Henry's work on Baptism and the Lord's Supper in 1783, and some memoirs of Thomas Strange of Kilsby, but his friends regretted that his modesty had prevented him from publishing much more. Robins remained in Daventry as a bookseller and druggist until his death.

He was succeeded by Thomas Belsham (1750–1829), who became a student at Daventry in 1766, and had been assistant tutor there from 1771 to 1778. Belsham later recalled that "I went to Daventry in August 1776, and remained there as a student till 1771 . . . Under Dr. Ashworth I studied Divinity and Philosophy, and paid such attention to my lectures as to obtain the approbation of my tutor. But I was exceedingly deficient in reading, which I much regret."[174] Following his assistant tutorship Belsham became minister of Angel Street Church, Worcester. On 30 July 1781 he wrote to "the Trustees, Communicants and Subscribers of the Protestant Dissenting Congregation at Daventry" accepting their unanimous call to the pastorate, and at the same time he assumed the tutorship in divinity at the Academy.[175] Belsham was another whose pilgrimage took him from Arianism to Unitarianism, of which he became an ardent apologist. This change of view occurred during his Daventry days and, with commendable integrity, he resigned his post in 1789, and accepted a tutorship at the new Hackney College, where he served from 1789 to 1796. He was pastor of Gravel Pit, Hackney from 1794 to 1805, and at Essex Street, London from the latter date until 1829. A great shaper of the Unitarian denomina-

---

171. For Furneaux (1726–1783) see ODNB. An alumnus of Moorfields Academy, he received the DD of Aberdeen University in the same year as Caleb Ashworth, 1767.

172. Taylor, NRO DVURC 24, 1.

173. Belsham quoted by Jeremy, *The Presbyterian Fund*, 65. For Robins see Watson, *A Brief Memoir of the Rev. Thomas Robins*; Coleman, *Memorials of the Independent Churches in Northamptonshire*, 198–206.

174. Williams, *Memoirs of the late Thomas Belsham*, 78.

175. For his letter see NRO DVURC 24, 8.

tion, he is almost as well known for exceeding even Ashworth in corpulence, so that when he went to preach at Chowbent a hole had to be cut in the wall to allow him access to the pulpit.[176] With Belsham's resignation the Academy returned to its former home in Northampton under John Horsey (1754–1827), an alumnus of Homerton College, who had been called to the pastorate of Castle Hill in 1777.

In the meantime three others had served as assistant tutor at Daventry. Benjamin Carpenter (d. 1816) was a student from 1768 to 1873, when he served as classical tutor for a few months only before taking his first pastorate at Bloxham and Milton (1773–1775). He subsequently served at West Bromwich (1776–1778), Stourbridge (1778–1795) and again from 1807 to 1815; and at Clapham (1795–1798) and his home town of Bromsgrove (1798). We have already seen that he was among those who resisted the advocacy of Unitarianism by Priestley and Belsham and, indeed, he entered the pamphleteering lists against Belsham, who replied in print to him.[177] John Taylor (1754–1817) was enrolled as a student in 1772, and was classical tutor from 1776 to 1782, when he became a Quaker. He removed to Manchester, where he kept a school. Timothy Kenrick (1759–1804), who entered the Academy in 1774 stayed on as tutor in mathematics and natural philosophy from 1778 until 1784, when he succeeded the venerable high Arian Micaijah Towgood at George's Meeting, Exeter, with which he coupled a tutorship in the third Exeter Academy, which he founded in 1799.[178]

It remains to mention those who studied under Ashworth and subsequently became academy tutors elsewhere. William Enfield (1741–1797) began his studies at Daventry in 1758. He ministered at Benns Gardens, Liverpool from 1763 to 1770, and then became tutor at Warrington Academy until 1785. In the latter year, as we have seen, he removed to Octagon Chapel, Norwich, where he remained until his death. His sermons tended towards the moralistic rather than the theological, and he published a

---

176. For Belsham see ODNB; John Williams, *Memoirs*; Urwick, *Nonconformity in Worcester*, 110-12. When William Enfield left Warrington for Octagon Chapel, Norwich in 1785, Belsham was approached by supporters of Warrington Academy to succeed him. Belsham felt that although he was at that time a high Arian, he was too orthodox for the Warrington situation. See Nightingale, *Lancashire Nonconformity*, II (ii), 221.

177. For Carpenter see Evans, *Midland Churches*, passim; *The Monthly Repository* 12 (1817) 4-7, 51-52.

178. For Kenrick see ODNB; Murch, *A History of the Presbyterian and General Baptist Churches in the West of England*, 437-44.

number of works, a hymnal, and *Institutes of Natural Philosophy, Theoretical and Experimental* (1783). He dedicated the latter to Joseph Priestley, and in 1784 he was made an LL.D. of Edinburgh University. Gifted though he undoubtedly was, he "does not appear, even in the estimate of his friends, to have wisely exercised the authority entrusted to him as the rector of the Academy."[179] Following his resignation the Academy was removed from Warrington. William Bull (1738-1814),[180] who entered the Academy in 1759, stands out as a tutorial alumnus who remained faithful to evangelical Calvinism. He was minister at Newport Pagnell from 1764 until his death, and in 1782 he established his Academy there, with the financial support of John Thornton of Clapham and the encouragement of John Newton and other evangelicals. Bull's was one of a new breed of academies in that its objective was specifically the training of ministers, not the general higher education of Dissenting youth. The study of the Bible was elevated, and Newton advised Bull to give no place in the curriculum to science or philosophy, though logic crept in later.[181] I come finally to Robert Gentleman (1745-1795), who entered Daventry Academy in 1863. He was called to Swan Hill Chapel, Shrewsbury in 1767, and in 1775 he opened a boarding school there. His views having now become Arian, in 1779 he became tutor at the Presbyterian Fund's Carmarthen Academy and pastor at Lammas Street Chapel. In 1784 he accepted a call to minister to Kidderminster's Arian seceders in the New Meeting, remaining there until his death.[182]

That Thomas Belsham, perhaps the Daventry alumnus at the furthest remove from Ashworth's theological position could write in the following terms is testimony to the integrity of both men:

> Dr. Ashworth was a man of considerable abilities and learning, and of unaffected modesty. He possessed a clear apprehension, a sound and discriminating judgment, and a tenacious memory; and his application to the duties of his profession was indefatigable and highly meritorious . . . [T]hough he professed those principles which are called Moderate Calvinism, he opposed no obstacle to freedom of enquiry . . . I willingly embrace this

179. Halley, *Lancashire: its Puritanism and Nonconformity*, II, 405.

180. For Bull see ODNB; McLachlan, *English Education under the Test Acts*, 241-45.

181. See Sell, *Philosophy, Dissent and Nonconformity*, 12, 47-48.

182. For Gentleman see ODNB; Evans, *Midland Churches*, 156; Elliot, *A History of Congregationalism in Shropshire*, 22-24; McLachlan, *English Education under the Test Acts*, 55-57.

opportunity of paying a small tribute of gratitude and affection to the memory of a judicious and laborious instructor, a kind, a prudent, and a faithful friend.[183]

Others were less approving. In 1821 the celebrated Baptist minister, Robert Hall, wrote a "Memoir of the Rev, Thomas Toller" of Kettering in which he said that

> At the time of Mr. Toller's admission into the Daventry academy, the literary reputation of that seminary was higher than that of any among the dissenters; but, partly owing to a laxness in the terms of admission, and partly to the admixture of lay and divinity students, combined with the mode in which theology was taught, erroneous principles prevailed much; and the majority of such as were educated there became more distinguished for their learning, that for the fervour of their piety, or the purity of their doctrine . . .

Hall then refers to Priestley's favourable verdict on the academy, and continues:

> [T]he Theological professor prided himself on the steady impartiality with which he held the balance betwixt the contending systems, seldom or never interposing his own opinion, and still less betraying the slightest emotion of antipathy to error, or predilection to truth. Thus a spirit of indifference to all religious principles was generated in the first instance, which naturally paved the way for the prompt reception of doctrines indulgent to the corruption and flattering to the pride, of a depraved and fallen nature.[184]

It may be that Alan Clifford has something similar in mind, though he does not say so, when he advises us that with the removal of Doddridge's Academy to Daventry there "opened a less glorious chapter in the history of the Academy."[185] On the other hand we may confidently suppose that the Unitarian, Alexander Gordon, thought it a mark of Daventry's distinction that "Under Ashworth, Daventry Academy became a leading centre of learning for liberal Independents and Presbyterians."[186]

---

183. Belsham, *Zeal and Fortitude in the Christian Ministry*, 40 n.
184. Hall, *Works*, IV, 307–8.
185. Clifford. *The Good Doctor*, 104.
186. A. Gordon and Terry, "Caleb Ashworth," ODNB.

A caveat may, I think, be entered in both directions. In the first place, Doddridge had been content to have the liberal Samuel Clark as his assistant and to entrust the running of his Academy to him during his absence; and Doddridge, like Ashworth and Clark—and John Jennings before them, encouraged the open discussion of a wide variety of ideas. It is not surprising if, in doctrinally lively times, such a method should result in the alteration of opinions. Moreover, neither Doddridge nor Ashworth regarded their institutions as closed seminaries, but as academies providing a higher education. It would be pleasant to think that their ideals had come down to that minority among our present-day university departments of Religious Studies, conducted by ostensibly liberal scholars, in which Christianity is the one major religion which is barred from the curriculum. On the other hand we should not forget William Bull and others like him, who were able Daventry alumni of a decidedly evangelical stripe, more concerned with depth of spirituality than with breadth of curriculum.

It has further been charged that the Daventry of Ashworth's day did not produce men distinguished for their scholarship. But it had a wider brief that this, and if its alumni did not bequeath Gill-like bodies of divinity, the intellects of Priestley, Palmer, Bull, and Belsham, to name but a few, were undoubtedly on the sharper side of blunt. Nor should we overlook the alumni who went into secular employment: the Johnstone brothers who became significant physicians, or Joseph Dawson who ended where he most truly belonged, in mining. As for those who worked in pastoral charge and in Dissenting academies: from Ashworth's twenty-three years as principal have come no fewer than eleven entries in the *Oxford Dictionary of National Biography*—roughly one every two years; with which may be compared Mansfield College's record of eighteen ministerial entries in 120 years; roughly one every six years. By this reckoning Daventry's achievement during Ashworth's tenure was not insignificant. And over and above teaching and pastoral work Ashworth wrote text books, compiled a tune book, wrote a treatise on music with special reference to singing in the sanctuary, and masterminded and superintended the building of the Academy and the refurbishment of the chapel and other properties. Those writers who refer to his "prodigious labours" are not wide of the mark; and if it is alleged that Ashworth was no great scholar himself, the reply is that his genuine modesty made him most reluctant to publish, but that the funeral orations he published at ten year intervals reveal a lucid writer a careful thinker and a compassionate man. Hugh Worthington's verdict is just: "Dr. Ashworth was a man, who, though not distinguished by that acumen of genius and vigour of imagination, which some have possessed, yet by strong sense, inflexible resolution and indefatigable labour, acquired a store of theological learning, not often exceeded, and through a long train of years discharged the office of Divinity Tutor, with a respectability and success, which have seldom been equalled."[187]

The local man, Thomas Taylor, may give the final verdict on Ashworth the academy tutor. In his notes on the early history of Daventry Independent Church he refers to the Academy, "over which [Ashworth] presided with considerable reputation 23 years."[188]

VI

Caleb Ashworth died of congestive heart failure at 4.00 on Tuesday 18 July 1775. Belsham was there at the time, and he has described Ashworth's agony during his last days.[189] On 17 November 1775 his daughter, Miss H. Ashworth, wrote to Mercy Doddridge in the following terms: "we had a great loss in my Dear fathers not being sensable for some days before his Death: a very great sufferer he was: but happy State where Sin and Sorrow seace."[190] In the meantime Ashworth's funeral had taken place and he had been buried in the family tomb in the Daventry churchyard. We learn that the funeral oration was given by his successor, Thomas Robins, and that although "The town is what is called *high* . . . the principal gentlemen could not refrain from attending [Ashworth's] successor's sermon on his decease; not sitting, however, within the walls of the meeting-house, though they walked through the aisles to select their station."[191] Despite the encouragement of Samuel Palmer, Tayler, Fawcett, and Orton, Robins declined to publish his sermon.[192] In view of this, and by way of a "public testimony of respect," Palmer wrote his own sermon and it was published. It did not, however, include the history and character of Ashworth, for he himself had prohibited this. In his Preface Palmer did, however, allow himself to say that "if it had not been for this prohibition, nothing more needed to have been said, than that [Ashworth] was the immediate

---

187. Anon., "Memoir of the late Rev. Hugh Worthington," 562 n.
188. NRO DVURC 24, 1.
189. Williams, *Memoirs of the late Reverend Thomas Belsham*, 105.
190. NCL MSS L.1.4.56.
191. Thomas, "Supplementary hints," 80.
192. See Palmer, Orton's *Letters to Dissenting Ministers*, II, 160, 163 and n.

successor of the illustrious Dr. Doddridge, and was nominated by him to this office."[193] He dedicated his sermon to the Daventry students.

Palmer's text is Luke 10:2, "The harvest is truly great, but the labourers are few: Pray ye therefore the Lord of the harvest, that he would send forth labourers into his harvest." He divides his text in the obvious way: the harvest is the Redeemer's; it is great; the labourers are few; and prayer must be offered to God that their number may increase. Throughout Palmer has the need for ministers and the work of the Dissenting academies much in mind:

> We as Protestant Dissenters have reason to lament, that the number of ministers among us is far short of what it was when our fathers made that noble sacrifice to Christian liberty and the rights of conscience, which laid the foundation of our dissent. And Oh how much inferior are many of their sons of the present age in ability, devotion and zeal! The number of our ministers rather continues to decline. Many of our congregations are destitute, and are breaking up for want of suitable supplies, and the number of candidates for the ministry on our academies is not proportioned to the demands of our churches.[194]

What is Palmer's diagnosis of the cause of this unhappy state of affairs? First, the ministry is arduous and is a life of self-denial; the office promises no favourable worldly prospects; the Dissenters are divided among themselves; many hearers lack zeal and manifest "a strange ignorance of their avowed principles" so that they "run after every new preacher of almost any denomination who has the name of a 'gospel-preacher,' though in reality he has nothing but zeal, often nothing but noise to recommend him, or some other talent for making the thoughtless multitude gaze."[195] At this point Palmer inserts a footnote in which he points out that he has nothing against Methodists as such, and commends their ministers "as far as they preach the gospel and act agreeably to it . . . [Nevertheless] there are many irregularities among them . . ."[196] He then continues to exhort his hearers to pray for more labourers of the right sort, and this involves praying also that the "*schools of the prophets*" may be blessed, so that they will aim "not to train up *mere* scholars, (who are great curses to the Church) but *good*

---

193. Palmer, *The Want of Labourers in the Gospel Harvest*, Preface.

194. Ibid., 13. I am sure that I am not alone in having heard identical laments from those alive today.

195. Ibid., 14.

196. Ibid., 15 n.

Ministers of Jesus Christ."[197] In a Postscript he expresses the wish that some young ministers would spend a few years in "some of the darkest and most irreligious parts of this kingdom, where no regular societies are formed. Or where the Interest is entirely or almost extinct."

Among the endowments of the Daventry church are listed £200/0/0 from the will of James Floyd, and £100/0/0 of stock left by Caleb Ashworth.[198] On 15 March 1777 Thomas Robins, Wm. Barlee, and William Bull signed a document stating that they had received from John Ashworth the sum of £22/2/6, to be added to the £57/0/0/ given by his later father; the money to be used for buying £100/0/0 of stock, the interest to be used towards the support of three boys in the "Protestant Dissenting Charity School in Daventry."[199]

The inscription on Caleb Ashworth's tomb reads as follows:

>Here rest in hope,
>The remains of the Rev. Caleb Ashworth, D.D.;
>Pastor of a congregation of Protestant Dissenters,
>And director of the academy in this town.
>He died
>July 13, 1775, aged 54.
>With indefatigable application,
>With genuine well-regulated zeal,
>And with growing reputation and success,
>He exerted his eminent abilities
>And extensive acquaintance with sacred and human literature
>In the service of his great Master,
>And in promoting the important interests
>Of learning, religion, and charity.
>"Blessed is that servant whom his Lord when
>he cometh shall find so doing."[200]

In Thomas Belsham's opinion, "Dr. Ashworth was a great and good man. He had his foibles, and so have we all. These will be buried in the dust, while his many and great excellencies will remain long engraven upon the hearts of survivors. May they ever remain engraven upon our hearts, and

---

197. Ibid., 25.
198. NRO MSS, DVURC 24, 1.
199. NRO MSS, DVURC 24, 6.
200. Coleman, *Memorials of the Independent Churches of Northamptonshire*, 196.

may it be our ambition to follow him in those respects in which he followed his Divine Master!"[201]

One poignant remark remains to be added. I referred to Miss Ashworth's letter to Mercy Doddridge following her father's death. Three years later, in a letter of 18 June 1778, Job Orton writes, "I hear that Miss Ashworth died last week of a bad fever, just as she was going to be married to a considerable merchant in London. How awfully is the family melted away in a few years!"[202]

BIBLIOGRAPHY

(a) Manuscript sources

New College, London MSS, L.1.4.34; L.1.4.56; L.12.1; 54/3/44; L.57.10; L.12.1; L.177, 178, 180, 184, 215, 217, 218, 237, at Dr. Williams's Library, London.
DVURC [Daventry United Reformed Church] 24.1; 24.2; 24.3. 24.5; 24.8; 25(a) and (b); NPL 651, 655, 656,1125, 1132; at Northamptonshire Record Office, Northampton.

(b) Dictionary

A number of references are made to articles in *The Oxford Dictionary of National Biography*. Oxford: Oxford University Press, 2004.

(c) Other published works

Allard, W. *Memoir of Joseph Bealey: the Late Minister of a Congregation Meeting for Worship in the Presbyterian Chapel, at Cockey Moor.* Manchester: J. Aston, 1814.
Anon. Memoir and notes on the funeral sermon delivered on the death of Benjamin Carpenter. *The Monthly Repository* 12 (1817) 4–7, 51–52.
———. "Memoir of the late Rev. Hugh Worthington." *The Monthly Repository* 8 (1813) 561–75.
———. "Memoir of the late Rev. Noah Hill." *The Monthly Repository* 10 (1815) 186–88.
———. *The Unitarian Heritage: An Architectural Survey of Chapels and Churches in the Unitarian Tradition the British Isles.* Sheffield: Unitarian Heritage, 1986.
Arnold, Thomas, and J. J. Cooper. *History of the Church of Doddridge.* Kettering and Wellingborough: Northamptonshire Printing and Publishing Co., 1896.
Ashworth, Caleb. *A Collection of Tunes, Part I . . . with an Introduction to the Art of Singing.* 2nd ed. London: J. Buckland, 1765.

---

201. Williams, *Memoirs of the late Reverend Thomas Belsham*, 105.
202. Palmer, Orton's *Letters to Dissenting Ministers*, I, 199.

———. *Hope, the Christian Mourner's Relief. A Sermon Occasioned by the Death of the Rev. Mr. James Floyd, Who died July 21 1759, in the 55th Year of his Age. Preached at Daventry, July 29*. London: J. Buckland, 1759.

———. *The Principal Rules of Hebrew Grammar, compiled from some of the most considerable Hebrew Grammars*. Cambridge: 1763.

———. *Reflections on the Fall of a Great Man. A Sermon preached to a Congregational of Protestant Dissenters at Daventry in Northamptonshire on Occasion of the Death of the Late Reverend Isaac Watts, D.D.* London: J. Waugh, 1749.

———. *The Regards a Christian Congregation owe to their deceased Ministers represented and urged, in a Sermon preached at the Old Meeting in Birmingham, On Occasion of the much lamented Death of the Reverend Mr. Samuel Clark, Who departed this life December 6, 1769, In the Forty-second Year of his Age . . . To which is added the oration delivered at his Interment, by William Howell*. London: J. Buckland, 1770.

———. *Treatise on Trigonometry*. London, 1768.

Belsham, Thomas. "A List of Students educated at the Academy in Daventry under the Patronage of Mr. Coward's Trustees, and under the successive Superintendence of the Rev. Caleb Ashworth, D.D., the Rev. Thomas Robins, and the Rev. Thomas Belsham." *The Monthly Repository* 27 (1822) 163–64, 195–98, 284–87.

———. *Zeal and Fortitude in the Christian Ministry Illustrated and Exemplified. A Discourse delivered at Hackney, April 8, 1804, on occasion of the Death of the Rev. Joseph Priestley, LL.D., F.R.S., &c. Published at the Desire of the Congregation. To which is annexed, A Brief Memoir of Dr. Priestley's Life and Writings, and a Letter from his Son, Mr. Joseph Priestley, containing Particulars of his Last Sickness*. 2nd ed. London: J. Johnson, 1804.

Binfield, Clyde. *Pastors and People. The Biography of a Church: Queen's Road Coventry*. Coventry: published by the church, 1984.

Browne, John. *History of Congregationalism and Memorials of the Churches in Norfolk and Suffolk*. London: Jarrold, 1877.

Burder, George. "Memoir of John Butterworth." *Evangelical Magazine* (1804) 243–49.

Clifford, Alan C. *Philip Doddridge of Northampton: A Tercentenary Tribute*. Norwich: Charenton Reformed Publishing, 2002.

Coleman, Thomas. *Memorials of the Independent Churches in Northamptonshire*. London: John Snow, 1853.

Cowgill, Rachel, and Paul Holman. *Music in the British Provinces*. Aldershot: Ashgate, 2007.

Davidson, Hilary. *Choirs, Bands and Organs. A History of Church Music in Northamptonshire*. Oxford: Positif Press, 2003.

Deacon, Malcolm. *Philip Doddridge of Northampton*. Northampton: Northamptonshire Libraries, 1980.

Densham, W., and J. Ogle. *The Story of the Congregational Churches of Dorset, From their Foundation to the Present Time*. Bournemouth: W. Mate, 1899.

Drage, Sally. "The Larks of Dean: Amateur Musicians in Northern England." In *Music in the British Provinces 1690–1914*, edited by Rachel Cowgill and Peter Holman, ch. 10. Aldershot, UK: Ashgate, 2007.

Drage, Sally, and Peter Holman. Programme Notes to the CD, *While Shepherds Watched*. London: Hyperion Records (CDA66924), 1996.

Elliot, Ernest. *A History of Congregationalism in Shropshire*. Oswestry: Woodall, Minshall, [1898].

Evans, G. E. *Midland Churches: A History of the Congregations on the Roll of the Midland Christian Union.* Dudley: *Herald* Printing Works, 1899.

———. *Vestiges of Protestant Dissent.* Liverpool: F. and E. Gibbons, 1897.

Farrer, William, and J. B. Brownbill. *A History of the County of Lancaster*, VI, 1911.

Foster, James. *A Sermon Preached at White's Alley, on Sunday, October 31, 1742. On Occasion of the Death of the Reverend Mr. John Ashworth.* London: J. Noon, 1742.

Gordon, Alexander. *Addresses Biographical and Historical.* London: The Lindsey Press, 1922.

———. *Freedom After Ejection: A Review (1690-1692) of Presbyterian and Congregational Nonconformity in England and Wales.* Manchester: Manchester University Press, 1917.

Guppy, Paul. Programme Notes to the CD, "Repeat their Sounding Joy." West Gallery Music from Wyresdale, Lancashire, 1999.

Hall, Robert. *The Works of Robert Hall, A.M. With a brief Memoir of his Life by Dr. Gregory: and Observations on his Character as a Preacher, by John Foster.* 2nd ed. 6 vols. London: Holdsworth and Ball, 1833–34.

Halley, Robert. *Lancashire: Its Puritanism and Nonconformity.* 2 vols. Manchester: Tubbs and Brook, 1869.

Hampton, John D., revised by E. N. Staines. *History of the Lisbon Chaplaincy.* 2nd ed. Lisbon: Church Council of St. George the Martyr, 1989.

Hardman, James S. "Caleb Ashworth of Cloughfold and Daventry." *The Baptist Quarterly* N.S. 8 (1936–37) 200–206.

Herford, R. Travers, and E. D. Priestley Evans. *Historical Sketch of the North and East Lancashire Unitarian Mission and its Affiliated Churches 1859-1909.* Bury: Fletcher and Speight, 1909.

Holman, Peter. "Performing Psalmody: A Personal View." In *Georgian Psalmody 2: The Interaction between Urban and Rural Practice.* Corby Glen: SG Publishing, 1999.

Hosken, T. J. *History of Congregationalism and Memorials of the Churches of our Order in Suffolk.* Ipswich: W. E. Harrison, 1920.

Hunsworth, G. *Memorials of the Old Meeting House, Kidderminster*, [1874].

James, John. *The History and Topography of Bradford.* London: Longman, Brown, Green and Longmans, 1841.

Jeremy, Walter D. *The Presbyterian Fund and Dr. Williams's Trust, with Biographical Notes of the Trustees, and Some Account of their Academies, Scholarships and Schools.* London: Williams & Norgate, 1885.

Joyce, Jeremiah. "Memoir of the late Rev. Hugh Worthington." *The Monthly Repository* 8 (1813) 561–75.

Langley, Arthur S. *Birmingham Baptists Past and Present.* London: The Kingsgate Press, [1939].

McLachlan, Herbert. *English Education under the Test Acts.* Manchester: Manchester University Press, 1931.

———. *Essays and Addresses.* Manchester: Manchester University Press, 1950.

———. *The Unitarian Home Missionary Society College.* London: Sherratt & Hughes, 1915.

Manning, James. *A Sketch of the Life and Writings of the Rev. Micaijah Towgood*, 1792.

Matthews, A. G. *Calamy Revised* (1934). Oxford: Clarendon, 1988.

Murch, Jerom. *A History of the Presbyterian and General Baptist Churches in the West of England; with Memoirs of some of their Pastors.* London: R. Hunter, 1835.

Musson, A. E., and E. Robinson. *Science and Technology in the Industrial Revolution*. Manchester: Manchester University Press, 1969.

Nicholson, Francis, and Ernest Axon. *The Older Nonconformity in Kendal*. Kendal: Titus Wilson, 1915.

Nightingale, Benjamin. *Lancashire Nonconformity*. 6 vols. Manchester: John Heywood, 1890–93.

Nuttall, Geoffrey F. *Calendar of the Correspondence of Philip Doddridge, DD (1702–1751)*. London: Her Majesty's Stationery Office, 1979.

Orton, Job. *Memoirs of the Late Reverend Dr. Philip Doddridge*. Shrewsbury, 1766.

Overend, Frederick. *The History of Ebenezer Baptist Church, Bacup*. London: The Kingsgate Press, 1912.

Palmer, Samuel. *Letters to Dissenting Ministers and to Students for the Ministry, from the Rev. Mr. Job Orton, Transcribed from the original Short-Hand, with Notes Explanatory and Biographical. To which are prefixed, Memoirs of his Life by Samuel Palmer*. 2 vols. London: Hurst, Reed, and Orme, 1806.

———. "Memoir of Dr. Caleb Ashworth." *The Monthly Repository* 8 (1813) 693–96.

———. *The Want of Labourers in the Gospel Harvest, considered and improved: in a Sermon Preached July 30, 1775, on Occasion of the much Lamented Death of the Reverend and Learned Caleb Ashworth, D.D. Tutor of the Dissenting Academy at Daventry in Northamptonshire*. London: J. Buckland and W. Harris, 1775.

———. [Palmer, Samuel]. "Brief Memoirs of the Rev. Mr. Samuel Clark, Late Minister at Birmingham." *The Monthly Repository* (1806) 617–22.

Parry, Abel Jones. *History of the Cloughfold Baptist Church from 1675 to 1875*. Manchester: John Heywood, [1876].

Priestley, Joseph. "Joseph Priestley's Journal while at Daventry Academy, 1754," transcribed from the original shorthand by Tony Rail and Beryl Thomas. *Enlightenment and Dissent* 13 (1994) 49–113.

———. *The Theological and Miscellaneous Works of Joseph Priestley*, edited by J. T. Rutt (1817–1831). Bristol: Thoemmes, 1999.

Sell, Alan P. F. *Church Planting: A Study of Westmorland Nonconformity*. 1986. Reprinted, Eugene, OR: Wipf & Stock, 1998.

———. *Dissenting Thought and the Life of the Churches: Studies in an English Tradition*. Lewiston, NY: Mellen, 1990.

———. *Hinterland Theology: A Stimulus to Theological Construction*. Milton Keynes, UK: Paternoster, 2008. Eugene, OR: Wipf & Stock, 2009.

———. *Philosophy, Dissent and Nonconformity 1680–1920*. 2004. Reprinted Eugene, OR: Wipf & Stock, 2009.

Sellers, Ian. *Our Heritage. The Baptists of Yorkshire, Lancashire and Cheshire 1647–1987*. Leeds: The Yorkshire, and the Lancashire and Cheshire Baptist Associations, 1987.

Seymour, Jane. "The musicians of Rossendale." *West Gallery* 6 (1994); amended version at http://www.wgma.org.uk/Articles/Larks/article.htm.

Sibree, John, and M. Caston. *Independency in Warwickshire*. Coventry: G. and F. King, 1855.

Stell, Christopher. *An Inventory of Nonconformist Chapels and Meeting-Houses in Central England*. London: Her Majesty's Stationery Office, 1986.

Taylor, Thomas. Notes on the early history of Daventry Independent Church. See Manuscripts above: DCURC 24.1.

Thomas, Thomas. "Supplementary Hints to the Rev. Mr. Palmer's Memoir of Dr. Ashworth." *The Monthly Repository* 9 (1814) 10–12; 78–80.

Thompson, John Handby. *History of the Coward Trust: The First Two Hundred and Fifty Years 1738–1988.* Supplement to *The Journal of the United Reformed Church History Society*, 6; and *The Congregational History Circle Magazine* 3 (1988).

[Thornton, Alfred]. *1672–1972: Daventry Congregational Church . . . 300 Years of Witness.* Daventry: Dacre Press, [1972].

Turner, J. Horsfall. *Nonconformity in Idle with the History of Airedale College.* Bradford: T. Brear, 1876.

Urwick, William. *Nonconformity in Herts.* London: Hazell, Watson, and Viney, 1884

———. *Nonconformity in Worcester.* London: Simpkin, Marshall, Hamilton, Kent, 1897.

Watson, George. *A Brief Memoir of the Rev. Thomas Robins, late of Daventry, Northamptonshire; with a Sketch of the Sermon Preached on the Occasion of His Death.* London, 1810.

Whitley, W. T. *Baptists of North-West England, 1649–1913.* London: Kingsgate, 1913.

Wilkinson, John T. "The Rise of Other Methodist Traditions." In *A History of the Methodist Church in Great Britain*, edited by Rupert Davies, A. Raymond George, and Gordon Rupp, ch. 7. 4 vols. London: Epworth, 1964–88.

Williams, John. *Memoirs of the Late Reverend Thomas Belsham: Including a Brief Notice of His Published Works, and copious Extracts from His Diary, together with Letters to and from His Friends and Correspondents.* London, 1833.

Wilson, Walter. *The History and Antiquities of Dissenting Churches and Meeting-houses in London, Westminster, and Southwark.* London: Button, 1808–12.

Wylie, Robert J. V. *The Baptist Churches of Accrington and District.* Accrington: Wellington, 1923.

3

Scottish Religious Philosophy, 1850–1900[1]

A PREAMBLE IS UNAVOIDABLE. First, although biblical studies and doctrinal and practical theology fall outside my remit, we do well to remember that some of the philosophically-minded authors to be considered could turn their hands to these and other intellectual pursuits. The age of the polymath had not yet entirely passed, the age of the disciplinary specialist was still in the making. I shall not be able to include all of those who contributed philosophico-religious ideas to Scottish thought, and in particular I shall not be able to introduce a number of those who, with emotions varying from regret to hostility, opposed Christian intellectual positions and were answered by those who espoused them.[2]

Secondly, it will be necessary to take account of the fact that some of the writers with whom I shall be concerned outlived the nineteenth century, and published works of interest during the early years of the twentieth century.

Thirdly, the impact of what Gilbert Ryle called "the laicizing of our culture" and "the professionalizing of philosophy" had yet to be felt.[3] In

---

1. Abbreviations: DECBP : *Dictionary of Eighteenth Century British Philosophers*, edited by Yolton, Price and Stephens; DNCBP: *Dictionary of Nineteenth-Century British Philosophers*, edited by Mander and Sell; DSCHT: *Dictionary of Scottish Church History and Theology*, edited by Cameron; ODNB: *Oxford Dictionary of National Biography*.

2. For example, J. S. Mill and his interlocutors. Of those Christian authors I shall introduce here, Robert Flint, Robert Mackintosh, and James Orr appear briefly in the pages of my *Mill on God*.

3. Ryle, Introduction to *The Revolution in Philosophy*, 4.

Scotland especially the senior philosophical posts in the universities were in the hands of ministers of religion to a significant degree, and it was not unusual for appointments to be influenced by denominational considerations. To an extent hard to comprehend nowadays, Scottish society at large was occupied with biblical, doctrinal and ecclesiastical debates. People took sides over modern biblical criticism, the status of the Scottish Church's confessional standards, and the relations between Church and state; and any of these, or all of them in combination, could divide churches and split families. These matters coalesced in such a way as to influence Scottish university appointments in philosophy. After more than a century of secessions from the Church of Scotland the question of patronage came to the fore once more during the eighteen-thirties, with many complaining that under the patronage system non-evangelical ministers were being intruded upon parishes that did not wish to receive them. Following what became known as the Ten Years' Conflict, in 1843 the Disruption occurred when Thomas Chalmers led one-third of the ministers and up to half of the lay representatives out of the General Assembly. They constituted themselves as the Free Church of Scotland. Denying that they were (like the earlier Seceders) ecclesiastical voluntaries, they regarded themselves as the Church of Scotland, Free. They established colleges in Edinburgh, Glasgow, and Aberdeen, and owing to their expertise in "godly politicking"—an occupation in which the United Presbyterian[4] John Cairns seems to have excelled—they ensured that A. Campbell Fraser, Professor of Logic at the Free Church's New College, Edinburgh, and not J. F. Ferrier, was appointed at Edinburgh University in 1856 in succession to William Hamilton; that Alexander Bain was not appointed at St. Andrews in 1858, or John Nicol at Glasgow in 1864, or T. H. Green at St. Andrews in the same year; and in 1868 the outstanding scholar, Robert Flint, who had remained with the Church of Scotland and whose spirit could not have been less partisan, was passed over at Edinburgh in favour of the seceder

---

4. Not , therefore, "a minister of the breakaway Free Church" as stated by Alexander Broadie, *A History of Scottish Philosophy*, 305. One month before the professorial election was due to be held Cairns published his *Examination of Ferrier's Theory of Knowing and Being*. According to his biographer Cairns was "an absolute and ruthless anti-Hegelian." See MacEwen, *Life and Letters of John Cairns*, 396. MacEwen reminds us, *ad loc.*, that "In Germany the Hegelian philosophy had been closely connected not only with the Tübingen Schol of theology but with still grosser rationalism . . ." This did not at all appeal to the evangelicals. Letters and pamphlets flowed, and Cairns followed up with *The Scottish Philosophy: A Vindication and a Reply*, 185. For Cairns (1811–1892) see also DNCBP, DSCHT, ODNB.

Henry Calderwood.[5] Edward Caird attributed his success in securing his Glasgow Chair in 1866 to the fact that he had "done nothing"[6]—that is, he had not come forth as a "party" man—least of all as a man of the "wrong" party.

Fourthly, on the other hand, as W. R. Sorley observed of "English" philosophy (under which rubric he, like James Seth and others, included the Scottish—the age of devolved government not having yet arrived), "Many of its great writers have been men of leisure or men of affairs, who were not occupied with philosophy professionally but were attracted by the perennial interest of its problems."[7] Among the latter the Scots Alexander Bain, J. H. Stirling and James Lindsay were prominent.

Finally, how are we to construe "Scottish" in the title of this chapter? Are we to understand "the religious (philosophical) thought of Scots (at home and abroad)"? Or ought we to consider all who philosophized in Scotland—which would admit the Welshman Henry Jones and the Englishman A. E. Taylor? Or ought we to concern ourselves with "religious-*cum*-philosophical thought in Scotland that was characteristically Scottish?" Partly because I have discussed the Cairds and other idealists elsewhere,[8] I take the last route (though reserving the right to discuss the exile Robert

---

5. No doubt those nineteenth-century evangelicals who were conversant with the Scottish intellectual tradition regarded these academic victories as appropriate recompense for the "Moderate" succession of John Simson, Francis Hutcheson and William Leechman at Glasgow University in the eighteenth century. Strongly confessional Calvinists regarded the more optimistic anthropology of the Moderates as wrong in itself, for it implied that sinners had moral and epistemological abilities that their status actually denied them—a view perceived as demeaning to Christ's saving work. See further, Davie, *The Democratic Intellect*, ch. 14; though beware of a certain partiality which enables Davie to describe Calderwood as "a narrow-minded extremist" (319), and to speak of Fraser, Calderwood and Veitch as having "captured [their] chairs in the interests of extreme evangelicalism" (328). See also MacEwen, *The Life and Letters of John Cairns*; and Thomson, *Ferrier of St. Andrews*. The following ordained persons held philosophy chairs in Scottish universities during the second half of the nineteenth century: Henry Calderwood (United Presbyterian: Edinburgh), William Fleming (Church of Scotland: Glasgow), Robert Flint (Church of Scotland: St. Andrews, Edinburgh), A. Campbell Fraser (Free Church: Edinburgh), and William A. Knight (Free Church: St. Andrews). As we shall see, a number of philosophically-inclined theologians held chairs in the theological colleges of the several denominations.

6. Caird confided thus to R. M. Wenley; see Adams and Montague, *Contemporary American Philosophy*, II, 390.

7. Sorley, *A History of British Philosophy to 1900*, 301. James Seth's book is *English Philosophers and Schools of Philosophy*.

8. I have discussed the Cairds elsewhere. For John see *Defending and Declaring the Faith*, ch. 4; for Edward see *Philosophical Idealism and Christian Belief*.

Mackintosh, whose professorial chair was in England). There remains the begged question, What is denoted by the term, "characteristically Scottish religious-*cum*-philosophical thought?" The answer is, that thought which, to a greater or lesser degree is indebted to Thomas Reid's Common Sense philosophy. The justification of this appropriately vague answer will become clearer as we proceed.

I

When Thomas Reid (1710-1796) declared that "Wise men now agree, or ought to agree in this, that there is but one way to the knowledge of nature's works; the way of observation and experiment"; and when he further remarked that "All that we know of the body, is owing to anatomical dissection and observation, and it must be by an anatomy of the mind that we can discover its powers and principles,"[9] he was doing more than placing himself in the scientifically inductive line of Isaac Newton; he rightly understood himself as reaching back to Bacon's *Novum Organum* (1620). He also knew that "when we turn our attention inward and consider the phaenomena of human thought, opinions and perceptions, and endeavour to trace them to general laws and first principles of our constitution, we are immediately involved in darkness and perplexity."[10] Undeterred, he set out to advance a theory that would make good what he perceived as the deficiencies of Locke's sensationalism, Berkeley's psychological idealism, and Hume's scepticism.[11] By means of a careful analysis of self-consciousness he aspired to offer an account of those principles, both necessary and contingent, that were antecedent to experience. Whereas Oswald and Beattie appealed to the "common sense" of humanity regarding such beliefs as those concerning the reality of the natural order, personal identity, causation and freedom— all of which a Hume could show were epistemologically valueless and subject to illusion, Reid sought a more philosophically sophisticated and secure basis from which to launch his critique. He was as persuaded as Hume that the scientific approach of observation and ex-

---

9. Reid, *An Inquiry into the Human Mind*, 11, 12. For Reid see DECBP, DSCHT, ODNB.

10. Ibid., 16.

11. I am well aware of the extensive discussions that have been engendered regarding the appropriateness or otherwise of these terms as descriptive of the three writers (for example, Locke allied reflection with sensation, and was a rationalist in ethics); but this is what Reid understood himself to be doing.

periment was the correct one, but in deriving his principles from a careful analysis of self-conscious experience he turned the tables on Hume. Far from appealing to the common sense of humanity, in the popular sense of the term, as the guarantor of truth, he argued that Hume's sensation was an abstraction that could not be dissociated from an experiencing self.[12] Negatively, Reid held that the mind is not a passive recipient of ideas that are the alleged objects of thought. Positively, he took the activist line that "By the *mind* of a man, we understand that in him which thinks, remembers, reasons, wills."[13] Judgement and belief, as well as simple apprehension, are, in Reid's view, integral to the operation of the senses. Thus in this natural realism self-consciousness and sense perception are brought together. Hence Andrew Seth's suggestion that "by maintaining a theory of Immediate Perception, Scottish philosophy destroys the foreignness of matter to mind, and thus implicitly removes the only foundation of a real dualism."[14] While it may justifiably be argued that Reid's multiplication of intuitions, and his delineation of necessary and contingent principles leaves something to be desired, it must be conceded that his investigation of self-consciousness paved the way in Scottish religious thought for a Christian apologetic that was at the mercy neither of sensationalism nor of the vaguer types of mysticism.

The realisation was not slow in dawning, however, that religious experience concerns ultimate mystery that falls outside the range of introspective self-observation. Reid and William Hamilton (1788–1856)[15] could only grant the fact, and the latter, influenced by Kant's conviction that we can acquire knowledge of phenomena only, not of noumena, adumbrated his doctrine of subjective relativity, namely, that there is no way whereby we may transcend the relation of knower and known. He balanced this with the claim that there is also objective relativity in that in any known object there is a plurality of relation. At this point J. F. Ferrier

---

12. In an analogous way McCosh, who had studied under Hamilton and Chalmers, was later to turn the tables on John Stuart Mill, whose sensationalism, McCosh declared, relied upon the very intuition that Mill had ruled out. See Mill. *An Examination of Sir William Hamilton's Philosophy*; McCosh. *An Examination of Mr. J. S. Mill's Philosophy*. See also Sell, *Mill on God*, 52–53.

13. Reid. *Essays on the Intellectual Powers of Man*, 20.

14. Seth, *Scottish Philosophy*, 76–77. Seth later added "Pringle-Pattison" to his name in fulfilment of the terms of a will. I discuss his thought in *Philosophical Idealism and Christian Belief*.

15. For Hamilton see DNCBP, DSCHT, ODNB.

(1808–1864)[16] broke with his mentor and friend and, repudiating agnostic relativity, went in quest of a more rigorously rational defence of common sense. He invoked the idea of organic emergence and contended that the self that orders the several experiences of common sense remains distinct from them. That is to say, while agreeing with Reid that the several states of mind are known to self-consciousness, they are known by the self as the subject of them all. Influenced by, though not slavishly attached to, Spinoza's method, Ferrier diverged from Scottish intuitionism towards a deductive rationalism. Some found Ferrier teetering on the brink of monism; James Seth characterized his position as that of absolute idealism,[17] and Broadie justifies that label thus: "This is a version of the doctrine of 'absolute idealism', 'absolute' because it concerns the character that something must have if it is to exist absolutely and is not to exist merely relatively to something else, and 'idealism' because the doctrine affirms that there is no world except as an object in relation to a subject of consciousness."[18] For all that, Ferrier regarded himself as developing, not repudiating, Scottish Common Sense philosophy, and testified that while he had read Hegel's works he had quite failed to understand them.

From our present point of view Ferrier's significance is that he exemplifies, at one extreme, the degree of definitional elasticity of which the term "Common Sense" was capable, whilst the other extreme is represented by Oswald and Beattie who construed the term in the more popular sense of the common judgments of humanity. In between we find such an author as Henry Calderwood (1830–1897),[19] himself a former student of Hamilton. In his book, *The Philosophy of the Infinite: A Treatise on Man's Knowledge of the Infinite Being, in Answer to Sir William Hamilton and Dr. Mansel* (1854), he, like Ferrier, repudiated the agnosticism he found in his teacher's work, but did so by aligning himself with the intuitionism of Reid and Stewart, and not by taking Ferrier's deductive rationalist way. The nub of his case was that it is open to human beings to have a real, though incomplete, knowledge of the infinite.

It is not difficult to understand why those who intended to uphold the tradition as adumbrated by Reid, and even by Hamilton, should have regarded Ferrier as a traitor, his protestations of fidelity to the Scottish philosophical tradition notwithstanding. His philosophy was not "safe,"

---

16. For Ferrier see DNCBP, ODNB.
17. J. Seth, *English Philosophers*, 239.
18. Broadie, *A History of Scottish Philosophy*, 311.
19. For Calderwood see DNCBP, ODNB.

and to this charge the evangelicals added their judgment that his theology was not "sound." They were not concerned that Ferrier turned his guns on the English Coleridge and F. D. Maurice,[20] but when he denounced the anthropological pessimism of Thomas Chalmers and other high Calvinists which led them to believe that sinful man "can, and must, *do nothing for himself*,"[21] thereby undermining moral responsibility, this was Moderatism, and a step too far.[22] From the evangelical point of view Ferrier espoused the wrong philosophy, the wrong theology, and belonged to the wrong Church (of Scotland). When he further opposed Chalmers's idea of removing epistemology from the Scottish course in moral philosophy in favour of compulsory political science and jurisprudence, he earned a further black mark.[23] It must also be granted that, although he had earlier practised as an advocate at law, Ferrier was not always his own best advocate. Thus, following his failure to succeed to the Edinburgh Chair he published a pamphlet in which he both declared his loyalty to the Scottish school of philosophy and also sardonically observed that "It is well known that a candidate for a philosophical chair in the University of Edinburgh need not now be a believer in Christ or a member of the Established Church; but he must be a believer in Dr. Reid, and a pledged disciple of the Hamiltonian system of philosophy."[24] This suggests that he was a very clever person who was not always very wise.

It remains only to add that the successful candidate for the Edinburgh Chair, Alexander Campbell Fraser (1819–1914),[25] aroused the ire of Ferrier when in 1856 he published a paper entitled, "Ferrier's theory of knowing and being." Ever keen to resist monistic gnosticism, Fraser branded Ferrier's rationalistic version of common sense theory "a kind of

---

20. As he did in *Blackwoods Magazine*, June 1840. For a sample see Davie, *The Democratic Intellect*, 263–64.

21. Ferrier, *Philosophical Works*, II, 244.

22. Many evangelicals were influenced in this matter by Ralph Wardlaw's Congregational Lecture (the first in the series, delivered in 1833), *Christian Ethics; or Moral Philosophy on the Principles of Divine Revelation*. To Davie (*The Democratic Intellect*, 267) Wardlaw was "a sectarian enthusiast." In fact he was a distinguished Congregational divine, albeit an anthropological pessimist. For a less prejudiced account see Sell, *Philosophy, Dissent and Nonconformity*, 154–57.

23. For philosophy in the Scottish universities see, in addition to Davie, *The Democratic Intellect*, Veitch, "Philosophy in the Scottish Universities."

24. Ferrier, *Scottish Philosophy, the Old and the New*, 7.

25. For Fraser see DNCBP, DSCHT, ODNB; Sell, *Commemorations*, ch. 10.

Scottish Hegelianism."[26] Ferrier replied in his *Scottish Philosophy, the Old and the New*.

Against the intellectual-ecclesiastical background all too briefly sketched, I shall introduce some philosophically-inclined Scottish religious thinkers who, during the second half of the nineteenth century, tended more towards their native philosophical tradition than to the post-Hegelian idealism which became increasingly prominent, especially at Glasgow under the Cairds and Edward Caird's student, Henry Jones. By way of further placing these thinkers I shall first consider the judgments they passed upon their prominent philosophical predecessors and contemporaries;[27] I shall then discuss their contribution to apologetics and their responses to some of the particular intellectual challenges of their day. I proceed in chronological order of thinkers from Descartes onwards.

II

James Iverach (1839–1922) became Professor of Apologetics and New Testament Exegesis at the Free Church (subsequently United Free) College, Aberdeen in 1887. In 1904 his book, *Descartes, Spinoza and the New Philosophy* appeared. Descartes, we learn, went in quest of "all the presuppositions, and all the points involved in the fact of knowledge. He did not ask Kant's question, How is knowledge possible?"[28] In the event he did not complete his analysis of the principles involved in knowledge. He stopped short, and instead offered his method of systematic doubt. Whereas his original intention was to reach universal and necessary truth, the objective of his method of doubt was certainty. He substituted "for a process of analysis a process of abstraction,"[29] whereby he separated thought from its object, the mind from the world. He thus "introduced that dualism which spoilt the fruitfulness of his philosophy, and gave rise to that abstract rationalism which divorced philosophy from experience, and gave rise also to that empiricism which divorced experience from thought."[30] With Descartes

---

26. Fraser, "Ferrier's theory of knowing and being," 312. More than forty years later Fraser defended Hamilton against Ferrier's charges in his *Thomas Reid*.

27. I restrict myself to thinkers from Descartes onwards, and to overall judgments passed upon them: I cannot here offer a critique of my authors' expositions as such.

28. Iverach, *Descartes, Spinoza and the New Philosophy*, 44. For Iverach see DNCBP, DSCHT; Sell, *Defending and Declaring the Faith*, ch. 6.

29. Ibid, .46.

30. Ibid., 53.

> the Ego is taken to be the form of consciousness, and directly affiliated to this is the phaenominalistic spiritualism of Berkeley, the monadological spiritualism of Leibniz, and the transcendental idealism of Kant. The idea as the content of consciousness has given rise to the Ego as absolute substance of Spinoza, the Ego as absolute activity by Fichte, and the Ego as absolute reason by Schelling and Hegel, and the Ego as absolute will by Schopenhauer, and as individual will by Wundt. Taking the Ego as empirical principle, and subordinating it to its objects, we have the empirical philosophies from Locke to Herbert Spencer.[31]

In Iverach's opinion everything in Descartes' philosophy turns upon his proof of the existence of God, and his most damning criticism is that Descartes invoked God and his power to heal the dualistic breach Descartes had made between mind and body:

> he uses principles which he holds to be truths evident by the light of reason to prove the existence of God, and then he seeks to guarantee the validity of reason by the veracity of God . . . [I]t is not a worthy procedure to bring in the notion of the Deity to save a system from bankruptcy . . . If the consciousness of self is the first certainty, and if we cannot abstract from it, then to seek to go beyond it is futile. But Descartes did not trust his own first principle.[32]

Analytically, Descartes argues that imperfect human beings have the idea of a most perfect Being and, since they could not produce this idea themselves, it must have a cause in that Being. Synthetically, he starts from the ontological argument and contends that the idea of God is an axiom from which all else flows. Whereas Anselm's ontological argument failed to show that the idea of God is a necessary one, Descartes finds the idea given in our experience and we cannot expunge it. He is thus led to believe that our self-consciousness is inseparably joined to our consciousness of God. The idea of God is thus necessary, and divinely given. Descartes could not, however, answer the question, "If God is the sum of all perfection, how can we explain the manifoldness and imperfection of the finite?"[33]

Iverach proceeds to argue that Cartesian dualism leads to the deeper dualism between "the idealist and the mechanical schools of thought."[34]

---

31. Ibid., 54.
32. Ibid., 62, 63.
33. Ibid., 90.
34. Ibid., 93.

This arises from the fact that Descartes "proceeds, not by analysis, but by abstraction, and when he limits matter to extended substance he is simply attributing reality to an abstraction, and is as scholastic as any schoolman."[35] Again, "He left unclear the relation of will and understanding, the relation of soul to body, and the relation of God to both; . . . his definition of the nature of mind and of the nature of body made it impossible that there should be any interaction between them."[36]

By contrast, "the essence of the system of Spinoza" is "the wholeness of the whole."[37] His was the quest for the highest good, human perfection. Spinoza does not seek the origin of our ideas; rather, he sets out from the conviction that true ideas are self-evident, and that "We think truly when we apprehend things through their essential nature or through their proximate cause,"[38] in other words, when we "have in idea the real nature of the object of thought."[39] Spinoza is concerned with concrete being, with the particularity of objects of thought, and he seeks to avoid abstractions. Whereas Hume held that distinct perceptions are distinct existences and that the mind cannot perceive any real connection among distinct existences, to Spinoza it is axiomatic that "our fixed and necessary ideas had eternal realities correspondent to them."[40]

To Spinoza, God, or Substance, is one, without limit or change. The problem at once arises, "How can the concreteness of the whole and its wholeness consist with the changeableness of the *Natura naturata*?"[41] To this question Spinoza has no satisfactory answer. Again, in the interests of the inevitable necessity of things he ignores or explains away freedom and final cause: to him these are illusions prompted by human ignorance and finitude. At the same time he insists that his position poses no threat to the moral life. Indeed, he argues that "The more the knowledge that things are necessary is applied to particular things, the greater is the power of the mind over the emotions . . . Universal necessity lifts us out of our isolation, and enables us to see ourselves as included in the universal Being, and one with God."[42] At this point Iverach seems to yield to bafflement, concluding

35. Ibid., 123.
36. Ibid., 130.
37. Ibid., 132.
38. Ibid., 152.
39. Ibid., 153.
40. Ibid., 161.
41. Ibid., 190.
42. Ibid., 235.

that "it is our business to take from [Spinoza's message] as much as we find possible for us in these days of ours."⁴³ It may well be, however, that he had reached the word limit of the series for which he was writing. I have elsewhere presumed to say that such was Iverach's patience in laying the groundwork that "In both book and sermon he could spend so much time on preliminaries that weighty matters were crowded together at the end, or even omitted altogether."⁴⁴ Certainly one reviewer complained that "The major theological part of Spinoza's writings and the main part of his political philosophy are untouched"⁴⁵ in *Descartes, Spinoza and the New Philosophy*. Elsewhere, however, Iverach did turn his attention to pantheism, albeit with reference to later writers, and I shall return to him shortly.

George Berkeley falls next to be considered, and here the authority is Alexander Campbell Fraser, whose edition of Berkeley's works is still in print, that of T. E. Jessop notwithstanding, and whose *Berkeley* (1881) remains of interest for the way in which Fraser relates Berkeley to other philosophers, not least to Hume and Reid.⁴⁶ We learn that by concentrating upon Berkeley's earlier works Hume is able to welcome his phenomenalist nominalism, and to present him as a sceptic superior even to Bayle. In so doing, Fraser declares, "Hume ignores the Berkeleyan appeal to common sense on behalf of the beliefs (a) that the interpretable phenomena of sense, viewed objectively, are the real things; and (b) that in his moral consciousness of *himself*, as a free self-acting spiritual person, each of us reaches the ontological reality of substance and cause, and the spiritual basis of things—the datum universalised in 'Siris.'"⁴⁷ Hume thus exaggerates an aspect of Berkeley's thought, and mistakes the part for the whole. In the reaction against Hume the three elements that went to make up Berkeley's philosophy became disengaged:

> The subtle argumentative analysis and negative phenomenalism . . . was the Berkeley to whom Hume and afterwards John Stuart Mill avowed allegiance. The appeals to common faith or common sense, in our consciousness of self, and in connection with the favourite thought of significant and interpretable sense phenomena . . . forecast Reid, while they recall the *cogito* of

---

43. Ibid., 242.
44. Sell, *Defending and Declaring the Faith*, 120.
45. Duncan, Review, 95.
46. For Fraser's account of his philosophical pilgrimage see *Biographia Philosophica*.
47. Fraser, *Berkeley*, 214 n.

> Descartes. Lastly, the philosophical rationalism of "Siris," which sees in the phenomenal things of sense the creative working of that *intellectus ipse* in which each separate conscious spirit shares, in its way anticipates Kant and Hegel.[48]

The upshot was that "By the rigid application of the phenomenal criterion, the spiritual intellectualism of Berkeley was made by Hume to disappear."[49]

Fraser grants that Hume's scepticism cannot be refuted either by Reid's appeal to the trustworthiness of our ineradicable beliefs, or by Kant's analysis of the necessities of thought, for "To show, by means of suspected faculties, that the 'experience' which has been charged with illusion, because only phenomenal, really presupposes more than phenomena, is to presume as real what the sceptic asks to be proved real. There is always an abstract possibility that our faculties may be false; but if even self-consciousness and memory must be vindicated before they can be used, we can never get to work at all."[50] Moreover, scepticism "is always practically refuted, by the imperishable trust which reason reposes in its own validity; so that no human mind can permanently surrender to it."[51] Fraser concludes that Berkeley's thought

> becomes, when we pursue it further than he did, a sublime intuition of the phenomenal realities of sense, inorganic and organic, as established media for the intellectual education of finite spirits by means of physical sciences; for intercourse between individual moral agents, and for a revelation of the Eternal Spirit, in whom the merely phenomenal things of sense, and moral agents too, have their being. It includes the fundamental faith that the universe exists for an eternal moral purpose, so that our experience in it, with the conditions of thought and belief presupposed in the experience, must be practically trustworthy and reasonable.[52]

"A philosophy grounded on Faith," Fraser declares (*pace* Ferrier), "was the highest lesson of Reid and his successors, especially Hamilton, in Scotland . . ."[53] We shall come to Fraser's own account of such a philosophy in due course.

---

48. Ibid., 217.
49. Ibid., 221.
50. Ibid., 224.
51. Ibid., For Calderwood's critique of Hume see his posthumous, *David Hume*.
52. Fraser, *Berkeley*, 233–34.
53. Ibid., 230.

Scottish Religious Philosophy, 1850–1900

First, however, we must consider the reaction of a Scottish religious philosopher-theologian to the Hegelian way of pursuing Spinoza's quest of wholeness and of joining together what Hume had put asunder, and what Kant's phenomena-noumena disjunction had, in its own way, forbidden. I summon Robert Mackintosh (1858–1931), a sharp-minded, self-styled refugee from the High Calvinism of the Free Church of Scotland, who found a congenial home in Congregationalism, and after a pastorate in Dumfries became Professor of Apologetics at Lancashire Independent College, Manchester.[54] His book, *Hegel and Hegelianism* appeared in 1903. I am here concerned only with his judgment on Hegelianism, for it is the judgment of one who, like James Denney, James Orr and others, but decidedly unlike Henry Jones, was taught at Glasgow by Edward Caird, but was finally unpersuaded by his Kant-influenced absolute idealism.

In Mackintosh's opinion, while intuitionalism "finds its chance in the misadventures of empiricism,"[55] Kant broke from intuitionalism

> by substituting *one system of necessity* for the many necessary truths or given experiences from which intuitionalism takes its start . . . [Yet] Kant's idealism is incomplete. On one side, the world we know by valid processes of thinking cannot, we are told, be the real world. Or, beginning from the other side; neither the reality which ideal thought reaches after, not yet the reality which our conscience postulates, is the valid world of orderly thinking. The great critic of scepticism has diverged from idealism towards scepticism again, or has given his idealism a sceptical colour, mitigated—but only mitigated—by faith in the moral consciousness.[56]

Hegel does not flinch. He boldly affirms the rationality of the universe; he strenuously denies the dualism of fact and principles and declares that all is as it must be. To the extent that he rebuts Kant's scepticism, Mackintosh approves of Hegel. But he seriously questions his dialectical method whereby he even "undertakes to show to candid minds that incompatible assertions not only may but must both be true."[57] This, Mackintosh thinks, subverts the systematic coherence that Hegel thought he had achieved. What Mackintosh wishes to do is to rectify the relation between the real, *qua* rational, and thought:

---

54. For Mackintosh see DNCBT, DTCBP, DSCHT, ODNB; Sell, *Robert Mackintosh*.
55. Mackintosh, "Theism," 747.
56. Ibid., 749.
57. Ibid., 750.

> The existence of a world of natural realities in time and space we do not think is genuinely deducible, though, when it is presented in experience, we can see that it is congruous to thought. And—what is still more important—the revelation of reality made in the philosophy of spirit is—to us men at least—something quite different from a set of new phases in the consciousness of an object. We must be in earnest in establishing a distinction between Divine and human consciousness. We must make the difficult assertion of the limitation of human knowledge.[58]

By contrast, Hegelianism knows too much. It "understands all mysteries,"[59] whereas Christians "*know* a love which *passes knowledge*."[60] Thus both sceptics and philosophical dogmatists are mistaken.

Robert Flint (1838–1910)[61] was, in his judicious way, as generous as possible to absolute idealism. While regretting that "The adherents of the philosophy of the Absolute must be admitted to have fallen, in their revulsion from agnosticism, into many extravagances of gnosticism," it remains the case that "A God who is not the absolute as they understood the term, not the Unconditioned revealed in all that is conditioned, and the essential content of all knowledge at its highest, cannot be the God either of a profound philosophy or a fully developed religion. The philosophy of the Absolute was, on the whole, a great advance towards a philosophical theism."[62] Nevertheless, "the idea of God is not one which can be rightly apprehended merely through intellect speculatively exercised or operating on the findings of science. It requires to be also apprehended through moral experience and the discipline of life."[63] In two long sentences Flint positions himself between unmitigated intuitionism and outright absolutism:

> Those who urge us to put all probable evidence aside, and fall back exclusively instead on intuition, or faith, or feeling, which cannot themselves at the utmost yield more than probable evidence, as sources of absolute certitude, ask us to abandon a practically strong and sure foundation for one which is comparatively weak and suspicious. And those who go further, and

---

58. Mackintosh, *Hegel and Hegelianism*, 287.
59. Ibid., 290.
60. Ibid.
61. For Flint see DNCBP, DSCHP, ODNB; Sell, *Defending and Declaring the Faith*, ch. 3.
62. Flint, *Agnosticism*, 586
63. Ibid., 599.

ask us to put our trust in the speculative dialectics or metaphysical hypotheses of some individual philosopher, as, for instance, of Hegel or Green, will generally be found to recommend us to build on what is merely a fog-bank—a process which will assuredly not lead us to a certainty that cannot be subverted or shaken.[64]

Positively, Flint declares that "Complete religious certitude is reserved for those who shut their eyes against no kind of good evidence to spiritual truth; who ... assent to the truth as it is in Christ ...; and who ... faithfully strive to act up to its demands ... Then ... we shall get the perfect certitude we seek. Until then we have no right to expect it, nor is it desirable that we should get it."[65]

James Iverach expressed his general agreement with reference to idealism:

> To speak of the absolute and unconditioned as synonymous with God, is simply to alter the conception of God ... [T]he idealistic philosophy makes religion to be simply an aspect of itself, and does not leave us a God into whose fellowship we may enter, in whose service we may find perfect freedom ... We need a God who can speak to us, and if He cannot speak directly to us ... the flower and fruit of religion will wither and die.[66]

He objected to the way in which Edward Caird had "calmly annexed" revelation and brought it within the sphere of natural process, with all the pantheizing tendencies thereby entailed.[67] Not surprisingly, in Iverach's view, "History and Fact are merely scaffolding useful for the introduction of Ideas, but as soon as the ideas are there the facts may usefully disappear."[68]

With this we approach more decidedly theological critiques of absolute idealism—such, for example, as that for absolute idealists evil can be but a stage on the way to a greater good. But I must leave such matters and, with Flint's reference to "probable evidence" ringing in my ears, turn

---

64. Flint, *Sermons and Addresses*, 333.

65. Ibid.

66. Iverach, *Theism in the Light of Present Science and Philosophy*, 307, 292. Among others who offered critiques of absolute idealism was Henry Calderwood in his *Handbook of Moral Philosophy*.

67. For a fuller discussion of Iverach and Flint on pantheism see Sell, *Enlightenment, Ecumenism, Evangel*, ch. 7.

68. Iverach, "Pantheism," 33.

to the approach of representative Scottish religious thinkers to Christian evidences and theism.

III

It is not too much to say that the second half of the nineteenth century was the golden age of Scottish apologetics; and it is equally true to say that the period marked a significant shift in apologetic style and content. To take the latter point first, the situation may be summed up under the slogan, "the decline of the evidences." That is to say, it became increasingly less fashionable, because less justifiable, to appeal to biblical miracles or the alleged fulfilment of prophecy as evidence of God's existence, activity and purpose. When Joseph Butler (1692–1752) endorsed the prevailing view that miracles and prophecy were reliable evidences of the truth of Christianity,[69] the deist Thomas Woolston (1669–1731) had already construed miracles allegorically, and the freethinker Anthony Collins (1676–1729) had already given prophecies similar treatment.[70] In the wake of Hume's devastating critique of miracles *qua* evidence; in the light of modern approaches to the biblical text (which prompted those who disapproved of them to mutter darkly about "the German problem") which, *inter alia*, increasingly persuaded Christians that miracles were signs to believers rather than evidence for the persuasion of sceptics, and that biblical prophets were at least as concerned with forthtelling as with foretelling; given the anti-intellectual thrust of those who persisted in millenarian speculation—something that was distressing to many Christians and fodder to the increasingly vocal breed of secularists; in view of all this many realised that older apologetic approaches would no longer work.[71] Of this Mackintosh was quite convinced: "Would you believe *any* doctrine, whatever its moral complexion, if it had miracles enough in its train? If you would, you are no Christian. If you would not, then a certain amount of moral excellence is at any rate a *sine qua non* of revelation, and in so far its evidence is partly internal."[72]

69. Butler. *Analogy*, II, ch. 7.

70. See Sell, *Enlightenment, Ecumenism, Evangel*, 119–21.

71. I do not, of course, intend to convey the impression that there was change by sudden agreement. The climate of ideas is more subject to occasional storms than to obliterating hurricanes. Moreover, exponents of the evidences are ever with us, albeit normally to be found to the right of mainline denominational and theological institutions.

72. Mackintosh. *Essays Towards a New Theology*, 359.

There is one other straw in the wind that suggested the need for a revision of apologetic method. Many Christians, among them Thomas Chalmers (1780-1847)[73] had traditionally believed that unbelief was a sin, and in their minds was the psalmist's observation that "the fool [that is, the immoral person] hath said in his heart, There is no God. They are corrupt . . . there is none that doeth good" (Psalm 14:1). The idea that unbelievers, agnostics, atheists and secularists could be morally upright took a long time to take root, yet traditional believers were increasingly confronted by precisely such persons.[74]

Standing at the threshold of our period, Chalmers adhered throughout his life to the traditional view of the evidential value of miracles that he had propounded in *The Evidence and Authority of the Christian Revelation* (1814). There is a certain irony in the fact that the evangelical Calvinist Chalmers here adopt precisely the same method as that followed by William Leechman (1706-1785), the Moderate professor at Glasgow University.[75] It is also interesting to note that James Buchanan (1804-1870),[76] who succeeded Chalmers as Professor of Systematic Theology in the Free Church (New) College, Edinburgh, published a two-volume work, *Faith in God and Modern Atheism Compared*, in which he eschewed intuitionism and concentrated on the natural, as distinct from the miraculous, evidences for the existence of God. This approach, which was indebted to Lardner and Butler, was epitomised by William Paley, of whose appeal to evidences Robert Mackintosh said, "When such exclusively 'external' arguments are urged, the contents of Christianity go for next to nothing."[77]

As an example of one who adopted a modified view of the matter I cite William Lindsay Alexander (1808-1884),[78] Professor and Principal of the Congregational Theological Hall, Edinburgh. He discusses prophecy in terms of foretelling (not forthtelling), and argues that while the fulfilment of prophecy does not prove the truth of the prophet's message directly, it does prove "the divinity of his commission . . . This proved, the truth of

---

73. For Chalmers see DNCBP, DSCHT, ODNB.

74. Interestingly, the freethinker Anthony Collins was (early) regarded as a highly moral person, even by those who repudiated his teaching.

75. See H. M. B. Reid, *The Divinity Professors*, 255. For Leechman see DECBP, DSCHT, ODNB.

76. For Buchanan see DSCHT, ODNB.

77. Mackintosh, "Apologetics," 192.

78. For Alexander see DNCBP, DSCHT, ODNB.

what he utters follows as a necessary conclusion."[79] But the days of this taking with one hand and giving back with the other were numbered. None saw this more clearly than Flint who, in the closing year of the nineteenth century reflected thus: "The evidentialist view . . . did great injustice to such a revelation as the Christian, and was, in fact, neither reasonable nor Christian. A revelation which presents mysteries as its substantive and distinctive message is a revelation which does not reveal, and belief in which is not belief in truth as such. Revelation is the manifestation of spiritual light, and spiritual light is what can be seen and felt by the spirit."[80]

I proceed chronologically through the apologetic authors. First, brief mention should be made of William Fleming (1792–1866)[81] who succeeded James Mylne in the Moral Philosophy Chair at Glasgow, and who at the beginning of our period published a theodicy entitled, *A Plea for the Ways of God to Man: Being an Attempt to Vindicate the Moral Government of the World* (1858), in which he discussed metaphysical, physical and moral evil, and held that "Philosophy is not complete but in Theology";[82] William Robinson Pirie (1804–85),[83] professor in Aberdeen, who, notwithstanding his debt to the Scottish philosophical tradition, had idealistic leanings, and who in his *Natural Theology* (1867) argued (not very impressively) that since human beings have a desire for God as father and friend, there must be a God, otherwise human nature would be a delusion; and William Honeyman Gillespie (1808–1875)[84] who was unusual both in being a Methodist, and also in propounding a version of the ontological argument for the existence of God in his book, *The Argument A Priori for the Being and Attributes of the Lord God the Absolute One and First Cause*, which was first published in 1833 and subsequently enlarged.

In his *Biographia Philosophica* Fraser provides a revealing account of his philosophical pilgrimage. Among a number of significant remarks is the following: "I seemed to find that in philosophy things must *at last* be

---

79. Alexander, "The evidence to the truth of Christianity supplied by prophecy," 18.

80. Flint. *Sermons and Addresses*, 306.

81. For Fleming see DNCBP.

82. Fleming, *A Plea for the Ways of God to Man*, vi. Fleming taught Robert Flint, and of the former R. M. Wenley wrote, "Fleming, familiarly called 'Moral Will', who had been transferred from the Chair of Oriental Languages to that of Moral Philosophy, seems to have been a hodman amidst his brethren of the Scottish school." Quoted by Macmillan. *The Life of Robert Flint*, 38.

83. For Pirie see DNCBP.

84. For Gillespie see DSCHT.

'left abrupt', as Bacon puts it."[85] He strove to find a way between what he perceived as scientific naturalism leading to the Unknowable, and the new "gnostic Idealism, bound by its profession to eliminate all mysteries, and at last to reach infinite science of Reality."[86] This is his account of what he did:

> I expanded Berkeley's divine language of vision into a universal sense-symbolism, and our moral consciousness of our own free agency into perfect moral agency at the heart of the Whole. Implicates of pure reason, which with Kant make human reason possible, led to implicates of moral reason, which presuppose the universe of reality to be morally constituted reality, although by us incompletely interpretable. I gradually came to think of this theistic faith, not as an infinite conclusion empirically founded in finite facts, but as the necessary presupposition of all human conclusions about anything.[87]

This is consistent with Fraser's judgment that far from being sceptical of sensation, Berkeley was a spiritual realist. At the same time Fraser concluded that Berkeley required correction by Reid and *vice versa*. Berkeley failed to "extract from the phenomena of perception the evidence of a substance different in kind from the self-conscious spirit which perceives them,"[88] while "the philosophy of Common Sense, as represented by Reid, did not rise to the conciliation of the natural order of the material with the originative freedom of the spiritual world, in which operating law in outward nature is recognised as immediate divine agency, or a part of a revelation of perfectly reasonable Will in and through a universe of things and persons."[89] Here we have the basis upon which Fraser developed the ethical theism that is most fully adumbrated in his Gifford Lectures.[90] His position may be summed up in one sentence: "If Nature is practically trustworthy, and fit to be scientifically reasoned about, the Omnipotent Spirit immanent in it must be perfectly good and design the goodness of all. This is final faith."[91] Fraser fully understands that "This is not direct argumentative proof: when we try to make it so it becomes circular reasoning. It is only the conscious expression of a postulate, without *tacit*

---

85. Fraser. *Biographia Philosophica*, 138.
86. Ibid., 184. Cf. his *Locke*, 296.
87. Ibid., 188–89.
88. Fraser, *Essays in Philosophy*, 49.
89. Fraser, *Thomas Reid*, 125.
90. *Philosophy of Theism*.
91. Fraser *Berkeley and Spiritual Realism*, 84.

practical assent to which human knowledge and human agency must dissolve in total doubt."[92] As we have seen, Ferrier would not have approved of Fraser's terminus in faith, and among others who did not was James Lindsay (1852–1923),[93] who propounded a more intellectualist theism.[94] To Fraser, however, "A philosophy grounded on Faith was the highest lesson of Reid and his successors, especially Hamilton, in Scotland,"[95] and he never repudiated his conviction that "The issue of a true philosophy is to disclose the horizon of mysteries by which the power of philosophising is bounded."[96]

Next in chronological order comes Alexander Balmain Bruce (1831–1899),[97] Professor of Apologetics and New Testament Exegesis at Glasgow Free Church College. His oft-reprinted work, *Apologetics: or, Christianity Defensively Stated* (1892), is far from being a hard-nosed philosophically analytical study. Bruce's primary objective was pastoral. The apologist's vocation, he declares, "is neither to confound infidels nor to gratify the passions of coarse dogmatists, but to help men of an ingenuous spirit, troubled with doubts bred of philosophy or science, while morally in sympathy with believers."[98] Bruce's method is informed by two positive and two negative motives. Positively, he upholds the scientific method. This means first, that he will not countenance the "unscientific" exclusion from consideration of the human being's moral sense, religious insights and faith; and secondly, that appeal may be made to religious literatures not as authorities, but as witnesses. His second positive motive is that of speaking to his age, which includes attending to the evolutionary *themes* of development and growth (Bruce does not offer detailed critiques of evolutionary *theories*). Negatively, Bruce is dissatisfied with older theistic argumentation, whilst at the same time holding that "If Christ's doctrine of God be true, there ought to be something in the world to verify it . . . The bankruptcy of natural theology is a gratuitous proposition."[99] For all that, Bruce does not think that

92. Fraser, *Philosophy of Theism*, 176.

93. For Lindsay see DNCBP.

94. See Lindsay. *A Philosophical System of Theistic Idealism*; Lindsay, *Autobiography*, 47.

95. Fraser *Berkeley*, 230. A. Seth described this book as "the ripest and most catholic expression of the national tendency in philosophy." See *Scottish Philosophy*, 208–9.

96. Fraser, "Introductory lecture on logic and metaphysics." In *Inauguration of the New College*, 179.

97. For Bruce see DSCHT, ODNB; Sell, *Defending and Declaring the Faith*, ch. 5.

98. Bruce. *The Chief End of Revelation*, vii. Cf. Bruce, *Apologetics*, 37.

99. Bruce, *The Moral Order of the World*, 351.

arguments from such external notions as motion, causation, design—or even from the idea, are valid. Rather, he starts from the assumption that God is, discusses the kind of God he is, and proceeds to our knowledge of God as revealed supremely in Jesus. Again, Bruce sets his face against all theories—agnosticism and materialism among them—that would deny what he has seen in Jesus. Working but a stone's-throw from the Cairds, he is especially concerned to repudiate absolute idealism not because he has no doctrine of immanence—he does; but because the immanently ideal Christ of idealism is not the historic Christ of biblical faith. Idealism thus tends in a pantheistic direction such that humans are deprived of genuinely free action, while evil, construed as a stage on the way to a higher good, undermines all moral distinctions. Throughout, Bruce's intention is to harmonize reason and faith.

Robert Flint, who was described as "undoubtedly the most learned man of his day in Scotland,"[100] and as "the last great apostle of Scottish moderation,"[101] is Scotland's supreme apologist (as well as being an indefatigable historian and analyst of European philosophy). He is also the most comprehensive, dealing as he does with *Theism* (1877); *Anti-Theistic Theories* (1879)—a rebuttal of atheism, materialism, positivism, secularism, and pantheism; and *Agnosticism* (1903). On the one hand Flint does not think that the traditional theistic arguments conclusively demonstrate God's existence, though he believes that they have a certain cumulative force and exhibit something of God's character. On the other hand, he does not argue that the failure of the 'proofs' opens the way for faith. He doggedly seeks rational grounds for believing and, with indebtedness to Butler and Paley, holds that these may be found by inference from God's self-manifestation in causation, intelligence and righteousness. On this basis we may, on *a priori* lines, affirm that our ideas of absolute being must apply to God alone. This is a philosophical and a religious necessity, for "The heart can find no secure rest except on an infinite God."[102] Theism might have sufficed if human beings had remained sinless, but they did not. Hence God's revelation of himself in Jesus Christ the Saviour. In Christ pre-eminently is "the truth to which all other truth tends as its centre or goal."[103]

---

100. Macmillan, *The Life of Robert Flint*, 326.
101. Davie, *The Democratic Intellect*, 335.
102. Flint *Theism*, 301.
103. Flint, *Sermons and Addresses*, 312.

As well as his objection to the pantheizing tendencies he discerned in absolute idealism, Iverach paid particular attention to evolutionary thought. "Evolution," he declared, "is the working hypothesis of most scientific men at the present time"[104] and as such Christian apologists had to reckon with it. Darwin's theory of natural selection held no terrors for him; on the contrary, Christians should rejoice in all that science could tell them concerning God's method of creation. There is no ground for conflict between faith and science, for "the concern of science is with the force itself and its way of working, and not with the origin and cause of it."[105] Iverach was by no means alone, however, in regretting the way in which the evolutionary theme had been exploited by some, and in particular by Herbert Spencer. Iverach pursued Spencer relentlessly and quite regularly. Among his charges were that Spencer claims that by organic evolution the homogeneous becomes heterogeneous, but fails to explain how this happens, or could happen; that Spencer wrongly seeks to explain the higher in terms of the lower—"One has sympathy with those who labour at an impossible task,"[106] he drily remarks. In passing we may note that in the light of an extensive scrutiny of comparative biology, Henry Calderwood concluded to "the impossibility of tracing the origin of man's rational life to evolution from a lower life."[107] In good Scottish fashion, Calderwood finds this confirmed by the deliverances of self-consciousness, the source of "the powers of a rational life."[108] The Living Source of all existence, he declares, is God immanent, yet transcendent: "we recognise the Supernatural within the Natural,"[109] and the first cause is the eternal personality, "related to the spiritual life of rational souls, as He can be related to no other type of existence within the wide sphere of Creation."[110]

As for Spencer's Unknowable, Iverach reminds us of Spencer's view that time, matter, space and force are all forms of it and then counters, "He . . . does not see that if the Unknowable is manifested, so far as it is manifested it can be known."[111] More generally, Iverach contends that

---

104. Iverach. *Christianity and Evolution*, 1.

105. Iverach, *Is God Knowable?* 193.

106. Iverach, *Theism in the Light of Present Science and Philosophy*, 94. See further Iverach, *The Philosophy of Mr. Herbert Spencer Examined*.

107. Calderwood. *Evolution and Man's Place in Nature*, 337.

108. Ibid., 338.

109. Ibid., 341.

110. Ibid., 342.

111. Iverach, *Christianity and Evolution*, 208.

naturalistic evolutionists cannot allow for purpose in the universe, and neither can the idealistic evolutionists: "Even Hegelian evolution, which is a greater and higher thing than Darwinism, leaves us without a future, and its outlook is bounded by the life that now is. Indeed, the highest product of evolution in the hands of Hegel seems to be a Prussian at the beginning of the present century—a respectable product of evolution certainly, but one that does not seem to have exhausted the resources of civilization."[112]

James Orr (1844–1913)[113] studied first at Glasgow University under Edward Caird, and then at the United Presbyterian Divinity Hall, Edinburgh, where the Professor of Apologetics was John Cairns. Following pastoral experience he was appointed to the Chair of Church History there and, on the union of his Church with the Free Church in 1900, he transferred to the Chair of Apologetics and Systematic Theology in the United Free Church College, Glasgow. He published on historical and theological subjects, and was skilled in popular apologetics as witness *The Faith of a Modern Christian* (1910). The full title of his major work, *The Christian View of God and the World as Centring in the Incarnation* (1893)—a work commended by Flint—proclaims his conviction that there is a Christian view of the world distinct from all others, and that at its heart is the incarnate Christ. Flint would not have disagreed with this, but Orr makes this the starting-point rather than the culmination of his apologetic method. He holds that "Christian apologetic can never be satisfactorily separated from the positive exhibition of the Christian system."[114] As for theism, he declares that "Proof in Theism certainly does not consist in deducing God's existence as a lower from a higher; but rather in showing that God's existence is itself the last postulate of reason—the ultimate basis on which all other knowledge, all other belief rests."[115] For this reason, he writes, "If I undertake to defend Theism, it is not Theism in dissociation from Revelation, but Theism as completed in the entire Christian view."[116] This is not, in his view, to deny the fact of intellectual common ground as between believing and unbelieving rational beings. Orr stands with Flint and Iverach in regard to evolutionary and post-Hegelian idealism. He repudiates Hume's sceptical divorce of reason from faith no less than the theological

---

112. Iverach, *Theism in the Light of Present Science and Philosophy*, 237.

113. For Orr see DNCBP; DSCHT; ODNB; Sell, *Defending and Declaring the Faith*, ch. 7; Scorgie, *A Call for Continuity: The Theological Contribution of James Orr*.

114. Orr, *The Progress of Dogma*, 322.

115. Orr, *The Christian View of God and the World*, 94.

116. Ibid., 77.

presuppositions of Ritschl and his school that tend in the same direction. Underlying all is Orr's concern to oppose any who would excise the supernatural from Christianity. He was utterly persuaded that naturalistic readings of the faith entailed the overlooking of Jesus's self-consciousness as Son of God, his sinlessness, his supernatural powers and his claims. Those who perpetrate such theologies "are never under a greater mistake than when they imagine that it is the preaching of this old Gospel of the grace of God—old, yet ever new—which is alienating the modern world from the Churches. It is not the preaching of this Gospel which is emptying the churches, but the want of it."[117]

Robert Mackintosh may sum up the general position taken at the end of our period by those Scottish religious thinkers who stood most obviously within the Scottish philosophical tradition. He is persuaded that Kant dealt the death blow to the classical *a posteriori* arguments for God's existence, by showing that they cannot "be strung on one thread, or proved to lead up to one and the same God, unless by the use of the inconclusive ontological argument."[118] Nevertheless a natural theology of some sort is necessary; it will always be incomplete; but it may lead people to the threshold of revelation. For example, despite the inadequacy of the cosmological argument *qua* rational demonstration "If there were nothing in this world which made it look like God's world, faith would be too utterly a paradox."[119] Moreover, humanity's knowledge of the moral law—which humanity did not institute, which it can violate, but not alter—is also suggestive of a divine inaugurator. But it is the revelation of God in Christ that is God's best word to us, and "one cannot know what the gospel of Jesus Christ is unless one knows it from the inside."[120] Thus, "In nature we find suggestions of God; in conscience, the postulate of God; in Christ, the affirmation of God . . . But all moral revelation is twofold—a revelation of grace and duty; a revelation of moral forces above us, and of moral obligations resting on us."[121] Whether, like Orr, they set out from the Christian world view, or worked their way towards it, none of the Christian philosophers here discussed could keep theology at bay.

---

117. Orr, *The Faith of a Modern Christian*, 234.

118. Mackintosh, *Essays Towards a New Theology*, 365. Though Flint thought that they would gain in impressiveness, albeit not in conclusiveness, if so combined.

119. Mackintosh, *Albrecht Ritschl and His School*, 255.

120. Mackintosh, *Essays Towards a New Theology*, 336.

121. Ibid., 389.

BIBLIOGRAPHY

Adams, G. W., and W. P. Montague. *Contemporary American Philosophy*. 2 vols. London: Allen & Unwin, 1930.

Alexander, W. L. "The Evidence of the Truth of Christianity supplied by Prophecy." In *The Credentials of Christianity: A Course of Lectures Given at the Request of The Christian Evidence Society*. London: Hodder & Stoughton, 1880.

Bacon, Francis. *Novum Organum*. Chicago: Open Court, 1994.

Broadie, Alexander. *A History of Scottish Philosophy*. Edinburgh: Edinburgh University Press, 2009.

Bruce, A. B. *Apologetics: or, Christianity Defensively Stated*. Edinburgh: T. & T. Clark, 1892.

———. *The Chief End of Revelation*. 2nd ed. London: Hodder & Stoughton, 1890.

———. *The Moral order of the World in Ancient and Modern Thought*. London: Hodder & Stoughton, 1899.

Buchanan, James. *Faith in God and Modern Atheism Compared*. 2 vols. Edinburgh: Buchanan, 1855.

Butler, Joseph. *The Analogy of Religion*. 1736. Reprinted, London: Ward, Lock, [1884].

Cairns, John. *Examination of Ferrier's Theory of Knowing and Being*. Edinburgh: Constable, 1856.

———. *The Scottish Philosophy: A Vindication and a Reply*. Edinburgh: Constable, 1856.

Calderwood, Henry. *Evolution and Man's Place in Nature*. London: Macmillan, 1893.

———. *David Hume*. London: Macmillan, 1898.

———. *Handbook of Moral Philosophy* (1872). 14th ed. London: Macmillan, 1888.

———. *The Philosophy of the Infinite: A Treatise on Man's Knowledge of the Infinite Being, in Answer to Sir William Hamilton and Dr. Mansel*. Cambridge: Macmillan, 1861?.

Cameron, Nigel M. de S. *Dictionary of Scottish Church History and Theology*. Edinburgh: T. & T. Clark, 1993.

Chalmers, Thomas. *The Evidence and Authority of the Christian Revelation* (1814). Philadelphia: Anthony Finley, 1817.

Davie, G. E. *The Democratic Intellect: Scotland and Her Universities in the Nineteenth Century*. 2nd ed. Edinburgh: Edinburgh University Press, 1964.

Duncan, George M. Review of J. Iverach, *Descartes, Spinoza and the New Philosophy*. In *The Philosophical Review* 14 (1905) 95–97.

Ferrier, J. F. *Philosophical Works of the Late James Frederick Ferrier* (1875), edited by Alexander Grant. 3 vols. Bristol: Thoemmes, 2001.

———. *Scottish Philosophy, the Old and the New: A Statement*. Edinburgh: Sutherland and Knox, 1856.

Fleming, William. *A Plea for the Ways of God to Man: Being an Attempt to Vindicate the Moral Government of the World*. Edinburgh, 1858.

Flint, Robert. *Agnosticism*. Edinburgh: Blackwood, 1903.

———. *Anti-Theistic Theories*. Edinburgh: Blackwood, 1879.

———. *Sermons and Addresses*. Edinburgh: Blackwood, 1899.

———. *Theism* (1877). 11th ed. Edinburgh: Blackwood, 1905.

Fraser, A. Campbell. *Berkeley*. Edinburgh: Blackwood, 1881.

———. *Berkeley and Spiritual Realism*. London: Constable, 1908.

The Theological Education of the Ministry

———. *Biographia Philosophica: A Retrospect*. Edinburgh: Blackwood, 1904.

———. "Ferrier's Theogy of Knowing and Being." In *Essays in Philosophy* (a collection of his papers from *The North British Review*). Edinburgh: W. P. Kennedy, 1856.

———. "Introductory Lecture on Logic and Metaphysics." In *Inauguration of the New College of the Free Church, Edinburgh, November* 1850, 159–87. London: Johnstone & Hunter, 1851.

———. *Locke*. Edinburgh: Blackwood, 1890.

———. *Philosophy of Theism* 1896). 2nd amended ed. Edinburgh: Blackwood, 1899.

———. *Thomas Reid*. Edinburgh: Oliphant, Anderson and Ferrier, 1898.

Gillespie, William Honeyman. *The Argument A Priori for the Being and Attributes of the Lord God the Absolute One and First Cause*. London, 1833.

Iverach, James. *Christianity and Evolution*. London: Hodder & Stoughton, 1894.

———. *Descartes, Spinoza and the New Philosophy*. Edinburgh: T. & T. Clark, 1904.

———. *Is God Knowable?* London: Hodder & Stoughton, 1884.

———. "Pantheism." *The Expositor* 7th series, 3 (1907) 493–507; 4:20–35, 153–68.

———. *The Philosophy of Mr. Herbert Spencer Examined*. London: Religious Tract Society, 1884.

———. *Theism in the Light of Present Science and Philosophy*. London: Hodder & Stoughton, 1900.

Lindsay, James. *Autobiography of Rev. James Lindsay, D.D.* Edinburgh: Blackwood, 1924.

———. *A Philosophical System of Theistic Idealism*. Edinburgh: Blackwood, 1917.

McCosh, James. *An Examination of Mr. J. S. Mill's Philosophy: Being a Defence of Fundamental Truth*. London: Macmillan, 1866.

MacEwen, Alexander R. *Life and Letters of John Cairns, DD, LLD*. London: Hodder & Stoughton, 1895.

Mackintosh, Robert. *Albrecht Ritschl and His School*. London: Chapman and Hall, 1915.

———. "Apologetics." *Encyclopedia Britannica*. 11th ed. II, 189–94.

———. *Essays Towards a New* Theology. Glasgow: Maclehose, 1889.

———. *Hegel and Hegelianism*. Edinburgh: T. & T. Clark, 1903.

———. "Theism." *Encyclopedia Britannica*. 11th ed. XIV, 744–58.

Macmillan, Donald. *The Life of Robert Flint*. London: Hodder & Stoughton, 1914.

Mander, William, and Alan P. F. Sell. *Dictionary of Nineteenth-Century British Philosophers*. Bristol: Thoemmes, 2002.

Orr, James. *The Christian View of God and the World as Centring in the Incarnation*. Edinburgh: Elliot, 1893.

———. *The Faith of a Modern Christian*. London: Hodder & Stoughton, 1910.

———. *The Progress of Dogma*. London: James Clarke, 1901.

Pirie, William Robinson. *Natural Theology: or, An Inquiry into the Fundamental Principles of Religious, Moral, and Political Science*. Edinburgh: Blackwood, 1867.

Mill, John Stuart. *An Examination of Sir William Hamilton's Philosophy* (1865), edited by J. M. Robson. Toronto: University of Toronto Press, 1979.

Reid, H. M. B. *The Divinity Professors in the University of Glasgow*. Glasgow: Maclehose, Jackson, 1923.

Reid, Thomas. *Essays on the Intellectual Powers of Man*, edited by Derek R. Brookes and K. Haakonssen. Edinburgh: Edinburgh University Press, 2002.

———. *An Inquiry into the Human Mind on the Principles of Common Sense* (1764), edited by Derek P. Brookes. Edinburgh: Edinburgh University Press, 1977.

Ryle, Gilbert. *The Revolution in Philosophy*. London: Macmillan, 1960.

Scorgie, G. G. *A Call for Continuity: The Theological Contribution of James Orr*. Macon, GA: Mercer University Press, 1988.

Sell, Alan P. F. *Commemorations: Studies in Christian Thought and History*. 1993. Reprinted, Eugene, OR: Wipf & Stock, 1998.

———. *Defending and Declaring the Faith: Some Scottish Examples 1960–1920*. 1986. Reprinted, Eugene, OR: Wipf & Stock.

———. *Enlightenment, Ecumenism, Evangel: Theological Themes and Thinkers 1550–2000*. Milton Keynes, UK: Paternoster, 2005.

———. *Mill on God: The Pervasiveness and Elusiveness of Mill's Religious Thought*. 2004. Reprinted Eugene, OR: Wipf & Stock, 1977. Reprinted Eugene, OR: Wipf & Stock, 2012.

———. *Philosophical Idealism and Christian Belief*. 1995. Reprinted, Eugene, OR: Wipf & Stock, 2006.

———. *Philosophy, Dissent and Nonconformity 1689–1920*. 2004. Reprinted, Eugene, OR: Wipf & Stock, 2009.

———. *Robert Mackintosh: Theologian of Integrity*. Bern: Lang, 1977. Reprinted Eugene, OR: Wipf & Stock, 2012.

Seth, Andrew. *Scottish Philosophy: A Comparison of the Scottish and German Answers to Hume* (1885). 2nd ed. Edinburgh: Blackwood, 1890.

Seth, James. *English Philosophers and Schools of Philosophy*. London: Dent, 1912.

Sorley, W. R. *A History of British Philosophy to 1900* (1920). Cambridge: Cambridge University Press, 1965.

Thomson, Arthur. *Ferrier of St. Andrews: An Academic Tragedy*. Edinburgh: Scottish Academic Press, 1985.

Veitch, John. "Philosophy in the Scottish Universities." *Mind* 2 (1877) 74–91, 207–34.

Wardlaw, Ralph. *Christian Ethics: or Moral Philosophy on the Principles of Divine Revelation*. London: Jackson & Walford, 1834.

Yolton, John W., et al. *Dictionary of Eighteenth-Century British Philosophers*. Bristol: Thoemmes, 1999.

4

Living in the Half Lights
John Oman in Context

THE GUIDE BOOKS WILL tell you that the county of Orkney lies some twenty miles to the north of the Scottish mainland, and that it comprises sixty-seven islands. The largest of these, known as Orkney's mainland, covers an area larger than all of the other islands put together. John Wood Oman was born on Orkney's mainland on 23 July 1860. To be precise, he was born at Biggins Farm in the parish of Stenness; and in those names there resides a clue to Orkney's history. For *bygging*, meaning 'a building,' comes from the Norse verb *byggia*, 'to build,' while *Stenness* is Norse for 'stone point.' These names remind us, therefore, that in the wake of the Scots Celtic Church of the sixth and seventh centuries, and of Orkney's absorption into the Kingdom of the Picts in the early eighth century came the Viking raids of the late eighth century, and rule by the Norsemen. Thus matters stood until 1472, when the Scottish parliament annexed Orkney and its more northerly neighbour, Shetland, at a cost of 50,000 florins for Orkney and 8,000 florins for Shetland. The financial beneficiary was King Christian I of Denmark, who needed the money towards the dowry required on the marriage of his daughter, Margaret, to King James III of Scotland. But the name Stenness, stone point, suggests an even earlier history, for the community is home to some prize examples of prehistoric megaliths, notably the Ring of Brodgar and the Stones of Stenness, the tallest of which rises to seventeen feet. These stones brooded over ritual activity until the sixth century.[1] Also in the vicinity is the neolithic village of Barnhouse, and

---

1. Bardgett, *Two Millennia of Church and Community in Orkney*, 18, referring to Ritchie, "Birsay around AD 800," 56.

Living in the Half Lights

the sizeable chambered cairn, Maeshowe, in which prominent individuals were buried some 5,000 years ago. In the midst of all this history, not to mention a rather bloodthirsty legend,[2] with Biggins Farm situated on flat land overlooking the sound, and with a view of distant hills, John Oman was born, the second of four sons of Simon Rust Oman and his wife Isabella Irvine Rendall. Their family was completed by two daughters

The nearest town to Stenness is the harbour town of Stromness ("headland of the current"), which was a whaling centre in the nineteenth century. In his younger days Simon Oman had risen to become master of a sailing vessel, but by now he was farming at Biggins. The remains of Pictish dykes made of turf with stone footings have been found in Stenness, and in the eighteenth century farmland was enclosed by turf dykes six feet in height.[3] There was a flourishing peat trade between Orkney and Edinburgh;[4] corn was grown and carefully threshed so that the stalks could be used either for thatching, or by young girl home-workers who plaited them for use by the makers of Orkney straw-backed chairs.[5] Cheese-making was widespread, and the export of salt geese and goose feathers brought further income to the area. Fenton relates that "A visitor saw a bare-headed, shoeless boy herding a flock of geese in Stenness in 1842."[6]

John Oman loved his homeland, and later in life he wrote two accounts of it.[7] He describes the sometimes hazardous route by which Orkney was reached in his day; he describes the land and the sea; he recounts the history of the islands and has a good deal to say about life as it was lived. In this last connection he does not shun the anecdote, least of all when the tale concerns ministers. He recalls a man whose wife and cow were blown off a cliff in a gale and fell to their deaths. Some months later the man met the minister, who consoled him in his loss. "'Deed Sir', was the disconcerting reply, 'as ye hae often said, but I never understood it as

---

2. See W. P. L. Thompson, *New History of Orkney*, 58. It tells of Ragnhild, who secured the deaths of a succession of husbands by promising to marry their murderers.

3. See Fenton. *The Northern Isles*, 13, 91.

4. Ibid., ch. 26.

5. Ibid., 358, 271.

6. Ibid., 507.

7. The manuscripts are among the Oman papers at Westminster College, Cambridge I refer here to the longer of the two. I am most grateful to Mrs. Margaret Thompson for making the Oman papers available to me, and also for supplying photocopies of a number of articles and reviews at a time when unaccustomed quantities of snow prevented ready access to Cambridge.

well before, the ways of Providence are wonerfu. When the wife and the coo were blown off the cliff I thought I had a sair, sair, loss, but I gaed ower tae Graemsay and there I got a far bonnier wife and a far better coo."[8] We learn of the minister of Sanday who neatly accommodated the alternatives within a prayer thus: "Keep thy protecting hand around all who travel by sea and bring them safely to their desired haven. But if in thine inscrutable providence it be thy will that helpless ships should be cast upon the shore, dinna forget the pair island of Sanday."[9] Mingling church, school and family, Oman writes,

> Before the days of the Secession the minister was often a very original character who did not believe in making too many new sermons. Mr. Clouston of Stromness ... had but four which he gave in rotation, so that each of them appeared like the quarters of the moon. My great-grandfather, whose name John Wood has come down till I am the fourth to bear it, was about the last man in Stromness to wear a long waistcoat and silver buckles on his shoes and was a strong supporter of the parish minister, but his son, the second John, who afterwards taught the youth of Stromness with such a strong hand that it is said he could send an offender off with one cuff from the far side of the room into the fireplace, made these stale productions more stale by repeating them, when well out of reach of his father's ears, word for word, well garnished with portentous coughs.[10]

Oman's early education was in the hands of a tutor who had been engaged by a neighbour to the family, to whose classes a few other boys were welcomed. But however much Oman may have learned from the tutor, it is not fanciful to suppose that two things impressed his young mind more than anything else. The first was the sense of permanence inspired by the history around him and by the solidity of his home life in a farmhouse in which his family had lived for generations. It is not without significance that he dedicated his Kerr Lectures on *The Problem of Faith and Freedom in the Last Two Centuries* to the memory of his father, "A scholar only of life and action, but my best teacher." The second decisive impression was that of his personal solitariness (which is not the same as loneliness). This, as he tells us in his most learned work, *The Natural and the Supernatural*,

---

8. Oman, "The Orkneys," ms., 7.
9. Ibid., 27.
10. Ibid.

he gained from his childish yet intense contemplation of the natural world around him:

> Nothing moves simple folk and children like the idea of aloneness in the ever-moving vastness of time, if this be filled with concrete individual forms on the one hand, and invested with ... the feeling of the undifferentiated holy on the other ...
>
> [A]n average sort of child, living under the conditions in which man had developed his powers of perception, with nature's work much in evidence around him and man's little, often alone under the open sky, and about as much on the sea as on the land, among simple stay-at-home people and some far-travelled folk and wandering gypsies, is at least as near the conditions in which man's perception developed as this Western modern world affords.
>
> The most noticeable feature of my earliest view of the world is of how minutely, definitely, decisively everything in it was individual.
>
> While my apprehensions of the countryside continually varied with sunshine and shadow, day and night, summer and winter, my general awareness of it was neither of a changing scene, nor of the aspect I preferred, nor was it of an average impression or a composite picture, but of something one in all its moods and aspects, much like awareness of a friend.
>
> To the very long sight of one who constantly looked from horizon to horizon, the depth of the sky was overwhelmingly impressive, and was the first object I think ever to hold my attention immovably ... [T]hough space was ... the illustration, the real impressiveness was in time ... Through this first came the idea that I was alone. I had been to church. I think the preacher had been expressing the absolute difference between good and evil under the material forms of heaven and hell. I went down to the edge of the water alone, and stood, a very small child, with the full tide at my feet ... It flashed upon me that, if I dropped in and floated out, with endless sea around, I should be alone for ever and ever.[11]

It is perhaps not surprising that at the age of fourteen Oman had no higher aspiration than "to ride a horse bare-backed and steer a boat in a gale";[12] or that an unnamed Cambridge Professor should later have

---

11. Oman, *The Natural and the Supernatural*, 132, 133, 135, 136–37. It is interesting to note that Oman contributed the article on "Individualism, Individual, and Individuality" to James Hastings, ed. *Dictionary of Christ and the Gospels*, I, 814–21.

12. Oman, *Honest Religion*, 36.

remarked of Oman, "When I think of the great man, heather, and salt winds, and mountain mists come to mind rather than a gown and lecturer's desk."[13] From Oxford there came similar testimony when, in the course of reviewing what he described as Oman's epoch-making work, *The Natural and the Supernatural*, Nathaniel Micklem declared, "It has been said to me that no one can understand Dr. Oman aright who does not see him standing on the prow of a Viking ship with the wind and the salt spray blown around him; certainly there is in his thought a robustness, a freshness, a virility and venture which smack of the sea and of heroic enterprises; there is breadth, a wholesomeness, a common sense which is infinitely refreshing to readers of ordinary theological and devotional literature."[14]

I

So much for Oman's geographical, historical and home context; but what of the ecclesiastical? In late medieval Orkney the parishes were grouped so that, for example, Firth, Orphir and Stenness had the services of one priest, Sandwick and Stromness, of another.[15] The Reformation in Orkney seems to have been more a matter of ecclesiastical reorganization than of doctrine, and a good deal of the reorganization had to do with the reapportionment of land. Thus in 1563 Patrick Bellenden "received the Stenness lands which had provided the endowments of the Precentor (Magnus Halcro) [of Kirkwall Cathedral]. On this property the Bellendens had their principal residence, the Palace of Stenness, which according to popular tradition stood so high that it was possible to see ships in Hoy Sound from the upper windows."[16] Alexander Dick, who conformed in 1574, was the only Cathedral dignitary to serve the Reformed Church;[17] of the others, the Precentor was accused by the Reformed of adultery.[18] In the 1560s the parish of Stenness continued to be linked with those of Firth and Orphir,

---

13. Quoted by George Alexander, "Memoir." In *Honest Religion*, xxxi.

14. Micklem, Review of Oman, *The Natural and the Supernatural*, 36. Micklem further judges that the book is "devastatingly Protestant and profoundly evangelical in temper and in thought."

15. Bardgett, *Two Millennia of Church and Community in Orkney*, 52.

16. W. P. L. Thompson. *The New History of Orkney*, 259. This is from ch. 18, the whole of which concerns the Reformation in Orkney.

17. Bardgett, *Two Millennia of Church and Community in Orkney*, 64.

18. Ibid., 63.

with Thomas Stevenson as minister.[19] Stromness was now partnered with Sandwick and Graemsay and served by a minister, Jerome Tulloch, and a reader, William Smith.[20] There is no suggestion in the literature that the priests who came over from Rome were committed to, or even well versed in, Reformed doctrine, while others subsequently appointed were beset by unwieldy charges covering sometimes inhospitable terrain. Without question Harry Colville, minister of Orphir, Stenness and Firth, stepped outside the *Book of Discipline* in the 1590s. His objective was to find evidence against Earl Patrick Stewart's brother and rival, John Stewart. To this end he "led the prosecution against Thomas Paplay and Alison Balfour [who were] accused of plotting Patrick's death by poison. The minister supervised the questioning of the suspects by torture—which was extended to Balfour's husband, son and seven-year-old daughter. Followers of John Stewart successfully murdered Colville in 1596,"[21] whereupon there ensued a pastoral vacancy.

Meanwhile the General Assembly had, during the 1570s sanctioned a church order which had no place for bishops, but bishops remained *in situ*, with the result that during the seventeenth century turmoil over the relative authority of bishops and presbytery continued, with episcopal lands frequently being a neuralgic factor. The Stuart Kings strove to enforce episcopalianism upon the Scottish Church, and it was not until the accession of William and Mary that, from 1690, Presbyterianism became the established religion across the whole of Scotland. Toleration was extended to episcopalians by the Act of 1712, but in Orkney a number of clergymen and lairds remained sometimes vociferously loyal to the Jacobite cause, and for this they were punished. In the wake of civil and ecclesiastical struggles the turn to the restraint of Moderatism, and the desire for ministerial respectability is not hard to understand. Not, indeed that all ministers were as respectable as they might have been. One lived in "open concubinage" with another man's wife both before and after his marriage. The Synod gave him four months to break with the woman, but in the meantime the Court of Justiciary tried the minister, found him guilty, and banished him to the plantations for life.[22] Among further deficiencies

19. Ibid., 61; cf. 98.
20. Ibid., 62.
21. Ibid., 73, referring to Anderson, *Black Pattie*, 49, 50; and Craven. *History of the Church in Orkney*, 66–70.
22. See Small, *History of the Congregations of the United Presbyterian* Church, II, 482.

were that on some islands the people had received the Lord's Supper on only one or two occasions in fifty years; and the intrusion of unwanted ministers under the patronage system caused real concern in some quarters. In one such case, at Orphir, a minister was to be ordained but the people secured the church so that nothing could be done. Nine months later the Presbytery sent troops from Caithness in order to ensure that the ordination went ahead, and during the ensuing struggle one woman was killed and several people were wounded.[23]

But some church members, not least because they heard of religious revivals in parts of mainland Scotland, became restive under the moralistic perorations of Moderate ministers, the perceived evil of patronage, and the general low state of religion in the county. Orkney which, unlike the Western Isles, had not imbibed a solid, still less a scholastic, version of Calvinism, was ready to receive a more evangelically open version of the Reformed faith.

In 1797 the godfather of Scottish revivalism, James Haldane, paid his first visit to Orkney. According to his biographer he "brought to the inhabitants a large outpouring of spiritual blessings."[24] Haldane's observations led him to the conclusion that, with very few exceptions, the islands of Orkney were "as much in need of the true Gospel of Jesus Christ, so far as respects the preaching of it, as any of the islands of the Pacific Ocean."[25] He preached in Stromness, where the minister, Mr. Hamilton, and his wife received him kindly; while in Kirkwall, where the fair was in progress, his hearers numbered from three to four thousand on weekdays and six thousand on Sundays. In his *Journal* Haldane notes with pleasure the seeds of the Gospel sown by an Orkney man who had been apprenticed to a "pious tradesman" in Kirkwall. This man went to Newcastle on business, and there he much appreciated the ministry of the Antiburgher minister, William Graham. On his return he gathered for prayer with others, and after a time they appealed to the Antiburgher Synod for a preacher.

This Orkney tradesman was John Rusland, or Russell. By August 1795 a church building to seat eight hundred was in progress, and in the following year the work was completed. The Edinburgh Presbytery of the Antiburgher Synod sent two supplies to Kirkwall: Chalmers of Haddington served in June and July 1796 and Culbertson of Leith in August and September. Chalmers presided over the opening of the church on 1 July.

23. Ibid.
24. Haldane, *The Lives of Robert and James Haldane*, 167.
25. Ibid., 169, from Haldane's *Journal*, 12 August 1797.

Six elders, who were nominated and unanimously elected by the members of the congregation, were ordained on 14 August. On 16 July 1797 the first communion service was held in the open air, with Stuart of Falkirk presiding. By now the membership stood at 196. The first minister, William Broadfoot, arrived in 1798, and by 1814 he could report that 1250 persons were attending Sunday worship, of whom at least three quarters were church members.[26]

News of this new venture spread around Orkney, and although their town was fourteen miles from Kirkwall, people from Stromness began making the journey to worship there. In 1802 the Synod provided a catechist for Stromness, and in 1803 money was collected towards a church of their own. In 1806 thirty communicants, including two elders, were disjoined from the Kirkwall church and constituted as a separate congregation. Their building, seating 643, cost £600. This was the church which John Oman and his family attended from nearby Stenness. Oman was born during the ministry of William Stobbs, the second minister, who had arrived in 1829 and remained until his death in 1863. In 1837 he reported that there were 544 communicants, that he conducted a two-hour Sabbath-evening school with an attendance of 310, and that between 200 and 300 people attended his monthly prayer meeting. Stobbs was followed by James S. Nisbet (1865–1874), who was succeeded by Thomas Kirkwood (1876–1880).[27] Nisbet and Kirkwood were the ministers John Oman would remember.

I have already said that Orkney, though ecclesiastically impoverished by the end of the eighteenth century, did not have a legacy of staunch Calvinism, and was therefore open to a more evangelical version of the Reformed faith. Indeed, one of the historians of the Secession Church declared that "In no part of Scotland perhaps has [the Secession Church's] beneficial influence been more extensively felt or visibly displayed, than in the interesting group of the Orkney isles."[28] Another concurs: "In no part of the British dominions has the Secession prospered more than in Orkney. It has planted congregations in almost all the islands; and exercised an influence peculiarly favourable to the moral and religious improvement of the islanders."[29] It is not too much to say that this Church became the

26. Small, *History of the Congregations of the United Presbyterian Church*, II, 482–83.

27. For a full account of the Stromness church see ibid., 490–92. Cf. MacKelvie, *Annals and Statistics*, 554.

28. A. Thomson, *Historical Sketch of the Origin of the Secession Church*, 146.

29. M'Kerrow, *History of the Secession Church*, 392.

folk church in many parts of Orkney during the nineteenth century. We need to understand the testimony of his Church if we are to understand Oman's developed ecclesiological positions and attitudes.

In 1733 Ebenezer Erskine, William Wilson, Alexander Moncrieff and James Fisher, who had been deposed from their ministerial charges by the General Assembly of the Church of Scotland, joined with Ralph Erskine and Thomas Mair in constituting themselves an Associate Presbytery. There were two neuralgic issues. The first was doctrinal. In 1722 Ebenezer and Ralph Erskine, together with eleven others, had presented a representation to the General Assembly of the Church of Scotland against the Assembly's repudiation of the book, *The Marrow of Modern Divinity*. The Assembly construed the book as teaching antinomianism and universalism, whereas Erskine and his friends, who staunchly upheld particular redemption, construed it as endorsing the free offer of the Gospel to all, for all have the warrant to believe. Here are the seeds of evangelical Calvinism.[30] The second issue, or constellation of issues, concerned polity and church order, and arose in part from the manner of their treatment by the Assembly. In 1734 they published *A Testimony to the Doctrine, Worship, Government, and Discipline of the Church of Scotland: or, Reasons for their Protestation entered before the Commission of the General Assembly, November 1733*. Among other things they opposed the intrusion of unwanted ministers upon congregations and the exclusion from communion of those who opposed the ministers thus appointed; the conferring of *quasi*-presbyteral power upon the Commission and Sub-commissions; the "prosecution of such measures as corrupted, or had a direct tendency to corrupt, the doctrines contained in our excellent Confession of Faith";[31] and the refusal to censure those who departed from it.

In 1747 we come to the Breach within the Associate Presbytery, and the formation of the General, or Antiburgher, Associate Synod. From 1744 onwards the citizens of Edinburgh, Glasgow and Perth were required to take the Burgess Oath if they wished to work in commerce, join a trade guild or be enfranchised. The terms of the Oath were: "Here I protest before God, and your Lordships, that I profess, and allow with my heart, the true religion presently professed within this realm, and authorized by the

---

30. For the complicated tale of which this is an all too brief summary, see McCrie, *The Marrow of Modern Divinity*; Anon., *Testimony of the United Associate Synod of the Secession Church*.; McKerrow, *History of the Secession Church*; Henderson, *The Religious Controversies of* Scotland; Lachman, *The Marrow Controversy*; Sell, *The Great Debate*, 55–57.

31. Anon., *Testimony of the United Associate Synod*, 45.

laws thereof: I shall abide therat, and defend the same to my life's end; renouncing the Roman religion called papistry."[32] To the Antiburghers this struck at the principle of the church's spiritual freedom and independence of other authorities. Over the next half century the Antiburghers toiled through one theological dispute after another, but they also engaged in productive overseas missionary work, and denounced the slave trade in 1788. The next excitement of importance from our point of view followed in 1804, when some in the Antiburgher Synod embraced New Light principles and published them in its *New Testimony*. That is to say it formally affirmed that the power of worldly kingdoms was limited to secular matters only. Interestingly, a formative work which encouraged the Synod to this conclusion was entitled, *A Review of Ecclesiastical Establishments in Europe: An Attempt to Prove that every Species of Patronage is Foreign to the Nature of the Church, and that any modifications which have ever been, or ever can be, proposed, are insufficient to regain and secure her in the possession of the liberty wherewith Christ has made her free*. The work appeared anonymously in 1792, but in his *Candid Vindication of the Secession Church* the author unmasked himself. He was none other than the William Graham of Newcastle whose preaching, heard by John Rusland/Russell of Kirkwall had been instrumental in securing the presence of the Antiburghers in Orkney.[33] With this the New Light Antiburghers became voluntaryists, and on this basis they were able to unite with the New Light Burghers in 1820 to form the United Secession Church.

The final piece of the jigsaw concerns the Relief Church. The Relief Presbytery was constituted in 1761, and, once again, patronage as applied by Moderate churchmen was a principal cause of the secession. The seceders were led by Thomas Gillespie, who was deposed from his Dunfermline parish in 1752; Thomas Boston of Jedburgh, who left his charge in 1757; and Thomas Colier/Collier, a native of Fife.[34] In view of the polity of the Relief Church it is perhaps not insignificant that both Gillespie and Collier had sojourned amongst English Dissenters. Indeed, Gillespie, having left the Divinity Hall of the Church of Scotland in Edinburgh at the suggestion of his mother, who had become a keen supporter of Erskine and the

---

32. Quoted by M'Kerrow, *History of the Secession Church*, 210.

33. Graham also published a handful of sermons. We further learn that he "was an excellent mathematician, and bestowed great labour and spent much money in endeavouring to discover an exact method of finding the longitude at sea." See MacKelvie, *Annals and Statistics*, 524.

34. Not therefore "an English dissenting minister," as stated by Needham in "Relief Church, 702(ii).

Secession Church, found that Church's Theological Hall in Perth not to his liking and left it after only ten days, and went on to the Independent/Congregational academy conducted by Philip Doddridge at Northampton.[35] "There," says J. H. Leckie, "he learned a 'Voluntary' doctrine of the relation between Church and State, being taught that 'the Civil Magistrate' had nothing to do with the religious opinions of citizens, nor had any right to confine the minds of men within the bounds of established creeds."[36] From there he proceeded to Hartbarrow, Westmorland,[37] as is clear from John Birkett's letter written from Kendal to Doddridge on 8 November 1740. Birkett informs Doddridge that the latter's suggestion that Gillespie serve at Hartbarrow for six months "on Mutual Trial" has been accepted, notwithstanding that "the Presbyterian Ministers of this North Class of Westmorland and Cumberland are extremely prejudiced against Scotch ministers in general" because of the Scots' "unwillingness to embrace every Wanton, Wild, Novel Notion, that is broach'd now-a-days."[38] The reference here is to the disquiet caused in some northern circles by the drift into "Arianism" of a number of English Presbyterian ministers. Gillespie was licensed by Doddridge and others on 30 October 1740, ordained in northern England on 22 January 1741, and received into the Presbytery of Dunfermline in March of that year, on the recommendation of Doddridge, Job Orton and thirteen other ministers.

Thomas Collier had served the pastorate of Ravenstonedale, also in Westmorland, for an unspecified period until 1761.[39] Originally Presbyte-

---

35. Barr, *The United Free Church of Scotland*, 67, writes, "It is not generally known that the famous Dr Philip Doddridge . . . was ordained a Presbyterian ere he became an Independent." This is just as well, for it is not the case. In evidence Barr reproduces Doddridge's ordination certificate which does indeed show that he was ordained a "presbyter," and that five of the eight ministerial signatories were Presbyterians. But (a) in the eighteenth-century there was a good deal of ministerial co-operation across what would later become regarded as "denominational lines" (denominations as we know them being creatures of the nineteenth century); (b) generally more than one English Presbyterian minister would be ordained at a time, and not always in the pastorate of any of them; (c) there is no question that Castle Hill, Northampton was an Independent/Congregational church, or that the practice in that tradition was that ministers were ordained in the pastorates they were called to serve.

36. Leckie, *Secession Memories*, 71.

37. Barr, *The United Free Church of Scotland*, 68, says that efforts to determine the place in *Lancashire* to which Gillespie went have proved unsuccessful.

38. See NCL MS L1/4/101 at Dr. Williams's Library, London; Nuttall, *Calendar*, no. 652; Sell, *Church Planting*, 116–17.

39. Though there is no reference to him in Nicholson and Axon, *The Older Nonconformity in Kendal*, or in Whitehead, *History of the Dales Congregational Churches*.

rian, the theology of its ministers oscillated during the eighteenth century. John Magee, who served from 1714 to 1733, was the first Ravenstonedale minister to be supported by the Independent Fund, and he must therefore be deemed to have been orthodox. Indeed, during his ministry some more radical Presbyterians seceded from the church. His successor, James Ritchie, a Glasgow University graduate, declined to subscribe to the Westminster Confession of Faith with the result that the church members "could not in conscience take the Lord's Supper at his hands."[40] There followed a fourteen-year-long legal battle which concluded in 1747 in favour of Ritchie, who by then had moved on; he and his supporters did, however, pay half of the costs of £820/0/0 incurred by the church. By 1753 Ritchie was an Arian.[41] The trustees of the church continued to exercise authority, and it was not until James Muscutt made it a condition of his accepting the call to the pastorate in 1811 that "the Church be re-organised and put upon the Independent or Congregational plan."[42] Thomas Collier was clearly not heterodox, or he would not have been welcomed as a coadjutor by Gillespie and Boston. Moreover, he was sympathetic to the Congregational church order, for he was called to the pastorate of the Colinsburgh Independent church "by the congregation in the presence of the great Head of the church... As Mr. Collier was from among the dissenters in England, this mode of forming a ministerial engagement with a Christian society would be perfectly familiar to him, and was in all probability accepted by himself."[43] This church owed its origin to a secession from the Church of Scotland in 1760, prompted by the intrusion of Dr. John Chalmers upon the people as minister. The majority of the congregation left the Parish Kirk and built a large church for themselves. Gillespie, himself out of charge, preached there and encouraged the flock in the direc-

---

However, Woodger and Hunter, *The High Chapel*, include a table of ministers in their front pages, from which we learn that Thomas Collier's date of arrival is not known, but his date of departure is given as 1761.

40. See Whitehead, *History of the Dales Congregational Churches*, 95; Woodger and Hunter, op.cit., 5, Nicholson and Axon, *The Older Nonconformity in Kendal*, 288–89.

41. See Nicholson and Axon, 289.

42. See Whitehead, 97; Woodger and Hunter, 8.

43. Struthers, *The History of the Rise of the Relief Church*, bound with A. Thomson's *Historical Sketch* and paginated consecutively, 284. See also Small. *History of the Congregations of the United Presbyterian Church*, II, 376–79. Neither Collier's name nor that of the Colinsburgh church appears in McNaughton's works: *The Scottish Congregational Ministry 1794-1993*, and *Early Congregational Independency in Lowland Scotland*, I. This suggests that the cause had but a brief independent life prior to its reception into the Relief Presbytery.

The Theological Education of the Ministry

tion of Relief, and was instrumental in securing the services of Collier. On the day prior to his induction Collier and the church members "observed a solemn fast; accommodating themselves also, in this matter, rather to the English Congregational than to the Scotch Presbyterian model."[44] The induction took place on 22 October 1761, with Boston delivering the admission sermon on 1 Corinthians 2:2, "For I am determined not to know any thing among you save Jesus Christ and him crucified."[45] On the same day Gillespie, Boston and Collier, together with one elder from each of their congregations, constituted "a presbytery for the relief of Christians oppressed in their Christian privileges."[46]

Among the principles of the Relief Church were the following:

> The calls, commands, and invitations of the word, are the ground of faith, and they are directed to mankind, as lost and perishing sinners of Adam's family.
>
> The Israelitish church, established in Palestine, was not a *voluntary* society, but the Christian church *is*.
>
> As [Christians] are *members* of the church of Christ they *belong* to a community entirely *different* from the civil state.
>
> In regard to other churches around them, the Relief held it unlawful to hear legal and unsound preachers who overturned in their discourses the doctrines of grace—and also to hear intruders who had violently thrust themselves into particular charges in the church of Christ, and who by so doing had robbed Christ of his *authority*, and his people of their *liberty*.
>
> [I]t is *real saintship* that entitles men to the sacred supper, *in the sight of God* . . .it is the *visibility* of saintship *before the world*, that entitles men to communion in the *eye of the Church*.[47]

It should be added in connection with the last point here that the Relief Church, unlike the Antiburghers, advocated a communion table open to all saints, whether or not they held to the National Covenant of 1638 and the Solemn League and Covenant of 1643; such adherence, they felt, should not be made a term of communion.

In 1821, as if in demonstration of its relative openness of spirit, the Relief Church made overtures to the recently-united Associate Churches;

---

44. Struthers, *The History of the Rise of the Relief Church*, 284.

45. Ibid., 285. It is therefore odd that Leckie should say that neither Gillespie nor Boston "seem to have addressed the gathering or to have taken any part in the proceedings." See *Secession Memories*, 90–91.

46. Ibid., 287.

47. Ibid., 301, 309, 311, 317.

thirteen years later the United Secession Church, having by now become more generally voluntaryist in attitude, reciprocated; and in 1847, after protracted negotiations, the United Presbyterian Church came into being—a Church comprising 518 congregations; and this was Oman's Church. On the occasion of the Church's Jubilee in 1897 Dr. Henderson neatly summed up the situation. With reference to the Secession and Relief strands he said,

> Both sections . . . proclaimed the same gospel of Jesus Christ; both stood for relief from the evils which were dominant in the Establishment; but to the one it was given to work out the problem of the relation in which Church and State should stand to each other; for in all its contending and testimonies, in all its breaches and divisions of Burgher and Anti-Burgher, of Old Light and New Light, this question was ever coming up. To the other was given the task of showing that a Church of Christ can look beyond its own narrow limits, recognise the brotherhood of all true believers, and hold fellowship with them, though in many points of doctrine and practice they may differ from itself. In the end, the time came when the one was more or less permeated by the spirit of the other, so that a union between them became possible.[48]

But a Church is more than its statements of belief and practices; it has an ethos too; and perhaps Professor James Orr captured this in his remarks on the Jubilee occasion. He suggested that the "spiritual movement" underlying both Secession and Relief "was at bottom one":

> No name was more savoury in the cottage homes of Scotland than that of Boston of Ettrick, and where did Boston get his light? He was converted by Ebenezer Erskine's father. And where did Gillespie, the founder of the Relief, get his religious impressions? From conversations with Boston of Ettrick. And who was Gillespie's mother? A good Seceder woman . . . And whose was the second great name in the history of the Relief?—Thomas Boston of Jedburgh, the Ettrick Boston's son.[49]

Around the newly united Church there soon began to swirl the tides of modern biblical criticism, the challenge of evolutionary thought, and the doctrinal implications of these. Forward-looking in attitude, the United Presbyterians were the first to reflect on the doctrinal spirit of the times

---

48. Henderson, "The Divine Leading," 233.
49. Orr, "The Contribution of the United Presbyterian Church," 97.

in relation to their formal standards of belief and practice. In 1879 they unanimously adopted a Declaratory Act according to which there would be liberty of opinion "on such points in the Standards not entering into the substance of the faith." That the result was so resoundingly affirmative was in no small measure due to the sincerity and skill of the highly regarded and greatly loved Principal of the Theological College, John Cairns, under whom Oman was shortly to sit.[50] In 1892, though after more of a struggle and at the risk of a secession which materialized in 1893, the Free Church followed suit in almost identical words. Evincing an almost English ability to sanctify muddle in a good cause, these Scots omitted to specify which were the points that did not enter into the substance of the faith. Nevertheless, the way was thus clear for the union of the United Presbyterian Church with the Free Church in 1900. Thus was constituted the United Free Church.

That John Oman imbibed the spirit of the United Presbyterian Church and never repudiated it is easily demonstrated from his writings. Let us take the main points one by one. First, a generous interpretation of Calvinism allowing for the free offer of the Gospel. Oman writes, "Extreme Calvinism I never came across, for I knew it only among a race who, whether for thought or action, divided humanity into men who went to sea and muffs who stayed at home, and for whom the sovereignty of God meant the assurance of being able to face all storms, and seek no harbour of refuge. Nor had they any idea of having to work up the salvation of their souls. The real opposite of Divine Sovereignty is striving and crying instead of turning in simplicity and trust to God.[51]

Secondly, the Church is "a religious, a Divine society, not to be identified with the civil society, and yet with a national significance on better justification than mere recognition by the State."[52] Oman characteristically emphasises the fact that to belong to the Church is not to take upon oneself a yoke of bondage; rather it is to experience the freedom that Christ gives, whereby we are enabled to obey God and do his will.

Thirdly, the obligation of fellowship with all the saints: "This is the true and practical expression of a belief in the Holy Catholic Church. It is nothing less than a denial of any rejection of any brother for whom Christ died, which is nothing less in the end than a denial or contempt for any

---

50. See MacEwen, *Life and Letters of John Cairns*, ch. 24; Cairns, *Principal Cairns*, 131–33.

51. Oman, *Honest Religion*, 165, cf. 38.

52. Oman, *The Church and the Divine Order*, 303.

man. The heart which prays continually for grace to recognize all who truly name the name of Christ despises no one."[53]

Fourthly, the protest against the elevation of ecclesiastical formulae above the Gospel:

> How often has the Church given way to this temptation, ceasing to strive for a unity in which, through the good-news of God in Jesus Christ, each one sees the same reality, drinks of the same spirit and gladly accepts as his own the same Divine rule, and seeing it instead by fixed creed, uniform organisation, and even by an ordering of recognised duties, all imposed purely from without to conserve what seems already won![54]

> From day to day life must be faced with a creed falling far short of omniscience. It is less an illumination than points of light in the darkness, rather lighthouses to direct the course than sun or moon to display the prospect. Except when satisfied with tradition or theory, none question the Apostle's description of our knowledge, as "seeing in a glass darkly."[55]

These principles Oman carried with him to the end of his days. They came to him not so much through the books he read as through the air he breathed in the ecclesiastical context in which he was reared. Devoted to that environment as he was, Oman spent his working life as one who lived in a diaspora. Passing over for the moment his higher education, I shall briefly sketch his cross-border ecclesiastical context, for his working life was spent as a minister on the roll of the Presbyterian Church of England.

The name of the Church seems innocuous enough, but it hides a rather complicated pre-history, which I shall try to break down into a few concise points. First, following the union of the Scottish and English crowns in 1707 a considerable number of Scots removed to England in quest of work and education. Presbyterian churches were constituted on English soil at Wooler in 1729, Newcastle in 1749, Maryport in 1776, and it was not long before the Scottish Presbyterian presence was felt in Liverpool and London. Most of those who joined such churches regarded the Church of Scotland as their home, though some had been raised in one or another of the Scottish dissenting churches. Secondly, for a complex of intriguing reasons which I cannot stay to elucidate,[56] the vast majority of the

---

53. Oman, *Vision and Authority*, 170.
54. Oman, *The Paradox of the World*, 277.
55. Oman, *Vision and Authority*, 217.
56. But see Sell, *Dissenting Thought*, ch. 5.

English Presbyterians of Old Dissent had become either Congregational or Unitarian by the end of the eighteenth century, or early in the following century. Thirdly, the expatriate churches in England were organized into presbyteries, and at first it was thought that an English Synod of the Church of Scotland might be constituted. Questions were raised, however, concerning the propriety and legality of a Scottish established Church having jurisdiction in what the General Assembly called a "foreign country" which had its own Anglican establishment. In the end the Presbyterian Church *in* England was constituted in 1842. It comprised the new Scottish churches on English soil, together with the orthodox minority of English Presbyterian causes which had not turned Congregational or Unitarian during the preceding decades. By 1876 it numbered 153 congregations. Fourthly, many members of the Presbyterian Church in England sympathised with the Disruption Church of 1843, and in the following year the English Church declared independence from the Church of Scotland, regarded the Free Church as a sister Church, accused the Church of Scotland of having compromised sacred principles, and prayed that it might see the error of its ways and repent. A minority of congregations within the English Church, including Crown Court in London, remained faithful to the Church of Scotland, left the English Church and became members of Scottish presbyteries. In the same year the Presbyterian Church in England opened its theological college in London, and it is significant that all of its original teachers were drawn from the Free or Secession Churches; and this brings me to the fifth point. An increasing number of Scots were arriving in England, as well as immigrants from Wales and Ireland, and by now a sizeable number of the Scots among them belonged to the Secession Churches which, as we saw, had united in 1847 to form the United Presbyterian Church. It was not long before the United Presbyterian Church had four presbyteries comprising 58 congregations on English soil, and these were formed into a Synod in 1863. They, as we know, were voluntaryists, and, of course, the Presbyterian Church in England had no option but to adopt the same position and throw its lot in with English Nonconformists. This facilitated the union in 1876 of the United Presbyterian Synod with the Presbyterian Church *in* England to form the Presbyterian Church *of* England. At the time of the union the Church had 259 congregations and 46,540 members. The considerable sacrifice, both in terms of fellowship and finance, willingly borne by the United Presbyterian Church as it dismissed 109 congregations should not go unremarked.

On completion of his higher education Oman was licensed as a probationer by the United Presbyterian Synod. For a few months he served the preaching station at Makerstown near Kelso, and whilst there he was able once again to meet his former minister at Stromness, Thomas Kirkwood. From Makerstown he became assistant to Dr. James Brown of St. James's Church Paisley, and from that base he preached at a number of vacant churches, but no call came. It may be that Oman did not have the gifts of pulpit oratory that some congregations expected: he was a preacher of the thoughtful, rather than the histrionic, sort; and there is evidence that he suffered from vocal problems.[57] It is also the case that at that time the number of available ministerial candidates exceeded the number of vacant charges. Whatever the reason, after four years of disappointment, Oman entered the ministry of the Presbyterian Church of England in 1890, on receiving a call to Clayport Street Church, Alnwick.[58] Brown of Paisley, though far from well, attended the welcoming celebrations.

The Alnwick church had been founded in 1753 by the Associate Burgher Synod. In November of that year John Brown of Haddington ordained three elders who had been called by the congregation. At first meetings were held in a room at the top of Canongate, then in another house, and from 1761 in their own building seating 300. The first regular minister, John Marshall, was ordained and inducted in 1766. The cause prospered and outgrew its premises, so that in 1803 a new meeting house was erected on the south side of Green Batt, with seating for 550. In 1845 John Ker, who went on to teach at the theological college, was inducted,

---

57. Bevans, *John Oman*, 123, cites a letter which relates that Oman was diagnosed as having a "corn" in his throat, and an observation of F. G. Healey to the effect that Oman "reckoned his vocal chords had been damaged by faulty elocution training." If the latter were the case Oman, sadly, was not alone. He writes, "As I was obviously in need of help, the advice of my friends was frequent and free; and I learned too late that it was uniformly mistaken," with the consequent "ruining of my vocal chords." See *Concerning the Ministry*, 110. Classes in elocution were, and still are, provided for ministerial students in many theological colleges, but all too often they are more concerned with how voices sound (accents, volume, light and shade) than with how they are produced. It is quite conceivable that Oman, and before him Principals Thomas Robins of Daventry Academy, Henry Rogers of Spring Hill College and Henry Roberts Reynolds of Cheshunt College, all of whom withdrew from preaching owing to vocal problems, could have been helped had competent guidance been available. For a specialist discussion of voice production and related matters see Karen Sell, *The Disciplines of Vocal Pedagogy*.

58. The churches of Alnwick would seem to have had a facility for calling scholarly ministers to their pastorates. Powicke (for whom see Sell, *Enlightenment, Ecumenism, Evangel*, ch. 1, was at the Congregational Church there from 1879–1886.

The Theological Education of the Ministry

and there was further church growth. The Duke of Northumberland's agent refused to renew the church's forty-year lease on the land, which was passed to the Church of Scotland for the erection of St. Paul's Church. Meanwhile Ker's congregation had a 700-seater church built, and there the distinguished preacher, whom Oman later commended to his students as exemplifying homiletic pathos,[59] held forth. In 1851 William Limont assumed the charge and remained there for forty-seven years. It was he to whom Oman came first as assistant and then as successor.

Though by no means an example of "ecclesiastical man," Oman took his preaching, teaching and pastoral duties seriously. "This was his extraordinary merit," wrote one, "that a man of such brilliant intellect, whose sermons were often hard to follow, could yet create this strong bond of affection and trust between himself and the humblest of his flock."[60] To his pastoral duties Oman added consistent study. He translated Schleiermacher's *On Religion: Speeches to its Cultured Despisers* (1893), and to the third edition of this book Rudolf Otto contributed the Introduction. In a letter Oman wrote, "I did Schleiermacher during the first years I was in Alnwick from sheer loneliness."[61] But after a few years he was lonely no longer, for in 1897 he married Mary, one of four daughters of Hunter Blair, J.P., of Gosforth, an elder in the church and a prominent boot manufacturer in Newcastle-upon-Tyne. In due time the Omans had four daughters, and John and Mary remained happily married until her death in 1936. A theological vacancy at New College, Edinburgh, for which Oman was considered, was filled in 1904 by H. R. Mackintosh, who secured a large majority at the General Assembly.[62] Oman's Kerr Lectures were prepared and delivered, and in the winter of 1907 he gave lectures at Syracuse University and Auburn Theological Seminary on "The foundations of belief." He was invited to take professorial positions in the United States and Melbourne, but he declined. In 1907, however, Oman accepted the Chair of Systematic Theology and Apologetics at Westminster College, Cambridge, and there he served for the next twenty-eight years. With this I come to Oman's intellectual context.

59. Oman, *Concerning the Ministry*, 142.

60. Staker, *A History of St. James' United Reformed Church*, 30. Much of the information in this paragraph is drawn from this tercentenary booklet. Among the church members was the chemist, J. L. Newbigin, for more than forty years the secretary of Alnwick Missionary Society. He was the grandfather of J. E. Lesslie Newbigin, to whom further reference shall be made.

61. Quoted by Healey, *Religion and Reality*, 159.

62. See Reith. *Reminiscences*, 47.

II

However competent Oman's Stenness tutor may have been in imparting the basics of education, it would seem that prescience was not among his gifts, for F. G. Healey relates that "When Oman's parents told the tutor that they thought of sending their boy to Edinburgh, the tutor replied, according to a contemporary of Oman's at Stenness, 'that he saw no promise to justify such an effort.'"[63] Undaunted, the Omans sent John to Edinburgh University when he was seventeen with the idea that he should in due course enter the medical profession. First, however, in 1882 he gained the degree of MA with first class honours in philosophy, and in addition he won the Gray and Rhind scholarships. His Professor of Logic was Alexander Campbell Fraser of the Free Church of Scotland,[64] while Henry Calderwood of the United Presbyterian Church held the Chair of Moral Philosophy.[65] While their names do not appear in the indices to Oman's major works we may not unreasonably suppose that from these two, both of whom stood broadly in the tradition of Scottish common sense realism flowing down from Thomas Reid, he learned cautions against the absolute idealism which was currently being propounded by John and Edward Caird in Glasgow University. Fraser disliked absolutism's pantheizing tendencies, and its "Gnostic" confidence that we could comprehend the reasonableness of the universe—a claim against which Fraser pitted the undeniable obstacle of moral evil. He was always aware of the limits of our knowledge and hence of the need to exercise prudence in assertion—a marked characteristic, this, of the articulated thought of John Oman. His realistic caution did not, however, prevent Fraser from arguing that from the generally trustworthy natural order we might legitimately infer a morally good Divine creator. He accompanied this claim with an argument to the effect that a universe which includes sin and suffering is preferable to a non-moral universe, not least because it affords a training ground for moral agents. Calderwood likewise exercised scholarly caution. Perceiving atheistic tendencies in his teacher William Hamilton's writings, he defended the view that human beings may have genuine, albeit partial, knowledge of the divine. He countered materialism, Hegelianism and, on the ground of the transcendent intelligence which informs every human

---

63. Healey, *Religion and Reality*, 158.

64. For Fraser (1819–1914), see ODNB; Mander and Sell, *Dictionary of Nineteenth-Century British Philosophers*; Sell, *Commemorations*, ch. 10.

65. For Calderwood (1830–1897) see ODNB; *Dictionary of Nineteenth-Century British Philosophers*.

mind, physicalism. A. S. Pringle-Pattison (then Andrew Seth) was at the beginning of his career when Oman was a student. Oman was not uninfluenced by the personal idealism of which Pringle-Pattison was a pioneer, and years afterwards he reviewed his old teacher's Gifford Lectures which, owing to the intervention of War between their delivery in 1913 and their publication in 1917, appeared to him as a period piece, albeit a lucid one marked by literary grace.[66]

Even more important than the instruction of his philosophical mentors was Oman's reaction to the *cause celèbre* of the day: the heresy trial of William Robertson Smith, who held the Old Testament Chair at the Free Church College, Aberdeen. Influenced by the documentary hypothesis of his teacher, Wellhausen, Smith contributed articles to the ninth edition of *Encyclopaedia Britannica* which prompted many in his own Church and elsewhere to question his view of the inspiration of Scripture. The case rumbled on for five years, and in 1881 Smith was deposed from his Chair though not expelled from the ministry, whereupon he repaired to Cambridge where he pursued his studies until his early death. We have no need to speculate upon the influence the trial had on Oman: we have it from his own mouth:

> When I went to the university, a raw lad from the ends of the earth, with little equipment except a vast responsiveness to the intellectual environment, the Robertson Smith case was shaking the whole land. I had no notion, in those days, of ever being interested in theology, and my ignorance of the matters in dispute was profound. But I read [Smith's] speeches, and, on one occasion, heard him. I seemed to find the same kind of knowledge as was making the world a place for me of incessant discovery and the same passion for reality as seemed at the moment life's supreme concern. At the same time I heard people who, not only did not know, but did not want to know, condemning him for vanity, because of this very loyalty to the results of investigation. Again and again I heard people declare that, even if all he said were true, regard for useful tradition and the ecclesiastical amenities should have kept him from saying it.[67]

Oman was appalled by this anti-intellectual, obscurantist stance, was deeply concerned that ordinary folk would reach, or be confirmed in, the

---

66. Oman, Review of *The Idea of God in the Light of Recent Philosophy*, 278–79. For Pringle-Pattison see ODNB; *Dictionary of Nineteenth-Century British Philosophers*; Sell, *Philosophical Idealism*, 83–92 and *passim*.

67. Oman, "Method in theology," 82–83.

belief that religion was "a kind of trade-union to impose upon mankind merely traditional beliefs,"[68] and was disgusted by the sanction the position received from ecclesiastical leaders. As he later put it, they were "more exercised about unity than veracity."[69] He was "shocked" when a lawyer and Free Church elder said to him, "'Granted that Robertson Smith is right, if it is truth, it is dangerous truth, and he has no right, as a professor of the Church, to upset the Church by declaring it.' I hope I have not since weakened in my loyalty to truth, but in those days I thought intellectual truth the one worthy pursuit in life: and this suggested that the Church was not interested in it. Had I been intending the ministry probably I should have been put off it, but this affected me somewhat as a call to my life's work."[70]

Accordingly, he entered the United Presbyterian Theological College, where the staff included John Ker, to whom reference has already been made, and the greatly loved ecclesiastical statesman and collector of languages, Principal John Cairns. Cairns was the right kind of Principal; that is to say, he was one of whom anecdotes could lovingly be rehearsed. Thus J. H. Leckie, who entered the College two years after Oman left it, recalled that on entering the classroom one day the students found that Cairns had inscribed an Assyrian inscription on the blackboard: "For two days he lectured on this inscription with the most assured belief that we were following every word, and there was deep regret in his face and in his voice when he said: 'And now, gentlemen, I am afraid we must return to our theology.'"[71] More to our present purpose are Oman's recollections on his Principal. "[A] great man has departed," he wrote on learning of Cairns's death, "for myself I would say the greatest man I have ever met." An accomplished linguist, Cairns would apologize for his poor Hebrew—"Hebrew in my day was very imperfectly taught," and then close his eyes and recite pages of the Hebrew Old Testament flawlessly. He was a humble man; he knew all the theologians of note in Germany; and "his mere presence in the world was a benediction . . . Of all things his laugh was most wonderful. It was like a mountain enjoying an earthquake . . . He was so careful not to hurt that sometimes he was not bold enough to criticise . . . He never seemed to perceive any evil in any mortal . . . The many things that make men little he did not perceive for a man only perceives

68. Ibid., 85.
69. Ibid., 82.
70. Oman, *Vision and Authority*, Preface to the 2nd ed., 1928, 9–10.
71. MacEwen, *Life and Letters of John Cairns*, 743; cf. Cairns, *Principal Cairns*, 138.

that into which his own heart opens a window . . . While here he lived the eternal life."[72]

If the Robertson Smith case had, as Oman said, shaken the whole land, the need to adjust to modern biblical criticism was by no means the only intellectual challenge facing Christians at that time. There was evolutionary thought and a bundle of "isms" including agnosticism, materialism, pantheism—all of which were slain by Robert Flint, the most learned apologist of the day; but he was by no means alone in defending the faith against attack. On the contrary, this was the golden age of Scottish apologetics.[73] Such writers as John Stuart Mill and Herbert Spencer came under regular scrutiny. Under the title, *Unbelief in the Eighteenth Century as Contrasted with Its Earlier and Later History*,[74] Principal Cairns had judiciously discoursed upon rationalistic trends in his Cunningham Lectures of 1880. As for Oman himself, he was particularly opposed to the post-Hegelian immanentist idealism being promulgated in Glasgow by the Cairds. For thinkers of this type, "The final word was immanent cosmic process, and rational man is but its highest vehicle and most conscious mirror. This is predestinarianism in a way to have taken away even Calvin's breath"[75] Later, in the midst of war, Oman lamented that Germany had constructed a myopic idealism out of Hegel, making the state the Absolute's final organ, to which the individual, lost in the crowd, had to do obeisance.[76] He returned to the theme in his greatest work, in which he complained that Hegelianism "does not merely dismiss the problem of the individual, but is the profoundest attempt to account for it on a scheme which, nevertheless, derives all rationality from absorbing him into the process of the Cosmic Reason."[77]

Over and above the excitements surrounding the Declaratory Acts, there was considerable doctrinal and more general theological publication

---

72. Oman, "Dr. Cairns. By one of his students," ms. at Westminster College, Cambridge.

73. See ch. 3 above; Sell, *Defending and Declaring the Faith*. For concurrent apologetic efforts in Nonconformity south of the Scottish border see Sell, *Philosophy, Dissent and Nonconformity*, ch. 5.

74. Edinburgh: A. & C. Black, 1881.

75. Oman, *Grace and Personality*, 32. He proceeds to argue that this is, nevertheless the logic of Calvin's own position. For immanentism, modern biblical criticism and evolutionary thought see Sell, *Theology in Turmoil*, chs. 1–3; for a fuller discussion of the first see idem. *Philosophical Idealism*.

76. Oman, *The War and its Issues*, 91.

77. Oman, *The Natural and the Supernatural*, 475.

Living in the Half Lights

during the second half of the nineteenth century. It is quite remarkable that Scotland could produce sufficient scholars to staff not only the four ancient University departments, but also the three new Free Church colleges required following the Disruption, the Secession Colleges, and still have a number of scholar-pastors in charges across the land. As if that were not enough, theologians from Scotland staffed many colonial institutions, and the Congregationalists were able to export Gilbert Wardlaw to Blackburn, A. M. Fairbairn to Bradford, Robert Mackintosh to Manchester, and P. T. Forsyth and A. E. Garvie to London.

Such was the apologetically and theologically vibrant environment in which Oman read for his degree of BD, and subsequently for his DPhil of Edinburgh. During his theological course Oman was able to spend two summer terms abroad. In 1883 he, together with his fellow-students James Gardner and B. R. Mein, was at Erlangen University, where he sat under the dogmatician F. H. Frank,[78] the biblical scholar, F. T. R. von Zahn, and the philosophical theologian, G. Class. Two summers later he was at Heidelberg, where he heard Adolph Hausrath on New Testament Introduction and Merx on the Psalms. As well as contributing substantial volumes in his field, the former wrote a number of historical romances under the pseudonym George Taylor—an achievement which, as far as I know, is unmatched by any other devotee of the Tübingen school of criticism. By a happy coincidence Adalbert Merx later studied the Sinaitic Palimpsest which had been discovered in 1892 by Agnes Smith Lewis who, with her twin sister, Mrs. Margaret Dunlop Gibson, was a benefactress of Westminster College, Cambridge. On leaving Erlangen Oman went on to Neuchâtel with a view to mastering French.[79]

In 1907, following his period as a United Presbyterian probationer and minister at Alnwick, Oman assumed the Barbour Chair of Systematic Theology and Apologetics at Westminster College, Cambridge, in succession to James Oswald Dykes, who had just retired from the combined position of professor and principal. Members of the appointing Synod had cast 402 votes in favour of Oman, against 101 for Patrick Carnegie Simpson. Oman's academic colleagues in the College combined academic prowess and ecclesiastical loyalty to a high degree. In 1908 John Skinner became Principal, a position he held until his resignation in 1922, when Oman succeeded him in that office, once again defeating Simpson, but

---

78. Whose position Oman outlines in *The Problem of Faith and Freedom*, 346–48.

79. See Alexander. "Memoir," xviii; Oman, "Reminiscences of continental travel" and "German student life," unpublished papers at Westminster College, Cambridge.

this time by "a slight majority."⁸⁰ Skinner had been on the staff since 1890. He held the Chair of Old Testament Literature and Apologetics,⁸¹ and became the first Nonconformist to receive the Degree of Doctor of Divinity of the University of Oxford. Charles Archibald Anderson Scott held the Chair of New Testament Language, Literature and Theology from 1907, and in 1920 he became the first Nonconformist minister to gain Cambridge University's D.D. Meanwhile in 1914 he had been nominated for the Chair of Church History, but on this occasion Carnegie Simpson, a distinguished ecclesiastical statesman, was successful. In the same year a rumour was started to the effect that Oman was to be nominated for the Chair at Glasgow United Free Church College which had fallen vacant on the death of Professor James Orr. On 17 February R. C. Gillie, the convenor of the Westminster College Committee wrote a letter for circulation in which he strongly expressed the view that Oman's removal would be a disastrous blow to the College; and the Birmingham Presbytery, on the motion of the Revd J. R. Gillies resolved to resist Oman's removal, and the London North Presbytery did likewise.⁸² Oman himself made it clear that he did not wish to leave Cambridge.

In his capacity as Principal, Oman sent a memorandum to a subcommittee established by the Moderator's Committee to review the Presbyterian Church's ministry. Oman wrote on the basis of enquiries he had made into the curriculum of theological colleges. The question was how broad the curriculum should become. "The strongest opinion" he reported, "I had from President Wilson. 'Stick at all costs to your four central subjects. Our method means utterly superficial knowledge...'" On this Oman remarked, "My experience as a teacher has rubbed into me the enormous difference between knowing a subject and knowing about it."⁸³ Accordingly he maintained the longstanding policy of focusing upon the

80. Report on 11 May 1922 among the Westminster College Oman papers.

81. Skinner was a native of Aberdeenshire, that nursery of Old Testament professors, of whom two, Skinner and W. G. Elmslie, taught at Westminster College. Others were A. B. Davidson, W. Robertson Smith and George Adam Smith.

82. See the Oman papers at Westminster College, Cambridge.

83. Typescript "Memorandum" at Westminster College, Cambridge. Cf. the second epigraph in this book, the source of which is Robert Franks's *Report* of 1926 to the subscribers to Western College, Bristol. According to John Huxtable, a Western College alumnus, "Franks used to say that it is better to read big books, even if you disagreed with them, than clutter your minds with pious little books which are like hayforks: they pitch you up and toss things about and land you where you were before." See *As It Seemed to Me*, London: The United Reformed Church, 1990, 11. For Franks and Huxtable see the Bibliographical Appendix below.

Old and New Testaments, Church History and Theology, and this with a view to fostering depth of understanding on the part of his students as courses proceeded from session to session.

When Skinner died in 1921, he was succeeded in the Old Testament Chair by William Alexander Leslie Elmslie, whose father, William Gray Elmslie, had earlier held the post. When Oman retired in 1935, the younger Elmslie succeeded him as Principal, while Oman's former student, H. H. Farmer, was called to the Chair of Systematic Theology.[84] On his retirement, Oman was promised a copy of Hugh Rivière's portrait of Oman made by the artist himself; and the Omans were given tickets for a two-week cruise to the Norwegian fjords.[85] The fact that it was an independent institution notwithstanding, by now Westminster College's contribution to the University of Cambridge was taken as a matter of course. This was in no small part to the distinguished service Oman gave to the Board of the Faculty of Divinity and the Degrees Committee. In addition he lectured in Comparative Religion from 1913–1922, served three terms as Stanton Lecturer in the Philosophy of Religion, was elected an Honorary Fellow of Jesus College in 1928, became an Honorary DD of the University of Oxford in 1928, and a Fellow of the British Academy ten years later—an honour he accepted with some hesitation because he felt he would not be able to make further contributions "to support the honour."[86]

Whilst at Cambridge Oman served his Church in a variety of ways. He undertook pulpit supplies in the Birmingham Presbytery on behalf of ministers who were called away during World War I. He visited the troops in France under the auspices of the YMCA and, deeply affected by the War, he published *The War and Issues* in 1915—a second edition being required the following year. He found during his visits to military camps and hospitals that "fundamental religious questions were constantly being discussed," and this "forced upon me the reconsideration of my whole religious position."[87] Following the cessation of hostilities he toured occupied areas;[88] and he was still reflecting upon the War in his last book,

---

84. For sketches of the academic staff see Elmslie, *Westminster College Cambridge*; Robson, *Our Professors*. Note that Robson curtails C. A. A. Scott's tenure of his Chair by ten years, 12.

85. Cottle and Cooper, "Westminster College Bulletin," 230.

86. Alexander, "Memoir," xxiv.

87. Oman, *Grace and Personality*, 5.

88. Obituary in *The Times*, 18 May 1939.

Honest Religion, published posthumously in 1941.[89] Though far from being a professional ecclesiastical statesman, he was nevertheless honoured by the call of the Presbyterian Church of England to be Moderator of its General Assembly in 1931.

It is characteristic of Oman that he kept in touch with his roots. Thus, for example, he paid return visits to Alnwick. On one such occasion *The British Weekly* reported that "Dr. Oman's ripe scholarship, combined with a most reverential mind, mark him as an outstanding preacher. The services throughout were very hearty."[90] On another occasion *The Alnwick Guardian and County* Advertiser devoted almost a full page, including a large photograph of Oman, to one of his return visits.[91] Again, he was present as a distinguished visitor at the General Assembly of the United Presbyterian Church in 1924.[92] In 1932 he joined William Temple and others in signing a letter to *The Times* urging that aid be sent to China where, during the summer of 1931, an area larger than England had been flooded.[93] Four years later he, together with the Baptist, M. E. Aubrey, the Congregationalists, Sidney M. Berry and A. J. Grieve, the Methodist, J. Scott Lidgett, and others, signed a letter regarding the four hundredth anniversary of the martyrdom of William Tyndale. The signatories' objective was to encourage churches, Sunday schools and brotherhoods to mark the occasion, and to commend a commemorative pamphlet published by the British and Foreign Bible Society.[94] Above all, however, during his Cambridge years Oman did the bulk of his writing, most notably his books, *Grace and Personality* (1917) and *The Natural and the Supernatural* (1931). While a full account of these cannot here be provided, we have not finished placing him in his intellectual context until we noted some of the intellectual influences, both positive and negative, upon him; certain trends of thought to which he paid no heed; and the way in which the main lines of his own thought were received.

Later in life Oman published his summary impressions of the varieties of continental thought, contemporary with himself, that he had encountered.[95] Of the Tübingen way of forcing facts to conform with

---

89. See, for example, *Honest Religion*, 5, 16.

90. *The British Weekly*, 1 April 1909.

91. *The Alnwick Guardian and County Advertiser*, 21 September 1912.

92. See Reith. *Reminiscences*, 274.

93. *The Times*, 21 March 1932, 10.

94. *The Times*, 26 September 1936, 13.

95. Oman, "Author's preface" to *Honest Religion*, xxxiv–xl. Unless otherwise stated, quotations in this paragraph are drawn from these pages.

Living in the Half Lights

Hegelian categories he declared that no other school "has risen to quite this height of glorifying the abstraction as universal oracle . . ."; and he elsewhere objected to the postulate of the Tübingen authors, namely, that "As soon as a book is shown to have been written with a purpose, it is to be discounted as an accurate historical report."[96] In opposition to this, and to a perceived pantheistic and non-moral interpretation of Christianity, the Ritschlians, for all their elevation of the Kingdom of God construed in *quasi*-Kantian terms of "the progressive moralisation of the race," could not show why "the model of moral form—the Pharisee—did not go into this kingdom before the publican and the sinner." On the other hand, Oman defended Ritschl against the charge that his repudiation of metaphysics entailed the denial of the objectivity of religious knowledge. Ritschl "had worshipped at [the shrine of the Transcendental Philosophy] only to find the cosmic process instead of God, and he had also been a disciple of the Tübingen school, till he found that its criticism was only subjection to this metaphysical idol."[97] Ritschl's point, says Oman, was that "a theoretical truth is one that can be forced upon any intelligent person by argument, and religious truth never arrives at that stage";[98] it requires "not merely intelligent consideration, but an attitude of the will. The Ritschlians were less Olympian than the Tübingen authors, and their contribution to raising the essential questions about early Christianity was much greater; yet their answers were determined by their outlook, far more than their outlook by their answers." For all that, Ritschl understood that "Personality is the prime religious basis. Men do not start from the Absolute and then add personality. They start from personality, and, by discovering that in spite of sin and evil they can . . . subject all things to moral and spiritual ends, they arrive at a belief in omnipotent personality."[99] For their part, the Apocalyptic School "denied all that was rational in its predecessors' view. But by the spectacles of its theory its vision was even more controlled" and "it still continued to measure with the old Kantian ethic, if not the old Kantian reason." Thus, Schweitzer argues that Jesus did not spiritualize, but ethicized the political ideal of late Jewish Messianic expectation in Kantian fashion, whereas Oman is utterly convinced that "If . . . there is anything certain about what Jesus did, it was to work a moral regeneration by a religious one, and that His ethical spirit was not of the Kantian order

---

96. Oman, *The Problem of Faith and Freedom*, 300.
97. Oman, "Ritschlianism," 472.
98. Oman, *The Problem of Faith and Freedom*, 365.
99. Oman, "Ritschlianism," 473.

to be merely poured into anything." The most recent School, he continues (citing Dibelius), "tests all by 'form' and what it calls 'set in life'. This might seem to show more regard to life and history, but . . . it is used just as another category to drill the records and has a great part of its impressiveness from becoming the slogan or battle-cry of a school . . . [T]here is nothing it says but may in certain cases be true: only it is not so universally true that a general ordering of all can be derived from it."

Oman's preference is for Rudolf Otto's view that "Jesus announced a Kingdom already present in spiritual power but which was to have further manifestation and consummation, yet this was to be of the nature of the prophetic vision of knowing God and having His commandment in the heart." His difference from Otto lay in the fact that he could not endorse the view that the holy is simply a matter of intense, value-free emotion: "As mere feeling," he writes, "the sense of the holy would be impossible to distinguish from the mere spooky feeling which is magical, at one end, and from the sense of the sublime which is artistic, at the other."[100] That is to say, abstracted from moral considerations, the "awesome holy" characterizes magical, superstitious, belief.[101] In making this point elsewhere Oman draws a delightful illustration from his youthful experience:

> When a boy of fourteen or thereabouts, I was riding through the Standing Stones of Stenness on a winter afternoon when dusk was settling into darkness. They stand on the top of a lone narrow neck of land between two lochs . . . The circle of stones had a look of ancient giants against the grey sky, and the gaping mounds which had been opened stood shadowy and apart. A more numinous scene, at a more numinous hour, could not be found on earth. And the feeling which suddenly struck me is not inaptly described as the *mysterium tremendum et fascinans*. But at the same moment it struck my old horse at least as vehemently as myself. He threw up his head, snorted, set his feet, trembled, and finally bolted at a rate I should have thought impossible for his old bones. Now there is little doubt that Prof. Otto is right in finding the reason why the early Briton erected this circle of stones on that particular spot in the peculiar eerie feeling it created rather than in merely intellectual ideas; but, as the feeling had probably not yet arrived at being religious for my horse, and

---

100. Oman, *The Natural and the Supernatural*, 61.

101. Ibid., 60–63. Oman's point was endorsed by English Nonconformity's most scholarly, and most undeservedly neglected, theologian of the twentieth century, Robert Franks. See his *The Atonement*, 21. For Franks see Sell, *Hinterland Theology*, ch. 10 and *passim*.

had ceased to be religious for me, it would be necessary to ask, what was the peculiarity which, without disrespect to his intelligence, I may assume my horse not to have attained and which, without excessive pride in my state of civilization, I may assume I had passed beyond, which made it for primitive man religious? . . . [Feelings aroused by nature] may stir and pass over into the holy . . . but are we not then in a new order? And is not the essence of it that it is an order of absolute value which, when it escapes from its material form, is just the ethical sacred, the sense of the requirements of a Spirit in the world which is absolute and of a spirit in ourselves in its image which has its worth in accepting as its own these absolute requirements and refusing to bring them down to the level of our temporal convenience?. . . . My horse, we may assume, had not reached this valuation, and I was at least learning to make it by less material ways.[102]

Apart from this ethical valuation, he continues, we have superstition, not religion, and we do not have a love which casts out fear. By separating the rational from the religious Otto "can do no more than say that they are connected *a priori*, which is not very satisfactory."[103] The upshot is that Otto's work "does little to satisfy thought," but "it does a great deal to stimulate enquiry and reflexion."[104] Integrity prompts the observation that to C. A. Campbell this was nothing other than an unjustified "attack" on Otto. To him it was the "incredible," but "sober truth" that Oman wrote as if all that Otto had said about the *fascinans* aspect of the numinous "simply did not exist." He felt that if Oman had paid as much attention to Otto's *fascinans* as he had done to his *tremendum*, his one-sided critique would have been balanced by the recognition that "The *fascinans* aspect is that in virtue of which the numinous consciousness is enraptured and entranced by the transcendent *worth* or *value* of the numen."[105] He would therefore have seen that Otto did not banish the moral as charged.

Lying behind Otto as a prominent influence upon Oman is Schleiermacher, with his experiential starting-point for understanding religion. Oman defends Schiermacher against the charges that there was nothing objective in his theology, that by feeling he meant sentiment, and that by absolute dependence he meant "mere mystical self-surrender."[106] On the

---

102. Oman, "The Idea of the Holy," 282–83.
103. Ibid., 286.
104. Ibid.
105. See Campbell, *On Selfhood and Godhood*, 343.
106. Oman, "Schleiermacher," 403.

contrary, for Schleiermacher, feeling "is neither sensation nor emotion, but the contract with reality, which, while it precedes clear intuition, is not a mere cause of it but passes into it. Thus religion and perception are both contacts with reality and united at their source."[107]

From time to time Oman was called upon to review the work of living theologians. Among the works allotted to him was Hastings Rashdall's *The Idea of Atonement in Christian Theology*. He finds that "The work is pervaded throughout by the conviction, not only that the study of history is a necessary preliminary to any serious reconstruction, but that, to a large extent, it will supersede the need for any such task."[108] He wryly remarks that Rashdall does not have much difficulty in selecting authors for discussion, "seeing he believes that all that is obnoxious to him was maintained only by a few dominating but deluded individuals, beginning with St Paul and culminating in Luther."[109] Rashdall rejects "every form of vicarious, substitutionary, or representative theory of atonement."[110] Anselm left us with a God who cared more for his own honour than for his debt-paying Son, but he did at least call forth Abelard's moral influence theory, with which Rashdall finds himself in general sympathy. Oman agrees with Rashdall that no atonement theory that conflicts with Jesus' teaching can be called Christian, but queries whether Rashdall's idea of God, namely, that he is a "kind of moral governor who justifies us as we are just," takes full account of the fact that "For Jesus there is only one condition of forgiveness—the God to whom we return."[111] Whereas Paul had a gospel for sinners, Rashdall's treatment of reconciliation is slight. Indeed, "he does not get very far beyond a morality which is still entangled with the old Pharisaic demand for an equivalence of merit and reward, which any doctrine of atonement that means anything must deny to be the final method of God's rule."[112]

When he turns to H. R. Mackintosh's book, *The Christian Experience of Forgiveness*, we find Oman diagnosing his response thus: "disagreement is probably rather from a difference of race and temperament and general outlook than from any clear difference of opinion . . . [T]here is something of a Celtic quality with which the ordinary Briton feels a little

---

107. Ibid., 404.
108. Oman, Review of H. Rashdall, *The Idea of Atonement*, 267.
109. Ibid.
110. Ibid.
111. Ibid., 272.
112. Ibid., 274.

overwhelmed."[113] He proceeds to posit two kinds of mind, the first, exemplified by Mackintosh, "takes naturally to Otto's awed holy; the other type instinctively shakes it off as a nightmare."[114] The types vary as to the difficulties they perceive: "Prof. Mackintosh very easily thinks of God as just doing things; it is an essential part of the [other's] idea of God that God is just another name for the ultimate real. Thus the problem of forgiveness is apt to be, for him, something exceptional that God does, while, for the other type it is something which is just because God is what He is, and we have found it out."[115] Oman further feels that Mackintosh so dwells on the suffering of the Cross as to minimize the victory of the Cross. To all of which I shall return shortly.

Karl Barth was probably the theologian by whom Oman was least likely to be influenced in a positive direction. Recalling the theological atmosphere he had experienced in Erlangen, Oman remarked that "if we had to choose between the older orthodoxy of the Erlangen School and the newer of the Barthian, the former has at least the Christian temper."[116] Oman objects to that way in which Barthians fault Schleiermacher's empiricism for rendering religion anthropocentric:

> It used to be said that Schleiermacher deserved his name, which means veil-maker, but Barth and his disciples deal in thicker and still more opaque material. Much of the criticism of this school is true, and they have done a great deal to clear the ground. I am not very learned in their works and cannot claim to know all that is maintained, but the effect so far seems to leave more of a quagmire than before. Schleiermacher is denounced as a high-priest of error. Ever since his day Protestant theology has wandered in the quagmires of pious emotion and not found objective God-given truth. This is preached with prophetic fire. But when we come to ask what is God-given truth, what is *Das Wort Gottes* which is the supreme truth, and how do we know it is God's word; so far as I have read, the writers clothe themselves in vagueness and become abusive.[117]

---

113. Oman, Review of H. R. Mackintosh, *The Christian Experience of Forgiveness*, 297.

114. Ibid.

115. Ibid., 297–98.

116. Review of A. Chapman, *An Introduction to Schleiermacher*, 214.

117. Oman, "Schleiermacher," 403.

Oman cannot see how human beings can do other than measure the universe and do so by using human measures. Even an infallible Scripture or an infallible papacy is humanly measured. But Barth and his followers deny that they are biblical infallibilists and affirm their acceptance of biblical criticism: "Therefore, it would seem an unavoidable conclusion that we must somewhere find our knowledge anthropocentric, and the question must arise of how it can be anthropocentric in such a way as to be objective knowledge. But apparently we go after strange Gods with Schleiermacher when we make the attempt."[118]

In view of the foregoing, Stephen Bevans seems wide of the mark when he writes, "It is rather ironic that Oman had such an antipathy to Barth. While differing radically in terms of theological method, both Barth and Oman would agree on the personal nature of God."[119] But (a) as between these two method is all, Barth being the disjunctive thinker, Oman the conjunctive; Barth eschewing apologetics, Oman writing *Honest Religion*; and (b) everything turns upon the connotation of "personal" in the term "personal God"; for Oman, God was the holy One, but he was never the wholly other One, and God's grace (*pace* Augustinianism and Calvinism) was persuasive not irresistible.[120] It is not inconceivable that Oman would have applied his words of 1923 to Barthianism: "Every now and then movements make a great impression by dogmatic assertion, but the sapping of the foundations goes on all the time, and, over a long period, it is always evident that they have not kept serious and thoughtful minds within the Christian Church, but that, what is still worse, they have been stirring doubt regarding the whole reality of a spiritual world."[121] Even student skits can convey truth, as when Westminster College students produced a booklet entitled "What I owe to Karl Barth, by John

---

118. Ibid., 404.

119. Bevans, *John Oman*, 121.

120. See, for example, the exposition of Horton, *Contemporary English Theology*, 135. Horton muses, *ad loc.*, that "Karl Barth seems to be urging us along that path [of Augustinian irrationalism and immoralism] as the only alternative to Pelagian pride of intellect and moral self-sufficiency." In fairness it must be granted that many Calvinists construed "irresistible" in "irresistible grace" not in terms of sheer omnipotent force, but in the sense that God's overflowing love towards the undeserving is so lovingly attractive that any resistance to it is quelled *ab initio*: the recipient would not wish to resist such grace. In this context they spoke of "the Father's drawing"—a very different thing from the Father's dragooning or compelling.

121. Oman, "Method in Theology," 85–86. This was Oman's Inaugural Lecture on assuming the Principalship of Westminster College.

Oman"; the pages in the booklet were blank.[122] When, in his last book, Oman declared that "there is no worse preparation for profitable dialogue than a mind school-mastering everything by dialectic,"[123] the innocent reader cannot help wondering whom he might have had in mind.

It would seem that outside the walls of Westminster College the Cambridge friend whose work Oman most greatly valued was F. R. Tennant. Oman reviewed the two volumes of Tennant's *Philosophical Theology*, welcomed the empiricist basis of the work, but regretted that "we deal with the environment as meaning," whereas Oman asks "what is meaning apart from value?" He would have pressed the "absoluteness of regard for the ideal value as sacred," which was foreign to Tennant's method.[124]

In the broader realm of contemporary philosophy Oman adjusted himself to the thought of a number of writers. For example, he opposed Samuel Alexander's view of space-time as "the matrix of all reality, from which all else in our experienced universe 'emerges'. In order to make a start at all, [Alexander] has to assume that it has qualities. But this is precisely the all-important step from motion to meaning, which nothing in the mathematical conception of space-time justifies him in taking."[125] Again, Oman had pertinent things to say concerning Henry Jones's Gifford Lectures, *The Faith that Enquires*. I am sure that Oman writes with utter sincerity, but the line between that and praising with faint damns, or writing with tongue in cheek, is not always easy to discern:

> Regarding a book which sets out to be philosophy, to say it is great preaching may seem doubtful praise. But there never was any doubt at any time that Prof. Jones's real gift lay in the region of moving appeal rather than in the severer disciplines of thought and reasoning . . . and this time . . . he has come into his kingdom . . . A superficial judgment judgement might give an impression of something like failure: and in one sense it is a quite correct impression. Yet the interest and value of the book are to be found in that very lack of logical success, because it

---

122. This incident is recalled by P. Carnegie Simpson, *Recollections*, 65.

123. Oman, *Honest Religion*, 30.

124. See the review of *Philosophical Theology*, I, 403–7; and II, 281–83. The quotations are from I, 406.Tennant contributed an obituary of Oman to *Proceedings of the British Academy* 25 (1939) 332–38.

125. Oman, *The Natural and the Supernatural*, 184. He refers to Alexander's *Space, Time, and Deity*.

> comes through a faith too vital and strong to be imprisoned in any intellectual form.[126]

The late author triumphed over suffering, and hence there is a "beautiful and heroic religious element in the book" which will enable theologians "readily to pardon the neglect of their own labours."[127] What is clear is that Jones's "real religion and active experience are no longer able to be contained in [his Hegelianism]."[128] Jones identified God and the Absolute, and rebuked F. H. Bradley for distinguishing between them, "But can any one read the book and suppose that the author's God is the name for the sum of the cosmic process?"[129] The strongest part of the book, in Oman's opinion, is Jones's demolition of Bosanquet's system as "mechanism masquerading as spiritual progress."[130] The book is also marked by "a mystical, non-ethical, purely emotional and submissive view of religion . . . which makes it easy to realize the long attraction for our author of the false peace of cosmic pantheism."[131]

Without question, the most devastating of Oman's reviews is that of Whitehead's *Process and Reality*. Having tried unsuccessfully to decline the task and return the book, he starts as he means to go on: "When Prof. Whitehead was a professional mathematician, thinking as a philosopher, his works interested me profoundly, but now that he is a professional philosopher, thinking and expressing himself as a mathematician, they have become, for me at least, of increasing difficulty with diminishing profit."[132] He finds many echoes of Hegel in the book, which "is the only philosophical utterance I . . . have ever found to be even more of an achievement in technical jargon than Hegel."[133] He trounces the view that mind is not an individual centre of activity, but is part of the production of "novel togetherness" as being not argument, but assertion. Moreover, "if we know the world in proportion as we stand over it and refuse every impression we do not know as our own meaning, and if only as we are independent

---

126. Oman, Review of H. Jones. *A Faith that Enquires*. *The Journal of Theological Studies* 24 (1923) 215.

127. Ibid.

128. Ibid., 216.

129. Ibid., Cf. Oman, *The Natural and the Supernatural*, 475.

130. Ibid.

131. Ibid. See further on Henry Jones, Sell, *Philosophical Idealism*, 73–83 and *passim*.

132. Oman, Review of A. N. Whitehead, *Process and Reality*, 48.

133. Ibid., 50.

do we find the universe respond to us, we must accept the fact, however incapable we are of explaining it."[134] As for God as a process of becoming in the universe, "God, to have any meaning, is not merely the sense of process, but the power whereby we subordinate process to higher ends. ... The question of God is not what the world is, or by process of nature is becoming, but of what can be made of the world, if it has a divine purpose in it by which we can at once deny it and possess it."[135]

As for trends of thought with which Oman might conceivably have engaged in writing but, as far as I can discover, did not, I would mention, to look no further than Cambridge, the philosophical contributions of G. E. Moore and Bertrand Russell, the emphasis in C. D. Broad's book, *Perception, Physics and Reality* (1914), upon the limits of knowledge—a recurrent theme in Oman's writings; and the amalgam of mathematics, logic and mysticism which was Wittgenstein's *Tractatus* (ET, 1922). In noting such omissions I do not imply an adverse judgment upon Oman, for time-lags are endemic in intellectual history, especially where interdisciplinary activities are in view. There would be as little point in complaining that the work of Oman and Buber, and those such as H. H. Farmer who were indebted to them, did not receive the attention of secular philosophers until the 1950s.[136]

But if he passed by the leading philosophical lights of Cambridge, Oman did cast an eye towards Oxford when A. J. Ayer launched his manifesto of logical positivism, *Language, Truth and Logic*, in 1936. Oman approves of Ayer's clarity of style; he chides Ayer for describing himself as an empiricist in the style of Berkeley and Hume when those two differed significantly on sensation and perception; when Ayer follows Hume in disposing of the reality of the ego on the ground that "it is never found keeping house alone," Oman retorts that "there is never any housekeeping in the mind without it"; he contends that if philosophy is to be restricted to the analysis of scientific ideas "it would have no right to the name of

---

134. Ibid., 52.

135. Ibid.

136. See Sell, *The Philosophy of Religion*, 194–95, for a brief account of the criticisms of C. B. Martin and Ronald W. Hepburn, and of the responses to Hepburn by John Hick and John McIntyre. With this note I recall with gratitude Ronald Hepburn, who set me on my doctoral way, and who died on 23 December 2008. I never have regretted seeking out a university (Nottingham) in which my supervisors would be a no-longer-persuaded Professor of Philosophy and a Christian philosopher of religion, the late James Richmond. When Hepburn was succeeded by Jonathan Harrison the challenge was in no way diminished.

love of universal wisdom" ("Quite so," I can hear Ayer chirruping); but he refrains from direct assault on the principle of verification as such. He concludes, "Apparently the whole position is imported from Germany, and what is wrong with Germany at present is seeing what it likes with the spectacles of theory and being able to ignore all the rest; and not seeing it as a whole with the eyed of the intellect enlightened by the imagination. In this it is different from Hume, who was a sceptic dealing with philosophical theories, not a dogmatist about all reality."[137]

What becomes clear from this review of positive and negative influences upon Oman is that in no case did he adopt the views of others without modification. On the contrary, in many accounts of the character of his own work the recurring note is that he was an independent thinker. He did not slavishly follow anyone: as Simpson said, he "was debtor to no man";[138] nor did he attract a school of disciples, though such alumni of Westminster College as H. H. Farmer, F. G. Healey and John Hick have acknowledged their indebtedness to him. Precisely because of his independence of mind it is hazardous to attach unqualified labels to him. He was neither an out and out empiricist, nor an out and out idealist. He has been called a liberal theologian, and he certainly was no biblical or confessional fundamentalist; but neither was he of the kind of whom P. T. Forsyth complained in a seafaring image that would have appealed to Oman: "too many are occupied in throwing over precious cargo; they are lightening the ship even of its fuel."[139] But if Oman was not a liberal who sought to discover how little could be believed whilst remaining in good ecclesiastical standing, neither was he one who sublimated a lack of traditional conviction in a flurry of Social Gospel activism.[140] Oman's liberalism, as we shall see, was characterized by his openness to new ideas, and by a refusal to bow to any authority, whether biblicist or ecclesiastical, which did not commend itself to his reason and conscience.

III

With this I come to the final major issue: having seen what Oman made of others, what did he contribute to the intellectual context in which he

137. Oman, Review of A. J. Ayer, *Language, Truth and Logic*, 24.
138. Simpson, *Recollections*, 65.
139. Forsyth, *The Principle of Authority*, 261.
140. For the ambiguity of both "liberal" and "conservative" see Sell, *Theology in Turmoil*, chs. 5 and 6.

lived? First, it would surely be impossible to deny that Oman's writings are marked by utter sincerity. "Sincerity," he declared, "must maintain a mind ever open to the truth and ever in pursuit of the truth, and the worst insincerity of all is that which has silenced the truth."[141] By this motto he lived and wrote; but note that "True sincerity is not a mere emotional response to impressions, but puts all its mind, as well as its heart, into interpreting signs."[142] As so often, he proceeds to illustrate from his early experiences:

> Have you ever seen an old fisherman studying the weather before committing his frail barque to the mercy of the sea? I think of one who for seventy years had braved the Atlantic, of how his long-sighted grey eyes used to search the horizon on a doubtful morning, and of the long experience behind them by which he interpreted every wisp of cloud and every shimmer of sunshine. To go out in good weather was a necessity of daily bread; to be out in bad might mean a watery grave. Many he had known who, having misread the signs of the sky, had gone out and never returned. Superficial impressions, therefore, had no weight with him . . .[143]

Sincerity takes us beyond what merely impresses "to the signs of the supreme and final realities by which our futures are ultimately determined."[144] Moreover, "no strong, independent, true character ever comes to birth except in solitary wrestling with serious thought and noble aspiration and high resolve."[145]

The serious thought which ever preoccupied Oman was that flowing down from the Rationalism of the eighteenth century and the Romanticism of the nineteenth. It is characteristic of his method that, far from embracing one and shunning the other, he carefully weighed both, and in each of them found both stimuli and cautions. This was consistent with his conviction that "There is no breadth of judgment without help from the past, but there is no using the past to good purpose without independent judgment on it of our own conscience of truth and right."[146] Painting with rather broad brush strokes he summarizes his findings thus: "The eighteenth century was occupied with the problem of the individual; the nine-

---

141. Oman, *A Dialogue with God*, 71.
142. Oman, *The Paradox of the World*, 7.
143. Ibid.
144. Ibid., 14.
145. Oman, *Concerning the Ministry*, 41.
146. Oman, *Honest Religion*, 13–14.

teenth with the problem of individuality."[147] He applauded the eighteenth century's "earnest love of truth," which "gave to its enquiries, in spite of their limitations, an abiding value; and [the] idolatry of the mathematical method was the chief cause of these limitations."[148] Thus, "Rationalism . . . conceived religion mainly as an intellectual affair of evidences about God as the maker of the world, and providence as the direction of it, and immortality as compensation for its injustices and perfections. The reason was not that religion ever seemed anything of the sort to those really interested in it, but that interest in religion was replaced by interest in scientific discussion . . ."[149] What particularly impressed Oman was Rationalism's testimony that "nothing is of real value for truth or beauty or goodness which is not of our own insight, choice and deliberate purpose. . . . [I]t achieved a clear understanding of the demand for absolute independence in moral judgment and moral decision, if they are to be truly moral."[150] Putting Descartes and Pascal together, he declares that "The ultimate standard is ourselves [Descartes], but it is ourselves in all our reach, in all we feel as well as all we think, in all we have attained, as well as in the bare faculty of following a deduction [Pascal]."[151] I would note in passing that when, nine pages later, Oman contrasts Pascal with the Jesuits, and says that "It is Christ, not the Church, that is our last court of appeal,"[152] it no longer seems to be "ourselves in all our reach" either. At various points in Oman's writings the question arises, By what steps does he proceed from the individual's authority to Christ's? Some have suspected him of occasional sleight of hand. But the phrase I wish to focus upon now is "ourselves in all our reach," for this is Oman's bridge to Romanticism.

Oman welcomed Romanticism's

> recognition of elements in human nature and in life which had been ignored, its attempt to live in a world and not in a vacuum, its thought of the universe no longer as a great machine of which the main problem was to find the driving wheel, but as a great work of art, the more glorious that it is still in the process of creation, its idea of man's mind no more as a mere calculating machine, . . . but as . . . a copy in finite form of the Eternal

---

147. Oman, *The Problem of Faith and Freedom*, 193.
148. Ibid., 54.
149. Oman, *The Natural and the Supernatural*, 6.
150. Oman, *Grace and Personality*, 29.
151. Oman, *The Problem of Faith and Freedom*, 61.
152. Ibid. 70.

Reason, not a mere faculty of abstractions, but a treasure-house of all the variety and individuality of the world.[153]

Such benefits notwithstanding, the Romantic Age missed much of importance "precisely because of its high-sniffing superiority to what went immediately before";[154] and, as we have already seen, Oman stoutly repudiated the view that "The final word was immanent cosmic process," with "rational man as but its highest vehicle and most conscious mirror."[155] In Oman's view the good fruits of both Rationalism and Romanticism are to be harvested, the rest rejected. Between them "they correspond to the two aspects of [the] problem" with which Oman wrestled throughout his writing life: "that knowing is meaning for the mind that knows, yet is knowledge of reality existing independently and in its own right."[156] Kant represents the former aspect, Hegel the latter.

Against the background of the thoughts just sketched, Oman went in utterly sincere quest of truth, and his quest was as ardent as his appreciation of the limitations of human thought was realistic. We saw how the question of truth *vis à vis* conventional convictions had been raised for him in a clamant way by the Robertson Smith case, and to the cause of truth he devoted his life. In his view, the "Search for Truth and Righteousness is just accepting God's invitation to 'Come and let us reason together.'"[157] Those who enquire into religion are particularly urged "to spare no pains in seeking truth."[158] Why? Because, as the Rationalists taught, "truth is not true for us, except as we ourselves see it; and that right is not righteous, except as we ourselves determine it; and that to determine our own beliefs by our own reason and our own duty by our own conscience, is man's highest and most personal concern, which he may not delegate with honour."[159] But what is truth? "Truth for us," he replies, "is what we know to be a right interpretation of experience when in perfect freedom we have allowed it to speak to us."[160] He answers the question, How to proceed?, with a rhetorical question of his own: "[I]s there any other way of finding our true bear-

153. Ibid. 208.
154. Oman, "Schleiermacher," 402.
155. Oman, *Grace and Personality*, 32. Cf. *The Journal of Theological Studies* 31 (1930) 404.
156. Oman, *The Natural and the Supernatural*, 165.
157. Oman, *Honest Religion*, 1.
158. Oman, *The Natural and the Supernatural*, 8.
159. Ibid., 100.
160. Oman, *Honest Religion*, 91.

ings than the spirit of Christ and His reconciliation to all God requires as well as all He appoints, without resentment and without evasion?"[161] This, however, presupposes faith in Christ; and Oman makes no bones about it: "Truth does not appeal to the heart until it is the faith upon which you cannot but act, and you do not act rightly except upon truth which is at once convincing and challenging."[162] Furthermore, genuine belief is "belief in a reality on its own testimony," and hence "belief in God must be a gift of God."

It is central to Oman's thought that the quest of truth is and must be the quest of a free individual. "Freedom," he remarks, "is . . . as essential for true faith as faith for effective freedom."[163] Indeed, "Freedom is not true freedom unless it is our own spiritual judgment in face of all in us that has merely natural appeal."[164] More specifically, he writes, "Christian liberty is nothing else than a sense of higher obligation. Christ has set us free not to please ourselves, not to sin or do right as suits our convenience, but He has set us free by giving us a deeper sense of our obligation to God."[165] Conversely, "There can be no freedom in the end without reaching God."[166] How, then, shall we be reconciled to God? Oman answers, "Regarding Christianity, the great question will not be its outward credentials, but whether it can place man in such a relation to God that his moral and religious needs shall both be satisfied, that he shall be right with himself and master of his life. . . . An Atonement must be its own witness to the hearts that have been atoned, or it is nothing."[167]

Small wonder, therefore, that Oman set his face against external authorities deemed infallible, whether confessional, ecclesiastical or biblicist. Against all such he contended that

> God does not conduct His rivers, like arrows, to the sea. . . . The expedition demanded by man's small power and short day produces the canal, but nature, with a beneficent and picturesque circumambulancy, the work of a more spacious and less precipitate mind, produces the river. Why should we assume that, in all the rest of His ways, He rejoices in the river, but, in religion,

---

161. Ibid. 51.
162. Oman, *Concerning the Ministry*, 59.
163. Oman, *The Problem of Faith and Freedom*, 24.
164. Oman, *The Natural and the Supernatural*, 306.
165. Oman, *A Dialogue with God*, 76.
166. Oman, *The Problem of Faith and Freedom*, 329.
167. Ibid.

can use no adequate method save the canal? The defence of the infallible is the defence of the canal against the river...."[168]

From Rationalism Oman had learned that God does not override the freedom of human beings by hurling infallibilities at them. Hence his recognition of the fact that while "A creed which expresses the living convictions of a church is a spiritual power of the first magnitude; a creed which merely sanctions authorised compromises is not concerned with religion at all, but is a worldly agreement for the legal interest of a corporation."[169] Indeed, "The highest creed taught merely from without becomes superstition."[170] Confessions belong to our "external heredity," and we have to go beyond them; and we have been learning that "great differences in doctrine can be consistent with true fellowship of the Spirit, and if a creed be used to insist on orthodox docility, the end would be no more unity than it would be freedom."[171] The same applies to the injunctions of the institutional Church and to the deliverances of an allegedly infallible Bible. The fact is that "Christianity has no means left to it whereby to compel consent from the outside."[172] For "If the infallibilities have been overthrown by inquiry and reason, they cannot be raised again by affirmation or even by the strongest conviction of their utility.... But the value, for truth and beauty and goodness, of our own insight, choice, and deliberate purpose, being once seen, can never again be wholly renounced."[173]

But, to repeat, Oman was ever conscious of the limitations of human knowledge. W. A. L. Elmslie recalled his saying that "There exists a larger scheme of life than any of us can ever yet know, which we can only serve as we serve the truth amidst the things which we do know."[174] "From day to day," said Oman, "life must be faced with a creed falling far short of omniscience. It is less an illumination than points of light in the darkness, rather lighthouses to direct the course than sun or moon to display the prospect. Except when satisfied with tradition or theory, none question the Apostle's description of our knowledge, as 'seeing in a glass darkly.'"[175] When one compares Rashdall "with St. Paul or even with Luther, one re-

168. Oman, *Grace and Personality*, 25.
169. Oman, *The Church and the Divine Order*, 325.
170 Oman, *Vision and Authority*, 24.
171. Oman, *Honest Religion*, 161, 163.
172. Oman, *The Problem of Faith and Freedom*, 327
173. Oman, *Grace and Personality*, 22.
174. Elmslie, *Westminster College*, 23.
175. Oman, *Vision and Authority*, 217. Cf. *Honest Religion*, 40.

alizes how little he cares to live in the half lights, and how all the really creative souls have had to live there all their time."[176] Happily, our "dim gropings after truth," failures and misunderstandings, "witness, not to the Divine failure, but to the Divine patience."[177]

IV

So much for Oman's objectives and manner. As to his method, Oman's theology is conjunctive, reconciling, harmonizing. With one particularly significant exception, to which I shall come in due course, he brings together ideas that are often perceived as opposites. As his former student, T. W. Manson, observed, such book titles as *Vision and Authority*, *Faith and Freedom*, and *The Natural and the Supernatural* exemplify Oman's "fundamental struggle to hold together things that, on the superficial view, seem to be incapable of reconciliation."[178] We have noted the way in which he related faith and freedom, but now we must consider what may be deemed the central relationship in his thought, namely, that of the natural and the supernatural. In the course of this examination we shall not be able to avoid another relationship, namely, that of religion and morality, for Oman's case is of the cumulative, spiralling kind rather than the linear. It is also necessary, as we proceed, to understand that Oman espouses a more than ordinarily hospitable epistemology. For this he was complimented by A. D. Lindsay, who described Oman's account as

> the best account of knowing I have ever read. He distinguishes four types of knowing: awareness, apprehension, comprehension, explanation. The originality of what he has to say lies mainly in his description of the first two types, consistently neglected by philosophers who are themselves so taken up with comprehension and explanation that they simply cannot see the other forms.... [T]o know truly we need faithfulness in action and sincerity of feeling, as well as clear intelligence, but no one ordinarily takes account of this in theories of knowledge ...[179]

---

176. Oman, Review of H. Rashdall, *The Idea of* Atonement, 270.

177. Ibid. 96.

178. Manson, "Introduction" to Oman's *Vision and Authority*, 8th ed., 1948, 2.

179. Lindsay, Review of J. Oman, *The Natural and the Supernatural*, 385, 386. For Oman's exposition see op.cit., 120–43.

Living in the Half Lights

The four types of knowing suggest that Oman's empiricism is by no means exhausted by the understanding of empiricism espoused by most scientists; and this in turn distinguished his approach from that of Tennant, who was much more in accord with scientific method as generally understood. What Oman was intent upon emphasising, however, was that to suppose that we gain a comprehensive view of reality by applying the scientific method is false. Indeed, he expostulates, "The notion that science gives the true picture of complete reality was the mere illusion of a dominant interest, which is no longer entertained by serious scientific thinkers."[180] He does not deny the sensational origin of much of our knowledge, but sensation is not the only avenue to knowledge. By contrast with scientific rigidity, "true theology leaves out nothing of the concrete varied world that is within the grasp of our finite minds, in the hope of seeing the things unseen manifested in the things which do appear."[181] Oman consistently maintained that there is "no reliable ground for faith except insight into reality, and no worthy and final goal except freedom in loyalty to its requirements."[182]

With this we are at the threshold of Oman's account of the natural and the supernatural. "As the natural world is known by sensation and its varied comparative values, so the supernatural world is known by the sense of the holy and its sacred or absolute values."[183] He further explains that

> the Supernatural means the world which manifests more than natural values, the world which has values which stir the sense of the holy and demand to be esteemed as sacred. . . . [The natural and the supernatural] are not in opposition, but are so constantly interwoven that nothing may be wholly natural and wholly supernatural. . . . We know the Supernatural as it reflects itself in the sense of the holy and has for us absolute value directly and without further argument: and the question is not that it exists, but how it exists in its relation to us and our relation to it.[184]

---

180. Oman, "Method in theology," 90. "No longer entertained"? Behold those scientists of the positivistic-evolutionary or reductionist sort who have graced our televisions and press in recent years! By Oman's reckoning they are not "serious scientific thinkers"—as, indeed, I had myself concluded.

181. Ibid., 93.

182. Oman, *Vision and Authority*, 11.

183. Oman, *The Natural and the Supernatural*, 69.

184. Ibid., 71, 72.

The Theological Education of the Ministry

At this point F. R. Tennant demurred. Oman, he says,

> rejects the view that the supernatural is known inferentially, as the assigned cause of the awe; and also the view that it is directly apprehended as to its essence or quality by any faculty akin to sense . . . its only "content" is its capacity to excite emotion and valuation. Yet if the "sense of" the holy involves immediate, as distinct from interpretative or suppositional, cognition of the invisible and intangible Supernatural, it would seem that there must be in it something so far akin to sensation as to be another instance of the "absolute positing" which, as Kant taught us, is involved in the existent, as distinct from the ideal essence of which no existence is a predicate.[185]

Behind this criticism lies Tennant's judgment that in writing as he does concerning "feeling" Oman conflates such elements as cognition, feeling and evaluation that are normally distinguished from one another.[186]

Undeterred by such a possibility, Oman elaborates his doctrine thus: "The Supernatural must be inquired into, like the Natural, as a world in which we live and move and have our being, if it is to be inquired into with profit . . . [T]here is no embodying the Supernatural apart from the Natural; and . . . the Natural is ready to become our possession and unfold its treasures as, in the power of the sacred, we stand over against it and above it."[187]

The phrase "and above it" suggests Oman's view that the natural is transformed by the supernatural: the two are not simply glued together, so to speak; rather, there is a mutual inter-penetration the result of which is a refined environment. Oman further insists that experience of the supernatural is objective in character; it is not a matter of a particular subjective feeling or attitude:[188] reality is in view throughout. He also grants that the validity of the experience turns wholly upon the question whether the "invisible world" exists or not.[189] How might such an existence be proved? He answers, "we cannot prove the reality of any environment while omitting the only evidence it ever gives of itself, which is the way in which it environs us."[190] It should be noted that the context of this remark is that of

---

185. Tennant, Review of *The Natural and the Supernatural*, 214.
186. Ibid., 213.
187. Oman, *The Natural and the Supernatural*, 72, 331.
188. Ibid., 23.
189. Ibid.
190. Ibid., 52.

proving the experience to ourselves, not of making it the basis of an argument designed in the hope of persuading others. It is integral to Oman's standpoint that none of the classical theistic arguments will put anyone in touch with reality. Perhaps we might say that his empiricism is the empiricism of immediate personal experience; the empirical order is not, for him, a bran tub from which we pull arguments and evidences and cobble them together as efficiently as we may. In his own words: "awareness of the reality of the Supernatural is not something added to the sense of the holy and the judgment of the sacred by some kind of argument, say from the natural world."[191] By this Tennant was exceedingly perplexed: "[I]f any argument seemed necessary to Dr. Oman," he declares, "the validity of religious belief should for him depend on the cogency of reasoning from sacred or moral values to a supersensible world; but even this he deems superfluous. . . . It is on this fundamental issue that I find myself most at variance with the author's position"[192] Oman would reply that the only way reality is known is by an immediate experience of it which renders argumentation superfluous.

The term "environment" recurs in Oman's writings, and in the present context he means by it the natural environment which is shot through with the supernatural, and *vice versa*. But then he takes a further step when he directly associates the environment with God: "Environment is not merely what we see with our physical vision," he writes; "It is still more that we see with the eyes of our soul—our imagination, our insight, our values, our inspiration, our faith in God's mind in it, and His purpose with man in the midst of it."[193] He further explains that "religion must be a large experience in which we grow in knowledge as we grow in humility and courage, in which we deal with life and not abstractions, and with God as the environment in which we live and move and have our being and not as an ecclesiastical formula."[194] There, once more, is the anti-ecclesiastical sting in the tail.

The question arises whether "the meaning of 'reality' is 'the personal God'" is a purely stipulative definition? If not, how does Oman make the leap from experienced reality to a personal, purposive, God—indeed, may he legitimately do so? John S. Morris has returned a negative answer to this question. He contends that Oman's way of moving from his religious

---

191. Ibid., 72.
192. Tennant. Review, 215.
193. Oman, *Concerning the Ministry*, 12.
194. Oman, *The Natural and the Supernatural*, 471.

evaluation of reality to an argument for the world as personal violates his epistemology of immediacy and lands him in what he wished to avoid—an apologetic stance analogous to that of other proponents of theism. As Morris puts it, "If Oman cannot logically move from knowledge of a Supernatural environment to assertions about the 'universe' and God then his argument becomes another version of the Natural Theology which he condemns."[195] In short, "If you start from experience you cannot validly end up with a metaphysical system claiming absolute truth."[196] As I understand matters, however, it is rather that Oman experiences reality as personal and then testifies to this; the truth, for him, is in the experience, it is not in any metaphysical system which may, or may not, be erected upon it. He is more concerned with the enterprise of the person who reaches out after reality, but this reaching out, he says, "presupposes a universe which responds to such independence and is only really known by it, which means that it also is in some true sense personal. . . . [W]e can speak of God as a person who, if he is not the Supernatural, is manifest through it."[197] Is the reader wrong to expect a justification of this claim? In the first place, are we not confronted by a *non sequitur*? Oman claims that a person who reaches out after reality and finds it in the universe has found something which is in a true sense personal. But since many of the phenomena of the universe are inanimate, yet no less awe-inspiring for that, has he not smuggled into the universe the idea of personality? Secondly, Oman makes a second leap when he says that God is the manifested person, the qualification, "if he is not the Supernatural [he] is manifest through it" being swiftly dropped. The problem would seem to be that Oman is so wedded to his experiential, "from below," starting point that there is not only an absence of theistic argumentation in his writings, but also, at crucial points, a revelation-shaped-blank which makes it appear that he proceeds by assertion only. It would seem that Oman's student, H. H. Farmer, had similar qualms, which he construed in terms of Oman's method (note the respectful third word):

> It is perhaps an unsatisfactory feature of Oman's profound discussion of religion in *The Natural and the Supernatural* that he does not make the personal nature of God and of His activity towards man regulative of his thought. . . . In the earlier half of [the book] he speaks of the Supernatural in a way that suggests

195. Morris, "Oman's conception of the personal God," 88.
196. Ibid., 89.
197. Oman, *The Natural and the Supernatural*, 340, 342.

Living in the Half Lights

that it is a merely static environment which man becomes aware of, explores, and gets to know through his sense of sacred values. ... Oman's own principle that in interpreting the Supernatural and its relation to us we should start from the highest that we know might well seem to require that the sense in which God and His approach to men are said to be truly personal should have been more deeply analysed and put more fully in control of the argument from the beginning; if this had been done, it would hardly have been possible to treat the Supernatural in the earliest sections of the book in the way just indicated.[198]

This comment seems to be a tacit request for a starting-point rooted in the revelation of a personal God who comes to us—even a request for a Christology and a soteriology. Another way of making the point would be to say that Oman's method, into which his deepest convictions cannot, I think, be squeezed, is too much that of a seeker on the journey towards faith, as distinct from that of the saint on the journey of faith.[199] It is as if at times he works within the environment of a Supernatural from which the gospel has been extruded.

Elsewhere, however, Oman proposes that it is, above all, through the experience of forgiveness that we give concreteness to our talk of the personal God: "if we find forgiveness a real and transforming experience," Oman writes, "we shall be able to speak of God as a person with the certainty that we are not merely seeing the reflexion of our own faces, but know that our own forgiveness of others is a reflexion of the highest perfection which is kind to the unthankful and evil."[200] What is odd here is Oman's description of the essence of sin as "estrangement from our true environment."[201] This seems a somewhat remote way of speaking of the disruption of the very kind of inter-personal relations he has been at such pains to delineate in other writings, not least with reference to the father and the prodigal son in Jesus's parable. It is an attenuation analogous to another to which I shall advert in the next section of this chapter.

First, however, we observe that Oman draws out the ethical implications of the individual-God personal relationship. Ever alive to the relations of faith and freedom, he argues that "absolute moral independence and absolute religious dependence are not opposites but necessarily one

198. Farmer. *Revelation and* Religion, 28 n.

199. See Oman, *Vision and Authority*, 56: "we can never be coming into the unity of the truth unless we are coming into union with all *seekers* after truth" (my italics).

200. Oman, *The Natural and the Supernatural*, 342.

201. Ibid.

and indivisible."²⁰² "We are persons," he continues, "and not merely individuals, precisely because we . . . attain our independence as we find ourselves in God's world and among His children. . . . [O]ur relation to God is personal after such a fashion that our religion is necessarily an ethic, and our ethic necessarily a religion."²⁰³ (Small wonder that Oman had a particular fondness for the Old Testament prophets). In more picturesque terms, he writes of moral progress that if it "is in response to higher environment, [the human being's] ability to recognize the manifestation of the high and holy, often in direct opposition to the pleasant and desirable, is no mere painting of imaginary pictures in the blackness on the corridor of his prison, but is a window open towards heaven, illumined by at least the first beam of the morning."²⁰⁴ He fully appreciates that "For mapping out from above God's operations, it must be admitted that we occupy no vantage ground," and that "Only if we can see grace as it works on earth and understand it as it affects our own experience, can we possibly hope to have either clearness or certainty,"²⁰⁵ he is persuaded that God is not one preoccupied with his own honour, but one who is concerned to "succour moral persons" deemed to be autonomous, who, in turn, make a personal response to God's personal grace-full gift of aid, and can do this only because they are truly free.²⁰⁶ Later, invoking italics for emphasis, he adds the important proviso, "grace is grace precisely because, *though wholly concerned with moral goodness, it does not at all depend on how moral we are*."²⁰⁷

V

Of Oman's revered Principal, John Cairns, it was said that "he came increasingly to regard the life of the individual Christian and the collective life of the Church as the most convincing of all witnesses to the Unseen and the Supernatural."²⁰⁸ As far as I am aware, Oman never made this ecclesial appeal when expounding the Supernatural. On the contrary, it may fairly be suggested that when he thought of the individual in relation to the

202. Oman, *Grace and Personality*, 33; cf. 57.
203. Ibid., 62, 78.
204. Oman, *Vision and Authority*, 27.
205. Oman, *Grace and Personality*, 45.
206. Ibid., 45–47, 81; cf. 159–60.
207. Ibid., 164.
208. Cairns, *Principal Cairns*, 141.

church his passion for bringing together themes that are often placed in opposition to one another dried up. To put the point in a nutshell, whereas he values the Reformation insight that every individual believer is a priest before God, needing no intermediary—least of all a sacerdotal one, he does not emphasise the idea of the priesthood of all believers together. In other words, he does not construe the priesthood of all believers as a corporate concept; he does not think in terms of the integral relationship of branches to Vine, or limbs to body. Positively, there runs throughout his writings the idea that the church is the gathering of the two or three in Christ's name. Thus, for example, he declares that

> A Catholic Ecclesia, a Church in its wholeness, we acknowledge wherever two or three are met in the name of Christ. That, and that alone, we acknowledge as fully as our Congregational brethren, both adequately and exclusively constitutes a Church of Christ. . . . [T]he fundamental thing about the order of the Church is that it ought to be non-legal, the government of each man by the Spirit of God and organisation through love. . . . The unit of it is the two or three freely met in Christ's name, and all wider co-ordination of it must be on the same principle of free association.[209]

Here once more is Oman's characteristic conviction regarding freedom; here, too, is the rather individualistic idea of a gathering of two or three persons with one another, each of whom is independently under the Spirit's government. Believers, or saints, are those who have been brought into a "relationship of trust and freedom with the God and Father of our Lord Jesus Christ," and their unity is "a unity of spirit thorough the one Spirit of God working in the individual members" who have been "individually reconciled to God."[210] Elsewhere he lists the "marks" of the church as follows: "(1) that it has unity in Jesus Christ as its one true Head; (2) that its one treasure is the gospel; and (3) that its one official is the organ of the priesthood of all believers."[211] By this last point he means that the official is the organ of, not the substitute for the priesthood of believers, and that there is "no religious distinction between clergy and laity."[212] It will be noted that even though in a footnote he has just adverted to the

---

209. Oman, "The Presbyterian Churches," 67, 73. Cf. Oman, *The Church and the Divine Order*, 11, 209; Oman, *The War and its Issues*, 55–56.
210. Oman, *The Church and the Divine Order*, 59.
211. Ibid., 210.
212. Ibid., 211.

Westminster Confession, Oman does not follow that standard in specifying "the doctrine of the gospel as taught and embraced, ordinances administered, and public worship performed" as marks of the church[213] - still less discipline, as specified in the earlier *Scots Confession*.[214]

It will also be observed that Oman does not answer those who contended that whereas the two or three gathered together in Christ's name may well describe a prayer meeting, it does not fully describe a New Testament church ordered under the gospel, with its several gifted and appointed members, its teaching function, its breaking of bread, and its baptismal practice. He does, however, take pains on more than one occasion to distinguish the Protestant from the Catholic ecclesiological principles in terms of the "two or three gathered": "What is the Church in principle? To the Catholic its determining principle is in the institution—its priesthood, bishops, councils, Pope; to the Protestant it is in the fellowship, in all that is involved in the two or three met in the name of Christ, in the succession of believers, in the bond of love."[215]

How, in practice, do the "two or three" comport themselves *vis à vis* their life together in fellowship? Are they a democratic assembly? Decidedly not, says Oman, as well he might. His emphasis upon the freedom of individual believers notwithstanding, he proclaims that "an individual possession is not necessarily individualistic,"[216] and that "Christianity is not individualism tempered by the ballot box."[217] In elaborating upon this he says the right thing but for an inadequate reason: "Christianity is 'ultra-democratic' not because it counts heads, but because it appeals 'to the image of God in all men.'"[218] While in no way wishing to deny the truth of that Quakerly utterance, we are landed once more in an attenuated position. The Church is not "ultra-democratic" because its members appeal to the image of God in all men, but because they seek, not their own will, but the will of the Lord of the Church, and because they discern this, insofar as they do, by the Holy Spirit through the Word within the

---

213. *The Westminster Confession*, ch. XXV.4; numerous editions.

214. *The Scottish Confession of Faith*, 1560, ch. XVIII, for which see Cochrane, ed. *Reformed Confessions*. For the addition see also John Craig's *Catechism* of 1561, in Torrance, *The School of Faith*, 160.

215. Oman, *The Church and the Divine Order*, 207.

216. Oman, *Vision and Authority*, 54; cf. 285.

217. Oman, *The Church and the Divine Order*, 318.

218. Ibid.

fellowship.[219] Oman's starting-point seems almost entirely confined to the "horizontal," human-to-human relationship to the exclusion of the Father who approaches in the Son by the Spirit.

The question arises, Why is Oman's ecclesiology so tilted towards the individual, rather than to the corporate understanding of the priesthood of all believers? A twofold answer may be offered. First, there is Oman's general intellectual position to the effect that "the Supernatural is an order of independent persons."[220] Secondly, there is his deep conviction that "God

---

219. This is the classical Congregational understanding of church meeting. In my favoured way of expressing the point: church meeting is a credal assembly in which the Lordship of Christ is confessed over the entire life and service of the church; in this sense it is a continuation of the church's worship, and the one who has been called to lead the saints to the throne of grace (and not someone who is good at "business meetings") should lead them in seeking the mind of Christ for their mission. In connection with Congregationalism, Oman must be corrected at one point. He says (*The Church and the Divine Order*, 279) that the desire of the Independents to be tolerated "as [part of the national Church]" at the time of the Restoration of the monarchy (1660) "shows how much [they] were still attached to the idea of a universal Christianity. Their present position is not the result of their theory of the Church, but a departure from it under what has influenced all Churches in the same direction—rationalism and evangelicalism." Now, working backwards, (1), Congregationalists were, like others, influenced by rationalism and evangelicalism. Crudely put, the former encouraged them towards a critical approach to the Bible and history, the latter led to a modification or dilution of their scholastic Calvinism and sent them out in mission at home and abroad. But their "theory of the Church" remained intact and was, indeed, a preservative against the eighteenth-century drift to "Arianism" and thence to Unitarianism which overtook a number of English and Welsh Presbyterian churches. See further, Sell, *Dissenting* Thought, ch. 5. (2) To the extent that Congregationalists wished for national comprehension, this would have been according to their polity as specified in the *Savoy Declaration of Faith and Order* (1658)—an polity that their compatriots in Massachusetts sought to apply with not entirely happy results. In general, Congregationalists would be more likely to say that an established national church is, potentially at least, an obstacle to catholicity, for the church knows no territorial boundaries. Following the Restoration and the ensuing punitive (albeit patchily applied) legislation, the Congregationalists shelved their establishment aspiration much sooner than the Presbyterians, some of whom entertained the forlorn hope of a state church on Presbyterian lines in England and Wales until the end of the seventeenth century. It is no shame to be attached to a "universal Christianity" if by that is meant the church catholic. Congregationalists (and their heirs in united churches) understand that it is by virtue of their membership in local, covenanted, fellowships that they are members of the Church catholic and, indeed, that there is no other way of belonging to the latter, for Christians are "*visible* saints," and one cannot be a Christian "in general." See further Sell, *Saints: Visible, Orderly and Catholic*. (3) The Independents/Congregationalists began to press for toleration during the Westminster Assembly, of which they were minority members, lest they should subsequently be swamped by Presbyterian order.

220. Oman, *The Natural and the Supernatural*, 341.

will do everything for man, suffer everything for him, give everything for him, but He will not override his will. If He cannot have free service He cares for no other."[221] Hence Oman's antipathy towards freedom-cramping ecclesiastical authority. Whilst agreeing that the Church "needs outward forms," he insists that "they are for the expression and operation of a unity that exists, not for compulsion to bring it into existence";[222] and in any case, although we need not rail at dignitaries or disallow "their usefulness in due place,"[223] "The Church is not a visible corporation, kept together by outward bonds of office and ecclesiastical order."[224] More provocatively still, he declares in connection with infallibilities whether ecclesiastical or biblicist, that "the old external dogmatic attitude of the Church cannot be maintained. . . . Uninquiring submission to external authority is neither God's method with man nor a desirable method of human obedience, but mere exaltation of necessity over freedom."[225] Moreover, "A God . . . credible only on clerical guarantees is a distressing as well as a worthless faith."[226] It follows that ecclesiastical machinery must never usurp the place of the fellowship, as has so often happened in Christian history. The fact is, he thunders, that "Nothing . . . has done more to mislead men about Christ than this notion that His Church can consists of officials and that His faith can be taught from the outside, and a man's conduct directed by any other authority than God's spirit in his heart."[227] Whereas some understand the falling away of many from the churches as requiring a strengthening of the Church's "external authority," Oman interprets the drift as indicative of the fact that the old external authorities have failed, and that "we ought rather to thank God that so slavish a method is no longer possible, and to see that the patient way of calling men to the liberty of the children of God is the quickest way after all."[228]

It is possible to have considerable sympathy with many of the points that Oman makes, and yet to feel that there is another side to the matter. For one who characteristically sought to hold together things that properly belong together, he is, where ecclesiology in concerned, strangely

---

221. Oman, *A Dialogue with God*, 88.
222. Oman, *Honest Religion*, 139.
223. Ibid., 140.
224. Oman, *The Church and the Divine Order*, 59.
225. Oman, *Vision and Authority*, 94; cf. 182.
226. Oman, "Method in theology," 86.
227. Oman, *A Dialogue with God*, 143.
228. Oman, *The Church and the Divine Order*, 317.

disjunctive, as when he writes concerning his own age, "Never was there an age which brought men so unavoidably to the issue that the basis of the Church is freedom, not authority, individual faith, not organised constraint, prophetic hope, not priestly tradition."[229] But there is both freedom in the Gospel and the authority of grace. While organised constraint has no place in Christianity, the conjuction of individual faith with corporate witness in the body of Christ is essential, for Christianity, though a personal religion, is not a private one; and while the contrast posited between prophetic hope and what I should call the sacerdotal tradition suggests the forward look which was ever in Oman's eye, the function of mutual witness, encouragement, reproof and love as exercised by the true priesthood of believers is a precious possession—which Oman would not, of course, have denied. Furthermore, given that Oman thinks that the gathered two or three cannot avoid having some organisational shape in the world, one could wish that he had been more generous concerning the church's several ministries and *foci* of life. He hardly has a good word to say for those who devote themselves to things ecclesiastical—except that they may be useful in their place. This, at least, was the feeling of a contributor to *The Presbyterian Messenger*, who regretted Oman's "often terrible critique" of institutional religion, and diagnosed in him a "temperamental inability to appreciate the opposite view," with the result that "Oman now and again tends to put asunder what God has joined," failing to understand that for "frail and groping beings such as we it is only through what he would call the 'lesser' mysteries that the greater can be appreciated."[230]

---

229. Ibid., 290.

230. Sinclair. "Living voices . . . Professor Oman," 430. Oman, as we have seen, had no patience with those who recommended silence where matters of truth were concerned lest the ecclesiastical boat be unduly rocked. This is a perennial issue in churchly fellowship, and there is something to be said in favour of the "ecclesiastics." Ministers sometimes face what W. D. Ross would have called a clash of *prima facie* duties. On the one hand they must state their convictions with integrity (Oman's position); on the other hand they must not needlessly break the fellowship of the church, and they are to lead *the people's* worship. Of Benjamin Fawcett of the Old Meeting, Kidderminster, where Calvinists, Arminians and "Arians" gathered, it was said that "he managed so far to conceal his opinions as to be very popular with his hearers, a large chapel being crowded at all the Sabbath-day services." Thomas Wright Hill, quoted by Hunsworth, *Baxter's Nonconformist Descendants*, 41. Fawcett was not necessarily "trimming," still less guarding his stipend. The high Arian, Micaijah Towgood, was commended by his biographer because "The main scope and tenor of his preaching was practical. He led not his flock for nourishment to the dry and barren hills of cold and unedifying speculation." See Manning. *A Sketch of the Life and Writings of Micaijah Towgood*, 92–93. When the young Joseph Priestley was at Needham Market , "though I had made it a

The Theological Education of the Ministry

For all that, it is not impossible to discern in Oman's writings a suggestion of that lateral thinking which, I believe, is urgently required if the unity of the Church catholic is to be more fully manifested (I do not say "created"—it is already given in Christ). Oman fully recognizes that what requires to be repudiated is the sectarian spirit which places obstacles in the way of fellowship of those are saints in the Lord and members of his Church. Nowhere is the problem more acute than at the Lord's table. As Oman writes, "That in the name of the Carpenter of Nazareth [the Lord's Supper] should be made the basis of a sacerdotal and hierarchical exclusiveness is perhaps as sad a perversion of the original purpose as anything in history."[231] Indeed, "from the time when the Church was founded on the bishop, not the prophet, from the time when it became a corporation with ruler and subject, the eucharist could no longer be the festival of the amazing fellowship where all were equally brethren of Christ, all equally kings and priest unto God . . . and where all a man was and all he had could be an offering of thanksgiving."[232] Augustine was responsible for this drastic turn of events. He introduced the "artificial view" that baptism "leaves an indelible mark" on the baptized person. This in time led to "the idea of an indelible mark of ordination upon the person who had power to imprint such a sacramental mark, and then the Church . . . was ready for an equally ecclesiastical and artificial view of the eucharist as a rite of priestly not personal sacrifice."[233] In all of this Oman sees the need to get behind what I have sometimes called "denominational small print" to that which already holds believers together. But, once again, his approach

---

rule to myself to introduce nothing that could lead to controversy into the pulpit; yet making no secret of my real opinions in conversations, it was soon found that I was an Arian. From the time of this discovery my hearers fell off apace . . ." See *The Theological and Miscellaneous Works of Joseph Priestley*, Ii 30; cf., XV, 23, XXI, 245. Thomas Belsham (one of my predecessors at Angel Street Congregational Church, Worcester) left the pastorate there in 1781 and became a tutor at the Dissenting academy at Daventry. Whilst there he became Unitarian in doctrine, resigned on conscientious grounds in 1789 and removed the academy in Hackney established by Rational Dissenters. He thereby preserved his own integrity, and at the same time recognized that the trinitarian worshippers served by the Daventry academy had the right to worship and teaching in that style. The underlying point is that the minister is not simply a private person, but a representative one; the moral is that some matters are best aired in discussion groups rather than from the pulpit. See further Sell, *Dissenting Thought*, 152–56; Sell, *Enlightenment, Ecumenism, Evangel*, 101–5, 374.

231. Oman, *Honest Religion*, 176. Cf. Oman, *Vision and Authority*, 170.
232. Oman, *The Church and the Divine Order*, 105.
233. Ibid. 164.

remains individually-focused, as when he says, "the greatest champion of the true unity is the man who most ardently seeks the truth and truth only and utterly, and who most uncompromisingly follows righteousness with entire consecration of aim and energy."[234] My own suggestion is that we go behind the sectarian talk which is enshrined in such propositions as, "When you submit to our order, or do things in our way, or read the Bible as we do then we will have full fellowship with you," by asking, What has God in Christ done for us all? I believe that he has called Christians into the one Church and therefore we should all accept the one Lord's invitation to his table in an utterly mutually reciprocal way, thereby manifesting the gift of unity we have all received and too frequently obscured in Galatian fashion by our several 'new circumcisions'.[235] It is the Gospel, not the individual's quest of truth, which should take precedence over all the inherited ecclesiastical practices which so rightly distressed Oman. As he said, "the best means of all for unity of fellowship is not available. Of all ways of showing how the love of the Father in the life without and the Fellowship of the Spirit within is one in the grace of Christ the greatest is the sacrament in which the symbols used sanctify the whole material life and make it transparently radiant with the spiritual."[236] This is as Christological—indeed, as Trinitarian—a mode of expression of the relation of natural and supernatural that I have found in Oman's writings, and it brings me to the heart of Oman's Gospel.

VI

What, for Oman, is Christianity's central message? In his major works we find his answer by a process of deduction rather than because he first placards it after the manner of a P. T. Forysth and then proceeds to elucidate its

---

234. Oman, *Vision and Authority*, 151. Cf. Oman, *The Paradox of the World*, 177.

235. I write this after some decades of participation in international dialogues between the Reformed family and others. While the gains in understanding are welcome, and while reunion has been facilitated in some cases, it seems highly unlikely that there will ever be uniformity of belief and practice across the whole church—nor need there be. If this is so, the only way forward is to ask in the first place not, where do we stand, how do we conduct our churchly life, but what has the God of sovereign grace done for us all? He has made us saints by calling, and saints are required to love their brothers and sisters. It is not loving to bar them from the table of the Lord. See further Sell, *Enlightenment, Ecumenism, Evangel*, ch. 11; Sell, *Confessing the Faith Yesterday and Today*, ch. 11; and, most fully, Sell, *The Great Ejectment of 1662*, ch. 4.

236. Oman, *Honest Religion*, 176.

ramifications. What is more, Oman's understanding of the central message is presented in a constellation of ways, some of which appear to be more lukewarm than others. Thus, writing of the Christ's saving work he says, "Love could do no more to show that it would do everything for man, everything except corrupt his will and replace his freedom, and so deprive him of his best heritage."[237] This might suggest that the Cross is somehow a display of loving outreach with special reference to Oman's concerns for voluntarism and freedom. On the same page things become a little clearer: "By the cross Christ has abolished the enmity between man and God, not merely be removing some outward causes of alienation, but by the demonstration of the succour which has nothing of the might which constrains, but is all of the might which persuades...."[238] But is sin merely an outward cause of alienation, given that we are urged by Oman to think in terms of the personal divine-human relationship? Is it not rather the wilful abuse of that relationship.[239] Again, if we are to understand that the succour that sustained Christ on the cross is available to us in time of trial, is this all that the cross signifies? What, for example, of mercy, forgiveness, new life? Later still in the same book we catch more of the note of victory: "It is the Christ overcoming sin and sorrow and death and defeat, who sets up God's will of love in the freedom with which it rules in Heaven, and so delivers us from the self-pity and self-love which is caused by the fear and the favour of the world."[240] The experience of many is that the cross does more than this. Further puzzlement is caused when Oman says that "To redeem man into a sinless freedom [the Divine love] must suffer with him sympathetically and vicariously. This suffering . . . is not an exceptional incident in the Divine method, but is a manifestation in time of what is eternal."[241] But (a) does not this mode of speech minimize the Bible's witness to the once-for-all-ness of the victory of the Cross?[242] (b) While I

---

237. Oman, *Vision and Authority*, 117; cf. 226.

238. Ibid.

239. There could hardly be a more clinically impersonal sentence than this: "We can go wrong through unveracity in thinking, sensuality in feeling or unrighteousness of decision, but all are varieties of the lack of true independence and, therefore, of freedom, this being failure to know a reality which so witnesses in its own right that no other witness has any right before it.' See Oman, *The Natural and the Supernatural*, 311.

240. Oman, *Vision and* Authority, 337.

241. Ibid.,343.

242. Cf. Langford, "The theological methodology of John Oman and H. H. Farmer," 235: "[I]t must be said that Oman is singularly free from interest in particular

think that there is much to be said for the view that God is not impassible, there is a case, not simply a pronouncement, to be made in favour of it.[243]

Are the difficulties lessened in what many regard as Oman's greatest work, *Grace and Personality*? A number of assertions give us pause. First, it seems a somewhat cool attenuation on the part of one to whom the parable of the Prodigal Son spoke so strongly to say that "reconciliation to God is primarily reconciliation to our lives by seeking in them only his ends. Its immediate significance is *reconciliation to the discipline He appoints and the duty He demands*."[244] Shortly he speaks more traditionally of God as in Christ reconciling the world to himself, and says that "The final triumph of this manifestation is the Cross, the obedience unto death of the Prince of Peace in the service of God's kingdom of righteousness."[245] But after this brief hint of what Aulén called the classical theory of the atonement, Oman reverts to something much more like a moral influence view of it: "In the Cross . . . above all else, we discern the gracious relation of our Father towards us, because there, as nowhere else, is the utter service of our brethren, unconditioned by our merit, shown to be the essential spirit of His family. The true meaning and power of the Cross we discover only as we have that spirit . . .'[246] After a further eight pages and a further oscillation we learn of "the gracious dealing of the Father with His children for victory over all the consequences of sin, without and within."[247] In the judgment of F. R. Tennant, Oman's understanding of grace was too restrictive. For Oman, he writes, "grace, or any divine action upon men,

---

historical situations or mediating *kairoi*. His theory of religious awareness does not emphasise the specific historical context . . ." This despite the fact that Oman can also say, "Revelation, being . . . concerned with the reconciliation of God's gracious relation to us by which alone we can discover that it is gracious, must be a work of history. What is more, it must be the work of history, the work which gives it meaning and treasures up its gains." *Grace and Personality*, 141.

243. Oman's contemporary, Robert Franks, for example, denied that God could suffer. See further Sell, *Hinterland Theology*, 606–10. On a number of occasions in his writings Oman dismisses views alternative to his own, and makes pronouncements, without argument. He brands Calvin a determinist in a quite uncritical way (which he must have known would be provocative); and, no doubt because he wishes to exclude satisfaction theories of the atonement, he brusquely disposes of the idea that God, whose honour has been abused by sin, needs to be reconciled to us. See, respectively, *The Natural and the Supernatural*, 286; *Honest Religion*, 99.

244. Oman, *Grace and Personality*, 110. His italics.

245. Ibid., 136.

246. Oman, *Grace and Personality*, 179–80.

247. Ibid., 189.

can only be regarded worthily when restricted to personal dealings with persons and, consequently to appeals to human reason and conscience. This restriction will be judged heretical by the larger part of Christendom ..."[248] Tennant does not explain further, but perhaps the reference is to the cosmic dimension of God's saving work in Christ (however that is most appropriately to be understood).

Oman, as we have seen, valued the modern historical method for the way in which it had helped to topple older *a priori* dogmatisms. "The historical method," he declared, "is to inquire, without presupposition, what God has actually done."[249] It is precisely because they felt that Oman's answer to his own question was vague, or an attenuation, that he came in for criticism. For a representative and balanced view we may heed Charles Duthie:

> There have been Christian thinkers . . . who have felt uncomfortable with the thought that God comes to dwell within. F. R. Tennant and John Oman were among them. Oman was afraid that we might construe God's grace as mechanical and irresistible. Grace, he kept saying, is just God being gracious and this gracious God always acts in a fatherly way, respecting the freedom He has given us. . . . Oman's thought is a welcome correction of all Christian systems which talk of God acting upon us as a physical force acts upon another physical force; but he missed something very big in the New Testament. God does indeed respect man's freedom and never treats us as less than personal; but He knows that our freedom is not complete and has been marred by our wrongdoing. Man may be God's child but he is God's erring and sinful child; and his condition is such that he needs to be forgiven, delivered, enlightened and empowered. . . . We can agree with Oman that the gracious God acts in relation to us both in accordance with His own nature and the nature he has given to us, and then go on to see how broad and deep this renewing action is.[250]

Duthie correctly adverts to Oman's horror of coercion, and of the forcing of allegedly infallible authorities upon free human beings. Least of all may the God of gracious personal relations be represented as bludgeoning people with grace against their free wills. This, I suspect prompted Oman to bypass almost completely traditional Christologies and, especially,

248. Tennant. "John Wood Oman," 337.
249. Oman, *Grace and Personality*, 20.
250. Duthie, "A God of Action," 9.

soteriologies. From normally passing references we are made aware of his abomination of the notion of retributive justice, of transactional, *quasi-*commercial theories of the atonement and, above all, of penal theories—"legal juggling of the most repellant kind," said he.[251] He neither cared for such theories nor offered his own by way of replacement.

For his part, H. R. Mackintosh regretted that in *The Natural and the Supernatural* there was not to be found a detailed discussion of revelation. Mackintosh was persuaded that God does not wait to be discovered, he comes to us. He therefore concluded, "If this be so, the final distribution of emphasis will be different from that of this great book."[252] We recall Oman's view that "Prof. Mackintosh very easily thinks of God as just doing things," whereas he himself thinks of God as "the ultimate real."[253] For his part, Carnegie Simpson, in his address at Oman's funeral service in St. Columba's Church, Cambridge, on 22 May 1939, said that Oman "was concerned, in religion, more with the foundation than with the edifice; and as regards the former, more, perhaps, with what God is than with what, in Christ, He has done for us men and our salvation."[254]

We are at last, I think, in a position to perceive the point at which Oman's theological approach is distinct from that of his contemporaries, some of whom felt that his work needed to be balanced by what one might call more Christological-*cum*-soteriological ballast. Oman's quest is of the Supernatural, of that reality which is the environment of the natural. This Supernatural, he concludes, is personal, and he then names it God—or, "at least" God's vehicle. We find ourselves in touch with the eternal as we deal "wholeheartedly with the evanescent," and with "God as the environment in which we live and move and have our being."[255] The gracious personal God leaves manifold signs of his presence, but awaits our free, uncoerced, approach. This, it may be suggested, explains the emphasis in his rather atomistic ecclesiology, according to which the Church is rather a collocation of independent, free, seekers, than an organism comprising saints who have been called by grace into union with Christ and with one another.

But let us be cautioned by the slogan, "By their sermons ye shall know them." To a quite striking degree the homiletic Oman is much more

---

251. Oman, *Honest Religion*, 117.

252. H. R. Mackintosh, Review of *The Natural and the Supernatural.*

253. Oman, Review of H. R. Mackintosh, *The Christian Experience of Forgiveness*, 297.

254. Simpson, *The Presbyterian Messenger*, 1939, 197.

255. Oman, *The Natural and the Supernatural*, 471.

inclined to strike soteriological notes which are normally muted in the major works so far considered in this section of my paper. A few almost random examples must suffice:

> The Cross . . . is a great affirmation that God's purpose is the salvation of His children into His Kingdom, the peace and glory and possessions of which only love can win, and for which only by love can anyone be won.[256]

> This power to reconcile us to God in all His way with us is summed up in the Cross, wherein every form of evil is made to work for good. Even death . . . is turned into the doing of God's will and the revelation of His pardoning love and the manifestation and victory of His righteousness and peace.[257]

> Christ suffered to bring us unto God. His sufferings stand between us and our sin. By his sufferings He triumphs over the world, the flesh and the evil one. All spiritual victories are contained in His death. When we suffer, we suffer with Christ who was made perfect through suffering . . .[258]

> The Cross of Christ is a symbol of triumph, of strength, of glory.[259]

> By the resurrection . . . a new light is shed upon the death of Christ and so upon the death of all who receive His grace. By death Christ has abolished death, but that is the smallest part of His work. By death He has also abolished sin.[260]

> Elsewhere we have much speculation regarding God. Only here have we perfect revelation. In Christ you have the glory which a full understanding of God's purpose with His world can bestow.[261]

To borrow H. R. Mackintosh's phrase, it is pointless to speculate upon what the "final distribution of emphasis" in his major works might have been had Oman brought to bear upon his method the more rounded Christian understanding hinted at in the above quotations. Might he, for example, come to the view that the Cross is *the* supernatural act of

---

256. Oman, *The Paradox of the World*, 84.
257. Ibid., 115; cf. 134, 166.
258. Oman, *A Dialogue with God*, 32.
259. Ibid., 49.
260. Ibid., 119
261. Ibid., 136.

sovereign grace in the sense that nature could neither have imagined nor engineered it, and that its purpose is to redeem and restore nature?[262] As it is one cannot resist the feeling that, like a number of other theologians, he believed more than could readily be accommodated within the boundaries of his chosen method. Oman was, nevertheless, a profound, sincere, honest ruminator upon theological themes who, like the fishermen among whom he was raised, pushed out into the deep waters. Two or three pages of Oman can be considerably more mentally bracing than whole volumes by some of the fashionable theological gurus of our time who, in a dogmatic and unscholarly way, parrot unanalyzed theological slogans for the delectation of their groupies. We might say that Oman's whole life was a response to the challenge posed by his loved and revered College Principal, John Cairns: "The best apology for Christianity is a life which makes the supernatural visible to ourselves and others."[263]

VII

Oman's works have been highly regarded by more discerning authors. Among Anglicans, Tennant surmised that those who agreed with it would regard *Grace and Personality* as "one of the greater treasures of theological literature," and thought that Oman was "one of the most original, independent, and impressive theologians of his generation and of his country";[264] J. S. Bezzant judged *The Natural and the Supernatural* "one of the two ablest and most thorough works on Philosophical Theology published a generation ago, the other being F. R. Tennant's two volumes so entitled";[265] J. K. Mozley said that *Grace and* Personality "is sufficient to place its writer

---

262. See further Sell, *Confessing and Commending the Faith*, ch. 5. When Oman thinks of sovereignty he too frequently thinks in terms of omnipotent force—something he rightly abominates. From my use of the term "sovereign grace" it will be clear that I think it frequently advisable to use one attribute of God adjectivally in relation to another. Sovereignty without grace might, as Oman feared, become sheer untoward force; but grace without power could hardly vanquish sin and the grave. The hymn, "Sovereign grace o'er sin abounding! Ransomed souls the tidings swell," remains a powerful blast from the Devonian shipwright, John Kent (1766–1843). Sadly, it is nowadays excluded from most mainline hymnals, not to mention increasingly ubiquitous screens on which "songs" are projected.

263. Quoted by MacEwen, *Life and Letters of John Cairns*, 562.

264. Tennant, "John Wood Oman," 335.

265. Bezzant, "The theology of John Oman." *The Modern Churchman* 9 (1965–66), 135.

among the most penetrating religious thinker of his generation,"[266] while C. F. D. Moule described the book "as one of the most exquisite books on religion ever written."[267] It is said that as he lay on his deathbed the Congregationalist, P. T. Forsyth, declared of *Grace and Personality*, "This is a book which I should like to put into the hands of every theological student."[268] From the ranks of the Reformed came numerous accolades. In the opinion of John Dickie, "No one in our day has written more penetratingly on the ultimate problems of religion and theology than Dr. Oman."[269] To the philosopher, T. M. Knox, *The Natural and the Supernatural* "is one of the three of four most distinguished contributions to philosophy which have appeared in English-speaking countries in the last forty years, and it is a scandal that hardly any of those now teaching philosophy in these islands have read it."[270] Finally John Hick, an alumnus of Westminster College after Oman's time there, deemed Oman "one of the most original British theologians of the first half of the twentieth century."[271]

But it is to Oman's students that we must turn for more personal reminiscences of Oman. Those who knew him said that he could be blunt, as when he remarked, on leaving the room following the presentation of a paper on *Grace and Personality*, "I do not recognise my own portrait."[272] His patience was tried by careless work, and he scorned what he called "the unlit lamp and the ungirt loin."[273] He was sometimes absent-minded, as when he fell asleep during a pastoral visit to a church member in Alnwick. He could appear formidable—an impression which "though no doubt it drew something from his fine physical stature and even more from his superlative equipment of intellectual power and vast knowledge was fundamentally that of character."[274] W. A. L. Elmslie, the first Westminster alumnus to be called to a Chair in the College, recalled that

266. Mozley, *Some Tendencies in British Theology*, 161.
267. So R. B. Knox, *Westminster College Cambridge*.
268. Healey. "The theology of John Oman," 543.
269. Dickie, *Fifty Years of British* Theology, 106.
270. T. M. Knox, Review of F. G. Healey, *Religion and Reality*, 547.
271. Hick, *Faith and Knowledge*, xix. I endorse Hick's adjective, provided that I may add that Forsyth was the most stimulating British theologian, and Franks the most scholarly Nonconformist theologian, of the period.
272. Healey, *Religion and Reality*, vii.
273. Farmer, "Theologians of our time. III. John Wood Oman," 132; cf. Farmer, "Death of Dr. John Oman," 9.
274. Farmer, "Theologians of our time," 132.

Oman possessed what one can but call an encyclopaedic range of learning: complete master of his own field of theology and philosophy, he could speak with the authority of real knowledge concerning a host of other subjects. He was a penetratingly just judge of character, but had absolute respect for the rights of personality. Therefore his students not only admired and revered him, they knew that they could also trust his guidance and rely upon his kindness.[275]

Another student spoke of the honesty and authority of Oman's teaching, and also of his "humorous stories, or taking part in party games in that homely and friendly atmosphere which Mrs. Oman and he have the secret of imparting."[276] Some students found Oman's class lectures difficult to grasp: to Lesslie Newbigin they were "obscure to the point of opacity" (a judgment which may tell us as much about the student as about the lecturer), but he valued Oman's chapel utterances;[277] and many found his well-illustrated and down-to-earth conversations held at the end of the lecturing week, and later gathered in *Concerning the Ministry*, of great benefit. T. W. Manson wrote of the influence upon students of Oman's "single-minded devotion to the truth," and testified that "There are many men in the ranks of the ministry to-day who are able to face the difficulties and perplexities of our time with some sort of inner serenity and courage because they once sat at the feet of a real hero of faith, one who never shirks a difficulty, is never content merely to defeat the opposition in argument, one who all through has striven for a unified vision of God, man, and the world, and wrought for nothing less than that whole truth that makes us free."[278] H. H. Farmer recalled that during the painting of Oman's portrait by Hugh Rivière three visitors called at the studio on three separate occasions. The first said, "That is the face of a fisherman"; the second, "That is the face of a philosopher"; the third, "That is the face of a saint." Farmer found these responses suggestive of Oman's wrestling with the facts, his reflective mind, and his humility.[279]

Following Oman's death on 17 May 1939, R. D. Whitehorn wrote, "In all his intellectual work he was concerned not with abstractions, but with the world as the home of free personalities capable of knowing God in "a

---

275. Elmslie, *Westminster College Cambridge*, 23.
276. E. W. P., "The new Principal," 155.
277. Newbigin. *The Unfinished Agenda*, 31.
278. Manson, "Dr. John Oman," 199.
279. Farmer, "Death of Dr. John Oman," 19.

gracious personal relationship," and therefore with the Christian evaluation of men and means, souls and things.... There has passed from among us a great teacher, a great thinker, a great Christian, and a great friend."[280]

I am sure that Oman, the Christian content to live in the half lights, saw a good deal of himself in both Pascal and Butler, of whom he wrote that they had "precisely the same overwhelming sense of the dimness of the light with which we are compelled to act and of the need of our whole nature, and not merely our faculty of argument, in searching for that faith which the conduct of life imposes on us."[281] But if there is one of his sentences which, more than any other, may stand as his own epitaph it is this: "To have thought God's thoughts, fathomed in some measure His creation, predicted His ways, penetrated in some measure into His working, sets man, even in this fleeting life, amid God's creatures with a radiance upon his brow which we may believe even death will not destroy."[282]

In those words are encompassed Oman's objective and his reward. The contemplative task they enshrine began for Oman when, as a solitary youth he experienced the call of the supernatural in the natural order of Orkney. Perhaps I may in conclusion resort to the kind of homely expression which this deepest of thinkers never shunned to use, and say that while you can take the man out of Orkney, you cannot take Orkney out of the man.

BIBLIOGRAPHY

(a) Manuscripts and Archives

New College, London MSS. L1/4/101; at Dr. Williams's Library, London.
The Oman Papers at Westminster College, Cambridge.
Robert Franks's Report of 1926 to the subscribers of Western College, Bristol; in the Congregational College Archives/Western College Bristol, at the John Rylands University Library of Manchester.

---

280. Whitehorn, "Obituary. The Rev John Oman." Roy Drummond Whitehorn was appointed to the Chair of Church History at Westminster College in 1933, and was Principal there from 1955 to 1963. He died on 14 November 1976, aged 85. See *Year Book of the United Reformed Church*, 1978, 271.

281. Oman, *The Problem of Faith and Freedom*, 425,

282. Oman, *A Dialogue with God*, 136; though in the text the last "His" is given a capital H. It must, however refer to "man," not God.

(b) Published Works

Alexander, G. "Memoir" of Oman, prefixed to John Oman, *Honest Religion*, London: Religious Book Club, 1941.
Alexander, Samuel. *Space, Time, and Deity*. London: Macmillan, 1920.
Anderson, Peter D. *Black Pattie: The Life and Times of Patrick Steward, Earl of Orkney, Lord of Shetland*. Edinburgh: John Donald, 1992.
Anon. *Memorial of the Jubilee Synod of the United Presbyterian Church May 1897*. Edinburgh: Publications Office, 1897.
———. Obituary of John Oman. *The Times* (18May 1939).
———. Reports of Oman's activities: *Alnwick Guardian and County Advertiser* (21 September 1912); The *British Weekly* (1 April 1909); *The Times* (21 March 1932), (26 September 1936).
———. *Testimony of the United Associate Synod of the Secession Church*. Edinburgh: for the Synod, n.d.
———. *The United Reformed Church Year Book*, London, 1978.
Bardgett, F. D. *Two Millennia of Church and Community in Orkney*. Edinburgh: Pentland, 2000.
Barr, James. *The United Free Church of Scotland*. London: Allenson, 1934.
Bevans, Stephen. *John Oman and his Doctrine of God*. Cambridge: Cambridge University Press, 1992.
Bezzant, J. S. "The Theology of John Oman." *The Modern Churchman* 9 (1965-66) 135-40.
Broad, C. D. *Perception, Physics and Reality: An Inquiry into the Information that Physical Science can Supply about the Real*. Cambridge: Cambridge University Press, 1914.
Cairns, John. *Principal Cairns*. Edinburgh: Oliphant Anderson and Ferrier [1903].
Cairns, John. *Unbelief in the Eighteenth Century as Contrasted with Its Earlier and Later History*. Edinburgh: A. & C. Black, 1881.
Cameron, Nigel M. de S. *Dictionary of Scottish Church History and Theology*. Edinburgh: T. & T. Clark, 1993.
Campbell, C. A. *On Selfhood and Godhood*. London: Allen & Unwin, 1957.
Cochrane, Arthur C. *Reformed Confessions of the 16th Century*. Philadelphia: Westminster, 1966.
Cottle, J. L., and A. S. Cooper. "Westminster College Bulletin." *The Presbyterian Messenger* (1935) 230.
Craven, James B. *History of the Church in Orkney: From the Introduction of Christianity to 1558*. Kirkwall: Peace, 1901.
Dickie, John. *Fifty Years of British Theology: A Personal Retrospect*. Edinburgh: T. & T. Clark, 1937.
Duthie, Charles S. "A God of Action." *The British Weekly* (8 October 1964) 9.
Elmslie, W. A. L. *Westminster College Cambridge 1899-1949*. London: Presbyterian Church of England, [1949].
E. W. P. "The New Principal: An Appreciation of Dr. Oman." *The Presbyterian Messenger* (1922) 154-55.
Farmer, H. H. "Death of Dr. John Oman: An Appreciation." *The Christian World* (25 May 1939) 9, 19.
———. *Revelation and Religion: Studies in the Theological Interpretation of Religious Types*. London: Nisbet, 1954.

———. "Theologians of Our Time. III. John Wood Oman." *The Expository Times* 74 (1963) 132–35.
Fenton, Alexander. *The Northern Isles: Orkney and Shetland*. East Linton: Tuckwell, 1997.
Forsyth, P. T. *The Principle of Authority* (1913). London: Independent Press, 1952.
Franks, Robert S. *The Atonement: The Dale Lectures for 1933*. London: Oxford University Press, 1934.
Haldane, Alexander. *The Lives of Robert and James Haldane* (1852). Edinburgh: The Banner of Truth Trust, 1900.
Hastings, James. *A Dictionary of Christ and the Gospels*. 2 vols., Edinburgh: T. & T. Clark, 1906, 1908.
Healey, F. G. *Religion and Reality: The Theology of John Oman*. Edinburgh: Oliver & Boyd, 1965.
———. "The Theology of John Oman." *Theology* 67 (1964) 543–46.
Henderson, A. "The Divine Leading in the Origin and Progress of the Secession and Relief Churches." In *Memorial of the Jubilee Synod of the United Presbyterian Church May 1897*, 225–34. Edinburgh: Publications Office, 1897.
Henderson, Henry F. *The Religious Controversies of Scotland*. Edinburgh: T. & T. Clark, 1905.
Hick, John H. *Faith and Knowledge: A Modern Introduction to the Problem of Religious Knowledge*. Ithaca, NY: Cornell University Press, 1957.
Horton, W. M. *Contemporary English Theology: An American Interpretation*. New York: Harper, 1936.
Hunsworth, George. *Baxter's Nonconformist Descendants: or, Memorials of the Old Meeting Congregational Church Kidderminster*. Kidderminster: Edward Parry, 1874.
Huxtable W. John F. *As it Seemed to Me*. London: The United Reformed Church, 1900.
Knox, R. Buick. *Westminster College: Its Background and History*. Cambridge: The University Library, 1979.
Knox, T. M. Review of F. G. Healey, *Religion and Reality*. In *The Journal of Theological Studies* (1966) 546–50.
Lachman, David C. *The Marrow Controversy, 1718–1732: An Historical and Theological Analysis*. Edinburgh: Rutherford House, 1988.
Langford, Thomas A. "The Theological Methodology of John Oman and H. H. Farmer." *Religious Studies* 1 (1966) 229–40.
Leckie, J. H. *Secession Memories. The United Presbyterian Contribution to the Scottish Church*. Edinburgh: T. & T. Clark, 1926.
Lindsay, A. D. Review of Oman, *The Natural and the Supernatural*. In *The Journal of Theological Studies* 33 (1932) 385–8.
McCrie, C. G. *The Marrow of Modern Divinity*. Glasgow: Byce, 1902.
MacEwen, Alexander R. *Life and Letters of John Cairns, DD, LLD*. London: Hodder & Stoughton, 1895.
MacKelvie, William. *Annals and Statistics of the United Presbyterian Church*. Edinburgh: Oliphant and Andrew Elliott; and Glasgow: David Robertson, 1873.
M'Kerrow, John. *History of the Secession Church*. Edinburgh: Fullerton, 1847.
Mackintosh, H. R. Review of Oman, *The Natural and the Supernatural*. In *The British Weekly* (29 September 1931).

McNaughton, William D. *Early Congregational Independency in Lowland Scotland*. Vol. I. Glasgow: The Congregational Federation, 2005.
———. *The Scottish Congregational Ministry 1794–1993*. Glasgow: The Congregational Union of Scotland, 1993.
Mander, William J., and Alan P. F. Sell. *Dictionary of Nineteenth-Century British Philosophers*. Bristol: Thoemmes, 2002.
Manning, James. *A Sketch of the Life and Writings of Micaijah Towgood*. Exeter: n.p., 1792.
Manson, T. W. "Dr. John Oman." *The Presbyterian Messenger* (1935) 199–200.
———. "Introduction" to Oman's *Vision and Authority*, 8th ed. London: Hodder & Stoughton, 1948.
Micklem, Nathaniel. Review of Oman, *The Natural and the Supernatural*. In *The Christian World* (22 October 1931) 36.
Morris, J. S. "Oman's Conception of the Personal God in *The Natural and the Supernatural*." *The Journal of Theological Studies* N.S. 23 (1972) 82–94.
Mozley, J. K. *Some Tendencies in British Theology from the Publication of* Lux Mundi *to the Present Day*. London: SPCK, 1952.
Needham, N. R. "Relief Church." In *Dictionary of Scottish Church History and Theology*, edited by Nigel M. de S. Cameron, 703–4. Edinburgh: T. & T. Clark, 1993.
Newbigin, J. E. Lesslie. *The Unfinished Agenda*. London: SPCK, 1985.
Nicholson, Francis, and Ernest Axon. *The Older Nonconformity in Kendal*. Kendal: Titus Wilson, 1915.
Nuttall, Geoffrey F. *Calendar of the Correspondence of Philip Doddridge, DD*. London: Her Majesty's Stationery Office, 1979.
Oman, John. *The Church and the Divine Order*. London: Hodder & Stoughton, [1911].
———. *Concerning the Ministry*. London: SCM, 1936.
———. *A Dialogue with God and Other Sermons* (1928). London: James Clarke, [1950].
———. *Grace and Personality* (1917). London: Collins Fontana, 1960
———. *Honest Religion*. London: The Religious Book Club, 1941.
———. "The Idea of the Holy." *The Journal of Theological Studies* (1934) 275–86.
———. "Individualism, Individual, and Individuality." In *Dictionary of Christ and the Gospels*, edited by James Hastings, I, 814–21. Edinburgh: T. & T. Clark, 1908.
———. *The Natural and the Supernatural*. Cambridge: Cambridge University Press, 1931.
———. "Method in Theology: An Inaugural Lecture." *The Expositor* 8th series, 26 (1923) 81–93.
———. *The Paradox of the World: Sermons*. Cambridge: Cambridge University Press, 1921.
———. "The Presbyterian Churches." In *Evangelical Christianity: Its History and Witness*, edited by W. B. Selbie, ch. 3. London: Hodder & Stoughton, [1911].
———. *The Problem of Faith and Freedom in the Last Two Centuries*. London: Hodder & Stoughton, 1906.
———. Review of A. J. Ayer, *Language, Truth and Logic*. In *The British Weekly* (26 March, 1936) 24.
———. Review of A. Chapman, *An Introduction to Schleiermacher*. In *The Journal of Theological Studies* 34 (1933) 214–16.
———. Review of H. Jones, *A Faith that Enquires*. In *The Journal of Theological Studies* 24 (1923) 214–17.

———. Review of H. R. Mackintosh, *The Christian Experience of Forgiveness*. In *The Journal of Theological Studies* 29 (1928) 296–99.

———. Review of A. S. Pringle-Pattison, *The Idea of God in the Light of Recent Philosophy*. In *The Journal of Theological Studies* 19 (1918) 278–79.

———. Review of H. Rashdall, *The Idea of Atonement in Christian Theology*. In *The Journal of Theological Studies* 21 (1920) 267–75.

———. Reviews of F. R. Tennant, *Philosophical Theology*. Vols I and I. In *The Journal of Theological Studies* 31 (1930) 403–7; 33 (1932) 281–83.

———. Review of A. N. Whitehead, *Process and Reality*. In *The Journal of Theological Studies* 33 (1932) 48–52.

———. "Ritschlianism." *The Journal of Theological Studies* 11 (1910) 469–76.

———. "Schleiermacher." *The Journal of Theological Studies* 30 (1929) 401–5.

———. *Vision and Authority, or The Throne of St. Peter* (1902). 2nd and 8th eds. London: Hodder & Stoughton, 1928, 1948.

———. *The War and its Issues: An Attempt at a Christian Judgment*. 2nd ed. Cambridge: Cambridge University Press, 1916.

Orr, James. "The contribution of the United Presbyterian Church to Religious Thought and Life." In Anon., *Memorial of the Jubilee Synod of the United Presbyterian Church May 1897*, 88–98. Edinburgh: Publications Office, 1897.

Priestley, Joseph. *The Theological and Miscellaneous Works of Joseph Priestley*, edited by J. T. Rutt (1817–1831). Bristol: Thoemmes, 1999.

Reith, George M. *Reminiscences of the United Free Church General Assembly (1900–1929)*. Edinburgh: Moray, 1933.

Ritchie, Anna. "Birsay around AD 800." *Orkney Heritage* 2 (2001) 54–64.

Robson, R. S. *Our Professors. Brief Notes of Men Who after Occupying English Presbyterian Pulpits Have Been Appointed to Chairs*. London: Presbyterian Historical Society of England, 1956.

Sell, Alan P. F. *Church Planting: A Study of Westmorland Nonconformity*. 1986. Reprinted, Eugene, OR: Wipf & Stock, 1998.

———. *Commemorations: Studies in Christian Thought and History*. 1993. Reprinted Eugene, OR: Wipf & Stock, 1998.

———. *Confessing and Commending the Faith: Historic Witness and Apologetic Method*. 2002. Reprinted, Eugene, OR: Wipf & Stock, 2006.

———. *Confessing the Faith Yesterday and Today: Essays, Reformed, Dissenting and Catholic*. Eugene, OR: Pickwick, 2013.

———. *Defending and Declaring the Faith: Some Scottish Examples 1860–1920*. 1987. Reprinted, Eugene, OR: Wipf & Stock, 2012.

———. *Dissenting Thought and the Life of the Churches: Studies in an English Tradition*. Lewiston, NY: Mellen, 1990.

———. *Enlightenment, Ecumenism, Evangel: Theological Themes and Thinkers 1550–2000*. Milton Keynes, UK: Paternoster, 2005.

———. *The Great Debate: Calvinism, Arminianism and Salvation*. 1982. Reprinted, Eugene, OR: Wipf & Stock, 1998.

———. *The Great Ejectment of 1662: Its Antecedents, Aftermath, and Ecumenical Significance*. Eugene, OR: Pickwick Publications, 2012.

———. *Hinterland Theology: A Stimulus to Theological Construction*. Milton Keynes, UK: Paternoster, 2008.

---. *Philosophical Idealism and Christian Belief.* 1995. Reprinted, Eugene, OR: Wipf & Stock, 2006.

---. *Philosophy, Dissent and Nonconformity.* 2004. Reprinted, Eugene, OR: Wipf & Stock, 2009.

---. *The Philosophy of Religion 1875-1980* (1988, 1996). Eugene, OR: Wipf & Stock, 2012.

---. *Saints: Visible, Orderly and Catholic; The Congregational Idea of the Church.* Allison Park, PA: Pickwick Publications, 1986.

---. *Theology in Turmoil: The Roots, Course and Significance of the Conservative-Liberal Debate in Modern Theology.* 1986. Reprinted, Eugene, OR: Wipf & Stock, 1998.

Sell, Karen. *The Disciplines of Vocal Pedagogy: Towards an Holistic Approach.* Aldershot, UK: Ashgate, 2005.

Simpson, P. Carnegie. "Dr. John Oman. Address given at the Funeral Service in St. Columba's Church, Cambridge, on 22nd May." *The Presbyterian Messenger* (1939) 197-98.

---. *Recollections: Mainly Ecclesiastical but Sometimes Human.* London: Nisbet, 1943.

Sinclair, Hugh. "Living Voices . . . Professor Oman." *The Presbyterian Messenger* (1915) 430.

Small, David. *History of the Congregations of the United Presbyterian Church from 1733 to 1900.* 2 vols. Edinburgh: David M. Small, 1900.

Staker, Jane. *A History of St. James' United Reformed Church, Alnwick: Incorporating Lisburn Street and Clayport Street Presbyterian Churches.* Newcastle-upon-Tyne, [1989].

Struthers, Gavin. *The History of the Rise of the Relief Church.* Bound with Thomson, below, and paginated consecutively.

Tennant, F. R. "John Wood Oman 1860-1939." *Proceedings of the British Academy* 25 (1939 332-38.

---. Review of Oman, *The Natural and the Supernatural.* In *Mind* 41 (1932) 212-18.

Thomson, Andrew. *Historical Sketch of the Origin of the Secession Church.* Edinburgh: A. Fullerton, 1848.

Thomson, William P. L. *New History of Orkney.* Edinburgh: Mercat, 2001.

Torrance, Thomas F. *The School of Faith: The Catechisms of the Reformed Church.* London: James Clarke, 1959.

Whitehead, Thomas. *History of the Dales Congregational Churches.* Keighley, UK: Feather, 1930.

Whitehorn, R. D. "Obituary: The Rev. John Oman." *Cambridge Review* (26 May 1939).

Woodger, Phyllis L., and Jessie E. Hunter. *The High Chapel: The Story of Ravenstonedale Congregational Church.* Kendal: Titus Wilson, [1962].

5

Clarity, Precision, and on towards Comprehension

The Intellectual Legacy of N. H. G. Robinson (1912-1978)

NORMAN HAMILTON GALLOWAY ROBINSON was born at Troon, Ayrshire, on 7 October 1912. He was the oldest son of George Robinson and his wife Barbara (*née* Fraser), who came from Fife.[1] George had been a sea captain, but from the time of his marriage he worked at Troon shipyard. George and Barbara had five sons and one daughter. Norman and another son became ministers, two sons were teachers, and one went to sea. The daughter became a missionary to the Gold Coast. Norman was educated at Ayr Academy, and at the universities of Glasgow (MA, DLitt), Oxford (BA), and Edinburgh (BD, DD). He gained first class honours in Philosophy at Glasgow, and was awarded the Clark Scholarship, which took him to The Queen's College, Oxford. The teachers who particularly influenced him were, A. A. Bowman Professor of Moral Philosophy, and H. J. Paton, Professor of Logic and Rhetoric, at Glasgow; Oliver Franks, tutor

---

1. For the bare bones of the first three paragraphs I am indebted to *Who Was Who*, 1971-1980. Information has been added from Mr. Frazer Robinson, to whom I am especially grateful; former church members and students; and an obituary notice by Matthew Black in the University of St. Andrews *Alumnus Chronicle*, June 1979, 65-66. A photocopy of Black's notice was kindly supplied by Mrs. Rachel Hart, Muniments Archivist of St. Andrews University. For a brief sketch of Robinson's life and thought see Stuart Brown, ed. *Dictionary of Twentieth-Century British Philosophers*.

in philosophy at Oxford; and John Baillie, Professor of Divinity at Edinburgh.[2] In 1936 he married Mary Elizabeth, only daughter of Christopher (known as Christie) and Catherine Johnston (they also had three sons) of Portrush. Norman and Mary had two sons, Frazer and Gordon, and two daughters, Catherine and Maureen.

Ordained in the Church of Scotland, Robinson served at Sandsting Parish Church, Shetland (1939–1943), South Church, Fraserburgh, Aberdeenshire (1943–1948), and at the High Kirk of Rothesay, Isle of Bute (1948–1954). He is remembered for his kindness, for his diligence in pastoral care, and for the lucidity and depth of his sermons. Whilst in pastoral charge he wrote a number of articles and published his first two books: *Faith and Duty* (1950), for which John Baillie wrote a Foreword; and *The Claim of Morality* (1952), for which he earned his Glasgow DLitt, and to which John Macmurray contributed an Introduction.[3]

In 1954 Robinson became Professor of Divinity and Dean of the Faculty at Rhodes University, Grahamstown, South Africa. His sojourn there was brief, for two years later he was appointed to the Chair of Systematic Theology at St. Andrews in succession to Donald Baillie, adding Divinity in 1967 on the amalgamation of Chairs following the retirement of E. P. Dickie. He served as Dean of the Faculty of Divinity from 1968 to 1964, and on a number of committees. He was an external examiner for other universities, and a guest lecturer in Britain and North America. Articles and reviews flowed from his pen, and his two books, *Christ and Conscience* (1956) and *The Groundwork of Christian Ethics* (1971) were published. To his students he was kind and warm-hearted. One of them recalls that "his lecturing style was declamatory—like a solid, old-fashioned Scottish preacher"; and not all of them were as passionate as he was concerning the differences between Barth and Brunner. A postgraduate student remembers him as a painstaking, but not a clone-making, supervisor who was "usually breezy, with a twinkle in his eye—although he dearly loved to 'scrap' theologically with other theologians."[4]

The World Council of Churches appointed Robinson an observer of the Anglican-Lutheran consultation on marriage (1970–1974), and in the

2. For Bowman (1886–1960) see Stuart Brown, ed. *Dictionary of Twentieth-Century British Philosophers*; for Franks (1905–1992), Paton (1887–1969) and Baillie (1886–1960) see ODNB.

3. The following abbreviations are used in this chapter: CC: *Christ and Conscience*; CM: *The Claim of Morality*; FD: *Faith and Duty*; GCE: *The Groundwork of Christian Ethics*.

4. Quoted by Matthew Black, "Obituary notice," 66.

latter year he was appointed by the World Alliance of Reformed Churches to the trilateral dialogue on marriage between that body, the Roman Catholic Secretariat for Promoting Christian Unity and the Lutheran World Federation.[5] Closer to home, he served as Convener of the Church of Scotland's Panel on Doctrine, and as Moderator of the Presbytery of St. Andrews.

Norman Robinson died, untimely and in harness, on 9 March 1978. His colleague, Matthew Black remembered him as "a scholar-churchman, a congenial colleague, a faithful teacher, and a warm friend."[6]

Reviewers of Robinson's books spoke of his deep knowledge of philosophy and theology and ethics, and a number of them applauded his critical acumen. A few, however, felt that his own argument would on occasion have stood forth more clearly if he had not introduced so many discussions of the work of others along the way.[7] Undeniably, the roll-call of those to whose writings he paid close attention is lengthy, including as it does Bentham, Hobbes, Shaftesbury, Hutcheson, Price, Ross, Prichard, Joseph, G. E. Moore, F. R. Tennant, Wittgenstein, H. D. Lewis, John Baillie, Barth, Brunner, Bonhoeffer, Bultmann, Tillich, Nels F. S. Ferré, Ian Ramsey, Reinhold Niebuhr, Paul Ramsey, J. A. T. Robinson, Harvey Cox, and Paul Lehmann. I think, however, that to suggest that careful attention to these and others deflected Robinson from the main thrust of his argument is to misunderstand his method, which is best summed up in Pringle-Pattison's phrase, "construction through criticism." Robinson was always concerned to deal with one complex issue at a time, and to adjust his thought to that of others, utlilizing what he deemed to be of benefit, and rejecting what was not. Had he not worked in this way, other reviewers might have complained that he had taken insufficient account of alternative views. For his method to succeed he needed patience, analytical skill and considerable learning; and these he possessed in abundance. No scholar was less inclined than he to jump on the passing band-wagons of philosophical or theological fashion.

As it happens Robinson's four books are on ethical themes. If we were to confine our attention to these, however, we should miss the broad sweep of his thought. My objective in what follows is to draw from Robinson's

---

5. The resulting report is entitled, *Theology of Marriage and the Problem of Mixed Marriages.* For an account of the dialogue see Sell, *A Reformed, Catholic, Evangelical Theology*, 216–18.

6. M. Black, "Obituary notice," 66.

7. See, for example, Ward's review of GCE, 109.

total corpus some of his main theses, and to set them in what I trust will be an appropriate sequence. I shall not, of course, be able to discuss each thesis in detail, but I hope that my findings will encourage others to return to a thinker whose contribution has been insufficiently recognized. I shall then note some matters of varying degrees of importance which arise from his work.

I

Thesis 1. *There can and should be positive relations between philosophy and theology.*

That there had been a breach of fellowship between philosophy and theology was clear for all to see in the mid nineteen-sixties. Robinson cites the logical positivism of A. J. Ayer as exemplifying the break-down of relations from the philosophical side; for on a strict interpretation of the principle of verification, namely, that those propositions only are meaningful which are either analytic or empirically verifiable, not only religious, but also aesthetic and ethical discourse, was branded strictly non-sensical, literally meaning-less. From the side of theology Barth, while he had done well to recall theology to the paramount fact of God's supreme revelation in Christ, showed a marked indifference to philosophy and, indeed, wished to divorce theology from it. As Robinson drily noted, "Clearly, no conversation can proceed, or even get under way, where the respective contributions of different parties are from the outset subject to such radical criticisms, complete nonsense on the one side and total irrelevance on the other."[8] However, what I might call "in-house" challenges were posed on both sides. The verification principle came under attack from other philosophers and theologians[9] while Emil Brunner and Barth had their celebrated contretemps over general revelation.[10]

On this latter point Robinson stood much closer to Brunner than to Barth. Barth was consistently hostile

> when philosophy assumes the form of natural theology. Behind this attitude there lies his conviction that philosophy finds in human reason a norm which is other than the revelation God has given of Himself in Jesus Christ His Son, and thus proves

---

8. Robinson, "Faith and Truth," 145. Cf. FD, 21.

9. See Sell, *The Philosophy of Religion*, ch. 5; Sell, *Confessing and Commending the Faith*, 99–106.

10. See Sell, *Confessing and Commending the Faith*, 269–71.

> itself blind to the sheer transcendence of God over sinful humanity and to the extensive corruption that sin has wrought in human nature. On the other hand, Barth recognises that sinners or not we must think, and that "if we open our mouths, we find ourselves in the province of philosophy." Philosophy . . . is inevitable, but . . . entirely unimportant.[11]

Certainly Robinson was not concerned to uphold natural theology in the sense of supposing that the traditional theistic arguments yielded a copper-bottomed demonstration of God's existence. Nor was he of the opinion that grace supplements nature, as the Thomists held, or that it supplants it. Rather "man is made *whole* by grace," and "becomes a *new* creature."[12] What he objected to in Barth's position was that "radical Protestantism is radical authoritarianism in the sphere of religion, but it is so because it is first of all and primarily radical *empiricism* in theology, if this word may be used to indicate a reliance upon that which is given and not just upon that which is given to sense."[13] At this point Robinson sees a link between Barth's position and the radical empiricism of logical positivism.[14] Underlying Barth's theology, he continues, is "a metaphysical preconception concerning the relationship between creatures and their Creator."[15] Having recourse to a radical doctrine of total corruption as entailing the obliteration, not merely the defacement, of the *imago dei*, Barth leaves no point of contact between natural humanity and God, and any place which he accords to reason is only to a reason completely determined by God's revelation.[16] But, protests Robinson, "The truth is that faith as conviction, as trust, as loyalty, as obedience, as love, cannot be completely determined; there is an ineradicable element of personal spontaneity, without which the conviction, loyalty and love would not be mine—or anyone's—and would not therefore be conviction, loyalty and love."[17]

---

11. FD, 6, quoting K. Barth, *Credo*, 183.

12. Robinson, "Barth or Bultmann?" 289. Robinson died while this article was in proof, and to it the editor, H. D. Lewis, appended a gracious tribute in which he said that Robinson "made many substantial and very perceptive contributions to theology and the philosophy of religion," and that "He combined a liberal outlook with a deep and learned understanding of traditional theology." Ibid., 290.

13. CC, 95.

14. Ibid., 90.

15. Ibid., 103.

16. Ibid, 137–39.

17. Ibid, 167.

Robinson's conclusion on the underlying question of Barth, natural theology and philosophico-theological relations is that "Barth would have nothing to do with human truth whether advancing in opposition or sympathetic alliance. All that human truth could achieve in the matter of God's existence would be to prove something about man, not conceivably anything about God; but the inevitable result of this intransigent attitude is to represent truth of revelation, not as something inescapable, but as thoroughly esoteric and as quite irrelevant to all human problems and all human questions."[18]

With such an understanding of the truth of revelation Robinson would have nothing whatsoever to do: theology was not thus to be fenced off from the rest of moral and intellectual endeavour. On the contrary, writing in the aftermath of World War II he declared that "the apologetic task is an essential part of the Christian commission, and it would be a grave tragedy indeed if, in the hour of the world's confusion, the Church were to allow its apologetics to be swallowed up by dogmatics."[19] As he elsewhere put it, Barth's "complete indifference to the apologetic question would leave theology defenceless against the relativism of the modern world."[20] In a word, he deeply regretted the fact that twentieth-century theology had put a "spoke in the wheel" between the disciplines of philosophy as theology, and this in a way which led to "the denial of any neutral meeting-place of believer and unbeliever."[21]

---

18. Robinson, "The Problem of Natural Theology," 325. He goes on to point out that when T. F. Torrance seeks to defend Barth on this point by suggesting that Barth reaffirmed the truths of natural theology "within the understanding of faith," Robinson retorts that this is no longer to deal with *natural* theology. Ibid., 329. For a discussion of particular points of interpretation see Illtyd Trethowan, "Professor N. H. G. Robinson and Natural Theology," 463–68.

19. Robinson, FD, ix; cf. Robinson, *Theology and the Personal*, 13. Robinson was puzzled by Daniel Jenkins' halting between apologetics and dogmatics, for the latter held both that the fact that the unbeliever "is in contact with God whether he is prepared to admit it or not, is what makes conversation with him possible and hopeful from the believer's point of view," and that the idea of general revelation was to be rejected. See Robinson's review of D. T. Jenkins, *The Christian Belief in God*, 92.

20. Robinson, "Barth or Bultmann?" 278.

21. Robinson, "Faith and Truth," 148.

Thesis 2. *Philosophical developments subsequent to logical positivism are more open to Christian discourse.*

In this connection the way in which Wittgenstein supplemented[22] his earlier findings on meaning with considerations of language use was of great importance. As Robinson wrote, "[I]t is now seen [that] language is legitimately used to perform many tasks besides that of describing and informing, it is used to issue commands, to offer advice, to express emotion, even to ask questions, and in such cases, although the sentences used may be neither true nor false, they are none the less unquestionably significant. Moreover, the recognition of such a multiplicity of uses opens up the possibility of a more positive account of religious language, for after all, as Wittgenstein pointed out, "this language-game is played.""[23] The critical question was, however, whether linguistic analysts were willing to grant that religious assertions made genuine truth claims. Some, clearly, were not, and Robinson cautioned all such that "if we attempt to correct the elimination of theological or of religious language by a method which certainly involves the elimination of religious *belief* we are simply defeating our own ends."[24]

In face of such reductionism, Robinson insisted upon the ontological import of religious language: "[R]eligious language has always been ontologically, not just logically, oriented, that is to say, oriented towards a distinctive reality, not simply towards a word that behaves peculiarly; and to minimise or to eliminate this objective reference would break the nerve of religion."[25] In Christian discourse "the word 'God' performs a twofold function in that at one and the same time it posits the ontological apex or ultimate and it expresses a union or communion, a sense of rapport,

---

22. I use "supplemented" as shorthand for the view that there was not a "late" Wittgenstein who was utterly distinct from the "early" one. See further Sell, *Confessing and Commending the Faith*, 106–17, especially 109.

23. Robinson, "Faith and Truth," 146. He quotes Wittgenstein, *Philosophical Investigations*, para. 654.

24. Robinson, "The Logic of Religious Language," 7.

25. Robinson, "The Logical Placing of the Name 'God,'" 133; cf. ibid., 139–40. Incidentally, it is in this paper that we find what is probably the driest remark in the whole of Robinson's *corpus*. He refers to those who pursue the line taken by the former Bishop of Woolwich (J. A. T. Robinson) in advocating the abandonment of the idea of "God up there." Norman Robinson dissents thus: "it seems to me that there is sense in speaking of the higher part of a person without being taken to mean the hair of his head when he is standing on his feet and the soles of his feet when he is standing on his head." Ibid., 148.

with that ultimate."[26] It must therefore be held that "religious language, if properly used, does grasp the reality by which the man of faith has himself been grasped." It is "about the 'Thou' who is worshipped, to whom prayers and praises are offered . . . it grasps Him whose reality invariably overflows all that is said in religious language. There is then a pervasive deficiency in religious language, but it is the deficiency of those who see through a glass darkly, not the deficiency of those who can see nothing but shadows cast upon the wall."[27]

Thesis 3. *Undue intellectualism is to be avoided, and the personal elevated.*

For all his commitment to matters philosophical, Robinson was wary of undue intellectualism—not least that fostered by some approaches to natural theology, especially since this could so easily minimise the importance of the personal. Indeed, in his Inaugural Lecture at Rhodes University he contended that "modern thinking since the scientific revolution of the seventeenth century has largely failed to take account of the personal."[28] Setting out from Hobbes, and with reference to Russell, he argued that more important than what science has to say along materialistic lines is what it omits to say about the personal. Its radical epistemological empiricism not only excludes God, but human persons as well. To redress the balance, Robinson has recourse to Kant. While Kant's idealism "as represented by his distinction between appearance and reality . . . constituted the fundamental weakness of his position,"[29] his strength is that he both gives due place to scientific knowledge whilst showing its limits,[30] thereby allowing room for what he calls the Primacy of the Practical, that is, for the system of personal relationships. On this his ethics turns.[31] Space is also found for the religious realm, though for Kant, unfortunately, this seems to entail simply belief in three objects, God, freedom and immortality, these being construed as an appendix to morality. Nevertheless, in Kant's phi-

26. Ibid., 142.
27. Robinson, "Faith and Truth," 159.
28. Robinson, *Theology and the Personal*, 1.
29. Ibid., 5.
30. Consistently with this, and against W. H. Walsh, Robinson holds that when Kant said, "I deny knowledge to make room for faith," he was not accepting "the scientific world-view as a criterion," but denying "scientific knowledge in certain directions or dimensions where only faith was competent." See his article, "Is Providence Credible Today?" 222.
31. See CM, 249. Cf. Robinson's critique of F. H. Bradley's "non-social" morality, ibid, 328 n.

losophy taken as a whole their lies the hope of a modern synthesis which will be much more satisfactory than the "uneasy alliance of scientifically inspired philosophy and some relic of religion,"[32] such as is found in the writings of Hobbes, Russell and Wittgenstein. Robinson laments the way in which modern philosophers have taken a leaf out of the scientist's book and excluded the personal from consideration—an abstraction which is necessary in scientific research, but which in philosophy leads to "a one-sided and radically defective philosophy."[33]

Robinson sees hopeful signs in the fresh emphasis upon the personal by such thinkers as Martin Buber, the existentialists and others. These remind us that we stand not only in relation to a world of objects, but in relation to an equally ultimate world of subjects. Along this path we may overcome the "egocentric predicament" of modern thought, and to this cause theologians have much to contribute, provided that they do not, like Barth, so emphasise the personal character, or subjectivity, of God that the subjectivity of human beings is swamped. This is not to deny the importance of Barth's profound insight that "God is not an object of our thought but the supreme and sovereign subject in that intersubjective situation, which is the ultimately real situation and from which all other situations are abstractions."[34] Nevertheless the human is not to be violated, not least because "God the Supreme Person sent His Son into the world . . . because He loved the human persons whom He made after His own image . . ."[35] The recognition that at the heart of Christian faith is a personal relationship with God is "the outstanding, peculiar and characteristic merit of modern theology."[36]

Robinson puts the point elsewhere in terms of the encounter theology of such theologians as H. H. Farmer:[37]

> [T]he idea of encounter draws our attention to the fact that language, treated as a self-contained totality or as a self-contained source of a wide diversity of meaningful statements in a wide variety of linguistic forms, is an abstraction. Language appears, and linguistic analysis takes place, within a social context. Language is a means of communication between persons; and the

32. Robinson, *Theology and the Personal*, 7; cf. Robinson, CC, 202–6.
33. Ibid.
34. Ibid., 15.
35. Ibid., 16.
36. Idem., CC, 9.
37. See Robinson, "Is Providence Credible Today?" 229.

> picture of an impersonal language, however rich in linguistic possibilities, hovering over the world or ordinary experience, of tables and chairs and so on, is, when drawn clearly, a quite incredible one. . . . Monologue made absolute becomes nonsense; it depends upon that which it disowns.[38]

Hence, in relation to the linguistic situation, "it is open to the theologian of encounter to claim that his basic idea is an analogy dictated by that situation, since dialogue is a form of meeting and encounter."[39] "At the centre of the Christian faith," he declares, is "not a belief *about* someone or something but a meeting *with* someone."[40]

Thesis 4. *Ethics is a normative science in which primacy is accorded to the practical.*

Robinson holds that ethics is a normative science. It is not concerned to raise epistemological and metaphysical questions such as those surrounding the freedom of the will;[41] nor is it occupied with descriptions of behaviour. Rather, ethics has to do with the norms and standards of behaviour: with what ought to be done, with duty. But what makes an act right or wrong? Utilitarians, for example, look to the likely consequences of action, but these cannot be infallibly predicted or controlled, and hence consequentialism fails to satisfy. Others suggest that the key to an action's rightness lies in the actor's motive. But Robinson argues that while motive and intention combine in the act, it is the actor's intention which is the subject of moral approbation or disapprobation. Thus an act is judged to be a right act in view of the actor's intention. The matter is complicated by the clash of *prima facie* duties which people experience. A given act may appear to be more appropriate than another in a particular situation, but what makes it so? There cannot be degrees of rightness (*pace* certain intuitionists); hence the conclusion that in any given situation the right act is that whereby the actor intends to realize the good conceived as "an all-inclusive form of life, a comprehensive system of personal relationships, which is *the* good, the ideal."[42] The moral goodness of motives and the goodness of consequences, Robinson concludes, "point beyond themselves

---

38. Robinson, "The Logic of Religious Language," 14.
39. Ibid.
40. Robinson, CC, 3.
41. Though in his later book, GCE, 42, he says that the question of freedom and responsibility is relevant to Christian ethics and to theology.
42. Robinson, CM, 329.

to this more fundamental conception, that of the good; while the various rules of right action reveal themselves as echoes of a more comprehensive demand, the single self-consistent claim which the Good life makes upon the attention of men, who are essentially fallible beings."[43]

Underlying Robinson's approach is his conviction concerning the primacy of the practical, for which he was indebted to Kant. But whereas Kant "seems to have thought of the practical and the theoretical as different exercises of the same abstract, disembodied reason,"[44] Robinson construes the distinction as one between a situation in life and a situation in thought. Of these the former is more fundamental than the latter, and the latter is an abstraction from it. Thus, "by stressing original dimensions of the human situation in life rather than postulates of practical but abstract reason, the principle of the primacy of the practical can be given a clearer and more stable meaning."[45]

Thesis 5. *Theology is not to be divorced from natural morality.*

Just as the point of contact between believers and unbelievers is to be maintained against those theologians who would fence off theology from all other thought, so the deliverances of natural morality are pertinent to the theological enterprise. Thus, for example, in opposition to Emil Brunner's view that sin has totally corrupted the content of natural man's morality but not its form, Robinson declares that in this context "content" and "form" are abstractions which cannot thus be sundered.[46] Such a consideration notwithstanding, both Barth and Brunner are generally dismissive of natural morality, and both sharply distinguish the ethics of the Christian from it.[47] But this would seem to admit the "intolerable supposition" of "two quite separate, independent and absolute claims upon human life, the divine claim and the moral claim."[48] Accordingly, Robinson contends,

> any presentation of the Christian faith which gives a predominantly negative view of morality carries with it the evidence of

---

43. Ibid.

44. Robinson, "Is Providence Credible Today?" 224; cf. Robinson, "The Problem of Natural Theology," 331.

45. Ibid., 226.

46. See Robinson, FD, 45, 47.

47. Yet, says Robinson, Barth does grant that we all have "some knowledge of some moral law," but he does not say how morality is related to religion. On which Robinson drily remarks, "Presumably, this is another of those questions towards which the only proper theological attitude is a profound lack of interest," FD, 25.

48. Robinson, GCE, 43.

its own inadequacy, for invariably one or other of two things happens. Either the formulation of the Christian faith which professes to have no use for morality finds itself constrained silently to re-introduce morality and so to convict itself of self-contradiction; or else it is compelled by the inner necessity of its own logic to portray the grace of God in a way which is anything but gracious and to represent the miracle it performs, not as one of grace at all, but after the same pattern as a marvel of mechanics. And there is no way of escape from this dilemma. If the activity of God towards the human soul is not understood in moral terms, it is invariably understood in mechanical terms, in a way, that is to say, which is not moral but less than moral.[49]

Along the mechanical route the moral experience of human beings can no longer be a point of contact between them and God, and the entire divine-human relationship is not so much vitiated as rendered impossible from the outset. Barthians tend to forget "what the Bible never forgets, that it is always *men* who are addressed . . . though they be clothed in the sullied garments of a fallen humanity . . ."[50] Thus while Robinson is prepared to allow that Barthianism is an evangelical theology, it is one of the "non-ethical, metaphysical and radically empirical" type.[51]

Along the Barthian line, any possibility of common ground in morality on which Christians and unbelievers might stand together, and any point of contact between natural humanity and the divine revelation are removed: "Indeed the concept of moral responsibility never appears in Dr. Barth's theological system as anything more than an island lying off the continent of his more characteristic thought . . ."[52] To Brunner, "Natural morality . . . is a work of human sin."[53] Against this Robinson maintains that "Whatever changes the Christian religion may work in the moral outlook of men. . . . morality . . . is not the product but the indispensable presupposition of the Christian revelation and the Christian gospel."[54] Not, indeed, that the position of those liberal theologians who have held that "moral man is simply embryonic Christian man, Christian man in the making" is any more satisfactory, for "In natural morality the finite creature makes the measure of himself finite too . . . and so comes under

49. Robinson, FD, 58–8.
50. Ibid., 53–54.
51. Robinson, CC, ix, 10, ch. 4.
52. Ibid.,102.
53. Robinson, FD, 40.
54. Robinson, GCE, 32; cf. ibid., 260.

the judgment of the Infinite."[55] Even so, Barth is right to insist on the supreme authority of Christ; the liberals are right not to repudiate natural morality: "each has contended for something which the other has failed to bring into the account."[56]

Thesis 6. *Jesus Christ is the norm of Christian theology.*

Robinson first carefully distinguishes two senses in which language about norms is used. We might say that "a normative science is one which studies norms that are and would be recognized apart from their systematic examination in this science."[57] This is the definition he favours. Jesus Christ is "the norm of all professedly Christian thought about God and His purpose of salvation, and neither theology nor any other human science can usurp Christ's place." It follows that "Theology . . . is concerned with a norm or standard of Christian thought and belief, but it does not and cannot produce a norm any more than ethics of itself can provide a rule of conduct."[58] There is, however, a further sense of 'norm' in which it is supposed that "a normative science provides and produces norms which would not be recognized apart from the existence of the science itself."[59] As we might by now expect, Barth is rebuked for adopting this exclusivist and self-defeating definition: "the appeal to the divine revelation as providing the justification of theological intransigence and of theological indifference to everything not specifically theological is in the end, and must always be, an appeal to a certain *human understanding* of the revelation."[60]

The question arises, In what sense is Christ the norm of theology? Robinson replies, "The New Testament Christians found in Christ not only the revelation of God but the way, the truth and the life; and to ignore this fact is to commit oneself to an unduly intellectualist version of their religion. The basic Christian reality appears to be not revelation, but an encounter, a fellowship, a living relationship. . . . This reality, of which divine revelation is a moment or an aspect, is a world reconciled to God in Christ, a fellowship of love."[61]

---

55. Robinson, "Natural Law, Morality and the Divine Will," 28, 29; cf. CC, 73–74.
56. Ibid., 28.
57. Robinson, "Is Theology a Normative Science?" 245.
58. Ibid., 246.
59. Ibid., 245.
60. Robinson, CC, 24–25.
61. Robinson, "The Future of Christology: II," 169. Robinson casts this point in trinitarian terms, and with specific reference to the Church in "Trinitarianism and Post-Barthian Theology," 200.

Thesis 7. *Christ is the moral sovereign, and hence Christian ethics is inseparable from Christian dogmatics.*

What is at issue here is the conviction that Christ is more than a moral authority who could stand aside once his followers had risen to his level of moral insight: he is the Lord; and he calls people to follow him in all the manifold aspects of life—life renewed and empowered by the Holy Spirit. Hence, "Christian ethics must remind itself that the word 'Christ' is to stand for the revelation of God, God in his reconciling act, and the name 'Jesus' for the historical *locus* of this act."[62] Because Christ is sovereign, his moral authority will never be superseded; it is final. Because of who Christ is—both Lord and Saviour—it is not possible "to separate his significance for Christian ethics from his significance for Christian dogmatics."[63] Because of who we are—sinners in whom God's image is defaced (but not obliterated)—"the Christian life must be represented as both Christocentric and redeemed, and its ethic as not only, quite properly, a theological ethic, but also as an ethic of redemption."[64] All of which is to say that "Christian ethics is not just related to dogmatics but is a part of dogmatics."[65] The doctrine of vocation is "the natural connecting link between dogmatics and ethics" because it concerns on the one side the vocation to receive the gift of God, and on the other, the call to service in the world.[66] In Robinson's view this understanding of Christian ethics could not develop so long as moral theology was construed as a casuistical system operated under ecclesiastical authority: "So long as the discussion was . . . cut short by the blank wall of a *de facto* authority and more basic issues were obscured, Christian ethics could not properly take shape."[67]

Thesis 8. *A normative study, Christian ethics occupies the same ground as general ethics, but it transforms the entire landscape.*

As with general morality, so with Christian ethics: it is a normative study. "Quite explicitly," Robinson says, "Christian ethics is concerned with the normative use of the word 'Christian'. It sets itself the task of

---

62. Robinson, GCE, 109.
63. Ibid., 116.
64. Ibid., 119.
65. Ibid., 216.
66. Robinson, "The Place of Vocation in Christian Ethics," 27.
67. Robinson, "Christian Ethics," 263–64.

giving a systematic account of the life that Christians ought to live, and of the claim that God in Christ makes upon them."[68]

Robinson does not intend that the dogmatic foundations of Christian ethics should be understood as in any way rendering natural morality redundant. This would be to ghettoize Christian ethics and breach relations with moral philosophy. On the other hand he does not agree with those who have suggested that Christianity merely supplies a fresh motive of gratitude for salvation to the motives operative in those who follow the path of general ethics; or that it simply adds the theological virtues of faith, hope and love to those enjoined by the natural law—on the contrary, the so-called theological virtues "do not crown [the good life], they constitute it."[69] Christian ethics is not, A. B. D. Alexander thought, a branch of general ethics.[70] Rather, (taking his cue from his teacher, Bowman), "Christian ethics occupies the same ground as general ethics but in doing so introduces a radically different conception of the moral life"[71]—one in which the autonomy of the self-contained moral consciousness is surrendered in faith and loving obedience to "the rule and overlordship of Christ as containing within himself the whole duty of man."[72] Indeed, "Christ not only judges our natural morality at its spring, in its very standards and ideals, but He recreates it and renews it. He does this by substituting the unmeasured requirements of love for the specific demands of law."[73] In a word, Christian morality is "a radical reorientation of natural morality."[74] Robinson never forgets that

> Men are moral beings apart from the Church and Scripture, and when Christian thought takes the form of Christian ethics it does not lead men into an entirely new country where a quite different language has to be learned, it does not land them on the moon, but enters a field already occupied. The Christian is certainly in some sense a new creature, but that clearly means, not another species altogether, but a creature, a man transformed or renewed, whose transformation and renewal cannot be articulated apart from some understanding of his existence

---

68. Robinson, GCE, 15.
69. Robinson, "Christian Ethics," 281. Cf. GCE, 127–30, 170–72.
70. See Robinson, GCE, 27.
71. Ibid., 172. For Bowman's view see FD, 106–7.
72. Robinson, GCE 172. Cf. ibid., 268–70, 272; CC, 19, 20.
73. Robinson, CC, 75.
74. Robinson, GCE, 122.

independently of that renewal. No more then can the ethical side of that transformation be understood apart from some comprehension of the human condition which is the subject of renewal.[75]

Robinson returned to this theme in his last published article, in the concluding paragraph of which he wrote,

> Whatever interpretation we offer of the situation of grace it must, one would think, be consonant with both declarations that man is made *whole* by grace and that he becomes a *new* creature; and neither the Thomist idea of supplementation, whereby grace is said to complete and perfect nature, nor the Reformers' idea of supplanting, whereby the old nature is said to be replaced by the new, measures up to this demand. Neither simple addition nor total replacement can quite grasp together both the radical newness of the new man and his continuing personal identity with the old one; and yet both are required to do justice to the dynamics of the Christian life, the life of the new man still very much in conflict with the old. For the Christian Christ is not only the judgment of this world but at the same time the victory which overcometh the world; and it is this total comprehensiveness of both the judgment and the re-affirmation which ensures that the human decision of faith is not in any sense "a work performed."[76]

In the light of the foregoing it is not difficult to see why Robinson felt that "morals provide a battleground of strategic importance, perhaps *the* battleground of strategic importance for the settlement of the issue between a religious understanding of reality and an understanding which grants no validity to religious insight."[77]

II

I trust that the theses I have extracted from Robinson's writings, encompassing as they do moral philosophy, theology and Christian ethics, fairly represent the main lines of his thought. Of necessity I have described them only briefly: the author's detailed discussions comprise their justification. While I find myself largely in agreement with Robinson's approach—not

---

75. Ibid., 16.
76. Robinson, "Barth or Bultmann?" 289–90.
77. Robinson, "The Universality of Sin" *Theology* 51 (1948) 449.

least with his determination to keep open lines of communication between theologians and philosophers, I should like to note a few particular matters arising from what I take to be a very worthwhile body of writings.

Robinson sets great store by the appeal to what he calls "the ordinary moral consciousness."[78] This phrase calls to mind Thomas Reid's recourse to the common sense of mankind, though, perhaps surprisingly, Reid is not among the many philosophers to whom Robinson refers. Robinson insists that the ordinary moral consciousness "is of course the last court of appeal in ethics."[79] The problem here is that even if we could know that all persons in the world were in conscientious agreement on the propriety of a particular judgment, this would not render that judgment necessarily correct. Moreover Robinson himself seems to be well aware of the difficulty of determining what the deliverances of the ordinary moral consciousness are, for among his objections to the Thomist idea of natural law is one to the effect that the idea "exaggerates the extent of the moral agreement between different races, different periods, and, indeed, different individuals."[80] It is arguable that the ordinary moral consciousness is similarly placed. Undeterred, Robinson declares that "The whole of ethics is based on the assumption that, by and large, moral judgments are true . . ."[81] The "by and large" in this sentence begs the question, How do we know which moral judgments are true, and how is this to be determined? Presumably by appeal to "the ordinary moral consciousness." But then, according to Robinson, "Duties, unlike rights, do not presuppose a *general* recognition." Thus, "If I consider it my duty to perform act A then it is my duty so to act even if in doing so I am resisting the prevailing moral convictions of the surrounding society. But my right to A depends upon general recognition."[82] But can one not go against "the ordinary moral consciousness" when dutifully performing an act, and does not this possibility throw into question the favoured criterion?

Over and above the logical puzzles posed by "the ordinary moral consciousness," there are theological considerations which bear upon it. Consider, for example, the fact of sin. Robinson rightly points out that the doctrine of the universality of sin is not reached at the conclusion of an

---

78. Some of the points to be made in this paragraph were raised by J. Kemp in his review of CM, 277–79.

79. Ibid., 308.

80. Robinson, "Natural Law, Morality and the Divine Will," 24.

81. Robinson, CM, 197.

82. Ibid., 255.

empirical enquiry into human vice and virtue. Rather, it is an insight of faith: "by faith we know what we are or would be without faith, all equally sinners, falling short of the glory of God. By faith we know what our purely natural 'virtue' is or would be, totally corrupted by pride, self-will, and selfishness. By faith also we know what faith itself is, that it is the gift of God lest any man should boast."[83]

God's revelation in Christ convicts us of having asserted "our human lordship over the human world," with the result that we are "at loggerheads with God."[84] We recall that Robinson does not subscribe to the doctrine of total moral corruption, but follows his teacher, John Baillie, in holding that a totally morally corrupt person, being unable to do other than evil, would not be able to sin, given that sin consists in voluntary rebellion against the good.[85] My way of construing "total" in "total depravity" is to say that it is extensive rather than intensive. That is to say, sin infects what we do and think across the board (mixed motives in ethical choices come to mind), but nothing that we do is wholly bad. In Robinson's words, "natural morality suffers from an all-pervading defect, its sinfulness."[86] The question thus arises, What are the epistemological consequences of sin *vis à vis* that "ordinary moral consciousness" to which Robinson so frequently appeals? To phrase the question more technically, what are the noetic effects of sin, and how might the question be determined? I should have welcomed further illumination at this point.

A related question concerns Robinson's commitment to the Kantian dictum, "I ought implies I can." In *The Claim of Morality*, his significant work on moral philosophy, Robinson says that "If anything is certain in ethics it is that 'I ought' does imply 'I can.'"[87] Elsewhere he remarks that Kant's dictum "has frequently been used, to limit what ought to be done and not as a guide to what can be done."[88] Now when Christian ethics claims the territory of general ethics, as Robinson says that it does, we find that "the 'I ought' of natural morality and obligation is not replaced . . . but is overshadowed by the 'Thou shalt' of the divine imperative."[89] But this would seem to entail a significant transformation of the Kantian

---

83. Robinson, "The Universality of Sin," 453.
84. Robinson, CC, 67.
85. See Robinson, FD, 28; cf. ibid., 142, GCE, 280.
86. Robinson, GCE, 100.
87. Robinson, CM, 131.
88. Robinson, CC, 52.
89. Ibid., 76.

"I ought therefore I can" into the Pauline "I ought but I cannot—who will help me?"[90]

All of this presupposes the truth of Robinson's affirmation that "The Christian religion is concerned from beginning to end with a personal encounter between God and man . . . "[91] Here, as we saw, he is indebted to Farmer, but also to Buber and to John Baillie. In the course of his discussion of "The logic of religious language" Robinson insists against any who would abstract from the real-life situation in which language is used, that "Language appears, and linguistic analysis takes place, within a social context."[92] This seems unexceptionable in so far as humans are concerned. But can we so easily speak of encountering God, or being encountered by him? This question was much debated in Robinson's day—not least by his fellow Scot, Ronald Hepburn in his book *Christianity and Paradox* (1957). I have not found a critique of Hepburn in Robinson's writings, though there may be one. But I do think that encounter language requires to be distinguished from inherently problematic theistic *arguments* from religious experience. It is more of the nature of testimony, of witness.[93]

That Robinson would agree with this is suggested by his observations on the familiar, and problematic, distinction between "belief in" and "belief that," with Christianity being deemed to be predominantly concerned with the former. H. D. Lewis was not without justification in noting that Robinson tended in this unfortunate direction in *Christ and Conscience* (1953),[94] but by 1961 we find him declaring that

> while we may not be able to prove the existence of God by rational argument we may none the less *contradict* the Christian faith on rational grounds, so that if faith in God may not *presuppose* belief that God exists it must *include* it, faith *in* God must be in, through and beyond many beliefs about Him. Certainly these beliefs cannot really stand apart from, and independently of, faith in God, but equally that faith apart from them would be devoid of content; and when both sides of this situation are clearly seen an alternative to the rigid separation of faith and truth appears on the horizon, what might be called the logic

---

90. See Romans 7:19.
91. Robinson, CC, 76.
92. Robinson, "The Logic of Religious Language," 14.
93. See further Sell, *Confessing and Commending the Faith*, 342–44.
94. See his review in *Journal of Theological Studies*, NS 9 (1958) 199–201.

of encounter, the logic of truth which is dialogical and not just monological.[95]

With this the balance is restored.

From many other points of interest in Robinson's work—among them his important distinction between hearing Scripture as a narrative as it were external to ourselves and hearing it clamantly when, by the Holy Spirit, its import comes home urgently to *us*[96]—I select his discussion of collective responsibility, for this has a certain topical interest at the time of writing. In March 2007 many in Britain will mark the two hundredth anniversary of the Slave Trade Abolition Bill. In this connection some have been calling for the Prime Minister, Tony Blair, to apologize to the descendants of African slaves who were so cruelly treated. Some popular pundits have gone so far as to suggest that we today are personally guilty because of what happened two hundred years ago (though I have not noticed that the same pundits are sufficiently consistent as to endorse the doctrine of imputed guilt flowing down from Adam—assuming that they have heard of it).[97] In a formal statement Blair has expressed sorrow and regret at what happened, but he stopped short of apologizing. Some construed this as a device, in an increasingly litigious society, for forestalling possible expensive claims for reparation on the part of the aggrieved. I hope, however, that Blair stopped short of apologizing because his advisers instructed him carefully on the ethics—and possibly even on the theology—of the matter. The philosopher, H. D. Lewis, blended ethical and theological remarks on the question in the period of Barthian ascendency, and took Robinson, among others, to task for their sympathy with the idea of collective responsibility.

Writing in the aftermath of the Second World War, Lewis was convinced that the doctrine of inevitable and universal sinfulness, so enthusiastically embraced by some theologians of the Word, was disastrous in that it cut off moral responsibility at the root: "there can be no more certain deflation of the sense of individual value and the dignity of personal life than the abrogation of individual responsibility in the properly moral sense. To weaken the sense of individual worth in this particular way is

---

95. Robinson, "Faith and Truth," 155.
96. See Robinson, CC, ch. 8.
97. I have reflected on collective responsibility in connection with the need of the reconciliation of memories between fractured parts of the one church, and also in regard to liturgical matters—especially prayers of confession. See Sell, *Aspects of Christian Integrity*, 65–68.

very plainly to play into the hands of irresponsible totalitarian régimes."[98] In particular, Lewis argues that the doctrine of collective responsibility and the concomitant idea of universal sin undermine the notion of individual guilt, thereby removing responsibility from individuals, who can be morally responsible only for their own thoughts and acts, and guilty only of sinful ones.[99]

That Robinson sees the point of the challenge is clear. He grants "the difficulty of holding together in the matter of sin, universality and individual responsibility; and again and again theology has failed by dwelling upon one side to the extent of doing violence to the other."[100] He sees that "If the universality of sin is stressed then man's responsibility for it seems inevitably to be called in question; while if an attempt is made to safeguard human responsibility the result is to cast some measure of suspicion upon the contention that sin is a genuinely universal feature of man's earthly life."[101] He then proceeds to explain that "The ground of our belief in the universality of sin is the revelation of God in Jesus Christ His Son, and our response and obedience to it. It is by faith that we know that all men are sinners."[102] No extenuating circumstances brought to bear in particular cases of wrongdoing can annul the truth that all have sinned.[103] Furthermore, human beings collectively "constantly accept, affirm, and acquiesce in the one world as a human enterprise . . . ,"[104] but from this it does not follow that "human responsibility for sin is denied or diminished."[105] On the contrary, people are "responsible for that which they unreservedly accept and affirm and for that in which they wholeheartedly acquiesce."[106]

Robinson thus wishes to affirm both a general collective human-social solidarity whilst at the same time agreeing with Lewis that individual responsibility "can never be transferred from one person to another, and that for every individual action it is always and only the actor himself who is morally answerable."[107] We might perhaps say that the Christian answer

---

98. Lewis, *Morals and the New Theology*, 108.
99. See ibid. 68–69; Lewis, *Morals and Revelation*, ch. 5.
100. Robinson, FD, 113.
101. Ibid., 128.
102. Ibid., 130.
103. Ibid., 132.
104. Ibid., 139.
105. Ibid., 140.
106. Ibid.
107. Robinson, CC, 27.

to the question, "Am I my brother's keeper?" is a resounding "Yes"; but from this it does not follow that I am objectively morally responsible for the wicked—or the good—things my brother does. The companion fact that the Christian answer to the question, "Have all sinned?" is equally in the affirmative should temper any adverse judgment of our brother with at least a modicum of humility and compassion.

I am well aware that my brevity has not done full justice to this tantalizing issue, but enough has been said, I think to show that in addressing this question Robinson stepped onto an ethico-theological hornet's nest of considerable importance.

III

The title of this chapter was suggested by Mrs. Robinson's reply to my letter of condolence on the death of her husband. She wrote that Norman's personal goals had been "to achieve firstly 'clarity', secondly 'precision' and finally 'comprehension'. The first two of these had certainly been achieved, but as he maintained, no-one lives long enough to achieve the third." No doubt; but there is good reason to think that Norman Robinson came nearer to comprehension than most of those who have braved the intellectually choppy waters which were his natural habitat.

BIBLIOGRAPHY

Anonymous. *Theology of Marriage and the Problem of Mixed Marriages.* Geneva: World Alliance of Reformed Churches, and Lutheran World Federation; Vatican City: Secretariat for Promoting Christian Unity, 1977.

Barth, Karl. *Credo: A Presentation of the Chief Problems of Dogmatics with Reference to the Apostles Creed.* London: Hodder & Stoughton, 1936.

Black, Matthew. "Professor Norman Hamilton Galloway Robinson." *Alumnus Journal of the University of St. Andrews* (1979) 65–66.

Brown, Stuart. *Dictionary of Twentieth-Century British Philosophers.* Bristol: Thoemmes Continuum, 2005.

Hepburn, Ronald W. *Christianity and Paradox.* London: Watts, 1958.

Kemp, J. Review of Robinson, *The Claim of Morality.* In *Philosophical Quarterly* 2 (1952) 277–79.

Lewis, H. D. *Morals and Revelation.* London: Allen & Unwin, 1951.

———. *Morals and the New Theology.* London: Gollancz, 1947.

———. Review of Robinson, *Christ and Conscience.* In *The Journal of Theological Studies* NS 9 (1958) 199–201.

Robinson, N. H. G. "Barth or Bultmann?" *Religious Studies* 14 (1978) 275–90.

———. *Christ and Conscience.* London: Nisbet, 1956.

———. "Christian Ethics." In *Preface to Christian Studies*, edited by F. G. Healey (chapter 12). London: Lutterworth, 1971.
———. *The Claim of Morality*. London: Gollancz, 1952.
———. *Faith and Duty*. London: Gollancz, 1950.
———. "Faith and Truth." *Scottish Journal of Theology* 19 (1996) 144–59.
———. "The Future of Christology." *The Expository Times* 77 (1966) I, 136–40, II, 167–70.
———. *The Groundwork of Christian Ethics*. London: Collins, 1971.
———. "Is Providence Credible Today?" *Scottish Journal of Theology* 30 (1977) 215–31.
———. "Is Theology a Normative Science?" *The Congregational Quarterly* 31 (1953) 245–52.
———. "The Logic of Religious Language." In *Talk of God*, edited by G. N. A. Vesey, ch. 1. London: Macmillan, 1969.
———. "The Logical Placing of the Name 'God.'" *Scottish Journal of Theology* 24 (1971) 127–48.
———. "Natural Law, Morality and the Divine Will." *Philosophical Quarterly* 2 (1952) 23–32.
———. "The Place of Vocation in Christian Ethics." *Theology* 53 (1950) 172–78.
———. "The Problem of Natural Theology." *Religious Studies* 8 (1972) 319–33.
———. Review of D. T. Jenkins, *The Christian Belief in God*. *Scottish Journal of Theology* 18 (1965) 91–92.
———. *Theology and the Personal*. Inaugural Lecture delivered at Rhodes University. Grahamstown: Rhodes University, 1952.
———. "Trinitarianism and Post-Barthian Theology." *The Journal of Theological Studies* 20 (1969) 186–201.
———. "The Universality of Sin." *Theology* 51 (1948) 448–54.
Sell, Alan P. F. *Aspects of Christian Integrity*. 1990. Reprinted, Eugene, OR: Wipf & Stock, 1998.
———. *Confessing and Commending the Faith: Historic Witness and Apologetic Method*. 2002. Reprinted, Eugene, OR: Wipf & Stock, 2006.
———. *The Philosophy of Religion 1875–1980*. 1988, 1998. Reprinted, Eugene, OR: Wipf & Stock, 2012.
———. *A Reformed, Evangelical, Catholic Theology: The Contribution of the World Alliance of Reformed Churches 1875–1982*. 1990. Reprinted, Eugene, OR: Wipf & Stock, 1998.
Trethowan, Illtyd. "Professor N. H. G. Robinson and Natural Theology." *Religious Studies* 9 (1973) 463–68.
Ward, Keith. Review of Robinson, *The Groundwork of Christian Ethics*. In *Religious Studies* 9 (1973) 108–10.
Wittgenstein, Ludwig. *Philosophical Investigations*. 2nd ed. Oxford: Blackwell, 1958.

6

Geoffrey Nuttall in Conversation

AFTER SOME YEARS OF friendship with the late Geoffrey Nuttall, the most distinguished British historian of Puritanism and Dissent in the twentieth century, I braced myself and said, "One of these days people will be reading obituaries in which your life and achievements are recorded. But how shall we know what you have thought about it all unless you tell us?" Happily, he warmed to the idea of reflecting upon his pilgrimage, and a series of chronologically-ordered two-hour conversations took place. Since the questions I posed may readily be inferred from the answers given, I have not interrupted the flow of Geoffrey's thoughts with my interjections. Between our meetings Geoffrey would refresh his memory from his diary, and so involved in the process did he become that on more than one occasion our conversational sessions were followed by letters, received by me the following day, which contained further information on the points we had covered, some of it spilling onto the outside of the envelope flap. What follows are Geoffrey's thoughts and reminiscences in his own words, supplemented by quotations from some of the letters I received. Geoffrey spoke and wrote in the knowledge that future publication was envisaged, and he was more than willing to share his thoughts. There is thus no breach of confidence in what follows. I have supplied the footnotes and the *Postscript*.

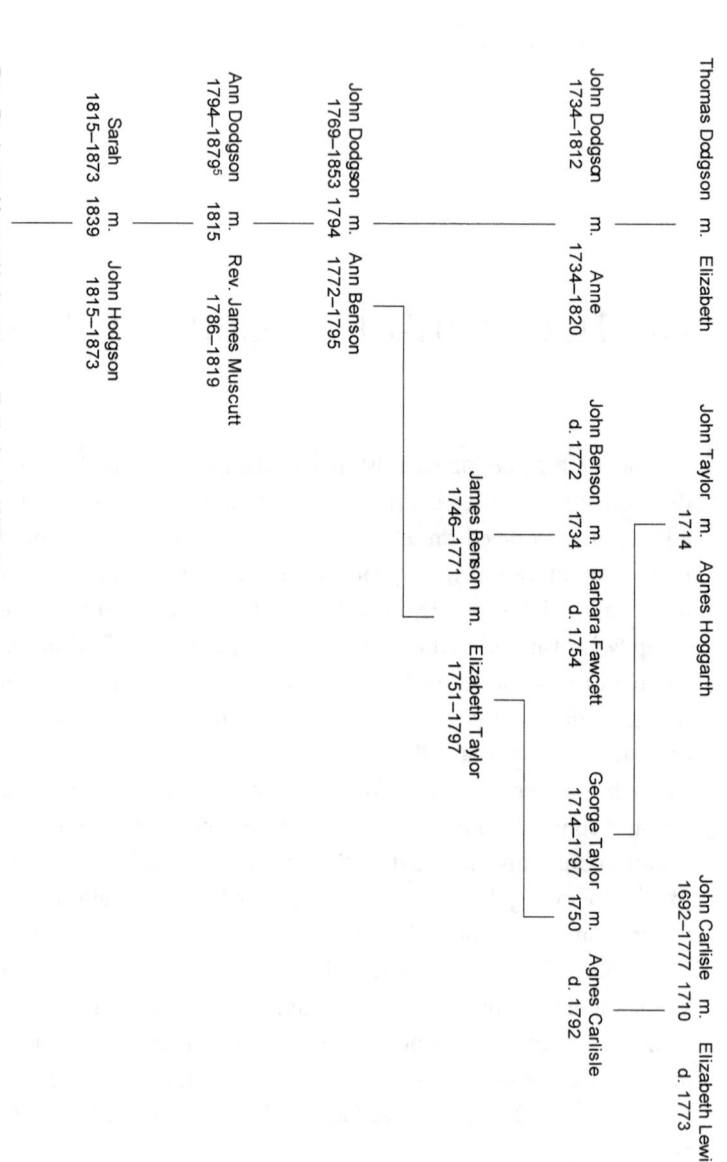

1. This year of death appears on two of Geoffrey's handwritten family trees. However, it does not accord with his reference to Ann as "living securely at Cockermouth all her ninety-six years." See *The Puritan Spirit*, 14.

Geoffrey Nuttall in Conversation

Family, Childhood, and Schooldays

I was born at Colwyn Bay on the 8th of November 1911. I have never thought of myself as a Welshman, but I can read and speak the language, and I have always been interested in Welsh Dissent and Nonconformity. I have written on Walter Cradock, Vavasor Powell, and Morgan Llwyd,[2] and also on Howel Harris.[3] I was gratified when the University of Wales conferred its Honorary DD upon me.[4]

You will be interested in the Sedbergh branch of my family on the previous page.[5]

As you can see, the name "Muscutt" appears as the second name of my maternal grandfather, the Reverend Dr. James Muscutt Hodgson, whose grandfather was James Muscutt.[6] Grandfather Hodgson became a Professor at Lancashire Independent College, and then Principal of the Scottish Congregational College.[7]

2. *The Welsh Saints.*
3. *Howel Harris.*
4. In 1969.
5. I was minister there and at Dent from 1959 to 1964.
6. For Muscutt (1786–1819) see E. M., Obituary, 410; Anon., Information, 277. Trained at Hackney College, he supplied at Darlington before 1811, in which year he went to Ravenstonedale, where he was ordained on 12 June. He left for Cockermouth in 1815, and remained there until his death on 7 August 1719. He was energetic in preaching in surrounding villages but "unhappily the domestic circle did not always afford him those kind and necessary attentions, which are of so much importance to the comfort of the ministerial office" (Anon., Information, 277). Nevertheless, "fervent piety, prudent zeal, and Christian disinterestedness, were happily blended and conspicuously displayed through the whole of his life." (E. M.410).
7. For Hodgson see *The Congregational Year Book* (hereinafter CYB), 1924, 97; Mander and Sell, *Dictionary of Nineteenth-Century British Philosophers*; Sell, *Philosophy, Dissent and* Nonconformity, 197–99 and *passim*; Kaye, *For the Work of Ministry*. He was born at Cockermouth, graduated MA of Glasgow (1862) and later became DD (Glasgow, 1888) and DSc (Edinburgh, 1882). He trained for the ministry at Lancashire Independent College (1862–66) under the Principalship of Henry Rogers. Following a pastorate at Uttoxeter (1866–75), he taught at his *alma mater* from 1875–94, when he became Principal in Edinburgh (1894–1916). For Henry Rogers (1806–1877) see CYB (1878) 347–48; *Dictionary of Nineteenth-Century Philosophers*; ODNB; Dale, Memoir of Rogers prefixed to the 8th edition of the latter's *The Superhuman Origin of the Bible*; Sell, *Dissenting Thought and the Life of the* Churches, chs. 17, 18; idem, *Philosophy, Dissent and Nonconformity*; Kaye, *For the Work of Ministry*.

The Theological Education of the Ministry

The minister at Newlands, Lincoln, of my great-grand-parents, was Caleb Scott,[8] who became Principal of L.I.C.[9] They kept up with him, and my grandmother went from Salisbury to stay at the College, where she met J. M. Hodgson, who was on the staff (after a pastorate at Uttoxeter—where perhaps you will take me one day). They were engaged on his 27th birthday, 18.viii.1878, and were married on 6.viii.1879 (a date inscribed, with their initials, in their serviette rings) at Fisherton St. Church in Salisbury—the first wedding in the new church (built in part through the munificence of my g.g.f., to whom there was a mural inscription beside the pulpit) replacing the chapel in Endless St., where my g.g.f. was minister after leaving Newark. They spent their honeymoon at Rosthwaite, which is why this name is (still!) on the gatepost of their home, 1 Demesne Road, near the College.[10]

This is how I come into the family tree (see below).

---

8. For Scott (1831–1919) see CYB, 1920, 112–13; Thompson, *Lancashire Independent College*; Kaye, *For the Work of Ministry*. He was educated at Silcoates School, trained for the ministry at Airedale College where his father Walter Scott (1779–1858) was Principal; served at Newland, Lincoln (1854–65), and then became Tutor (1865–9) and President (1869–1902) of Lancashire Independent College. He was Chairman of the Congregational Union of England and Wales in 1902. "The centre of all his thought was the Fatherhood of God," wrote R[obert] M[ackintosh], CYB, 1920, 113. A BA, LLB of London University, he became Hon. DD of St. Andrews in 1890. For Walter Scott see Kaye, *For the Work of Ministry*; Kenneth W. Wadsworth, *Yorkshire United Independent College*.

9. Lancashire Independent College, in Whalley Range, Manchester.

10. Letter of 1 January 1982.

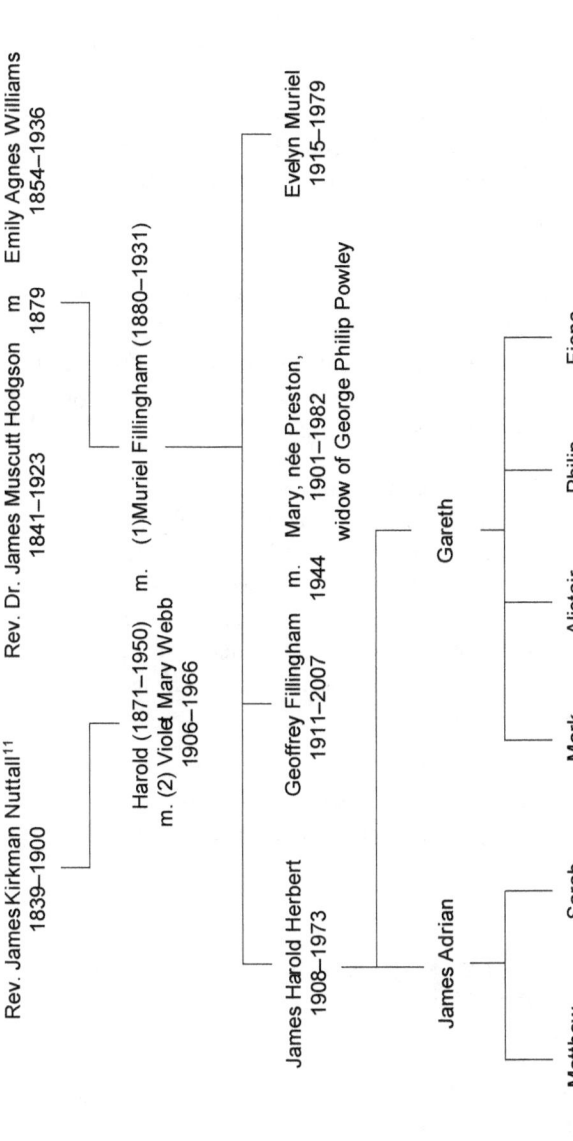

11. For J. K. Nuttall (1839–1900) see CYB, 1901, 198–99. He was born at Tottington near Bury on 1 December 1839, and trained at Rotherham Academy under the Principalship of F. J. Falding. He served at Bowling Green, Bradford (1865–74), where he was ordained on 22 February 1868; Fawcett Street, Sunderland (1874–84); Grange, Sunderland (1884–91); and Great George Street, Liverpool (1891–1908). For Frederick John Falding (1818–1892) see CYB, 1894, 191–93; Wadsworth, *Yorkshire United Independent College*; Kaye, *For the Work of Ministry*; Sell, *Philosophy, Dissent and Nonconformity*. He was an alumnus of Rotherham, and a Dr. Williams Scholar at Glasgow University, of which he became MA, DD. In 1888, on the union of Rotherham with Airedale College, he became Principal of Yorkshire United Independent College, Bradford, where he remained until his death.

The Theological Education of the Ministry

Grandfather Hodgson died when I was twelve. I remember him as a sweet and loving gentleman. His wife was quite different. She was the daughter of Charles Williams, maltster, of Salisbury, and when she died A. J. Grieve[12] recalled her as being "upright, downright and forthright." People who know me for my direct way of speech sometimes think that I got the idea of "truthing it in love" from the Quakers. Actually it came from Grandmother Hodgson. Her grandfather was the Rev. Charles Williams.[13] He was involved with the Religious Tract Society and wrote a number of books. He married a Smeeton—the Smeetons were a prominent Leicestershire-Northamptonshire Nonconformist family, and it is from the Smeetons, rather than from the Williamses that I inherited my strong Nonconformist genes.[14]

Three of my grandparents were lifelong teetotallers—J. M. Hodgson a vehement one; his wife, the maltster's daughter became one. At Cockermouth Congregational church in the 1850s Great-grandfather John Hodgson refused to become a deacon unless alcoholic wine was removed from the Lord's table; so they removed it. My parents, too, were teetotallers, and I was never anything other than a teetotaller.

> My father was MA, MD of Edinburgh, and being the son of a Congreg. minister was sometimes to be found in the Hodgsons' home, 50 Craigmillar Park. In 1904 he went back to it when on a visit to Edin., and on 4.iii.1905 became engaged to their daughter, whom he married on 30.vi.1906 at Augustine church. He was a G.P. in Colwyn Bay, which is why the name of the house in Conway Road, earlier (and now again), Erskine House, where I grew up, was Craigmillar.[15]
>
> Among Ray's books I verified from Tissington Tatlow's *Story of the S.C.M.* (1933), p. 903, that my father was Inter-collegiate Sec. in Edinburgh 1897–98, and from Lovett's *History of the*

---

12. For Grieve (1874–1952) see CYB, 1953, 508–9; Surman [son-in-law], *Alexander James Grieve*; Taylor and Binfield, *Who They Were* (hereinafter WTW). Grieve was President of Lancashire Independent College from 1922–1943.

13. For Williams (1796–1866) see CYB, 1867, 326–27; ODNB. Following pastorates at Newark (1823–33) and Endless Street, Salisbury (1833–35), he became editor of the Religious Tract Society (1835–47) and a prolific author. He retired to Sibbertoft, Northamptonshire, where he gathered a congregation in his house.

14. For references to the Smeetons see Nuttall, *The Puritan Spirit*, 255, 267.

15. Letter of 1 January 1982.

LMS (1899), ii.740, that my grandmother's sister Florence arrived in India in 1895![16]

My father, a lapsed Freemason, specialized latterly in eyes and x-rays. At the time he had the only x-ray equipment our side of Chester. The large house accommodated not only a surgery and waiting room, but an x-ray room and a developing room. From the age of six I felt that I must be a minister. One day my father asked me if I was going to be an engine driver. I replied, "I've told you before that I'm going to be a minister, so please don't trouble me any more!"

My mother was a great influence on me. She was an MA of Edinburgh. She taught us to play the piano, and we had a pianola too. Sadly, she died aged 50, when I was nineteen and just about to sit for Mods. In 1937, at the age of 66, my father married Vi, a woman exactly half his age. She was the daughter of a manufacturer of notepaper in Hyde, Cheshire. She had trained at St. Thomas's Hospital, London, and was a State Registered Nurse, but she did not practise. She was a faithful Christian, raised an Anglican but became a Congregationalist. She died of cancer in Worthing in 1966.

My brother went to Clifton College and became a chartered accountant with Pilkingtons in St. Helens. For a time he was church secretary at Eccleston Congregational church, but then he turned into a non-churchgoing man of the world. He drowned in the Mediterranean—swimming too soon after a meal—and was cremated in Falmouth.

My sister Evelyn and I were great friends in childhood. I first went to church while we were on holiday at Church Stretton. My Mother thought that if I misbehaved so far away from home the family would not be disgraced. On a later visit I, as a sensitive child, was pleased to sing, "Jesus the children are calling" as a solo—without crying. At home I attended St. John's Methodist Church, Colwyn Bay, where my father was a circuit steward. We went there because the Congregational minister at Colwyn Bay was too fundamentalist. Evelyn and I played in the grounds—and in the pulpit—of the church. My mother never became a member there. When I was eleven, she took Evelyn and me for another holiday to Church Stretton. At one point I held forth for forty minutes on the Reformation. Mother said, "Write it down." So I did, and that was my first church history essay. Evelyn went to Wentworth College, Bournemouth. She was much

---

16. Letter of 14 March 1983. The books were those of Raymond Arnold. Florence Williams was prominent in the establishment of the Women's Christian College in Madras. She served in India from 1895 to 1915. See Goodall, *A History of the London Missionary Society*, 76, 622.

involved in the Girl Guide Movement, and was in charge of the Guiders Training Centre at Bentley, near Farnham, and then at Larne, Northern Ireland. She was not a teetotaller. She liked horses and became an Anglican for social and geographical reasons. When our mother died she devoted six years to the care of our father, and when the young stepmother came along her nose was rather put out of joint. Through circumstances she had not had many opportunities to meet people of her own age, and she never married. She died of a tumour in the skull in Liverpool in 1977, and was buried in the Parish churchyard at Henllan, near Denbigh. Mary and I kept in touch with her until she died.

> While eating my breakfast on this New Year's morning, I have been reading my piece of ancestor worship in B[aptist] Q[uarterly] xxviii (1979), 184-90.[17] I must say I think it is rather charming! even if one has to keep a clear head to be sure who is exactly who. You will probably think it a bit macabre if I tell you it was drafted in the train going to, and returning from, Liverpool and the hospital where my sister had just died: actually, I found the activity sustaining—I suppose it put bereavement in a larger context, and gave me a sense of life's continuance.[18]
>
> Two 'influences' from those early days did not surface in utterance:-
>
> 1. 'Lala' my nurse from birth to the age of six, Mary Hayes of Workington, who became on marriage Mary Mesney and called one of her sons Geoffrey after me, and is still alive, aged 90, living with her married daughter at Chatteris. We lost touch after she left me till 1973, when I was 61 (i.e. for 55 years!), but have been in loving and frequent communication since then, and I saw her last in Leamington in July. She remembers my Grandmother Nuttall (d. 1916) well, as well as my other Grandmother and *her* Mother d. 1919, and of course both my parents—it is rather remarkable since I am now 70!
>
> 2. 'Lew', i.e. Annie Edith Lewis, a native of Leominster, who was in the Post Office at Colwyn Bay, and was devoted to me (and Evelyn), taking us our for a walk *every* Sunday afternoon, and writing to me *every* week while I was away at school. She is not living now.
>
> Both were strong characters and firm Christians.[19]

17. The Smeetons and Fillinghams are among those discussed in this article.
18. Letter of 1 January 1982.
19. Letter of 24 September 1982.

When I was twelve my mother, Evelyn and I began to attend Rhos-on-Sea Congregational church, where the minister was Arthur A. Bourne.[20] He could *pray*. He was a confirming rather than an inspiring influence. He gave me a copy of Augustine's *Confessions*. I never went to Sunday School, but learned religion from Mother on Sundays and from hymns around the piano. An early favourite of mine was "O Jesus, I have promised." One day at church a lady gave me a card bearing the words of the hymn, "Still with Thee, O my God," and said she would give me 6d if I learned it. So I did. No ministers really influenced me when I was growing up, though I did hear Sangster when he was in the Conway Circuit;[21] and during my teens I heard R. F. Horton[22] preach at Lyndhurst Road. I read his autobiography whilst at school, and thought him a model minister, honest and earnest. I became a church member at Rhos when I was sixteen.

At the age of nine I was sent to Baswich House School, Weeping Cross, near Stafford. I hated leaving home. My uncle, George Francis Atterbury Osborn, was Headmaster.[23] He was a mathematician, but he taught me Greek, and we used to read *Medea* together. I wanted to go to Cambridge University, where my uncle had been a student, but it turned out otherwise. I continued with piano lessons at Baswich House and passed the Lower Division examination. One day one of the teachers, a Roman Catholic, took me into a Roman Catholic church on the way to Stafford,

---

20. For Arthur Alfred Bourne (1877–1954) see CYB, 1956, 509–10. He began as a private school teacher in London, and then became lay pastor at Radlett, where he completed the Congregational Union Examinations. He then served at New College Chapel, London, and Hunstanton, arriving in Rhos in 1925. During his time there new premises were built. Ministries in Harpenden and Matlock followed. "Arthur Bourne was a man whose library and whose conversation reflected the culture which he possessed." Ibid., 510.

21. For Sangster (1900–1960), subsequently minister at Westminster Central Hall, see Vickers, *A Dictionary of Methodism in Britain and Ireland*.

22. For Robert Forman Horton (1855–1934) see ODNB; WTW; Horton, *An Autobiography*; Peel and J. Marriott, *Robert Forman Horton*.

23. It would therefore seem that Geoffrey enrolled at the school in the year in which the distinguished scientist, Nevill Francis Mott (1905–1996), for whom see ODNB, left it. According to Bourne and Donaldson in *The Victoria County History of Staffordshire*, V, 4, Baswich House had been built by Thomas Salt (d. 1871) [a relative of the antiquarian, William Salt after whom the Willam Salt Library, Stafford, is named]. "It is an irregularly planned mansion of red brick with oriel windows of wood and many small gables, and is a good building of its kind. A single-story picture gallery and a billiard room were added by Thomas's son, Thomas (d. 1904). The property was in use as a preparatory school before the Second World War. In 1952 it was acquired by the Staffordshire County Council as a Police Motor Training Centre."

and splashed me with holy water—for luck! My health was never robust. I was easily upset gastrically. At Baswich House I had a rest day every week, which I spent in bed. To date I have been in hospital on seven occasions.

From Baswich House I went on to the Quaker foundation, Bootham School, York.[24] With me I took Albert Goodrich's *A Primer of Congregationalism*. Goodrich himself had given this book to my mother when she was fourteen, and she gave it to me when I was thirteen.[25] I won a scholarship to Bootham, and also the entrance prize, but because I was not a Friend I could not have money, so I received books instead. I hated Bootham, despite the fact that there was no fagging or flogging there. My brother, who had gone to Clifton College, said that I wouldn't have lasted a week there. The Headmaster was Arthur Rowntree, but the teacher who influenced me most was A. Neave Brayshaw. Apart from my family, I was more influenced by Brayshaw and, later by Selbie,[26] than by anyone else. Once a fortnight Brayshaw took boys on visits to old churches, and at Easter-time he organized parties to Normandy. Kenneth Harrison was on one such continental trip. He was the son of the librarian of York Minster. A biochemist, he became a Fellow of King's College, Cambridge, then an alcoholic, and then disappeared from view. William Bewley of the Jacobs Biscuits dynasty was also a contemporary of mine at Bootham.

Until Bootham I had never been to a Quaker meeting, but rather took to it while I was there. I also became a pacifist—as much from reading Plato's *Crito* as from reading the Bible. There was a good deal of pacifist propaganda at Bootham. Pacifism taught me not to retaliate when persecuted at school (and I suppose I could seem "pious" and priggish), but I had not yet learned to be forgiving, loving and reconciling—Mary, much later, softened me and taught me to look for the good in people. Bootham taught me not to trust anyone. I spent as much time as I could in the

---

24. For Bootham School during this period see F. E. Pollard, *Bootham School York 1823–1933*.

25. Did this staunch Congregationalist mother think that Goodrich's small volume would protect her son from undue Friendly persuasion? For Goodrich (1840–1919) see CYB, 1920, 97–98; McNaughton, *The Scottish Congregational Ministry* (though read Hackney for Hoxton). Trained at Hackney College, he served at Braintree (1865–76), Elgin Place, Glasgow (1876–90); and Chorlton Road, Manchester (1890–1912). He was Chairman of the Congregational Union of Scotland in 1885 and of England and Wales in 1904.

26. For William Boothby Selbie (1862–1944), the first student and the second Principal of Mansfield College, Oxford (1909–32) see CYB, 1945, 441; ODNB; WTW; Kaye, *Mansfield College*. For Geoffrey's memoir of him see, *The Puritan Spirit*, ch. 31, sec. 1.

library—and, indeed, was the librarian for a period. The academic bias at Bootham was scientific, not classical. I had five Greek teachers in three years! For the last two years I had only six hours of teaching a week, and this reinforced my status as an autodidact. I matriculated two years before anybody else—very bad psychology!—at fourteen I came top of the matriculating class with distinctions in English, Latin and Greek. At sixteen I went to Oxford for a year's coaching by E. A. Upcott who, as Selbie later recounted, "gnashed his teeth" at the way I had been taught at Bootham— or, rather, not taught.

Towards the end of my schooldays my father went to see Selbie for advice as to where I should go to train for the ministry. Selbie suggested Oxford for Mods and Greats (not history), and then on to Mansfield for ministerial training. Then I had an interview with Selbie. He quizzed me about my dreams.[27] Then he asked, "Are you nervous of people?" to which I replied, "Well, I don't seem to be nervous with you." I sat the Mansfield entrance exam before going to Balliol College. It included a paper on "The history of Independency."

BALLIOL AND MANSFIELD

During my first year in Oxford I lodged with Mrs. Buchanan Gray, the widow of George Buchanan Gray, who had taught Old Testament at Mansfield.[28] His wife was a cousin of Grandmother Hodgson. When she became ill, I went to live with the Selbies for three weeks.

I had a high opinion of A. D. Lindsay, Master of Balliol.[29] I liked his book, *The Essentials of Democracy,* for its pat on the back for church meetings. I was not at all impressed by the Fellows of Balliol. The only one from whom I derived any benefit was C. G. Stone, tutor in Roman History, who wrote *The Social Contract of the Universe.* He had a terrible stammer. As for his subject, I had no interest in it at all, so I wrote a paper on the Cluniac order during Roman History lectures. I enjoyed Plato and Aristotle, heard Gilbert Murray[30] on Agamemnon, and H. A. Joachim on what became his book, *Logical Studies.*[31] Joachim's son, Joseph, was one of my two great

27. Selbie was by no means alone in being interested in the "new psychology" of those days.

28. For Gray (1865–1922) see CYB, 1923, 107; ODNB; WTW.

29. For Lindsay (1879–1952), philosopher and educationalist, see ODNB.

30. For Murray (1866–1957), classicist, see ODNB.

31. For Joachim (1868–1938), philosopher, see ODNB; Brown, *Dictionary of Twentieth-Century British Philosophy.*

friends at Balliol; the other was Richard Southern.[32] Closest of all, though, was Roy Niblett, who came to do a BLitt. at St. Edmund Hall, and whose roots were in Nonconformity. He held prestigious posts in education, and became Director of the London University Institute of Education.[33] I did not join societies, or go much to the Oxford Union debates, but I did go for walks with friends, and went to exhibitions at the Victoria and Albert Museum and the National Gallery. I was Student Librarian of the College. Since I was busy with scholarly pursuits other than those on the Mods and Greats syllabi, I got a third for both.[34]

Selbie had retired from Mansfield by the time I arrived there, but I was in regular contact with him. I also knew J. Vernon Bartlet, now retired from Mansfield's Chair of Church History, and I learned much from him.[35] Going to Mansfield was like a cold douche after Balliol. I lodged in homes and was friendly with the children—more so than with my somewhat lightweight, never-set-the-Thames-on-fire Mansfield contemporaries. I found the scholar to be a relatively lonely person at Mansfield. I liked the Bursar, J. Harrison Milnes,[36] and my best student friends were Antony Spalding and Dafydd ap Thomas, who became Professor of Hebrew at Bangor. There was not much devotional life in the College, though Selbie's successor, Nathaniel Micklem, *read* morning prayers.[37] This stuck in the gullet of a number of students, so they drew up a "Grand Remonstrance" protesting that they had no wish to be trained as priests. Before agreeing to sign the document, I rewrote it. When it was presented to Micklem he recognized my style and was wary of me ever afterwards. I avoided his lectures, and got permission to read Aquinas's *Summa Contra Gentiles* in the original *in lieu* of attendance. I was enrolled for the BD, which involved examinations and a thesis. I protested to Micklem about having to answer a question on W. P. Paterson's book, *The Rule of Faith*. But I passed the exam and then went for a three-week walking holiday with Spalding in

---

32. For Southern (1912–2001), historian, see ODNB.

33. For Niblett (1906–2005) see WTW; *Who Was Who* (hereinafter WWW) 2002–5; obituary in *The Guardian* (11 May 2005).

34. Evidently the Oxford degree regulations, unlike those of some other universities, did not contain a clause requiring the possession of a first or an upper second honours degree by those wishing to proceed to further and higher degrees.

35. For Bartlet (1863–1940) see CYB, 1941, 392–93; ODNB; WTW; Kaye *Mansfield College*.

36. For Milnes (1876–1964) see CYB, 1964–65, 444–45.

37. For Micklem (1888–1976) see CYB, 1977, 266; ODNB; WTW; Micklem, *The Box and the Puppets*; Kaye, *Mansfield College*.

Scotland. After one more year at Mansfield I submitted my BD thesis on "Faith and Reason in the Works of Bishop Peacock." I received very little guidance, though I did pay one visit to C. C. J. Webb.[38] The examiners were Claude Jenkins[39] and H. L. Goudge.[40] The thesis was never published, but it formed the basis of an article in the *Transactions of the Congregational Historical Society*: "Bishop Peacock and the Lollards."[41] I learned much from Wheeler Robinson, who gave better care and attention to my written work than any other tutor. I discussed my ideas for a book on the Holy Spirit and the Puritans with him.

I liked T. W. Manson[42] and C. J. Cadoux,[43] but felt that Cadoux's lectures were uninspiring. I greatly appreciated his book, *Catholicism and Christianity*—especially the conclusion. Micklem and Cadoux the pacifist, evangelical modernist, and ardent traditional Congregationalist, were at odds on many things, and I felt that I was harmed by my friendships with Cadoux and Selbie—and also with Albert Peel, another Congregational historian of some intransigence and considerable wit.[44] All of these had reservations about the way in which some seemed to be throwing overboard precious aspects of our heritage in the interests of liturgical reform and ecumenism; and those deemed guilty did not like them for it. I became Peel's protégé at *The Congregational Quarterly*, and this increased my feeling that I was a marked man. He wanted me to take over the editorship of the *Quarterly* but I declined and continued as reviews editor. I blame Howard Stanley for the death of the *Quarterly*. It had become a well-respected journal, but he withdrew support from it and it died.[45]

---

38. For Webb (1865-1954), Nolloth Chair of Philosophy of Religion, see ODNB; Ross, "Clement Charles Julian Webb"; Patrick, *Idealism and Orthodoxy at Oxford*; Sell, *Philosophical Idealism*.

39. For Jenkins (1877-1959), historian and clergyman, see ODNB.

40. For Goudge (1866-1939), see WWW 1929-40.

41. See "Bishop Peacock and the Lollard Movement," reprinted in Nuttall, *The Puritan Spirit*, ch. 4.

42. For Manson (1893-1958), biblical scholar, see ODNB; McKim, *Dictionary of Major Biblical Interpreters*; and ch. 8 below.

43. For Cadoux (1883-1947) see CYB, 1948, 489-90; ODNB; WTW; Kaye, *C. J. Cadoux*; Kaye, *Mansfield College*.

44. For Peel (1887-1949) see CYB, 1950, 523-24; ODNB; WTW; Argent, "Albert Peel: The Restless Labourer."

45. For Stanley (1901-1975) see *Yearbook of the United Reformed Church* (hereinafter URCYB), 1977, 271-72; WTW.

The Theological Education of the Ministry

At the beginning of my Mansfield course I conducted my first service—at Marston. My text was the verse on my nursery mantelpiece, "Lo, I am with you alway, even to the end of the world." I spoke on the reality, the comfort, and the challenge of the divine presence. At the climax of my sermon the woodwork of the reading desk came away in my hand. No pastoralia was taught at Mansfield. During my time in Oxford I heard guest lectures from Albert Einstein, Bertrand Russell, William Temple, E. W. Barnes and Charles Raven. Among the books which influenced me were volume two of Troeltsch's *The Social Teachings of the Christian Churches*; Anderson Scott's *Christianity according to St. Paul*; J. Skinner's *Prophecy and Religion*; and Leyton Richards's *The Christian's Attitude to War*.[46] I also enjoyed Silvester Horne's *A Popular History of the Free Churches*. At the end of my course, on Selbie's recommendation, I went for a year to Marburg. I went on the Procter Scholarship, and I had also won the Buchanan Prize for Hebrew two years running, with help from Dafydd ap Thomas. Wheeler Robinson said my Hebrew wasn't very good, but since there were no other applicants and the money was there, I could have it. I had tea with Rudolf Otto, though he was no longer teaching. I attended lectures by Rudolf Bultmann, and met Theodore Sippell, the great scholar of Puritanism. He gave me a non-partisan view of the Puritans.[47]

WARMINSTER

Mansfield College had an association with the Congregational church at Warminster, and that is how I got an introduction to it. The church was of long-standing, though there had been a Trinitarian separation from the Presbyterian church in 1719.[48] Warminster had a population of 7,000. It had been a liberal Nonconformist malting town, but by now it had become conservative, Anglican and military. It was a self-important place. The church had 106 members and congregations of about 40 in the morning

---

46. I suspect that this is a reference to Richards, *The Christian's Alternative to War: An Examination of Christian Pacifism*.

47. Rufus Jones, the American Quaker scholar, was among others encouraged by Sippell.

48. The building in Common Close, now shorn of its tall pinnacles, in which Geoffrey ministered dates from 1840. See Stell. *Nonconformist Chapels and Meeting-Houses in South-West England*, 245. The certificate for the 1840 building was signed on 21 February 1840 and issued on 2 March 1840. That for the original building on the site was signed on 6 January 1720. See Chandler, *Wiltshire Dissenters' Meeting House Certificates and Registrations*, nos. 228, 1547.

and 30 at night. Numbers were somewhat swollen by evacuees after the Second World War broke out.

I was ordained on 4th May 1938. Micklem gave the charge to the church, Arthur Bourne gave the charge to me. The provincial moderator was at an ordination elsewhere, so the Rev. Alfred Antrobus,[49] secretary of the Wilts and East Somerset Congregational Union, presided. The Rev. J. L. Buddell,[50] Arthur Bourne's successor at Rhos, also took part. I gave a *proper* declaration of faith and experience. Doddridge's "My gracious Lord, I own Thy right To every service I can pay," was among the hymns sung.

> I have remembered that another of the hymns we sang was one which had appealed to me as describing the work to which I was called ever since prep. school days: "We give Thee but Thine own," with the lines:
>
> To God the lost to bring,
> To teach the way of life and peace,
> It is a Christlike thing.[51]

My father and step-mother came to the service, and so did a Smeeton cousin. *The Warminster Journal* reported the event.

Out of my stipend of £250 p.a. I had to pay £75 p.a. rent for the house I lived in—the church's manse was let to a retired clergyman. The house had its own tennis court, of which young Congregationalists and Baptists made good use. I had a housekeeper who, with her husband, lived in rent free in return for looking after me. Antony Spalding, Albert Peel, and Wilton Rix[52] were among those who visited me; and once a term I went to Oxford. In 1941 Antony Spalding gave me my set of the *Dictionary of National Biography*.[53]

I had Mondays off, read on Tuesdays, and then began to prepare for Sundays.

---

49. For Antrobus (1874–1948) see CYB, 1950, 505.

50. For James Leonard Buddell (1884–1979) see URCYB, 1980, 249–50. He was at Rhos from 1935 to 1947.

51. Letter of 17 December 1982.

52. For Rix (1881–1958) see CYB, 1960, 435; WTW.

53. These volumes gave Geoffrey endless hours of amusement as he proof read the books, made marginal comments and corrections, and devised numerous lists of names under subject categories.

The Theological Education of the Ministry

> The list (I *think* made at Warminster) of "Writers who have influenced my style and thought" are (in this order, with the last name *added*): Church, Donne, Virginia Woolf, Bryce, St. Bernard, Erasmus, Bunyan.
>
> It was very good to have you here, quite apart from any of this stuff arising from our occupation during the last two hours![54]

I did not enjoy pastoral duties, but I did them faithfully. I visited the housebound once each week. Ever fearful of clericalism and professionalism in the ministry, I did not catechize my members in their homes.[55] I took the liberal line that the first thing was to get to know the people and then you would be able to pray with them when necessary; it didn't usually work. I was quite good with the uneducated. I could deal with people who had aspirations, or were educated. But if people were devoid of both aspirations and education, I was at a loss. The Vicar of Warminster would not speak to me in the street, but I had the use of the library at St. Boniface [Anglican] Missionary College. I often used to wonder whether I would ever marry, even though I seemed to be regarded as an eligible bachelor. Some thought that I had led another up the garden path—but she was a Methodist, and she married into that fold. There had been an "understanding" with a young lady which I terminated; and a short engagement of two to three months to an Anglican in Bath with whom I got in touch through the Warminster organist. Her father objected to the relationship, so she ended it without seeing me, and subsequently married a clergyman.

I often wondered whether I would be left in Warminster all my days. It was not easy being a pacifist minister in a military town like that. I never preached pacifism, and would only pray for those who had gone to war with a good conscience. But the members knew that I was a pacifist, and they didn't like it. I gave pastoral care to some soldiers, and wrote to a number of them for some time. Captain Walker, a Scottish Congregationalist, invited me to give four lectures to his platoon, which I did. I was co-secretary of the West Wilts Refugee Service, and of the Free Church ministers' fraternal. I edited the *Mansfield College Magazine* and wrote reviews and obituaries for it.

In the summer of 1942 I visited Wells with a party of soldiers. I fell, and had persistent sciatic pain. In late October I went home to Colwyn Bay in a car provided by the Womens Voluntary Service. Eventually I was

---

54. Letter of 29 September 1982.
55. Unlike Richard Baxter, for example.

seen by Sir Henry Cohen, who diagnosed a slipped disk and advised an operation. The operation was carried out at the Radcliffe Infirmary, and it was completely successful. After a period of convalescence at home I went back to Warminster. After the break of three to four months something was broken on both sides. In April 1943 I was invited to Woodbooke,[56] and began my work there as a Fellow on 1st October. The Warminster folk gave me a parting gift of £17, with which I bought some of Erasmus's *Letters*.

Woodbrooke

At Woodbrooke I found a relatively youthful, largely pacifist, vital group embracing eleven nationalities, and I began to live again. My duties as a Fellow were to write, and to act as a student-staff go-between. I was not required to give lectures or to attend them. My honorarium was £250 per annum. During vacations I went home to Colwyn Bay. Whilst at Warminster I had begun my research for *The Holy Spirit in Puritan Faith and Experience*. I spent my first three weeks at Woodbrooke going through my notes, and then I wrote the first seven chapters at the rate of one a week. The other Fellow in 1923–33 was Isabel MacGregor Ross, a descendent of Margaret Fell. My great friend at Woodbrooke was Hugh Doncaster.[57] He had a sensitive, tender conscience, but was morally strong and not at all priggish. He married a Congregationalist—a daughter of E. R. Hughes—and she became a Friend.

It was at Woodbrooke that I met Mary.[58] She grew up in Fleetwood, and was the fifth of six children—three boys and three girls. Members of her family—ships chandlers and ironmongers—had been founders of Fleetwood Congregational Church, but she broke away on leaving for teacher training at Anstey, the specialist physical education college. Before she left, the Fleetwood minister, Leslie Artingstall,[59] had already influenced her towards pacifism. After Anstey she went to Street, Somerset,

---

56. The Quaker College in Birmingham.

57. For L. Hugh Doncaster (1914–1994) see the obituary by Milligan and Nuttall, 52.

58. For an appreciation see Nicholls, "Mary Nuttall," on my copy of which Geoffrey corrected "Pawley" to "Powley," and the date of their marriage from 1945 to 1944. See also Wicken, "Mary Nuttall 1901–82."

59. For Artingstall (1885–1952) see CYB, 1953, 504. He was at Fleetwood from 1916 to 1919.

The Theological Education of the Ministry

to teach at Clark's training school. She joined the Quakers in Street, and felt that she had come home. Mary had always felt battered by words in Congregational worship, whereas I had been called to be a minister, and wanted a more Christocentric form of worship than was to be found in modern Quakerism—though the Quakers are an example to us of many Christ-like ways of behaviour and practice.

After Street, Mary went to Englefield Green, where she met George Powley. They married and went to live in Leicester, where Mary taught, and became increasingly active in the Friends Home Service Council. After a time Powley became ill, and spent some time at The Retreat in York, though he was not a Quaker. He became very withdrawn, and his life sadly ended on the railway line at Ewell, near his boyhood home. An open verdict was recorded. George and Mary had no children.

It now became difficult for Mary to continue teaching PT because the subject was so intertwined with OTCs[60] and the like. So she came to Woodbrooke the year before me. She was a warm, outgoing person, who didn't much like the idea of marrying a minister. We did not have an official engagement, but we regarded July 2nd as the day on which we made our pledges to each other. For relaxation I used to knit, but Mary would never help me with that. We enjoyed reading poetry; we read *Murder in the Cathedral*. Whilst at Woodbrooke I was a member of King's Norton Congregational church, whose minister was Ian Ogilvie.[61]

Mary was a member of Stirchley Meeting—a poor and struggling cause—and the question arose as to where we should be married. I said I wouldn't mind being married in a Friends Meeting House provided it were an old seventeenth-century one. So it was that during the summer vacation of 1944 we were married at Colthouse, near Hawkshead.[62] We were married from Isabel Ross's house at Far Sawrey—next door to Beatrix Potter's. We spent our honeymoon at the Borrowdale Hotel—this had been arranged by the Rev. J. B. Clark of Keswick,[63] one of Grandfather

---

60. Officers Training Corps.

61. Was he, perhaps, known as Ian or is this an uncharacteristic trick of memory? In CYB and McNaughton. *The Scottish Congregational Ministry 1794-1993*, 245, he is recorded as Kenneth Gowan Ogilvie. He was at King's Norton from 1944-1946.

62. The Meeting House at Colthouse was built in 1688 and registered in the following year. See Butler, *The Quaker Meeting Houses of Britain*, I, 300-302.

63. James Birkett Clark (1882-1968) served with the LMS, and then at Keswick (1931-1945). See CYB, 1969-70, 429.

Hodgson's former students. Whilst in Borrowdale we met T. W. Manson, who was staying at Rosthwaite.[64]

I was determined to submit my work for the DD as soon as possible and, in January 1945 I succeeded. Claude Jenkins was again one of my examiners; the other was Newton Flew.[65] There was a look of horror on the face of the Regius Professor, Leonard Hodgson,[66] when this young man of 34 carried off the prize. The degree of DD had been opened to Nonconformists in 1920. My Methodist examiner, R. Newton Flew,[67] had been the first to achieve it, and I was the second.

New College

On returning to Woodbrooke one day after a cycle ride with Hugh Doncaster, I found a message from Sydney Cave, Principal of New College, London,[68] inviting me to an interview to be held at Memorial Hall for the vacant position at his College. It had never occurred to me that I would ever work in London, and I didn't particularly want to go there. But as things turned out London was good to me. It gave me many opportunities of a scholarly kind, and the closeness to Dr. Williams's Library was a boon as far as my work, and my trusteeship there, was concerned. I came to be in touch with three or four canons of Westminster including Abbott and Carpenter; and with Max Warren, the missionary statesman and later sub-dean of Westminster.[69] I gave the Charles Gore Lecture in Westminster Abbey; I belonged to the London Society for Christians and Jews; and to the London Society for the Study of Religion, of which I was both

---

64. How difficult it is to escape the saints—even on honeymoon! My wife and I also spent ours in Borrowdale. We walked three miles to church in Keswick on the day after our wedding to find no fewer than four ministers—Norman Charlton, Cyril Grant, Kenneth Wadsworth and Glyn Evans and their wives—beaming at us as we came through the door.

65. For Flew (1886-1962) see DMBI; ODNB.

66. For Hodgson (1889-1969) see ODNB.

67. Flew graduated DD in 1930—the first Nonconformist to do so by examination.

68. For Cave (1883-1953) see CYB, 1954, 506-7; ODNB; WTW; Hart, *Dictionary of Historical Theology*; Bocking, "Sydney Cave (1883-1953)"; Sell, *Nonconformist Theology*.

69. For Edward Symes Abbott (1906-1983), Edward Frederick Carpenter (1910-1998), and Max Alexander Cunningham Warren (1904-1977) see ODNB.

secretary and later president. I was also the Ancient Merchant's Lecturer, and the Drew, Hibbert and F. D. Maurice Lecturer.[70]

But all of this was in the future. In April 1945 I duly met Cave and the London Moderator, Alan Green, who was also Chairman of the New College Governors.[71] I was awarded the position and my duties were to teach Church History, elementary Hebrew and Roman History. My salary was to be £650 per annum, and I would have to find my own house. After the meeting Cave took me to tea in a café, and I learned a little more about the College—it was the one College I knew nothing about. At the time of my appointment the College was still occupied by the Wrens,[72] so my first classes were held above a shop in Finchley Road. Gradually the College was restored to us, and for a time I lectured on bare boards in the Principal's house. Cave was a shy man who kept folk at a distance. Certainly the junior staff members were not regarded as colleagues. I seemed to do any pastoral work that was required. W. A. Davies was there—he was sweet but incompetent.[73] Madoc Davies taught elocution. A. J. B. Higgins came in 1946 to teach New Testament. He was a good, honest, but unimaginative scholar.[74] He was saturnine of temperament, and used to get angry with the students. His best work is *The Lord's Supper in the New Testament*. He and his wife had met in the Sunday School at Haverfordwest. He was a high church Congregationalist and on leaving New College he became an Anglican.[75]

There was an inrush of students from the forces, and some of these caused Cave considerable distress because of their intransigent conservatism, and I was saddened by this. With one exception I was not greatly troubled by them. I launched a series of preliminary talks on such topics as heaven, with a view to easing them back into the world of thought rather than action. But Cave disapproved, so the series abruptly stopped.

70. Among others, for which see Geoffrey's entry in *Who's Who*.
71. For Green (1889–1961) see CYB, 1962, 460.
72. Women's Royal Naval Service, founded in 1916.
73. For William Archibald Davies (1879–1966) see CYB, 166–67, 451–52. His entire ministry was in ministerial training, first at Mansfield (1909–1913) (though he is not indexed in Kaye, *Mansfield College*), then at New (1913–1946).
74. Trained at Lancashire Independent College, Higgins was a protégé of T. W. Manson. He later earned Manchester's rarely-awarded DD.
75. By this we should understand that Higgins was of the Church Order Group sort. Geoffrey would have regarded himself as a high church Congregationalist in the proper sense of the term, namely, that which asserts the sole Lordship of Christ in his Church, than which there is no higher churchmanship.

Trevor Davies joined the staff in 1948.[76] He was not a success. He published *Sublimation* in 1947. He was affable enough, but rather superficial. Holding Richmond Hill together was more up his street, and he went off to do that in 1951. He was not replaced. In 1953 Cyril Blackman took the position vacated by Higgins.[77] He had been teaching at Cheshunt, and I had known him at Mansfield. Loveable and absent-minded, he was a respectable second-line New Testament scholar: not so perceptive as Higgins, but a nicer person. After him came the Methodist, Francis Glasson. He had scholarship and honesty (though he could only see what he saw), and was always friendly.[78] The junior tutors were, in succession, Ronald Bocking, Roger Tomes and Roger Scopes.

Cave died of leukaemia in 1953. For such a fussy man, he met his end with great calmness. John Huxtable came in his place. I had known him at Mansfield, but we had not had much contact since.[79] During Huxtable's tenure I was the University of London's Chairman of the Board of Studies in Theology (1957–59) and Dean of the Faculty of Theology from 1960 to 1964. I had been admitted to the Board after three years of lecturing, and following the approval of my publications by about eleven scholars including Abbott, Cave, Clogg and Waterhouse.[80] But Huxtable did not have the academic standing to become a member of the Board. He was invited to attend Board meetings, but was not permitted to speak until some years had elapsed. This placed the College somewhat at a disadvantage. On the other hand Huxtable put us on the map ecclesiastically. I think he had really wanted the secretaryship of the Congregational Union but, much to the surprise, and even distress, of some,[81] Howard Stanley was appointed, and that set Huxtable's ecclesiastical statesmanship back for ten years, until he did achieve his goal in 1964. Among my King's College colleagues

---

76. For J. Trevor Davies (1907–1974) see URCYB, 1975, 293.

77. For E. Cyril Blackman (1908–1989) see URCYB, 1989–90, 192.

78. For Thomas Francis Glasson (1906–1998) see DMBI.

79. Cf. Huxtable. *As It Seemed to Me*, 32: "Geoffrey F. Nuttall, who was lecturer in Church History, had been a fellow student with me at Mansfield, where we had taken relatively little notice of one another." For Huxtable (1912–1990) see also URCYB, 1991–92, 229; ODNB; WTW.

80. For F. Bertram Clogg (1884–1955) and Eric Strickland Waterhouse (1879–1964), both of Richmond College, see DMBI.

81. Because Stanley, the Lancashire Moderator, was perceived as being of an aggressive disposition, and, in 1947, he had been vocal in opposition to draft proposals for union with the Presbyterians. For his change of heart see WTW, 215; Sell, *Testimony and Tradition*, 289–91.

were Peter Ackroyd, the Samuel Davidson Professor of Old Testament, Christopher Evans, Dennis Nineham, E. L. Mascall, Geoffrey Parrinder, H. D. Lewis, and Sydney Evans—the Dean of King's College, a politician and academic lightweight.[82] I got on well with all of them—rather surprisingly since I have the reputation of being "difficult."

> E. O. James (1888–1972)[83] was the name I could not remember. He was always friendly, and a strong supporter of (my) devotion to *scholarship*. W. R. Matthews, also, was always friendly.[84] Once when he came in to join (as one invited *ab extra*, but as a former Dean he hardly counted as *extra*) a Discussion Group which, from its onlie [sic] begetter we used to call "Nineham's Conversazione," I said to him "Where would you like to sit?" and he replied "I rather thought I would sit by you"! and I remember walking back with him once from King's to Ludgate Circus on his way to the Deanery. But was never inside that Deanery, as I often was at Westminster, and have been at Winchester, and Salisbury and Exeter, and could yet be at York, for R. D. C. Jasper and I always sat together at the Board of Studies in Theology. ... I have preached at St. Martin's, incidentally!

Cave used to talk much about security of tenure. He was a professor, I was a recognized teacher of the University. This recognition, said Cave, made for security of tenure, and he kept a close watch on stipends, which had to be within sight of secular rates. Cave had held out the possibility of a professorship in due course, but it never materialized because the College could not afford it. In Huxtable's time the University threw recognized teacher positions to the wind, and the theological colleges became responsible for appointing their staff without any vetting by the University, and for paying them. This was dressed up under the rubric of giving the colleges greater autonomy. But it meant that I lost security of tenure and no further watch was kept on my salary, which remained fairly stationary during Huxtable's ten years. I was doing the work of a professor, and had the repute of a professor, but without the title or the salary of a professor.

---

82. For Ackroyd (1917-2005) see WWW 2001–5. For Mascall (1905-1993), Anglican theologian, and Lewis (1910-1992), philosopher, see ODNB. For Edward Geoffrey Parrinder (1910-2005), history of religions, see DMBI; WWW 2001–5. For Sydney Evans (1915-1988) see WWW 1981–90.

83. For Edwin Oliver James (1888-1972) see ODNB.

84. For Walter Robert Matthews (1881-1973) see ODNB; W. R. Matthews, *Memories and Meanings*; H. P. Owen, *W. R. Matthews*; Sell, *Four Philosophical Anglicans*.

Charles Duthie,[85] who succeeded Huxtable in 1964 did much more to look after his own and his colleagues' salaries: mine was £2,600 p.a. when I retired in 1977.

I had no desire to move from New College—Mary thought that was a form of pride. When Cadoux died in 1947, Aubrey Vine[86] and I were invited to apply for the vacant Church History post at Mansfield. Neither of us was successful, and Erik Routley was appointed, apparently without interview. But I did apply under some pressure and rather reluctantly for Chairs at King's College, London, Manchester and Cambridge. I was interviewed at King's when C. W. Dugmore was appointed.[87] The others interviewed for the post were J. R. H. Moorman and J. C. Dickinson. Harold Roberts, Principal of Richmond College, spoke against me.[88] In the Manchester contest I was up against the Methodist Gordon Rupp, and he was successful.[89] I had crossed swords with him when he was teaching at Richmond College. He had wanted to pass a student, I to fail him. The independent third examiner agreed with me. After that Rupp never let me examine at Manchester, and when he left there for Cambridge he advised his successor, Basil Hall, never to employ "ferocious" Geoffrey as an examiner. No doubt Rupp is sound enough on the Reformation, but his work leaves something to be desired when he gets onto English soil. My second defeat by Rupp occurred at Cambridge, for which Chair Ullmann and Frend, who left Cambridge for Glasgow, had also applied.[90] My candidature was supported by David Knowles[91] and Norman Sykes. My friend, the American Quaker, Roland Bainton, often wondered whether I would welcome an appointment in the United States, and a more specific offer came from a charming Congregationalist, pacifist, professor in Chicago, whose name escapes me.

---

85. For Duthie (1911–1981) see McNaughton, *The Scottish Congregational Ministry*, 202; Sell, *Hinterland Theology*, ch. 11 and *passim*.

86. For Vine (1900–1973) see URCYB, 1973–74, 282–83; Sell, *Christ and Controversy*, 167–72.

87. For Dugmore (1909–90) see WWW 1981–90.

88. For Roberts (1896–1982) see DMBI.

89. For E. Gordon Rupp (1910–1986) see ODNB; DMBI.

90. For Walter Ullmann (1910–1983) see ODNB; for W. H. C. Frend (1916–2005) see WWW 2001–5. "Defeats" notwithstanding, Geoffrey contributed to Gordon Rupp's *Festschrift*, and vice versa. See Nuttall, "John Horne of Lynn," and Rupp. "A devotion to raputure in English Puritanism."

91. For Michael Clive Knowles [religious name David] (1896–1974) see ODNB.

> The name of the charming American who wanted me for Chicago . . . is the Rev. Howard Schomer. I wonder if you ever met him?[92]

But I stayed at New College. I was College Librarian. I devoted a good deal of time to the collection, and was relieved when, following the closure of the College, it proved possible to transfer the books to Dr. Williams's Library. Lovell Cocks preached at the closing service of New College. He was one of the last surviving students of P. T. Forsyth, and could always be relied upon to say something deep, lively and to the point on special occasions.[93]

Very occasionally the denomination invited me to do things. I was a member of the commission which, in the 1960s, prepared *A Short Affirmation of Faith* and the longer *Declaration of Faith*. Others involved included Alec Whitehouse, John Heywood Thomas and Cunliffe-Jones.[94] John Marsh was also on it, but he would never give me the serious attention that the others did. He wasn't grounded in Congregationalism.[95] I preferred the meetings when Howard Stanley wasn't present. He didn't understand what was going on, but liked to throw his weight around. His predecessor, Leslie Cooke, was always more responsive and open.[96]

As I look back it seems to me that I served *under* Cave, *with* Huxtable, and *over* Duthie. Although our attitudes to many things differed, I was closest to John Huxtable. I agreed more with Charles Duthie than with the other two, but Charles played his cards close to his chest, and didn't *stand* for things: he was understanding of student difficulties to the point of undue leniency.

Over the years I have examined a number of doctoral candidates, and have been pleased to encourage scholars young and old from various parts

---

92. Letter of 14 March 1983. Schomer was President of Chicago Theological Seminary (1959-66), and a prominent advocate of human and civil rights. He was a friend of Martin Luther King, and marched with him in Selma, Alabama. He died on 28 June 2001, aged 86. I never met him. His papers are at Harvard University.

93. For Harry Francis Lovell Cocks (1894-1983) see URCYB, 1984, 258-59; ODNB; WTW; Sell, *Commemorations*, ch. 13.

94. For W. A. Whitehouse (1915-2003) see URCYB, 2004, 332; for J. Heywood Thomas see WTW; *Dictionary of Twentieth-Century British Philosophers*; for Hubert Cunliffe-Jones see URCYB, 1991-92, 226-27; WTW; Wadsworth, *Yorkshire United Independent College*; Kaye, *For the Work of Ministry*.

95. For Marsh (1904-1994) see URCYB, 1995, 264-65; WTW; Kaye, *Mansfield College*.

96. For Cooke (1908-1967) see CYB, 1967-68, 435; WTW.

Geoffrey Nuttall in Conversation

of the world. But it saddens me that none of my New College students took my subject to an advanced level. I think that Wilfred Biggs[97] and John Taylor[98] could have done so, but no doubt the claims of the pastorate precluded this. So few New College students joined the Congregational Historical Society. I was President of the Society, and it was I who got the committee established: previously the officers had handled everything. I was also President of the Friends Historical Society, and am President of the Friends of Dr. Williams's Library. I also belonged to *Sub Rosa*, the ministers' luncheon club,[99] and I was Chairman of the General Body of Dissenting Ministers, and of the London Congregational Board (which is older than the London Congregational Union).

Assessments of Others

The now-departed historian I most admired was David Knowles, the historian of monasticism; the one still active whom I most admire is Patrick Collinson. Christopher Brooke and Ullmann do good work, and so does Dickens,[100] but he is a bore. I like Reg Ward, but do not always understand him.[101] I fear I'm prejudiced against Rupert Davies even though he was at Balliol.[102] He is bland and has no great scholarly weight; yet he bursts with self-satisfaction and maintains a wonderfully consistent smugness. George Yule of Aberdeen is a most affectionate soul, but he does very poor work and, intellectually, he's not more than third rate. Pennar Davies and Tudur Jones—than whom two persons could hardly be more different—

---

97. For Biggs (1918–1997) see URCYB, 1999, 291.

98. For Taylor see Bocking, "John Horace Taylor."

99. *Sub Rosa* was founded in 1791. Its origins lie in a dispute between some Homerton Academy students and their tutor, Daniel Fisher (d. 1807), an alumnus of Plaisterers' Hall (Zephaniah Marryatt, tutor), who taught at Homerton from 1771–1803. The students were expelled without being heard, and a minority of members of the King's Head Society and the Congregational Fund Board (the funding agencies) disapproved of this and began to meet over lunch to plan remedial action. The students were reinstated, and their supporting ministers concluded that they had enjoyed their lunch-time conversations so much that they resolved to continue meeting. Of this still continuing happy band I have the honour of being the current President.

100. For Dickens (1910–2001) see WWW 2001–5.

101. I managed to follow him at Manchester on his enjoyable romp through Modern History from 1485 to 1914; he subsequently went as Professor to Durham. He died on 2 October 2010, aged 85.

102. For Davies (1909–1944) see DMBI; ODNB.

are longstanding friends in Wales.[103] But my greatest historian friend is Jan van den Berg of Leiden, with whom I have collaborated on Doddridge.[104]

> Another time we had better look at my 3 ministers at Hampstead Garden Suburb, my 3 London Moderators, and other Congo's.[105]

The first London Moderator I knew was R. J. Evans.[106] He was a dear old thing. He was followed by Alan Green, who interviewed me for the New College post, and with whom I later fell out. I was Chairman of the Hodgson Trust—left in the eighteenth century by Robert Hodgson for the benefit of Calvinist ministers who did not give communion to those who took it on their knees. The trustees had to nominate ministers who were to receive the money. The secretary, A. R. Smart, took £25 p.a. for his services, and Alan Green constantly nominated his London men. But Green wasn't on the committee: we just met in his office. So I protested at his behaviour and he never forgave me. He was succeeded by Bill Simpson, a good, simple, deeply pastoral man.[107]

In my London days I was a member of Hampstead Garden Suburb Free Church and, on the whole, we were well served by our ministers. Frank Ballard[108] was a good old dog. He married Oman's daughter.[109] He was a strong Free Church Federal Council man, and got me involved in that. He was a good all-round man. He was a presence in the pulpit, and could be rather heavy; the services could last for an hour and a half. Stanley Andrews was my favourite. He wasn't so good as a preacher, but he was an admirable pastor, and so was his wife, Hope. Andrews was a Scot, who returned to Scotland and was "re-ordained" in the Church of Scotland. A very outgoing person. Peter Barraclough is a consistent preacher and

---

103. For William Thomas Pennar Davies (1911–1996) see WTW; Nuttall, "Pennar Davies." For Robert Tudur Jones (1921–1998) see WTW; Pope, "R. Tudur Jones 1921–1998"; Pope, "'A Giant of Welsh Protestantism'"; for the pair see Morgan, "Pelagius and a Twentieth-Century Augustine."

104. See *Philip Doddridge (1702–1751) and the Netherlands*.

105. Letter of 11 March 1983.

106. For Evans (1871–1967) see CYB, 1967–68, 441.

107. For William Charles Edward.Simpson (1907–2005) see URCYB, 2007, 337.

108. For Ballard (1886–1959) see CYB, 1960, 421–22.

109. For John Wood Oman (1860–1939), Professor (1907–1935) and Principal (1922–1935) of Westminster College, Cambridge, see ODNB; WTW; Hart, *Dictionary of Historical Theology*; Brown, *Dictionary of Twentieth-Century British Philosophers*; Healey, *Religion and Reality*; Bevans, *John Oman and his Doctrine of God*; Hood, *Oman and Macmurray*; Hood, *John Oman: New Perspectives*; and ch. 4 above.

leader of worship, no good at pastoral visitation, but excellent at funerals. He always takes the lead and can be over-sensitive when elders and others see things differently.[110]

My longstanding minister friends are the Baptist Raymond Brown,[111] and Ronald Ward, a good preacher and pastor, who has a lively and original mind.[112] And I always liked Norman Goodall.[113] And, of course, there's you. Of my former students I have kept in closest touch with Wilfred Biggs, Ray Arnold[114] and Eric Allen. My present minister, Peter Chave, conducts worship in a dignified manner and preaches thoughtfully and biblically.

Self-Assessment

I came to work on Baxter quite consciously as a counterweight against my special love for the more radical Dissenters. But having come to him, he gradually took possession of me. Doddridge is another central person in my thoughts. Reason and experience must be held together, and this is consistent with New Testament teaching; but Donald Davie goes along the old Enlightenment line and overlooks the experiential element.[115] I was brought up on Doddridge's hymns, and was prodded by F. J. Powicke to read Baxter when I was a teenager.[116] I was never drawn to Watts in the same way. I love his hymns, of course, but I think of him as a hypochondriac bachelor. I have no strong sense of his church fellowship, and he was somewhat withdrawn and didn't write many letters. Baxter and Doddridge were great letter writers. In any case, I prefer provincial types to metropolitan, and have spent most of my time with them.

I have never had a book refused, and have never had to hawk my wares around from one publisher to another. I wrote to order when I felt committed to the project, but *The Holy Spirit in Puritan Faith and Experience* and *Visible Saints* were my own. The former is the weightier of the two; the latter is not as good. I have not found much to correct in them

---

110. For Barraclough (1925–1992) see URCYB, 1994, 265–66.

111. Dr. Brown preached at Geoffrey's funeral service at Bourneville on 8 August 2007.

112. For Ward (1917–1006) see URCYB, 2008, 308.

113. For Goodall (1896–1985) see URCYB, 1985–86, 197; ODNB; WTW.

114. For Arnold (1923–2004) see URCYB, 2005, 328.

115. For Davie (1922–1995) see ODNB.

116. For F. J. Powicke (1854–1935) see CYB, 1937, 705; WTW; Sell, *Enlightenment, Ecumenism, Evangel*, ch. 1.

subsequently. I have rarely been upset by a reviewer. My writings don't usually have a long gestation period: ideas come to me and I follow them up. I think that my best devotional work is *The Holy Spirit and Ourselves*, and that the book on Dante is the best written—though it was extreme audacity on my part to attempt it at all: I am not a scholar of Dante or of Italian. Of all my works, I use my *Calendar of the Correspondence of Philip Doddridge* most frequently: it is a very good source book, though there are some indexing errors. I don't return to my *Richard Baxter* much, and almost never to *From Uniformity to Unity*. I regard my *Christian Pacifism in History* as a superior pot-boiler. I wanted to show that I was not just a narrow seventeenth-century historian.

I feel that I have given myself to New College and to our tradition, and I am saddened to think that the movement in the denomination is for the most part all the other way. Although my work has been recognized within the scholarly community, and although I glad to have helped make Puritanism and Dissent "respectable" subjects of academic study, the principles that have motivated me seem to be undervalued by most people in our Church. *The Holy Spirit in Puritan Faith and Experience* brought together the Holy Spirit, Puritanism, and experience, and you cannot get under the skin of the Puritans unless you keep those three together. My intention was to promote my Congregational convictions through my work, but nowadays my mind often turns to the title of Grandfather Hodgson's pamphlet, *Congregationalism Played Out—Then Cometh the End*. I fear that Congregationalism has folded up; and it's ecumenical claptrap to suppose that it has "died in order to live." I felt that I was doing my work for Congregationalism and for the Lord, but the denomination has not been a grateful recipient; I have failed, and this is painful. It is just conceivable that there will be a return, but it is not likely to come from the Congregational Federation or the Evangelical Fellowship of Congregational Churches.

Postscript

My wife and I were in regular contact with Geoffrey for some forty years (and how he loved to be teased by Karen), but even after all this time (though others knew him for much longer) it is not easy to sum him up. His was a multi-layered personality. As occasion demanded, his eyes could pierce with righteous indignation, twinkle with merriment and melt with sympathy. He could be generous to a fault, as many scholars, younger and older, discovered when they gravitated towards him, drawn by his willingness to encourage not just verbally but often in the form of reams of careful, referenced, criticism of their work. But he was not a "one track" friend. He showed great interest in Karen's doctoral work even though her field was far removed from his own, he being enamoured of (certain kinds of) hymns but, on his own admission, not well up in music. He took a lively interest in the doings of our children, to whom in their younger days he was Uncle Nuttall; and he was thrilled when our son became a Classical Scholar at Oxford and later moved into Renaissance Studies. He befriended my late mother when she moved to Queen Mother Court, Bournville (never Birmingham!), where he lived for some years, and he was always pleased to have conversations with my brother on his visits there from Finland. He was ever ready to be driven in quest of a Dissenting landmark; he welcomed many friends to his regular holiday haunt at Oberhofen am Thunersee, Switzerland; he would read Greek classics over breakfast, and Dante aloud to his visitors. He loved to speak of the philosophers—H.W. B. Joseph and H. H. Joachim among them—whom he had known in his Oxford days.

It cannot be denied, however—and it is clear from the tenor of some his remarks made in conversation—that he could "go off" people.[117] From some of his former students I have learned that if he came to the view that they were "not up to much" and showed little in their studies, or if they were uncritically ecumenical or biblicist, his patience would be sorely tested. I think that this was the outworking of a deep conviction that his energies had to be devoted to the fulfilment of his high calling to train ministers and stand up for "our people," and if some were disinclined to put heart and soul into this, so be it. On the other hand, if students were "not up to much" academically, but nevertheless strove to improve their grasp of matters intellectual, Geoffrey would spare no pains to help and encourage them.

Once he had made up his mind on an issue, or about a person, it was very difficult to persuade him otherwise. He admitted this as being an aspect of his "awkward squad" persona. When I told him that I was taking soundings concerning the possibility of forming an umbrella organization which would bring denominational historical societies and cognate libraries together with a view to cooperative research and publication, he abruptly pronounced, "It will never work. You'll never get the Strict

---

117. I have used the blue pencil only twice in reporting Geoffrey's opinions of others. I did so because in both cases there was another side to the question, and I felt that what he said would be needlessly hurtful to some still living.

Baptists and the Unitarians in the same room." But we did, and we do, and no one was more delighted than Geoffrey when he saw the Association's conference proceedings, and the first volume to appear of *Protestant Nonconformist Texts*, edited as it is by a Baptist, a Strict Baptist and a Unitarian.

Geoffrey felt that John Marsh, had erred in his Introduction to *A Book of Public Worship Compiled for the Use of Congregationalists* by John Huxtable, John Marsh, Romilly Micklem, and James Todd: "Throughout Dr. Marsh's Introduction (16pp.) our traditional repudiation of such books is not discussed, while dependence on the Spirit's leadings is not mentioned at all."[118] Behind this remark there lies, I think, both a deep suspicion of the "Genevans" of the Church Order Group, and an even deeper commitment to the art and craft of free prayer (something lifeless, even when grammatical, without the Spirit's prompting) of which Geoffrey himself was a master. Again, he could find little good to say about Lesslie Newbigin,[119] whom he regarded as a university-SCM Christian with no roots in the local church, who had subsequently become an ecumenical trimmer. Although Lesslie and Geoffrey ended on the same ministerial roll and lived in retirement in the same city they never met.[120] By contrast, he rejoiced in his friendship with Ron Webb, the Administrative Officer of the West Midlands Province, whom he regarded as a stalwart, salt-of-the-earth, Christian.

I have mentioned Geoffrey's sorrow at the sense of embattlement that Sydney Cave felt in connection with a nest of conservative evangelicals who were at New College in the late 1940s and early 1950s. This played to my pastoral advantage towards the end of Geoffrey's life. On one of our last visits Karen and I found that Geoffrey, now unable to read and lacking mental stimulation, would drift in and out of conversation. During one of his "out" moments I quietly asked, "Wasn't x one of your students?," mentioning the name of a prominent conservative evangelical. Back came Geoffrey with all guns blazing: "The heretic!," he cried, and thus conversation was resumed.

Given Geoffrey's disapproval of the "Genevan" tendency in Congregationalism, and of what he regarded as ecumenism of the uncritical—even

---

118. Geoffrey's review of *A Book of Public Worship*, 367. Marsh was raised in the Church of England.

119. For Newbigin (1909–1998) see ODNB; URCYB, 1999, 216; WTW; Wainwright, *Lesslie Newbigin*; D. R. Peel, "The Theological Legacy Of Lesslie Newbigin."

120. Geoffrey wrote a swingeing, exegetically-based, "not-for-publication" review of the report of the international Anglican-Reformed dialogue, *God's Reign and Our Unity*, the principal drafter of which was Lesslie Newbigin.

disloyal—sort, it is, on the face of it, surprising that I, a member of the old Church Order Group, and one who has worked in ecumenical contexts from the local to the global, should have got off so lightly. I think the answer lies in Geoffrey's awareness that my commitment to the visible saints as the locus of the Church catholic, and my willingness to confront sectarianisms whether catholic or evangelical would enable the voice of "our people" to be heard in those circles. Be that as it may, he was as supportive of my ecumenical activities as he was of my more strictly academic pursuits, and I am greatly indebted to him for this.

Sometimes Geoffrey would put me on the spot. "What do you make of Daniel Jenkins?"[121] he asked one day. I thought for a moment and replied, "I think he is a very good upmarket theological journalist." I intended this as a compliment, for Jenkins was a widely read, thoughtful, writer who could, apparently effortlessly and with great skill, communicate theological ideas to a wide readership. "Exactly so!" Geoffrey responded: "he certainly isn't a scholar like you and me." Discreetly passing over his observation about myself, I suspect that all who knew him would agree that, incontestably, there was no scholar quite like Geoffrey Nuttall—a judgment which applies equally to his published legacy, his traits, and, above all, to the strength and depth of his ministerial-*cum*-scholarly vocation, from which he would allow nothing to deflect him.

> As for my friends, they are not lost;
> The several vessels of Thy fleet,
> Though parted now, by tempests tost,
> Shall safely in the haven meet.
>
> Richard Baxter

BIBLIOGRAPHY

(a) Manuscripts

Personal correspondence with Geoffrey Nuttall.

(b) Published Works

Anonymous. *A Short Affirmation of Faith*. London: Congregational Union of England and Wales, 1961.

---

121. For Jenkins (1914–2002) see URCYB, 2003, 326; ODNB; WTW.

———. *The Congregational Year Book*. London: Congregational Union of England and Wales. Various years as specified in the footnotes.

———. *A Declaration of Faith*. London: Congregational Church in England and Wales, 1967. Reprinted in David M. Thompson. *Stating the Gospel: Formulations and Declarations of Faith from the Heritage of The United Reformed Church*. Edinburgh: T. & T. Clark, 1990.

———. *God's Reign and Our Unity: The Report of the Anglican-Reformed International Commission 1981-1984*. London: SPCK, and Edinburgh: The Saint Andrew Press, 1984.

———. Information regarding James Muscutt. *The Congregational Magazine* (1822) 277.

Argent, Alan. "Albert Peel: the Restless Labourer." *The Journal of the United Reformed Church History Society* 4 (1989) 319-36.

Berg, Johannes van den, and Geoffrey F. Nuttall, *Philip Doddridge (1702-1751) and the Netherlands*. Leiden: Brill, 1987.

Bevans, Stephen. *John Oman and his Doctrine of God*. Cambridge: Cambridge University Press, 1992.

Bocking, Ronald. "John Horace Taylor, 21.11.1921-27.01.2011." *The Journal of the United Reformed Church History Society* 8 (2011) 437-40.

———. "Sydney Cave (1883-1953): Missionary, Principal, Theologian." *The Journal of the United Reformed Church History Society* 7 (2002) 36-44.

Bourne, S. A. H., and Barbara Donaldson. On Baswich House School. In *The Victoria County History of Staffordshire*, edited by Margaret L. Midgley, V, 4. London: Oxford University Press for the Institute of Historical Research, 1959.

Brown, Stuart. *Dictionary of Twentieth-Century British Philosophers*. London: Thoemmes Continuum, 2005.

Butler, David M. *The Quakaer Meeting Houses of Britain*. 2 vols. London: Friends Historical Society, 1999.

Chandler, J. H. *Wiltshire Dissenters' Meeting House Certificates and Registrations 1689-1720*. Devizes: Wiltshire Record Society, 1985.

Dale, R. W. Memoir of Henry Rogers prefixed to H. Rogers, *The Superhuman Origin of the Bible*, vii-lxxii. London: Hodder & Stoughton, 1893.

Dancy, John. Obituary of Roy Niblett. *The Guardian* (11 May 2005).

E.M. Notice of the death of James Muscutt. *The Evangelical Magazine* (1819) 410.

Goodall, Norman. *A History of the London Missionary Society 1895-1945*. London: Oxford University Press, 1954.

Hart, Trevor. *Dictionary of Historical Theology*. Carlisle, UK: Paternoster, 2000.

Healey, F. G. *Religion and Reality: The Theology of John Oman*. Edinburgh: Oliver & Boyd, 1965.

Hood, Adam. *John Oman: New Perspectives*. Milton Keynes, UK: Paternoster, 2012.

———. *Oman and Macmurray: Experience and Religious Beief*. Aldershot, UK: Ashgate, 2003.

Horne, C. Silvester. *A Popular History of the Free Churches*. New ed. London: Congregational Union of England and Wales, 1926.

Huxtable, W. John F. *As it Seemed to Me*. London: The United Reformed Church, 1990.

Kaye, Elaine. *C. J. Cadoux: Theologian, Scholar, Pacifist*. Edinburgh: Edinburgh University Press, 1988.

———. *For the Work of Ministry: A History of Northern College and its Predecessors*. Edinburgh: T. & T. Clark, 1999.

———. *Mansfield College: Its Origin, History and Significance*. Oxford: Oxford University Press, 1996.
Lovett, Richard. *The History of the London Missionary Society, 1795–1895*. 2 vols., London: Frowde, 1899.
McKim, Donald K. *Dictionary of Major Biblical Interpreters*. Downers Grove, IL: InterVarsity Press, 2007.
McNaughton, William D. *The Scottish Congregational Ministry 1794–1993*. Glasgow: Congregational Union of Scotland, 1993.
Mander, William J, and Alan P. F. Sell. *Dictionary of Nineteenth-Century British Philosophers*. Bristol: Thoemmes, 2002.
Matthews, W. R. *Memories and Meanings*. London: Hodder & Stoughton, 1969.
Micklem, Nathaniel. *The Box and the Puppets*. London: Geoffrey Bles, 1957.
Milligan, Edward, and Geoffrey Nuttall. Obituary of L. Hugh Doncaster. *The Friend* (13 January 1995) 52.
Morgan, D. Densil. "Pelagius and a Twentieth-Century Augustine: the Contrasting Visions of Pennar Davies and R. Tudur Jones." *International Congregational Journal* 1 (2001) 41–54.
Nicholls, Marjorie. "Mary Nuttall." *The Friend* (16 July 1982) 877–78.
Nuttall, Geoffrey F. *Howel Harris 1714–1773: The Last Enthusiast*. Cardiff: University of Wales Press, 1965.
———. "John Horne of Lynn." In *Christian Spirituality: Essays in Honour of Gordon Rupp*, edited by Peter Brooks, ch. 10. London: SCM, 1975.
———. "Pennar Davies (12 November 1911—29 December 1996): *Complexio Oppositorum*." *The Journal of the United Reformed Church History Society* 5 (1997) 574–75.
———. *The Puritan Spirit: Essays and Addresses*. London: Epworth, 1967.
———. Review of *A Book of Public Worship*. In *The Congregational Quarterly* 26 (1948), 367.
———. *The Welsh Saints 1640–1660*. Cardiff: University of Wales Press, 1957.
Owen, H. P. *W. R. Matthews: Philosopher and Theologian*. London: Athlone Press, 1976.
Paterson, William P. *The Rule of Faith*. London, 1912.
Patrick, James. *Idealism and Orthodoxy at Oxford 1901–1955*. Macon, GA: Mercer University Press, 1985.
Peel, Albert, and J. A. R. Marriott. *Robert Forman Horton*. London: Allen & Unwin, 1937.
Peel, David R. "The Theological Legacy of Lesslie Newbigin." In *Ecumenical and Eclectic: The Unity of the Church in the Contemporary World. Essays in Honour of Alan P. F. Sell*, edited by Anna M. Robbins, ch. 6. Milton Keynes, UK: Paternoster, 2007.
Pollard, F. E. *Bootham School York 1823–1923*. London: Dent, 1926.
Pope, Robert. "'A Giant of Welsh Protestantism': R. Tudur Jones (1921–1998) and Congregationalism in Wales." *International Congregational Journal* 3 (2003) 13–35.
———. "R. Tudur Jones (1921–1998): Congregational Minister, Church Historian, and Welsh Nationalist." *The Journal of the United Reformed Church History Society* 6 (2000) 529–41.
Richards, Leyton. *The Christian's Alternative to War: An Examination of Christian Pacifism*. London: SCM, 1929.

Ross, W. D. "Clement Charles Julian Webb." *Proceedings of the British Academy* 41 (1955) 339–47.
Rupp, Gordon. "A Devotion to Rapture in English Puritanism." In *Reformation, Conformity and Dissent: Essays in Honour of Geoffrey Nuttall*, edited by R. Buick Knox, ch. 6. London: Epworth, 1977.
Scott, C. A. A. *Christianity according to St. Paul*. Cambridge: Cambridge University Press, 1927.
Sell, Alan P. F. *Christ and Controversy: The Person of Christ in Nonconformist Thought and Ecclesial Experience*. Eugene, OR: Pickwick, 2012.
———. *Commemorations: Studies in Christian Thought and History*. 1993. Reprinted, Eugene, OR: Wipf & Stock, 1998.
———. *Dissenting Thought and the Life of the Churches: Studies in an English Tradition*. Lewiston, NY: Mellen, 1990.
———. *Enlightenment, Ecumenism, Evangel: Theological Themes and Thinkers 1550–2000*. Milton Keynes, UK: Paternoster, 2005.
———. *Four Philosophical Anglicans: W. G. De Burgh, W. R. Matthews, O. C. Quick, H. A. Hodges*. Farnham, UK: Ashgate, 2010.
———. *Hinterland Theology: A Stimulus to Theological Construction*. Milton Keynes, UK: Paternoster, 2008. Reprinted Eugene, OR: Wipf & Stock, 2009.
———. *Nonconformist Theology in the Twentieth Century*. Milton Keynes, UK: Paternoster, 2006. Reprinted Eugene, OR: Wipf and Stock, 2012.
———. *Philosophical Idealism and Christian Belief*. 1995. Reprinted, Eugene, OR: Wipf & Stock, 2006.
———. *Philosophy, Dissent and Nonconformity 1689–1920*. 2004. Reprinted, Eugene, OR: Wipf & Stock, 2009.
———. *Testimony and Tradition: Studies in Reformed and Dissenting Thought*. Aldershot, UK: Ashgate, 2005.
Skinner, John. *Prophecy and Religion: Studies in the Life of Jeremiah*. Cambridge: Cambridge University Press, 1926.
Stell, Christopher. *Nonconformist Chapels and Meeting-Houses in South-West England*. London: Her Majesty's Stationery Office, 1991.
Surman, Charles E. *Alexander James Grieve: A Biographical Sketch*. Manchester: Lancashire Independent College, 1953.
Tatlow, Tissington. *The Story of the Student Christian Movement of Great Britain and Ireland*. London: SCM, 1933.
Taylor, John, and Clyde Binfield. *Who They Were: In the Reformed Churches of England and Wales 1901–2000*. Donington: Shaun Tyas, 2007.
Thompson, Joseph. *Lancashire Independent College 1843–1993*. Manchester: J. E. Cornish, 1893.
Troeltsch, Ernst. *The Social Teachings of the Christian Churches* (1923). Louisville: Westminster John Knox, 1992.
Vickers, John A. *A Dictionary of Methodism in Britain and Ireland*. Peterborough: Epworth, 2000.
Wadsworth, Kenneth W. *Yorkshire United Independent College*. London: Independent Press, 1954.
Wainwright, Geoffrey. *Lesslie Newbigin: A Theological Life*. Oxford: Oxford University Press, 2000.
Wicken, Joan C. "Mary Nuttall 1901–82." *The Woodbrooke International Journal* 7 (1982) 22–23.

7

Is Geoffrey also among the Theologians?[1]

ALMOST CERTAINLY THE LATE Geoffrey F. Nuttall would have returned a negative answer to the above question, and he would have recognized the allusion to 1 Samuel 10:11 (AV). In the strictly professional sense he was not a theologian. With reference to what he calls "the limits of Nuttall's range" Professor Clyde Binfield has remarked, "He is an ecclesiastical historian, but neither a theologian nor a philosopher."[2] He was, as is

---

1. The following abbreviations are used in this chapter:

    (A) THE WORKS OF G. F. NUTTALL

    BTL : *Better Than Life. The Lovingkindness of God.*
    CPH : *Christian Pacifism in History.*
    PS : *The Puritan Spirit. Essays and Addresses.*
    RB : *Richard Baxter.*
    HSO : *The Holy Spirit and Ourselves.*
    HSPFE : *The Holy Spirit in Puritan Faith and Experience.*
    RH : *The Reality of Heaven.*
    VS : *Visible Saints. The Congregational Way 1640–1660.*

    (B) JOURNALS

    CHST : *Congregational Historical Society Transactions.*
    CQ : *The Congregational Quarterly.*
    JURCHS: *The Journal of the United Reformed Church History Society.*

    (C) DICTIONARY

    ODNB : *Oxford Dictionary of National Biography.* Ocford: Oxford University Press, 2004.

2. Binfield, "Profile," 84.

widely known, an historian of distinction, applauded for his precision in argument, his assiduity in research, and his mastery of the linguistic and other tools of his trade. Articles have been written on Nuttall the Early Modern historian, the friend, the librarian, the scholar and humanist,[3] but not on Nuttall the theologian. This is not surprising when we consider that there are two things that constructive and systematic theologians might reasonably be expected to do, which Nuttall was not required to do, and did not attempt.

In the first place, he did not engage in great detail with current theological trends, though he did leave a few clues to his thoughts on some of them, and these illuminate his general theological stance. Among his earlier publications, one not listed in the published bibliographies,[4] is a lucid report of the 1937 Congregational Theological Conference on "Revelation and faith." It is notable for two things in particular. First, Nuttall brings out the striking contrast between the positions adopted by the theological liberal, Thomas Wigley, and the staunch Barthian, F. W. Camfield. Whereas the former distrusted intuition and advocated a rationalistic stance, the latter held that "man's reason, and man's world were completely lost in the impotence of sin, nor could he allow that in man's knowledge of God God is ever the object of man's thought, ever a *datum*."[5] These speakers and, indeed, the conference at large, prompted Nuttall's reflection, "I wished . . . that the discussion had kept throughout more closely to the realm of the personal, to which Principal Franks (may I call him an impenitent Christian humanist?) brought it back more than once."[6] Secondly, Nuttall contrasts the views of Hubert Cunliffe-Jones, "who somewhat dominated the Conference,"[7] and Robert Franks: "Mr. Cunliffe-Jones expressed the contrast by claiming that the Christian revelation was a revelation in history, with which thought must be made to fit in, and by rejecting Dr. Franks's philosophical method of constructing a metaphysic, into which revelation was then fitted"; on which Nuttall muses, "I should have thought that the more logical part of a metaphysic, the examination of the capacities and instruments of thought, was a *sine qua non* of theol-

---

3. See JURCHS V (1996). The articles are by Collinson, Brown, Bocking, and Tai Liu.

4. Tai Liu has contributed bibliographies of Nuttall's writings to Knox, *Reformation, Conformity and Dissent*, ch. 14, and JURCHS (1996) 534–43.

5. CQ 15 (1937) 503.

6. Ibid.

7. Ibid., 504.

Is Geoffrey also among the Theologians?

ogy simply *qua* thought."[8] Nuttall welcomed Cunliffe-Jones's emphasis upon history,

> but I was the more dismayed, when I learned what it meant. [He] rightly claimed that (for knowledge, if not existentially) there are no pure facts, that history is the interpreted fact, though the interpreting of it is history too; but he seemed unwilling to accept the corollary that there may be more or less of interpretation as well as different interpretations, and that we cannot treat the interpreted fact as if it had not been interpreted, we must judge the correctness of the interpretation. Absolute forms are as non-existent as pure facts, and the Christian revelation, just because it is historical, must submit to a criticism of the forms in which it was interpreted.[9]

Because of Cunliffe-Jones's reluctance at this point, Nuttall concluded that his approach to history was of the pre-Reformation sort:

> What I mean by a pre-Reformation emphasis is the implicit assumption that by the Christian revelation we must (not only *can* but *must*) understand the same as the Apostles meant and as the Church has always meant, and I call it pre-Reformation because it carries with it a theory of the unity of the Church over against heresy, which history disproves and Protestantism rejects. . . . We have to ask all the time, in the broadest historical sense, *quales homines interfuerint* (Calvin). . . . I am aware that this emphasis on the Spirit-guided use of the individual's judgment is increasingly out of favour now, when liberalism is dismissed *en bloc* as atomic, when "community" is in the air, and when Barth joins hands with Neo-Thomism in decrying personality; but I do not see how it can be avoided.[10]

In the light of the above report it is not fanciful to suppose that Nuttall had dogmatism of the Barthian kind within his sights when he wrote concerning ideas which "offer themselves with the apparent immediacy of perceptions," that "if we are to carry the conviction that what we have seen is *true* to others to whom our moment of vision has not been granted, we have to depend largely upon the normal forms of logical presentation."[11] This approach places Nuttall on the side of the aforementioned Robert

---

8. Ibid.
9. Ibid.
10. Ibid., 504, 505.
11. Nuttall, *To the Refreshing of the Children of Light*, 14.

213

Franks, whose principal objection to Barth was the latter's groundless assumption that the Word of God was equivalent to his own theology, and his abandonment on inadequate grounds of the apologetic aspect of commending the faith—faults on account of which Franks barred Barth from the pantheon of great theologians.[12]

More formally, in the Foreword to his justly admired book, *The Holy Spirit in Puritan Faith and Experience*, Nuttall did not hesitate to name names:

> The desire to lean upon a powerful external authority, which politically found expression in Fascism and National-Socialism, has favoured the claims of the the Roman Catholic Church and of a 'Word of God' in Scripture which judges but may not be judged. Rudolf Otto and Karl Barth have proclaimed a God who is *ganz Anderes* and a revelation which is purely divine and given, *sui generis*, containing no element of human, and therefore fallible, creation or even discovery. Neo-Thomists and Neo-Calvinists agree in laying emphasis upon dogmas and confessions, and tend to treat faith as assent to a static deposit, to a closed system, of doctrine, rather than as an ενέργεια springing directly from living, personal experience. In the reaction against an optimistic humanism which seemed hardly to need any doctrine of the Holy Spirit, human incapacity through Original Sin has been so exaggerated latterly as virtually to deny the doctrine.[13]

The second way in which Nuttall did not behave as a theologian might is that he did not discuss the several "departments" of systematic theology in order. This, of course, is a statement of fact which implies no adverse judgement whatsoever, for, to repeat, as an ecclesiastical historian he was in no way bound to do this, and we should not emulate those perverse reviewers who castigate authors for failing to do what they had neither the intention nor the need of doing. It would be foolish to lay the dogmatic scheme from creation to eschatology against Nuttall's writings with a view to ticking the doctrinal boxes. Were the attempt made we should find, for example, that he had little to say about creation, the attributes traditionally ascribed to God, theories of the atonement, and the Trinity (albeit his thought is pervaded by the conviction of a personal relationship with the

---

12. See Sell, *Nonconformist Theology*, 27, 30. For a full discussion of Franks's theology see Sell, *Hinterland Theology*, ch. 10.

13. HSPFE, vii.

Is Geoffrey also among the Theologians?

Father through the Son by the Spirit);[14] but such a finding would be trivial and of no utility, and would represent a profound missing of the point.

Far better to recall that, according to his own self-assessment, Nuttall's calling to be a minister of the Gospel was the primary claim upon him, his work as an ecclesiastical historian being a prominent way in which he fulfilled his vocation. Now it is all too evident that however hard they try (and some seem to try very hard), ministers of religion can never entirely succeed in avoiding theology. In some cases their encounters with the discipline yield effusions ranging from the platitudinous to the grotesque; but not in Nuttall's case. Although he never essayed a systematic theology and, as we have seen, viewed some such creations with more than a little scepticism, a sharp theological mind was in operation through all his historical writings, his preaching and his pastoral care. For this reason I feel bound gently to query a remark made by Professor N. H. Keeble at Nuttall's Memorial Service. He writes, "Geoffrey was interested . . . in the experience of faith rather than in theology, in communities of believers rather than in ecclesiology."[15] I suggest that this is too disjunctive a mode of expression, for to Nuttall the experience of faith was a theological experience—an experience of *God*, not, for example, something akin to an undifferentiated cosy glow. In this he was akin to Schleiermacher, on whom his friend and mentor, W. B. Selbie, had published a monograph;[16] and in communities of believers—the gathered, visible saints—he found the realization of his New Testament ecclesiology. Thus, whereas Professor Binfield declared that Nuttall was "not a theologian," he nevertheless discerned correctly that in Nuttall's view "Church history was a continuation of gospel history. It was an outworking of man's understanding of God.

---

14. In one of his few specific references to the Trinity Nuttall declares, "It is still arguable that the doctrine of the Trinity as commonly held is not in Scripture, any more than is the *word* Trinity (which, for that matter, will not be found in the proposed new Congregational *Declaration of Faith*, either)." See *Congregationalists and Creeds*, 7. It is less noteworthy that the doctrine "as commonly held is not in Scripture" than that the term is absent from the *Declaration*. For, while it is arguable that the New Testament contains the germ of, or of clues pointing towards, the doctrine of the Trinity, the doctrine was forged over time in a missionary situation and in face of alternative views. It is more than arguable, it is abundantly clear, that the 1967 *Declaration* of the Congregational Church in England and Wales (on the committee of which Nuttall served) is trinitarian in form.

15. The service was held at The American Church (Whitefields) in London on 16 November 2007. Keeble's address is found in Richards, *Geoffrey Fillingham Nuttall*. I quote from p. 21.

16. Selbie, *Schleiermacher*.

It was a *theological enterprise.*"[17] It thus transpires that when we attend closely to Nuttall's *corpus* we have no difficulty in detecting a number of interlocking theological themes which reverberate throughout, and are omnipresent as, for example, the cross is in the writings of P. T. Forsyth. These themes are the experience of the presence God in Christ by the Spirit, among the visible and voluntarist saints, as inspiring practical holiness, and as an harbinger of heaven.[18] I shall attend to each of these in turn, whilst at the same time recognizing that to be true to Nuttall we must attempt to think them concurrently: for him they were all of a piece. The history is at the service of these theological emphases. This is not to say that history is made to fit them, or is distorted by them. The point to the contrary was made by Nuttall himself: "theology must always be studied in the interplay of its full historical context."[19] Consistently with this it is more than implicit, it is placarded in his writings, that history must be studied with reference to the lives, beliefs, hopes and fears of those who are its actors. Nuttall's occasional references to "what is called intellectual history" was a faintly disparaging way of distancing himself from those historians (including some quite well known ones) who treated thought in abstraction from the human context within which it evolved. That he could never do; he was a "real people" historian.

I

Nuttall's understanding of history and of the historian's—or, at least, of his—task led him to declare that "we are not seeking to exclude the eternal but to discover it in the only place in which it is discoverable, in the temporal."[20] After all,

> The doctrine of the Incarnation, properly understood, is a historical doctrine: that God revealed Himself uniquely in a particular personality at a particular time. . . . Unfortunately the doctrine of the Incarnation has been torn from its context and interpreted in the light of conceptions of God un-Hebraic and unconcerned with either history or personality. These have

---

17. Binfield, "Profile," 92 (my italics).

18. In these theological concerns those of a philosophical bent may detect at least an echo of Kant's postulates (that is, conditions, not presuppositions) of thought: God, freedom and immortality.

19. PS, 234.

20. PS, 236.

produced doctrines accepted by traditional orthodoxy which are so patently unhistorical as the impersonality of Christ's humanity.[21]

This was not Nuttall's way. On the contrary, his examination of New Testament texts (in Greek, of course) was meticulous, and he was no less concerned than Calvin to pay heed to "the whole course of [Christ's] obedience."[22] Thus, for example, he writes, "[Christ's] suffering on the Cross cannot properly be separated . . . from his suffering in Gethsemane . . . It is . . . because of Jesus' whole life, but above all because of his death on the Cross, that Paul can cry, as in ecstasy, 'He loved me, and gave himself for me!' Many whose hearts would have remained hard to Christ's appeals throughout his ministry have been broken by his self-breaking on the Cross."[23]

This leads Nuttall to one of his most precise statements concerning the person of Christ: "[T]he whole burden of his life and message is to point men to God and assure men of God, as the One whose own being and purpose he sets forth in living image. In God alone is his inspiration and his security. He is as he is because God is as he is."[24] But he suffers. Does the Father, then, suffer? Nuttall goes so far as to say that "there must have been something analogous to the Cross in the heart of God himself. Only imagination and poetry have feet delicate enough to tread here."[25] The fact is that some theologians have worn hobnails at this point, whether for or against the divine impassibility. Nuttall pursues the matter no further—and good theologians know when to stop; but he has said enough to indicate his dissent at this point from Robert Franks, who staunchly upheld God's impassibility.[26] We should note, however, Nuttall's careful use of the term "analogy." He is in general well aware of the importance of the Creator-creature distinction, and with regard to the particular matter in hand he writes, "Between Jesus the man and his Father God there must be difference. To deny this would not only be blasphemous, it would make nonsense of the story and rob it of all possible religious significance. What makes the story unlike all others is that, alongside this difference and (somehow) *not* in contradiction to it, there was in the faith of those

21. Ibid., 236–37.
22. Calvin, *Institutes*, II.xvi.5.
23. BTL, 36, 67.
24. Ibid., 68.
25. Ibid., 70.
26. See Sell, *Hinterland Theology*, 608–9.

who told it, a oneness between Jesus and God of a kind without analogy in the experience of men . . . In Jesus God himself had drawn near. In Jesus' self-giving was the self-giving of God himself. The love of Jesus was one with the love of God."[27] The last two sentences quoted encapsulate Nuttall's own belief, but note the careful '(somehow)' and "in the faith of those who told it." The latter qualification states the fact but also begs the question of the reliability of the testimony.

In pondering the cross, Nuttall made much of the exemplary nature of Christ's suffering, in which connection he frequently had recourse to Quaker writers. "Fox's constant call to be ready and willing to endure suffering," he wrote, "is regularly associated with remembrance of Christ's cross."[28] Elsewhere he speculated that because "in this country our faith, whatever its peculiarities, be it Baptist, be it pacifist, is now tolerated, by taking away our opportunity to accept suffering for Christ's sake, [this may] weaken our principles or at least deprive us of a means of witness and ministry and persuasion."[29] But at the heart of Nuttall's thought on the Cross was the conviction that Jesus came to seek and to save the lost, and he invoked his much-loved Dante in making his point : "'In the middle of our life's way I found myself in a dark wood, where the straight path was lost: O how hard it is to say what it was like, the impenetrable, thorny thicket of this wood—the very thought of it makes me afraid again!' So Dante begins his great poem; and it was just for such fearful, lost souls in life's dark wood, where the trees are thick and the paths all overgrown, that Jesus came: to seek and to save them."[30] He further noted that the phrase "seeking and saving" was "so familiar that it is difficult to appreciate how remarkable it is: how new, strange and revolutionary: new and different from what characterizes all other religions."[31] As he elsewhere put it, "it is His seeking and saving which is a distinguishing mark of Jesus Christ."[32] He did not, however, expound what was done at the cross at any great length.

---

27. BTL, 75. When in RH, 69, Nuttall declares that "Christ's birth and death and resurrection have made a difference: *a difference not to God*, but to men's understanding of God" (my italics), he simply means that because of Christ we understand God in a fresh way; he is not asserting that God is non-susceptible to change.

28. Nuttall, "'Nothing Else Would Do,'" 653.

29. CPH, 64.

30. BTL, 60.

31. Ibid., 59.

32. CPH, 75.

Is Geoffrey also among the Theologians?

Before coming to the main thrust of Nuttall's position on the person and work of Christ it may be appropriate briefly to consider the question of the doctrine of salvation as it was raised in the disputes between Calvinists and Arminians. This, after all, is territory with which Nuttall's professional interests made him very familiar; but it also affords an example of his judicious, generally non-disjunctive, approach to argumentation:

> Antinomianism is not Calvinism; but it is Calvinism's peril. Every religious system has its peril. Catholicism can degenerate into superstition, Protestantism into a thin humanism. So Calvinism can degenerate into antinomianism of a dry, doctrinal kind, in which God's predetermination of all things not only precludes human action, including obedience to God's law, but makes it gratuitous for those already predestined to salvation. The curious thing is that Calvinism's opposite, whether Arminianism, universalism or enthusiasm, can also degenerate into antinomianism, though of a more practical kind. Here an emphasis on the unconditioned love of God for all men, or on the ability of men, by their reason of their innate goodness, to have some share in their salvation, at least by way of response to God's grace, can breed a tolerant compassionateness, and then a loose permissiveness, wholly antipathetic to the fulfilment of law divine or human.[33]

Except for the adjective in the first clause—for which we might substitute "Christian-humanistic," it is not difficult to imagine Nuttall nodding approvingly at the following obituary description of the Nathaniel Trotman: "His sentiments were strictly Calvinistic; his subjects purely evangelical. In his preaching there was the light of doctrine, without the dryness of system; the warmth of experience without the wild-fire of enthusiasm; the necessity of morality without the ostentation of pharisaism."[34]

Without question the major thrust in Nuttall's thought on the person of Christ was that it is with the risen and living Lord that we have to do. "From the beginning," he declared, "'Jesus and the resurrection' was the new message."[35] As to the resurrection itself, Nuttall observed that "It is sometimes argued that, if his tomb had not been empty, the authorities would surely have produced His body. It may be argued with almost equal force that, if His tomb was empty, it is strange that the apostles

---

33. Nuttall, "Calvinism in Free Church History," 425. Cf. Berg and Nuttall, *Philip Doddridge (1702-1751) and the Netherlands*, 13.
34. Quoted by Nuttall, ibid., 427
35. Nuttall, *Good Heavens!* 2.

made so little of it—*unless* they were less interested in this aspect of His resurrection than is much modern apologia."[36] They were fastening upon the experience which Nuttall described in the following terms: "One of the first implications of the resurrection of Jesus is that this relationship to him, this being with Him, is still possible: is possible, indeed, in a far wider way than before. Before, only a few could be with Him.... Now, no longer solely the twelve, not even the ten times twelve met together in Jerusalem, but all who will may come close to Him in discipleship, trust, love and self-abandonment."[37]

It is the same message, albeit couched in different terms, as that preached exactly three hundred years earlier by the Friend, Francis Howgill: "If you say you love him, manifest your love unto him, by following his Light revealed in you, which leads into the true Separation from Sin unto the Lord, to see his Presence near you, who will guide you with his Eye; ... and here you will see your Teacher not removed into a Corner, but present, when you are upon your Beds, and about your labour, convincing, instructing, leading, correcting, judging, and giving Peace to all that love and follow him."[38]

For the early Quakers, as for Nuttall (and in contradistinction from the Cambridge Platonists, for whom it was the divinely-illuminated reason and conscience),[39] the Light is a supernatural gift. As William Penn put it, "It is not our Way of Speaking to say the Light within is the Rule of the Christian Religion; but that the Light of Christ within us is the Rule of true Christians, so that it is not our Light but Christ's Light that is our Rule."[40] In the wake Penn—and of Paul—Nuttall contends that "the living Spirit of the Risen Christ is also a life-giving Spirit."[41] To that Holy Spirit I now turn.

---

36. RH, 65.

37. Nuttall, "The Heirs of Heaven," 10.

38. Nuttall, "Puritan and Quaker Mysticism," 529, quoting Howgill, *Dawnings of the Gospel-Day*, 1676.

39. See HSPCF, 18, where Nuttall, somewhat misleadingly, describes John Norris as being "another of the Cambridge School." There were, indeed, affinities between the thought of Norris and the Cambridge Platonists, but Norris, an Oxford man, was a generation younger than the Cambridge divines; he was greatly influenced by Malebranche, as they were not; and he argued that Robert Barclay had a constricted understanding of the Light. See further Sell, *Enlightenment, Ecumenism, Evangel*, ch. 1.

40. HSPFE, 44, quoting Penn, *Works*, II, 812.

41. RH, 69.

Is Geoffrey also among the Theologians?

II

Before enumerating Nuttall's pneumatological insights (for as with other doctrines he did not bequeath a fully-fledged pneumatolgy) it is necessary to indicate his general perspective on the matter. This is clearly seen in his finest book, *The Holy Spirit in Puritan Faith and Experience*. He explained his intention of giving a voice to the Separatists and early Quakers, and he distinguished these from Calvin: "Calvin himself, for all his stress on the Spirit's witness, yielding an intuitive certitude of Scripture as αυτοπιστος, has been pronounced justly [by P. Wernle] *kein Geistesmensch*."[42] In a footnote he added, "For Calvin the Holy Spirit is a necessity of thought rather than something known in experience."[43] I shall return to this problematic assertion in due course. As regards Greek thought, Nuttall declared that while the Greeks thought clearly "within the limits of what they had found about God," they had not found what the Hebrews had found: "The vital difference may be put in a word by saying that they has not found *Him*. Greek thought about God remains thought about a principle, a problem, something deduced, an ideal. Hebrew thought is about a *person* . . ."[44] Christian thought, not least early Quaker thought,[45] could not think of the Spirit without thinking of Christ, the Word made flesh, of whom we learn in the Bible, the message of which is conveyed to us by the same Spirit.

With this we come to the relation between the Spirit and the Word. Nuttall observed that whereas, prior to the Reformation, religious experience "had necessarily been coloured by the ecclesiastical medium," now it was "an experience of a directly biblical type, the experience which Scripture terms 'being filled with the Spirit.'"[46] This change raised the question of the locus of authority, on which matter Nuttall had this to say:

> In Christianity as a whole the question may be answered in one of three ways; authority may be found in the Church, the Bible, or the self. Each of these may be subdivided: the Church may be the Church as represented by the local priest, by tradition, by the Pope, or by a General Council; the Bible may be taken as a whole, or especial authority may be found in parts of it, or in the words of Jesus alone; the authority of the self may be thought of

---

42. HSPFE, 6.
43. Ibid., n. 5.
44. HSO, 3. That Nuttall should write this more popular book on the Holy Spirit was the idea of Mary, his wife.
45. See Nuttall, *The Refreshing of the Children of Light*, 11.
46. HSPFE. 21. Cf. CPH, 23, 53; "Law and Liberty in Puritanism," 19.

as dependent on the supernatural enlightening of the self by the Holy Spirit, or on the universal but still God-given gift of reason, or finally on reason itself, as the possession of man in his own right. The attitude which we adopt towards the Reformation and towards the history of Protestantism depends very much on the side we support in this controversy of authority; according to our decision we shall condemn the Reformation as mistaken or arrogant, praise it as the Golden Age in Christianity, or regard it as but the beginning of a movement towards freedom, a freedom which, through the clinging power of tradition, it could not itself immediately attain. Whatever be our attitude, however, the fact would seem to be that at the Reformation the authority of the Church (as then constituted) was denied, the authority of the Bible asserted, and the authority of the self, in experience and reasoning, foreshadowed.[47]

It was the conviction of the Puritans that by the Holy Spirit's inspiration the Bible was God's Word, and by the Spirit's enlightening its message was brought home to attentive readers: thus Spirit and Word belonged together. Whereas it was said of Quakerism's founder that "Though the Bible was lost, it might be found in the mouth of George Fox,"[48] in early Quakerism there developed a tendency systematically to disjoin Word and Spirit, not because Quakers scorned the written Word, but because they believed that the same Spirit who had inspired the apostles was now inspiring them. When Cromwell wrote that "As well without the Written Word as with it God doth speak to the hearts and consciences of men" he was, said Nuttall, endorsing a Quaker sentiment.[49] The next Quakerly step was that, to some, the Spirit became "the touchstone by which all else is to be tried, including the Bible itself."[50] Hence the protest of the Congregationalist, John Owen: "He that would utterly separate the Spirit from the Word had as good burn the Bible."[51] While in general sympathy with this, even Richard Baxter allowed the possibility of "extraordinary, confirmed,

---

47. Nuttall, "The Lollard Movement," 243–44.

48. Nuttall, "'Nothing Else Would Do,'" 652, quoting Croese, *General History of the Quakers*, 14.

49. PS, 175, quoting Cromwell, *Letters and Speeches*, Speech IV. According to the Dent Everyman edition, which was Nuttall's and is now, with his markings, in my possession, this is a conflation of two sentences in volume III, 84, the first of which is qualified by the phrase "in extraordinary circumstances."

50. HSPFE, 28.

51. Ibid., 31, quoting Owen, *Πνευματολογία* (1674) II.v.4.

revelation,"[52] the operative term being the middle one. John Robinson, the pastor to the Pilgrims, implied that those who read the Bible may be misguided in the conclusions which they, however honestly, draw from it. He was reported as saying of the Calvinists that "they stick where he [Calvin] left them; a misery much to be lamented; for though they were precious shining lights in their time, yet God had not revealed his whole will to them; and were they now living, saith he, they would be as ready and willing to embrace further light, as that they had received."[53] For his own part he was recalled as famously declaring that "the Lord has more light and truth yet to break forth out of his holy word,"[54] but this does not imply the necessary disjoining of Word and Spirit. Without question many Separatists and Puritans would have agreed with Calvin that "God did not bring forth his Word among men for the sake of a momentary display, intending at the coming of his Spirit to abolish it. Rather, he sent down the same Spirit by whose power he had dispensed the Word, to complete his work by the efficacious confirmation of the Word."[55] Again, Calvin, who was by no means unacquainted with enthusiasts, insisted that "the Spirit, promised to us, has not the task of inventing new and unheard-of revelations, or of forging a new kind of doctrine, to lead us away from the received doctrine of the gospel, but of sealing our minds with that very doctrine which is recommended by the gospel."[56] In a word, the Spirit would not contradict the Word—a position consistently held by many from Calvin to Nuttall.

While learning from his forebears that Word and Spirit may not be disjoined, and that the latter does not contradict the former, Nuttall was well aware that our approach to Scripture cannot be on all fours with that of the early Puritans, for whom "The sheet-anchor . . . was that Scripture contained the law of the Lord: a model or pattern for all life, social and national life as well as ecclesiastical, down to the smallest details of the individual's personal behaviour."[57] We, however, "no longer seek an infallible law in Scripture, and in the performance of what commands we do find there we think it right to leave considerable liberty . . ."[58] There are

52. HSPFE, 32, quoting R. Baxter, *Practical Works*, ed. W. Orme (1830) II, 198.
53. Ibid., 113, quoting J. Robinson, *Works*, ed. R. Ashton, 1852, I, xliv.
54. Ibid., 24, quoting ibid.
55. Calvin, *Institutes*, I.ix.3.
56. Calvin, *Institutes*, I.ix.1.
57. Nuttall, "Law and Liberty in Puritanism," 21.
58. Ibid., 22.

broader questions of interpretation too: "John Owen . . . held firmly and controversially to the divine inspiration of the points in the Hebrew text of the Old Testament; while a century later Job Orton, who 'in spite of his connection with presbyterians . . . always regarded himself as 'quite an independent,' and whom . . . 'both orthodox and heterodox dissenters have venerated . . . as a patriarch,' held that to distinguish between the Epistles and the Gospels, in the way universal among us to-day, was the clear mark of a Socinian."[59] All this granted, there is no reason to doubt that when Nuttall asserted that the Separatists "were not ashamed to acknowledge the converting power of God's Spirit in their hearts through His Word in the Bible, without the intervention of 'other men'"[60] he was also speaking for himself.

Like many in the Puritan tradition, Nuttall steered between the Scylla of biblicist legalism and the Charybdis of charismatic excess—"enthusiasm" as its early opponents branded it. As to the former, there was some chafing within Puritanism itself: "The Sabbatarianism, long sermons, psalm-singing, fast days and rigid morals which developed came to seem as much a piece of legalistic paraphernalia or abracadabra as the masses, penances and indulgences of unreformed Roman Catholicism has seemed," in which connection Nuttall quoted Walter Cradock of the Congregational church, Llanvaches, as saying, "I fear our fast dayes are the most smoky dayes in God's nostrills of all the dayes of the year,"[61] and drew the moral that "Scrupulosity, if wound too tight, eventually, and suddenly, springs back, or out into a new freedom."[62] In general, Nuttall elsewhere remarked, the Congregationalist's "appeal to 'the Bible alone' has been evangelical rather than rationalizing."[63] As to the latter, Nuttall looked back to the Lollards: "Ignorant, mistaken, fanatical the Lollards must often have been; but in their devotion to the Bible which they made their own, and in the sincere common sense with which they attacked the accumulations of tradition, they hold an important place in the evolution of English Church History."[64] James Nayler, the Quaker, understood that

---

59. Nuttall, *The General Body of the Three Denominations*, 4. The quoted words within this quotation are Alexander Gordon's in his DNB article on Orton.

60. Nuttall, "The Early Congregational Conception of the Church," CHST 14 (1944) 199.

61. Nuttall, "Law and Liberty in Puritanism," 22, quoting Cradock, *Divine Drops Distilled* (1650), 4–5.

62. Ibid., 26.

63. Nuttall, *Congregationalists and Creeds*, 7.

64. Nuttall, "The Lollard Movement," 250.

"the greatest and best gifts . . . from God are accompanied with the chiefest and worst temptations;"[65] and the pattern was repeated during the Evangelical Revival, on which Nuttall commented, "The excitement of Revival can tempt some natures and sensibilities into extravagance and fanaticism and, in the power of a freedom above the law, to shake off moral constriction; the inspiration claimed may come to be treated as independent of datum, medium or check in Scripture, history or the fellowship of the Church, in extreme cases even of Christ; personal assurance, impatient of reasoning's slower persuasions, can unfit for honest argument; and, taken together, this may drive an inquirer into deism or unbelief."[66]

Against all unbalanced enthusiasm, and with evident approval, Nuttall quoted Richard Baxter's words, "Doth the Spirit work on a man as on a beast or a stone? . . . No, the Spirit or God supposeth nature, and worketh on man as man; by exciting your own understanding and will to do their parts."[67]

III

This brings us to the place Nuttall accorded first to reason and then to will. Recognizing that Puritanism was rooted in the Renaissance as well as in the Reformation, Nuttall concurred with Robert Vaughan in holding that "the collocation 'enlightened Protestantism and sound reason' was a Puritan *sine qua non*."[68] Illustrations of this fact abound in Nuttall's writings. Thus, for example, he quoted John Owen: "The true Nature of Saving Illumination consists in this, that it gives the Mind such a direct intuitive insight and prospect into Spiritual Things, as that in their own Spiritual Nature they suit, please and satisfie it";[69] and Richard Baxter: "All that come into the world of nature, [Christ] enlighteneth with the light of Nature . . . ; And all that come into the world of grace he enlighteneth with the light of supernatural Revelation."[70] But Nuttall thought that Baxter went too far when he declared that "the Spirit and reason are not to be here disjoined, much less opposed. As reason sufficeth not without the Spirit, being dark and asleep; so the Spirit worketh not on the will but by the

---

65. Quoted by Nuttall, "Reflections on William Penn's Preface," 115.
66. Nuttall, "Methodism and the Older Dissent," 18–20.
67. HSPFE, 160, quoting Baxter's *Practical Works*, IV, 226.
68. Ibid., 36, quoting Vaughan, *English Nonconformity*, 161.
69. Ibid., 41, quoting Πνευματολογία, III.ii.16.
70. Ibid., 163, quoting Baxter, *The Quaker's Catechism* (1655), 7.

reason: he moveth not a man as a beast or stone, to do a thing he knoweth not why, but by illumination giveth him the soundest reason for the doing of it."[71] This, to Nuttall, precluded extraordinary modes of illumination by the Spirit which were above and beyond the range of our discursive reason—and, as we saw, Baxter elsewhere allowed the possibility of "confirmed" extraordinary revelations.

All of which is to say that while enamoured of reason, not least as an interpretative instrument and as that which checks the fantastic, Nuttall was far from being a rationalist. At the same time, he was concerned that "too keen a fear of reason, may lead paradoxically through the atrophying of the critical faculty, to something near an identification between God's ways and man's."[72] Positively, "Reason and conscience ... the instruments God has given men for discovering what is true and what is the right things for us to do, ... remain the *normal* means by which, as Christians, we become conscious of the guidance of His Spirit."[73] Thus, just as the Spirit was not to be disjoined from the Word, so the Spirit was not to be disjoined from reason, though his range is wider. This accords with Nuttall's judgment that "The Puritans were right in rejecting Quaker claims to infallibility; but in arguing that the Quakers could not possess the same Spirit as inspired the Apostles, for then they would be infallible, *quod erat absurdum*, they were wrong."[74]

In further expounding his view, Nuttall turns to Coleridge for the phrase, "whatever *finds* me, bears witness for itself that it had proceeded from a Holy Spirit . . . ,"[75] and adds, "In the sphere of theology such a criterion in experience is quickly condemned as thin and subjective."[76] I should have thought that the immediate difficulty with Coleridge's phrase is that people have been *found* by all manner of bizarre notions, and that therefore the posited criterion is far too elastic: but let that pass. The important concern is the reasoned appeal to experience, and in this connection Nuttall invoked his teacher, C. J. Cadoux: "Why should religious knowledge be the one field in which the limitation and infallibility of our minds are supposed to vitiate the process of our learning and allowed to sap our trust in the accessibility of truth? . . . [D]espite the margin of

71. Quoted ibid., 47
72. Nuttall, "The Lord Protector," 249.
73. HSO, 38.
74. HSPF, 172.
75. Ibid., 173, quoting Coleridge, *Confessions*, 10.
76. Ibid.

uncertainty, we have through our inward, spiritual powers—as through our powers of seeing and hearing—such measure of knowledge, light, and certainty as is sufficient for our daily need; and we have no right or reason to demand more."[77]

Nuttall made the point for himself by contrasting Bishop Pecock's epistemology with that of the Lollards:

> [I]n the last resort the authority Pecock advanced for his faith was not so different from that of the Lollards. If pressed, Pecock could only have admitted that the reason, by which articles of faith are to be proved, is its own intrinsic authority, which is a telling illustration of the non-rationalism, ultimately at one with the non-rationalism of a religious conviction, to which the rationalist is eventually driven back, for he would have found it hard to defend the authority of reason by reason. A pragmatic defence he could and did give: "we han noon other power"; but at least as implicit in the Lollards' biblicism... was the assertion of another power, in its own sphere as imperious and impregnable as reason, the power of divine inspiration. Reliance on the one power is in the end on exactly the same footing as reliance on the other; and to live entirely by logic would be as absurd as the life to which an uncritical biblicism also led.[78]

Elsewhere Nuttall made an analogous point with reference to Bernard of Clairvaux: "Bernard felt, as Dante was to feel, that after the sharp conclusion to which one is brought by the power of the Holy Spirit every logical demonstration must be dull (*ottusa*). Nor should such an attitude be dismissed as obscurantist. To obscurantism it may lead; but so may scholastic reasoning lead to aridity and barrenness."[79] Not the least important reason for Nuttall's delight in Dante's works was the latter's recognition that "Reason's wings are short, and logical argument is a blunted instrument; truth is something which must be seen, shining, self-evident and sure, in its own light."[80] The status of allegedly self-evidencing truths is a matter over which much ink has been spilt but, intriguing—and important—though the question is, it cannot be pursued here.

Turning now to the will and the conscience, we must hear what Nuttall had to say concerning their freedom. In a paper published in the wake

---

77. Ibid., quoting Cadoux, *Catholicism and Christianity*, 174.
78. Nuttall, "Bishop Pecock and the Lollard Movement," 85–86.
79. Nuttall, "St. Bernard of Clairvaux and His Ideal," 224.
80. Nuttall, "A Reading of the *Paradiso*," 49.

The Theological Education of the Ministry

of the celebration of the tercentenary of the Great Ejectment of 1660–62, Nuttall drew the following lessons from the witness of the seventeenth-century radicals:

> I am persuaded of two things. The first is this: that of all the liberties for which we are concerned, first and fundamental is liberty of conscience, liberty for worship, freedom of communion with God. These religious radicals, to whom much in our heritage is owing, were concerned, like ourselves, that civic liberties lost should be regained and that many kinds of freedom should be granted more widely. But their first concern, from which all else sprang, was for liberty of worship according to conscience. Till that was gained they were willing to lose, for themselves, their liberties of person and property, let alone any equality of rights and opportunities.[81]

Moreover,

> These men could go to prison cheerfully, despite the indescribable filth and ill-treatment they had to face, despite all the loss of liberty, because at a deeper level they had already willingly let their liberty go. They did not think of themselves as free men, free men though in the world's eyes they believed they ought to be. They thought of themselves as the servants of God, and they went to prison at His call, in pursuance of His will, which, day in, day out, they had been striving to fulfil, in small things as well as in great.[82]

As George Hughes of Plymouth, ejected under the Act of Uniformity and now in prison, wrote to his similarly imprisoned son, "free communion with God in Prison is worth a thousand Liberties gain'd with the Loss of Liberty of Spirit."[83]

It is not fanciful to suspect that as he pondered these things, Nuttall's mind turned to the spirits in Dante's *Paradiso*, of whom he remarked that "The spirits' vision of Him, on which their blessedness depends, is all of grace, . . . In response to such munificence, the spirits willingly accept the divine providence and disposal of themselves as a necessity dictated by God's love."[84] If we add to this some lines that Nuttall's great-great-grandfather, Charles Williams, wrote for the opening of New College, London,

---

81. Nuttall, "Our Freedom as Christians," 369.
82. Ibid., 369–70.
83. Ibid., 368.
84. Nuttall, "A Reading of the *Paradiso*," 51.

on 11 May 1850, we have Christian liberty coupled with the ecclesiological and eschatological dimensions of the Spirit's work to which I shall come shortly. Williams charged "the future students and teachers of the College to lead others

> To all the freedom with which Christ makes free,
> And to the brotherhood of his Church on earth,
> Instinct with life, and love, and joy, and hope,
> Foretasting now the blessedness of heaven."[85]

To Puritans, Quakers and Nuttall alike, freedom of worship entailed the right and obligation to "Praise God with that joyful alacrity which beseemeth one that is ready to pass into Glory, and try whether this will not cure the peoples weariness."[86] He would likewise have endorsed Baxter's further words concerning preaching: "Preach with such life and awakening seriousness; Preach with such grateful holy eloquence, and with such easie method, and with such variety of wholesome matter, that the people may never be aweary of you;"[87] and to any preacher he would have applied Fox's general, experimental, exhortation: "You will say, Christ saith this, and the apostles say this, but what canst thou say?"[88] Nor would the words of Bunyan, who preached "what I felt, what I smartingly did feel"[89] have been far from his mind. Extempore proclamation was implicit in Bunyan's practice; it was the exercising of the gift of the Spirit; and it was something which caused Baxter to oppose untutored lay preaching.[90] As to public prayer, Baxter's advice was that ministers should "Pray with that heavenly life and fervour as may wrap up the souls of those that joyne with you, and try then whether they will be aweary."[91] More radical Puritans opposed all set forms in worship in the interests of openness to the Spirit, and among their number on this matter was John Owen, who disputed the issue with Richard Baxter, who could not see that singing the set words of psalms and hymns differed in principle from using set forms of prayer.[92] Nuttall struck

---

85. Nuttall, "With Heart and Mind," in his *New College, London*, 6. For the complete poem see *Evangelical Magazine* (1850) 353-54.

86. RB, 53, quoting Baxter, *The Divine Appointment of the Lord's Day*, 124.

87. Ibid., quoting ibid.

88. PS, 183.

89. HSPFE, 8, quoting Bunyan, *Grace Abounding*, para. 276.

90. See HSPFE, 81.

91. RB, 53, quoting *The Divine Appointment of the Lord's Day*, 124.

92. See HSPFE, 72-73. Cf. Nuttall and Chadwick, *From Uniformity to Unity*, 166-67.

his own balance in the following way: "There is no reason why extempore prayer and read prayer, 'prophesying' and formal preaching, silent meetings and sacramental services should not be recognized, all in their several ways, as capable of divine inspiration and as means whereby men come into personal communion with God through Christ. . . . So long as each practice is kept free from the mechanical, impersonal corruptions introduced by sacerdotalism, each may have its place in Christian worship." As he continued to reflect on the worship of the Congregationalists we may be sure that he spoke for himself:

> What was fundamental was not the "shadowish or figurative ordinances,"[93] but the baptism of the Spirit and the feeding on spiritual bread; was not episcopacy or ministerial ordination or ecclesiastical polity of any kind, for "the true Succession" was "though the Spirit,"[94] and the Spirit blew where it listed; was not in creeds or catechisms or liturgies or any forms which might quench the Spirit and darken what fresh light might be given. What was fundamental was the personal reception, both individually and communally, of the Spirit; was in the possession of the Spirit's gifts and graces; was in not grieving the Spirit.[95]

Here, once again, are ecclesiological matters to which I shall shortly turn, but before leaving the specific theme of freedom I must comment upon Nuttall's negative phrase, "not in creeds or catechisms." Adverting to the tradition into which he was born, Nuttall informs us that, historically, Congregationalists hesitated over creeds because they were man-made, whereas Scripture was given by God; because, "when once established, creeds take on a fixity proper only to what is given in the revelation itself"; and because they unduly elevate the intellectual over the experimental.[96] Underlying all of these, however, was the fact that "Congregationalists have taken vehement exception to the imposition of creeds."[97] This point weighed very strongly with Nuttall. He quoted the Independent John Cook with approval: "compulsion can no more gain the heart, than the fish can love the fisherman,"[98] and on his own account he declared in a broadcast talk that "the perception that the simple New Testament confession 'Jesus

---

93. HSPFE, 177, quoting Bunyan, *Works*, I, 425.
94. Ibid., quoting Cromwell, *Letters and Speeches*, Speech I.
95. HSPF, 177.
96. See Nuttall, *Congregationalists and Creeds*, 6, 8, 9–11.
97. Ibid., 2.
98. HSPFE, 104, quoting Cook, *What The Independents Would Have* (1647).

is Lord' not only excludes all human claims to lordship over the church but can only be made freely by willing minds that have not been forced. Both these positions are clearly stated in the Savoy *Declaration* [1658]."[99] Furthermore, with reference to that "simple" confession, Nuttall was in the tolerant line of Baxter and Doddridge. "Two things," wrote Baxter, "have set the Church on fire, and been plagues of it above one thousand years. 1. Enlarging our Creed, and making more fundamentals than ever God made. 2. Composing (and so imposing) our Creeds and Confessions in our own words and phrases."[100] Consistently with this, the Reformed pastor *par* excellence, who advised those wishing to attach "denominational" labels to him that if "meer Christian" did not satisfy them they could call him a "Catholick Christian,"[101] exhorted Peter Ince to "bottom upon Christ and the great fundamentals. Unite in those with men of holiness & righteousness. Prosecute that union affectionately & unweariedly: & keep you eye upon that glory where we shall be one."[102] In thus protesting, Baxter was expressing his deep concern for Christian unity, as, later, did Doddridge: "[I]t is one very important article of my faith that I am bound in duty affectionately to esteem and embrace all who practically comply with the design and the revelation an love of our Lord Jesus Christ in sincerity, how much soever they may differ from myself in their language or their conceptions about any speculative points."[103]

Just as Nuttall sought a middle way between charismatic excesses and rationalism, so in connection with Christian confession he sought a middle way between ecclesiastical credal rigidity and authoritarianism on the one hand and the utterly unconstrained right of private judgment on the other. Thus, he wrote, "when Rome, becoming Modernist overnight (as a Capuchin friar has remarked), goes beyond the *traditio passiva* of the Council of Trent to *traditio activa* as the living authority which justifies the proclamation of a new dogma, such as the Assumption of the Virgin, we draw back as uneasily as when we see private judgment leading Robert Robinson to something like Unitarianism."[104] He underlined the

99. Quoted by Binfield, "Profile," 83.

100. RB, 122, quoting Baxter, *The Saints Everlasting Rest*, pt. ii, Preface, fol. R7 verso margin. Cf. Howe, *Works*, V, 226;

101. RB., 121, quoting R. Baxter, *Church-History of the Government of Bishops and their Councils abbreviated* (1680). Preface, fols. a4, b1.

102. Ibid., 84, quoting Dr. Williams's Library MS, 1: 11.

103. Nuttall quoting Doddridge's confession in the Castle Hill, Northampton, Church Book, reprinted by Waddington, *Congregational History*, 287.

104. Nuttall, "Reflections on Books Reviewed," 75.

ecclesiological point elsewhere in these uncompromising terms: "To claim doctrinal infallibility whether for individuals or for the Church as a whole is as much Ranterism as to claim moral perfectibility. For it is to claim exemption from the limitations of time and place which are of the essence of history."[105] But the further reference to matters ecclesiological brings us to Nuttall's doctrine of the Church—a doctrine according to which the individual's discernment of the mind of Christ through the Word by the Spirit is both facilitated, and where necessary tempered, by the fellowship of visible saints.[106]

IV

In Nuttall's view the Church is constituted by the call of Christ and by his presence in its midst. In his address to the London Society of Jews and Christians he dwelt upon the importance for Christians of Jesus's words, "Ye did not choose me, but I chose you" (John 15:16). But "As a Christian I must not say that they are not found in the Lord's mouth; for the transformation from the Old Israel to the new is most sharply expressed herein, that the title 'the Lord', which before was given to God alone, is now given also to Jesus. . . . Christians, the Church, while remaining, as they believe, the chosen people of God, are also distinctively Christ's people . . ."[107] By the end of the second century the meaning of "people" had changed, as had the reference of the term "chosen": "No longer a distinct nation in their own eyes or a distinct race in the eyes of others, the distinction of Christians now lay inwardly in faith and obedience to God in Christ and outwardly in an outgoing life of love and service."[108] Within the Congregational tradition the corporate response to Christ's call is traditionally in the form of a covenant. That is to say, "The covenant is recognized as what formally constitutes a church: John Robinson says explicitly that 'a company consisting though but of two or three . . . gathered together in

---

105. PS, 234.

106. That this mode of discernment may have consequences of the most political kind is suggested by Nuttall's remark that "Apart from the providence of God as revealed in events, Cromwell's guidance, like that of most of the Puritans, came from a three-fold source: it came from the word of God in Scripture, from the answering word of the Spirit in his own heart, and from the support and restraint of God's people." See "The Lord Protector," 251.

107. Nuttall, "The Concept of the Chosen People in Christianity," 8.

108. Ibid., 9.

the name of Christ by a covenant made to walk in all the ways of God known to them is a church.'"[109]

Another way of expressing the Church's constitutive factor is to say that it is "the community of the Spirit"[110]—which is to say that the risen Christ dwells by the Spirit in the midst of the visible saints. Yet another way of making the point is to say that "Just as . . . the Reformers dissolved the monasteries, no longer believing that 'the religious life' should be confined to a spiritual élite, so now the Puritans replaced the mysticism which blossomed in solitude, apart from the world, by an intense assurance of God's nearness open to ordinary men and women in their daily experience *and found most easily in the fellowship of believers.*"[111] Richard Baxter underlined the point as crisply as any: "Thy presence makes a croud, a Church."[112]

As Nuttall ruefully reflected,

> Again and again, the Church, in its official form, has sunk low into disputations, persecutions of its own members, self-aggrandisment, conventional acceptance of the standards of the world round about it. And, considering the dead weight which in this way has so often been against any conception, any experience, of the Spirit as known to Paul, what is astonishing is not that the experience has been so little shared or sought but rather its constant renewal. . . . In England the Puritans with their "prophesyings," the Independents with their "Church meetings," the Quakers with their silent meetings for worship, the Methodists with their "class meetings," have all in their turn been among these [renewal] groups.[113]

That such a witness flowed directly down to Nuttall is clear from his own testimony: "The Christian's Master is the risen Lord, whose ministry remains as constant and living, as effective and transforming, as ever it was in Galilee . . . Still He attaches us livingly to Himself, still He shares with us His mind, His experience, all that His ministry costs Him, even the oft-repeated bitter cup."[114]

---

109. Nuttall, "The Early Congregational Conception of the Church," 198, quoting J. Robinson, *Works*, II, 132.

110. HSO, 54.

111. Nuttall, "Puritan and Quaker Mysticism," 527, my italics.

112. RB 124, quoting R. Baxter, *The Reasons of the Christian Religion*, 458.

113. HSO, 59.

114. Nuttall, "The heirs of heaven," 15.

The Theological Education of the Ministry

In my opinion Nuttall was correct in saying that the Church is not constituted by the sacraments, and he invoked a variety of persons in support. He quoted the Separatist Henry Barrow as saying that "many thousands that never attained the symbol of the Supper yet do feed of the body and blood of Christ unto eternal life";[115] and as for baptism, Richard Baxter, by no means the most radical of Puritans, declared that "it is a dishonourable doctrine against God and Christianity to say that God layeth his love and mans salvation so much on a Ceremony, as to damn or deny an upright holy soul for want of it . . . The thing signified is necessary to salvation."[116]

In view of Nuttall's stance, it is not surprising that he was deeply distressed by the report of the international Anglican-Reformed dialogue, *God's Reign and Our Unity*. Indeed, he wrote a trenchant critique of it which he passed to me. He felt that it was too damning—even by his standards—to see the light of published day. It would therefore be wrong of me to refer to it in detail. I can, however, say that he detected a number of exegetical sins and some pre-critical exposition; but what angered him most was the reiterated claim that the Church is constituted by the sacraments.[117] This not only undermined the gospel in his opinion, but it opened the way to sacerdotalism of the kind which prompted him to wonder "how a theologian so devoted to wholeness as Gore is can be so sectarian over episcopacy," and to declare that he "would not have episcopal hands, even Gore's, laid on his head for all the unity in Christendom."[118]

Supplementing his desire not to violate the Gospel at this specific point was Nuttall's broader conviction that "the truly Christian community . . . will be marked not by uniformity but by genuine unity," and "Genuine unity is possible only if there is a large measure of freedom."[119] The fact that such concerns flowed from Nuttall's pen in what might, *prima facie*, have seemed unlikely contexts is testimony to the anxiety he felt at

---

115. PS, 171, quoting H. Barrow, *A Brief Discoverie of the False Church*, ch. 4, in Carlson, *The Writings of Henry Barrow*.

116. RB, 66, quoting R. Baxter, *Plain Scripture Proof*, 1st pag., p. 199.

117. *God's Reign and Our Unity*, 33, 41. For a few published examples of Nuttall's disdain of woolly language and untoward attitudes in ecumenical circles see PS, ch. 22. Note also his remark upon the Church of South India. Of that Church's original ministers who had been drawn from Nonconformist traditions he said that they "have fastened on those who come after them what they decline for themselves" (namely episcopacy). See Nuttall and Chadwick, *From Uniformity to Unity*, 184.

118. Nuttall, "Charles Gore," 57, 61. Cf. Nuttall, *Congregationalists and Creeds*, 16.

119. Nuttall, "Our Freedom as Christians," 367.

some ecumenical tendencies. Thus, in his pamphlet on the Countess of Huntingdon's Trevecca College he writes,

> I do not see any justification for dismissing Trevecca's ecumenicity of the gospel as self-defeating because lacking in true churchmanship. The Trevecca method could at least claim that it led to many conversions and to the gathering of new congregations. Our own efforts after ecumenicity, with less and hesitant preaching and more frequent observance of the sacrament, are being accompanied by a falling-off in the number of communicant members; nor have we avoided, or yet successfully met, fresh difficulties over ordination. . . . With all their deficiencies [the Trevecca preachers] preached the gospel and kept the flame of faith alive. I sometimes wonder whether the independent undenominational evangelical mission preachers of today, who would be approved for ordination by few and whose sermons might be acceptable to none of us, are not performing a similar service in our own time, till present calamities are overpast and faith and reason again embrace.[120]

It follows from the foregoing that since Christ alone is Lord of the Church there is something irregular (the early Separatists would have said, "of Antichrist") about a state-established Church. In 1646 the saints at Bury St. Edmunds made no bones about it:

> And wee being convinced in Conscience of the evill of ye Church of England, and of all other states wch are contrary to Christ's institution, And being (according to Christes institutions and Comandements) fully Separates, not only from them, but also from those who Communicate with them either publickly or privately, Wee resolve by the grace of God, not to returne unto their vaine inventions, their human devices, their abominable Idolatries or superstitious high places, which were built and dedicated to idolatry.[121]

However, Nuttall carefully pointed out that in the course of the Separatist-Congregational tradition there were both those who advocated the complete separation of Church and state, and those who would have had an established Church provided it were of their favoured kind. The broad Congregational tradition is represented by Jeremiah Burroughes: "What Nationall Worship hath Christ instituted? Doth our birth in the Nation

---

120. Nuttall, *The Significance of Trevecca College*, 21.

121. VS, 49, quoting Browne, *History of Congregationalism . . . in Norfolk and Suffolk*, 394; Grieve and Jones, *These Three Hundred Years*, 20.

make us members of the Church? These things are so palpably plaine to any that will understand, that tis tedious to spend time about them."[122] John Owen came to endorse this position, declaring that "He that will not separate from the World and false-worship is a separate from Christ."[123]

In expressing his own view Nuttall took his point of departure from Anders Nygren, and concluded with what must surely be one of his most radical suggestions:

> In *Christus Victor* for last March [Nygren] re-presented the Lutheran doctrine of the two kingdoms: the kingdom of God, of Christ, of the Gospel and of the Word of God; in short, the Church; and the kingdom of the world, of evil, of the Law and of the sword; in short, the State; and never the twain shall meet. "It is against the will of God," Dr. Nygren writes, "to try to rule the world by the Gospel. God has ordained an entirely different government to rule the world." Now certainly we need to guard against making an identification, an easy merging, of the Church and the world, or of the Church and the State; but in fact it has often been those with a lively sense of the *difference* between the Church and the State who have been the most active in bringing Christian influences to bear, in order to *transform* the State and its functions. . . . These things can be done; and I never heard that any Lutheran declined a food parcel because it expressed the intrusion of the gospel of love into the alien kingdom of a warring world. . . .
>
> So far as I can see, this contrast between the ways of Christ's disciples and the ways of the rulers of the nations is not meant to be a wall of partition which nothing, not even the transforming power of Christ, can break down. It involves His disciples in a way of life which will be not only towards one another within the Church, but eventually towards the rulers of the nations themselves. If that is so, I think we must work for the abandonment of sovereignty internationally as well as within the nation; and if this should being about enslavement, the acceptance of it willingly and redemptively, would after all, be in line with the main burden of the Christian ethic. Not that I think that any nation is at present ready to abandon its sovereignty.[124]

---

122. VS, 64, quoting J. Burroughes, *A Vindication* (1646) 22, from Bartlet, Ἰχνογραφία or a Model of the Primitive Congregational Way, 22.

123. Ibid., 54, quoting J. Owen, *Eschol: . . . Or, Rules of Direction*, Rule V.

124. Nuttall, *Christian Love Manifested in History*, 2-3, 11.

Is Geoffrey also among the Theologians?

Turning now from the constitution of the Church we may come to what the older divines called its matter: those who comprise it. In the first place the Church comprises the called, visible saints. Separated unto Christ they are separated from "the world," and also from the Church of England into which "the world" has infiltrated. This, at least, was the Separatist view, as well as that of Burroughes, Owen and others. Nor were Congregationalists alone in advocating separation from the godless world. Concerning Bunyan, Nuttall wrote that "By implication *The Pilgrim's Progress* is a powerful plea for separatism. If there was a case for separating from the Roman Church, there was also a case for separating from a worldly Church. Mr. Formalist and Mr. Pliable might find a place in it, but they could not be members of the Church of Christ in Bedford, who are in principle already translated from death to life because they love the brethren, with a love greater than their own. This is another way of saying that for Bunyan ecclesiology has its roots in Christology and in awareness of Christ."[125] Likewise, Richard Baxter declared that "The Church's separation from the unbelieving world is a necessary duty: for what is a Church, but a society dedicated or sanctified to God, by separation from the rest of the world? II Cor. 6:17, 18."[126]

This stream of testimony flowed down into our own time through the witness and writings of Nuttall, his friendship with, and lectures to, Anglicans notwithstanding. He contrasted the Congregational understanding of membership with other views thus:

> In much modern discussion church membership is not considered of vital import, and the Church invisible is brought in to include those supposed in some sense to be Christians though outside the Church as organized: it is another effect of universalism. In the seventeenth century it was still the other way round: it was the Church visible which was the Church at large, the all-inclusive net containing fishes bad as well as good, while the Church invisible denoted the saints, the few, known only to God. With this distinction, which today those who allow it, as well as those who deny it, agree is "not biblical," the early Congregationalists were not concerned. Their concern was with the visible Church; and within the visible Church they allowed none but saints, and visible saints.[127]

---

125. Nuttall, "The Heart of *The Pilgrim's Progress*." In Brooks, *Reformation Principle and Practice*, 238.

126. VS, 55, quoting Baxter, *A Christian Directory*, III, 53.

127. VS, 160.

William Bartlet expressed the positive point in these terms: the Church is "a free society or communion of visible saints, embodied and knit together by a voluntary consent."[128] In his exposition of the matter Henry Burton specifically referred to the fact that the saints "freely enter into Covenant'"[129] In Nuttall's opinion, "That [the early Congregationalists] should . . . have perceived that in the new fellowship which was created, only a free response, in others no less than in themselves, was worthy of God's grace is the most remarkable thing about them."[130]

Nuttall was nothing less than realistic when he declared that "Whatever the name, some form of discipline is necessary for any self-respecting community, if only to manifest and preserve its identity."[131] But this is a pragmatic consideration. The early Congregationalists, no less than Nuttall himself, thought theologically in terms of godly discipline under the Gospel: discipline designed to honour God, maintain the integrity of the Church and reclaim the sinful. Every church polity, no doubt, has its pitfalls, and Nuttall was well aware that "In practice, there is . . . some danger of a tendency for those who believe themselves to be the elect to believe themselves also to be the *élite*."[132] It was necessary to recognize that the saints were also sinners, and at church meeting members would be received into the covenant of the ground of their profession of faith and their godly walk (whereas Presbyterians required an affirmation of faith only), and they would be expected to maintain a godly walk. If they did not, church meeting would prayerfully consider the situation, hoping that any discipline meted out would prompt repentance and restoration to fellowship.

As to church meeting itself, Nuttall considered that it was "The distinctive feature of the Congregational polity . . . in which not only chosen officers but every member had an equal share in the church's government."[133] In a broadcast talk he subsequently elaborated the point, with reference to the Congregational Church's *Declaration of Faith* (1967):

> In intention church meeting is not, as it may appear to be, a democracy, with equal rights for all. It is, rather, a carrying forward of the Protestant emphasis on the church as a gathered

---

128. VS, 72, quoting Bartlet, Ἰχνογραφία, 30.
129. VS, 107, quoting H. Burton, *The Protestation Protested* (1641) fol. C2 verso.
130. VS, 167.
131. Nuttall, "The Speldhurst Church Book," 560.
132. Nuttall, "The Concept of the Chosen People in Christianity," 11.
133. HSPF, 119.

Is Geoffrey also among the Theologians?

and worshipping community. The Lord whose presence gives reality to the church's worship also has a will, for the church to perform; and if His people reverently seek it He makes it known to them, not infrequently through the disciplined sensitiveness of the simple.[134] Corporate expectancy and corporate obedience are thus marks of the church meeting. Such a conception makes demands of every church member and also requires faith in God's enabling power. So, Congregationalists believe, does the New Testament.[135]

The brief of church meeting was, of course, much wider than the disciplining (which sometimes degenerated into the policing) of wayward saints. It concerned the church's witness and mission, but also right order as regards the sacraments. As Nuttall pointed out, the Congregationalists inherited from the Separatists the view that "the sacraments, being seals of God's Covenant, ought to be administered only to the faithful, and Baptism to their seed or those under their government";[136] and he proceeded to explain that "Not only a pastor . . . but a genuine *coetus fidelium*, was a *sine qua non*."[137] Because there was no such thing on board ship, John Cotton refused to baptize a baby, named Seaborn, who was born in mid-Atlantic.[138] Similarly, the Lord's Supper, as a sacrament of the Church was instituted for its members only. On all of which Nuttall had his thoughts:

> Baptists and Congregationalists were at one, so long as they held to a Calvinist theology and discipline, in associating the Lord's Supper and the church meeting. The presence at *both* was both an immense privilege and the duty of *all* church members, giving devotional and responsible meaning to membership, and of *none* but members; and the absence of members from either ordinance was an occasion for discipline. With our abandonment of Calvinism, we are still at one, but negatively. We no longer require attendance at either ordinance as a condition of membership; and we practise an open communion, in which we welcome all Christians, if not all men whatsoever, to the Lord's

---

134. When reading "Law and Liberty in Puritanism," 23, we may not be mistaken in suspecting that Nuttall enjoyed quoting Cradock's *Glad Tydings from Heaven*, 29: "the Spirit of God in the least Saint is better able to determine than all the Bishops."

135. Quoted by Binfield, "Profile," 83.

136. HSPFE, 94, quoting F. Johnson and H. Ainsworth, *Apologie or Defence . . . of Brownists*, para. 10, as quoted by Dale, *History of English Congregationalism*, 180.

137. HSPFE, 94.

138. Ibid., citing Winthrop, *History of New England*, I, 131; cf. Nuttall, "The Early Congregational Conception of the Church," 202.

> Table, and in some churches to the church meeting also. It is not surprising that church meetings are now often ill attended. With the duty, the sense of privilege—in the proper, Calvinist sense of being "chosen, called, faithful," has gone. The Lord's Supper is ill attended too. It would be worse attended, were it not that here ecumenical pressures encourage frequent observance, though on an understanding in terms of individual piety almost wholly foreign to the communal and domestic piety of our fathers. *They* at the table accepted their *mutual responsibilities* of holiness and love, and *together* boasted their Saviour's name before the scoffing age, knowing themselves to be
>
> A little spot enclosed by grace
>   Out of the world's wide wilderness.[139]

On associations and councils wider (I do not say "higher") than the local church meeting Nuttall did not have a great deal to say. He did, however, offer his "Impressions" of the Seventh International Congregational Council which met at St. Andrews in 1953. Among other things he noted that

> In the document which was issued after the Council it is stated that "We believe that the mind of Christ for His people is given to Councils by the same Spirit that guides the local church." This is true; but nothing is gained by shutting our eyes to the fact that a Council is not, and cannot be, "the same" as a local church. The people who compose a Council are met temporarily and *ad hoc*, they do not know each other and have not given themselves to one another in continuing fellowship and mutual support, they do not know their Moderator in the way they know their minister nor does he so know them; which, since for Christians the personal is normally the channel through which God makes Himself known, makes a difference that is vital and inescapable. This is not at all to deny that the mind of Christ may be discovered in Councils. It is to say . . . that we have yet much to do in working out, and in being faithful to, the procedure which is appropriate for Councils.[140]

For the ideal as it applies both to church meeting and to wider councils Nuttall turned to a poem entitled "The Association," written in 1790 by the Baptist Benjamin Francis:

---

139. Nuttall, "Calvinism in Free Church History," 424.
140. Nuttall, "The St. Andrews Conference," 327.

> The sacred page thy only rule and guide,
> "Thus saith the Lord" shall thy debates decide;
> While charity spreads her balmy wings
> O'er different notions, in indifferent things,
> And graceful order, walking hand in hand
> With cheerful freedom, leads her willing band . . .
> In thee, impartial discipline maintains
> Harmonious order, but aloud disclaims
> All human force to rule the human mind,
> Impose opinions, and the conscience bind.[141]

What, finally, of the Church's ministers? Taking his cue from the New Testament, Nuttall explains that there, "Leading the worship of the community was . . . not a matter of sex, of office, or even of what we nowadays call function. It was a gift of the Spirit. Only so could a man (or woman) venture on it: but when the gift was offered it was not to be refused."[142] If the call to ministry was from God—a *sine qua non* in Congregational eyes, the orderly call of the saints in Church Meeting gave practical effect to it.[143] Thus "Ordination is the public recognition that God's Spirit has made a man overseer of a particular congregation; it is the congregation which ordains, not the other ministers present."[144] William Strong specified the stages thus:" First, the Spirit doth gift the men, and qualifie them for the work . . . Secondly, . . . he doth stir up the hearts of men, to chuse men, & to call them forth unto the works whom he hath gifted, and qualified for it: . . . Thirdly, there is yet something more, and that is persons being thus chosen, there is a sanction, and a stablishment from the Holy-Ghost, that doth come upon them . . ."[145]

Thomas Hooker underlined the point that ordination "presupposeth an officer constituted, doth not constitute; therefore it is not an act of Power, but Order."[146] Precisely because the call to ministry had nothing to do with the conveying of sacerdotal *potestas*, it was perfectly possible for churches to continue in the absence of an ordained minister. As Nuttall put it, "in the Congregational tradition, while the ministry has been honoured and desired, it is a church without a covenant which is the monstrosity, not

---

141. Nuttall, "Assembly and Association in Dissent," 303–4, quoting Rippon, *Baptist Annual Register*, I (1794) following p. 16.

142. HSO, 57.

143. Cf. Binfield, "Profile," 94–95.

144. Nuttall, "The Early Congregational Conception of the Church," 200.

145. VS, 87, quoting Strong, *XXXI Select Sermons*, 113–14.

146. Ibid., 88, quoting Hooker, *A Survey of the Summe of Church Discipline*, II, 59.

a church without a minister."¹⁴⁷ Whilst recognizing, with Cromwell, that the true apostolic succession was "through the Spirit," he did grant that this view "has its perils, both intellectual and moral . . . it may degenerate into humanism of a debased kind, just as sacerdotalism, which is the diametrically opposed conception of the church, may degenerate into superstition. But it is a positive conception, with its own theological foundation and its own inner articulation."¹⁴⁸ Certainly, none of the possible pitfalls in Congregational ordination theory in any way tempted Nuttall towards more sacerdotal views. Thus, for example, when G. K. A. Bell said that "the unity of the Church is found in the unity of the episcopate," and that non-episcopal ministries lack "not ordination, but the special link with the Apostolic Ministry," Nuttall found it fortunate that Professor T. W. Manson "drives a coach an horses through" this position, and concurred with Manson that "There is only one 'essential ministry' in the Church, the perpetual ministry of the Risen and Ever-Present Lord Himself."¹⁴⁹

Two aspects of ordination services are of particular importance. First, "Ordination . . . was an occasion when not only the unity and fellowship of the church which had called the minister but the unity and fellowship between the churches in general found visible expression,"¹⁵⁰ both in the of the orderly dismission of the ordinand from the place of his previous membership, and in the attendance at ordination services of ministers and "messengers" from other churches. Secondly, during the service "you do not answer set questions with set answers, you make your own declaration of faith and experience, proclaiming the faith as it has come to you and telling what great things God has done for you."¹⁵¹

Finally, as to the minister's bearing, Nuttall charged those holding that high office "to deepen and enrich [their] devotional life for the service of others" by cultivating "the large outlook; the ordered life; and the tender spirit. The opposites of these—the narrow outlook, the disorderly life and the hard spirit—we all recognize as wrong and to be avoided."¹⁵²

---

147. Nuttall, *Congregationalists and Creeds*, 11.

148. Nuttall, "The Early Congregational Conception of the Church," 203–4.

149. Nuttall, Review Bell, *Christian Unity*; and Manson. *The Church's Ministry*, 361–62.

150. VS, 94.

151. Nuttall, *Congregationalists and Creeds*, 5.

152. PS, 246.

V

An important feature of Nuttall's theology is that it is a practical theology. Nuttall was in no doubt that while the saints were called out and separated unto the Lord, they were not called to quietism, but rather to witness in the world around. As he put it, "it would be difficult to deny that the Church is called out of the world: called out, it is true, that, back in the world, it may be the means of the world's redemption, but still called out first, to become, and in a sense perpetually to remain, different from the world, different from what the world, in its un-Christian state, can ever be."[153] It is unfortunately the case that the saints can be different in quite obnoxious ways, and Nuttall illustrated the point when discussing the early Congregationalists:

> Their separation . . . in obedience to Christ, was with an evangelical purpose. They came out, that they might no longer touch anything unclean; but they were also separated unto the gospel, for the work whereunto the Holy Spirit had called them. If, after reading their Bibles, they saw that work clearly in terms of the practice and demonstration of holiness, they were, surely, not wrong. Yet one wishes they might have seen it with equal clearness in terms of love; for they often seemed hard and unloving; and, while this does not require us to impugn the sincerity of their purpose, it is bound to affect our judgment of them, just as it undoubtedly impeded their achievement.[154]

It is not surprising that a theology that turns on the presence in Church and believer of the risen Christ by the Spirit should give due place to the claims of others for, as Baxter declared, the doctrine of the Holy Spirit is "a most practical article of our belief."[155] We might say that witnessing in the world marks the point at which the Spirit's challenge and guidance press home most urgently upon the saint's free will, demanding an obedient response:

> When the Spirit of the Risen Christ comes among us . . . *He sharpens* our perception of the difference between truth and falsehood, and between right and wrong . . . and He insists on our judging: first in the intellectual sense of deciding *what* is true or right and *what* is false or wrong, and then in the moral

---

153. CPH, 13.
154. VS, 162.
155. HSPF, 7, quoting R. Baxter, *Works*, II, 189.

The Theological Education of the Ministry

sense of deciding *where we stand*. He demands, as always, a free decision.... [W]e have enough light.... We are to acknowledge that we may be mistaken. We are to remember our finiteness and creatureliness, and to seek the spirit of true humbleness. But still a decision is called for.[156]

There are certain things that God wishes to have done, and others that he forbids. As with Jesus, so with the saints: "when Jesus spoke of God as Father and of Himself as God's Son, an essential part of his meaning ... was that God had a will to be done and that it was for himself to be obedient and to do it."[157] If we truly love God we shall wish to follow the promptings of his Spirit, notwithstanding that "Seeking, doing, not his own will but the will of the Father who sent him brought Jesus to the Cross."[158] The call to suffering for the Gospel's sake was often in Nuttall's mind, and in this connection he thought that there was "no better advice than that offered in a letter written in 1653 from Appleby Gaol by the early Quaker, James Nayler: 'Dear hearts, you make your own troubles by being unwilling and disobedient to that which would lead you. I see there is no way but to go hand in hand with him in all things, running after him without fear or considering, leaving the whole work to him. If he seem to smile, follow him in fear and love. And if he seem to frown, follow him, and fall into his will, and you shall see he is yours still.'"[159] Those who take this advice find that the Spirit comes to their aid, as the Puritan Morgan Llwyd well knew: "When the true shepherd speaks, and a man hears him, the heart burns within, and the flesh quakes, and the mind lights up like a candle, and the conscience ferments like wine in a vessel, and the will bends to the truth: and that thin, heavenly, mighty voice raises the dead to life, from the grave of himself, to wear the crown, and wondrously renews the whole like to live like a lamb of God."[160]

Persons thus possessed by the Spirit come to have a view of the world in which commonly-held values are turned on their heads. Nuttall quoted the former Master of his old College, Balliol, Oxford, thus: "In politics, government by consent is strictly a contradiction in terms. But because the Puritan tradition started with the experience of a society which rested on consent and abjured the use of force, it tended to conceive the state on

---

156. PS, 343.
157. BTL, 42.
158. Ibid., 45.
159. HSO, 41, quoting Swarthmore MSS, 3.66.
160. HSPFE, 140, quoting Llwyd, *Gweithiau*, I, 219.

the analogy of such a society."¹⁶¹ In commenting upon these words, Nuttall made it clear that he stood for the abjuring of force, "and its replacement by a more excellent way; by consent, by respect for minorities, by tolerance, by humanity, by tenderness towards sufferers, by the redemption of the wrongdoer: all of them expressions, manifestations, of Christian love."¹⁶² He upheld the radical Puritans as an example of those who "not only claimed liberty for themselves, they granted it to one another, and on positive Christian grounds." They knew that "Compulsion in religion not only makes hypocrites of the unwilling, it bruises and insults the willing mind."¹⁶³ Concerning religious toleration in particular, he more than once recalled Cromwell's remark, "I had rather that Mahommedanism were permitted amongst us than that one of God's children should be persecuted,"¹⁶⁴ though this was a step too far for Jeremiah Burroughes and John Owen.¹⁶⁵

Nuttall recognized that freedom and rights were closely related concepts:

> We work for human freedom because, as we say, men have a right to be free. I wonder, however, whether we can be altogether happy about saying this? On what grounds can we argue as Christians that men have a right to anything? If we ought to be grateful for the least that comes to us, as more than we deserve, does it not follow that we have no right to it? In any case, what an unchristian and intellectual thing it is to stand on your rights ... [We ought] not to be thinking of our rights at all.
>
> Does this mean that we ought not to work for *others'* rights and for *others'* liberties? No, that does not follow. But we shall be more effective workers for others' rights if they are not rights for which we are concerned for ourselves.¹⁶⁶

To advocate toleration and a concern for the rights of others was not, however, for Nuttall, to adopt a policy of *laissez-faire* tolerance. On the contrary and above all, he staunchly upheld the position that war was not

---

161. Nuttall, *Christian Love Manifested in History*, 4, quoting Lindsay, *The Modern Democratic State*, 117–18.
162. Nuttall, *Christian Love Manifested in History*, 4.
163. Ibid., 5.
164. See, for example, "Cromwell's Toleration," 285.
165. See Nuttall, "The Lord Protector," 253.
166. Nuttall, "Our Freedom as Christians," 372.

to be tolerated—a lesson he had learned during his schooldays at Bootham from the Quaker, A. Neave Brayshaw.[167] Accordingly, he endorsed the view of his teacher, C. J. Cadoux, that "'the acclimatization of the Christian conscience . . . to the use of the sword' was part of 'the general Christian surrender to the spirit of the world,'"[168] and he noted that the Socinians were probably the first in Christian history, in their *Racovian Catechism* of 1605, officially to declare war unlawful.[169] By contrast, he noted with dismay that the trinitarian World Council of Churches at its Amsterdam Assembly could on the one hand declare that "war is contrary to the will of God" whilst at the same time "be (seemingly) content to rest in permission for Christians to take part in a known sin, some writers even defending this very formula."[170] "Those who meet as brothers in Christ from many countries for common consultation," he went on, "cannot easily return home to prepare in measures of war against one another."[171] He ruefully concluded that "the Church's ministry of suffering has never been practised on the national level . . . because it is a ministry which none will dare to attempt save Christians in the power of their Lord, and no nation, as a nation, is, or has been, Christian."[172] Hence the paucity of persons willing to stand with the early Quaker, Isaac Penington, who wrote respecting the opponents Friends faced,

> [W]e come not forth against you in our own wills, or in any enmity against your persons or government, or in any stubbornness or refractoriness of spirit; but with the Lamb-like nature which the Lord our God hath begotten in us, which is taught and enabled by Him, both to do His will and to suffer for His namesake. And if we cannot thus overcome you (even in patience of spirit, and in love to you), and if the Lord our God please not to appear for us, we are content to be overcome by you.[173]

167. Nuttall, "The Logic of Discipleship" 298.

168. CPH, 7, quoting Cadoux, *The Early Church and the World*, 613, 625.

169. Ibid., 59. He was not so pleased with the same *Catechism's* definition of the Church as 'the company of those who hold and profess saving doctrine.' See *Congregationalists and Creeds*, 10–11. This formula does seem to privilege intellectual assent over existential commitment, and assertions of this kind have been read as if the doctrines did the saving.

170. Ibid., 69.

171. Ibid., 71.

172. PS, 302.

173. Ibid., 303, quoting I. Penington, *Works* (1681) I, 406.

Is Geoffrey also among the Theologians?

Nuttall was perplexed not only by the reluctance of some Christians to make the pacifist witness; in an address to The General Body of the Three Denominations (Baptist, Congregational, Presbyterian) he also regretted the general dilution of the Nonconformist Conscience:

> It will be sad if, along with the good old name of meeting-house and other things once common to us all, the Quakers are left the sole inheritors, by default, of what was known . . . as the Nonconformist Conscience. In a word, it is that for which we stand, if we stand for anything. If we no longer believe in it, then the General Body has had its day; but for many of us, thank God! it is still near our central life-stream.[174]

However it may have been with the Three Denominations, nothing could dim Nuttall's admiration of the Quakers where moral and social issues were concerned:

> The Quakers printed constant appeals to Parliament for legal reforms of social grievances: for the reduction of poverty, the care of beggars and debtors, for penal reform and the abolition of capital punishment, for the suppression of tithes, and so on. . . . Early Quakerism is remarkable for this combination of a deep and inward piety with a keen interest in social, political, and economic affairs. The latter is always a natural overflow. The piety remains primary, as in this passage from one described as "perhaps the sweetest and wisest of the early Friends," William Dewsbury: "Will you then live as the Quakers? Then you must live contemptibly: the mistress and man are hail-fellow well met . . . Here is now a new world; and the fashions of the old world are gone, all pride, haughtiness, grossness and trampling upon one another are gone; all slain, through the operation of Christ."[175] Moreover from Fox through Nayler to Penn there ran the consistent message that when injuries were sustained, it was not enough to refrain from revengefulness; forgiveness must follow.[176]

---

174. Nuttall, *The General Body of the Three Denominations*, 8.

175. Nuttall, "The First Quakers," in *History of the English Speaking Peoples* (no. 51, 1970), 1638.

176. Nuttall, "Reflections on William Penn's Preface to George Fox's *Journal*," 117. I should not wish to leave the impression that Nuttall's view of the Quakers was starry-eyed. On the contrary, he had challenging words to say to present-day Friends, some of whom, he thought, were in danger of losing the pearl of price. See, for example, "The Logic of Discipleship," 299–300: "[W]hen Friends exalt Meeting for Worship because its silence is acceptable to those of other religions or of none, and welcome as members

I end this section with Nuttall's testimony to the saving practicality of it all:

> We cannot hope to redeem men, to be used by God in redeeming them, unless with the early Christians we first know to what, distinctively, and for whom, unreservedly, we would do so; unless with the mediaeval sects we keep close to the Bible, the New Testament, the Sermon on the Mount, where we find our promise and pattern of redemption, and our orders for our own part in it; unless with Grebel and Menno we are willing to spend and be spent, though the more we love the less we be loved, grateful for even a small share in the fellowship of Christ's sufferings; unless with the early Quakers we think of men, simply as men, as both worth redeeming and as never past hope of redeeming. In every case, I believe, we may learn from these earlier pacifists. We may see all their varying sanctions taken up into our own prevailing view of that which we are vowed to as inseparable from the means of redemption.[177]

VI

Turning finally to eschatology, we find that Nuttall brought ethics and heaven into the closest possible relationship. In *quasi*-Kantian fashion he argued that "Just as the sense of duty implies not only freedom in which to do it but the Taskmaster to whom it is due, so the sense of justice demands a sphere in which justice may be realized, as it is not realized on earth. In a word, ethics demands the reality of heaven." Moreover, "Apart from the faith that God's will *is* done in heaven, much of the nerve of our faltering attempts to do it on earth would be cut."[178] Again,

> God is someone who has a will to be done: who has a kingdom, a dominion, a rule. This, in fact, is what heaven means: not a place where we are happy, but where God's will is done; and where the source and security of our joy is that his will is done. The only

---

those unwilling to commit themselves (in *any* sense) to Christ, what becomes of Friends' *witness*? Message, witness, discipleship, the way of the cross—all these go to the heart of things . . . [I]f in their work for reconciliation and peace [Friends] cease to point clearly and unashamedly to the suffering love of Christ on the cross and in their own lives as the source of their inspiration, they may still be pacifists but they will have no peace testimony."

177. CPH, 75–76.

178. RH, 29.

treasure in heaven that we can lay up will be as we treasure his will and seek to do it and *want* that it should be done.[179]

Although he did not pursue this aspect in any detail in his writings, Nuttall was clearly in sympathy with Charles Gore's remark that "what any society is to become will depend on what it believes, or disbelieves, about the eternal things."[180]

What prevented Nuttall's claims concerning the ethics-heaven relation from becoming academic in the abstracted sense was that they were derived from his strong sense of the risen Christ's presence: "The text on my nursery mantlepiece, and the text from which I preached my first sermon, was "Lo, I am with you always"; and as far back as I can remember, the reality of the Divine Companionship, as I came to call it, meant that Heaven was real too."[181] Precisely because of the Divine Companionship here and now, Nuttall could not think of heaven as concerning only the future, and we may justifiably suppose that on this matter he associated himself with Baxter: "It is not Heaven that I am begging for . . . but that I may see it from Mount Nebo, and have the bunch of Grapes; the Pledge, and the first-Fruits; that Faith and Hope which may kindle Love and Desire, and make me run my Race in Patience, and live, and die in the Joy which beseemeth an Heir of heaven!" On this Nuttall commented: "The *straining* here is forward-looking, but the *strain* is present, and is a consequence of *so much* 'Heaven on Earth' *already* that to *wait* is well nigh intolerable."[182]

Nuttall was far from thinking that heaven, immortality, was a natural right, the prerogative of all. He was quite blunt about it: "to assume immortality as man's natural right is not a Christian position," adding (perhaps with the memory of a certain kind of funeral service in mind), "to speak of someone who has shown no seriousness in his allegiance to Christ as now rejoicing in Christ's fuller presence must be accounted little short of blasphemy. It is unreal, too, as blasphemy always is."[183] Elsewhere he explained himself more fully:

> The Christian's faith . . . does not . . . primarily depend upon feeling at all, however naturally it may be accompanied by and

179. BL, 38. Happily, the strong disjunction in the first half of the second sentence is corrected in the second half of it.

180. Nuttall, "Charles Gore," 55.

181. RH, 9.

182. Nuttall, "Puritan and Quaker Mysticism," 526, quoting Baxter, *Dying Thoughts*, 188. Cf. RH, 41, 84–85.

183. Ibid., 16.

> give rise to feeling, and however rightly it may control his interpretation of feeling. Nor is there in his faith as such any sense of deathlessness directly and *per se*, such as is present in mystical feeling. Life after death, as the Christian conceives it, is not an indestructible implicate of his being, a right to which he is born . . . it is, rather, the gift of God, the outcome of an encounter between God and each soul, in which God takes the initiative as He did when he "raised" Christ: theologically, the transitive reference of "resurrection" is prior to the intransitive. The Christian's assurance of life after death is thus never a sheer *datum*, it is always consequent upon his faith, an inference from it we may say, albeit a necessary inference.[184]

What are the implications of heaven as entailing a relationship with the risen Christ for people of other faiths? Nuttall contended that the Christian's experience of being at one with God would differ from any such experience as may be found in other religions, because Christians entertain different beliefs about God, humanity and their relationship. In particular, Christians think in terms of the personal nature of the relationship, and of their unworthiness to enter into it. In his Drew Lecture on Immortality he twice quoted lines from the tombstone of his great-great-grandmother, Mary Smeeton, and from them he took the title of his lecture:

> They, alone, who Jesus love,
> They are whose hearts are fixed above,
> To Him entirely given—
> Whose only trust is in His blood,
> Who live by faith, and live to God,
> They are the heirs of heaven.[185]

He could appreciate that "Friends' discomfort at the thought that any may be 'shut out' has something noble about it and reflects the Christian compassion which has placed Friends so often in the forefront of the relief of suffering,"[186] but he insisted that any who argued that to deny universalism was to deny God's character were profoundly mistaken, for

> the universality it . . . wishes to attribute to, God's love, a relationship undifferentiated and unconditioned, has no foundation either in the Bible or in our experience of any kind of love,

---

184. Nuttall, "The Heirs of heaven," 17.
185. Ibid., 9, 18.
186. Nuttall, *To the Refreshing of the Children of Light*, 16.

divine or human, nor yet in any honest observation of the world in general. Its foundation, if it has one, is rather in that human craving for "fair shares" which Professor Farmer rightly insists is, while one of the most difficult, one of the most necessary things for Christians to grow out of... A religion which saved(!) the character of God at the expense of the Incarnation [many of the conditions of which were "not fair"] might be highly moral but would no longer be Christianity.[187]

Indeed, apart from the relationship with the one who overcame "the sharpness of death"—a relationship which implied "all the starkness of exclusivity," "any gospel... must soon evaporate."[188]

Nuttall did not rule out the possibility that "To life after death there may be many paths; but not to the being in paradise with Christ which alone is heaven."[189] The Separatist ecclesiology is here transposed into the eschatological key. Noting that the New Testament writers were "so absorbed in the shattering newness of the experience which has come to themselves that they are not much concerned with its exclusiveness," he advised that "Our concern should be less to speculate upon the lot after death of those not Christians, and more to seek to bring them while they are still on earth, to share the living faith which to us is precious."[190] Not, indeed, that people are to be terrified into faith by the threat of hell as in days of yore, "For we no longer think it right to try to dragoon people into belief."[191] On the other hand we may not extrude the concept of judgment from the New Testament or the teaching of Jesus:

> No one was either more responsible, or more responsive, to God than was Jesus. Equally, no one believed more implicitly in the divine judgment as part of the heavenly world.
> Only, the motive-power in Jesus' life was not fear; it was fidelity and devotion, born of love. So it must be for those who seek to live in the way to which Jesus calls them.... [Moreover] we know the quality of the Judge, that He is ever ready to have mercy and to forgive...[192]

---

187. Nuttall, "The Heirs of Heaven," 18.
188. Ibid., 18–19.
189. Ibid., 19.
190. RH, 81, 82.
191. Ibid., 19.
192. Ibid., 25.

Nuttall confessed that he much preferred to think of Jesus as the one who seeks the lost until he finds, but he could not overlook the fact that "there is much in scripture in favour of the concept of a chosen people," and he judged that "Both history and present experience suggest that Christianity has never been, is not, and is perhaps never likely to be, the religion of more than a few."[193] However few, Christians must "guard against pride and self-satisfiedness . . . 'Ye did not choose me, but I chose you.' I still want to hold on to these words of Jesus."[194]

And hold on to them he did. As the old divines might have said, a tincture of heaven pervaded Nuttall's life and writings, just as it did the hymns of his friend, Philip Doddridge, their ostensive subject-matter notwithstanding. Of his other great friend, Richard Baxter, it was said that he "was conversant in the invisible world."[195] So was Geoffrey Nuttall.

VII

At the outset I said that Nuttall did not construct a theological system in the sense of a tour through the several *loci* of systematic theology, and that there was no reason why he, as a Church historian, should have done such a thing. What he wrote of the Puritans might be said of his own writings: "The interest is primarily not dogmatic, at least not in any theoretic sense, it is experimental."[196] In another sense, however, his thought was theologically systematic. It flowed from a consistent and firmly-rooted view of the world at the heart of which was the experience of the God made known by the risen Christ through the Spirit. This stance is of more than ephemeral significance, it has the kind of permanence that Nuttall described in relation to Charles Gore:

> In the 1920s Streeter probably influenced more growing minds than Gore did; but to turn to Streeter now, after reading Gore, is like turning to Peter Sterry, say, after reading Richard Baxter. Both types of mind are needed: one is not "better" than the other; but the *Reality* and *Adventure* of the moment, which means much precisely because it is a tract for the times and has immediate appeal and assimilability, by the same token also dates; while a discussion which, as less contemporary, is originally

---

193. Nuttall, "The Concept of the Chosen People in Christianity," 12, 13.
194. Ibid., 13.
195. RB, 128, quoting Bates, *A Funeral-Sermon*.
196. HSPFE, 7.

Is Geoffrey also among the Theologians?

less telling, may have staying power and, in the long run, more significance.[197]

Nuttall's theology is one which appeals, time and again, to the Bible, but not to Tradition. It is, however, born out of the marriage of Scripture with a complex of Separatist, Dissenting and Nonconforming *traditions*. In a deep sense it is a theology of the people, and the central people in Nuttall's writings are the saints. One might almost say that in his works they are as visible as they were in their churches, and Nuttall knew that this set him apart from other historians—even from historians of Dissent: "By training, historians are warned to avoid being unduly biographical. By temperament they are also often shy of the deeper religious issues. The approach academics prefer is intellectual rather than devotional and institutional rather than personal. To chart and assess developments in devotion is not easy, especially when underlying sympathy is scant or even absent."[198]

As already indicated, Nuttall's vocation as Church historian was subsidiary to his vocation as a Christian and as a Christian minister. He urged members of the United Reformed Church History Society to be "eager, above all else, even as historians and students of history, to be disciples of Him who makes all things new."[199] To say that as well as being a fine historian he lived and breathed theology is simply to say that he lived in the presence of the God who claimed him and addressed him by the Spirit through the Word in the fellowship of saints. He was not, professionally, a systematic theologian, but nor was he merely incidentally theological.

What are we to make of his theological contribution? I shall offer a few reflections which arise directly from the account rendered. First, I feel I must qualify Nuttall's bald assertion that "For Calvin the Holy Spirit is a necessity of thought rather than something known in experience."[200] Admittedly, this is a remark in a footnote, but since Calvin has suffered a bad press both because of some of his disciples and because of uncomprehending foes something must be said. I suspect that in making this remark Nuttall may have been unduly influenced by those scholars and ministers of the preceding generation—the Congregationalists Robert Mackintosh and W. F. Adeney among them[201]—who had been burned by

197. Nuttall, "Charles Gore," 54.
198. Nuttall, "Methodism and the Older Dissent," 170.
199. Nuttall, "Chandler, Doddridge and the Archbishop," 56.
200. HSPFE, 6, n. 5.
201. For Mackintosh see Sell, *Robert Mackintosh*; for Adeney see Sell, *Hinterland*

Calvin*istic* scholasticism and were more than a little relieved to be rid of it. For balancing remarks we need look no further than Calvin's *Institutes*. By his "secret testimony" the Spirit brings home to us the word God speaks in Scripture (I.vii.4); apart from the Spirit the letter is dead and the heart untouched, "But if through the Spirit it is really branded upon hearts, if it shows forth Christ, it is the word of life . . ." (I.ix.3); the Spirit impels us to aspire after eternal blessedness (II.ii.6); unless we participate in the Spirit we cannot "taste either the fatherly favor of God or the beneficence of Christ" (III.i.2); by the Holy Spirit we are brought "into the light of faith in [Christ's] gospel" and we are regenerated (III.i.4); and the Holy Spirit teaches us how to pray aright, and tempers our emotions (III.xx.5). So one might go on, but enough has been said to show that to Calvin the Spirit is more than a necessity of thought, and that he is known in—indeed, is critical to, experience. If a clinching text were needed it is *Institutes* III.ii.7, where Calvin states that faith is "a firm and certain knowledge of God's benevolence toward us, founded upon the truth of the freely given promise in Christ, both revealed to our minds and *sealed upon our hearts* through the Holy Spirit" (my italics). When Nuttall writes, "the doctrine of the Holy Spirit is a doctrine of a personal God, revealed in a Person and present in personal relationships with persons,"[202] I can almost hear Calvin's "Amen!" Be that as it may, Nuttall, again following Paul, cannot think of the Spirit without thinking of Christ: "It is to Jesus that we must turn" in order to "seek further understanding of 'The character of the Spirit.'"[203]

Secondly, I have already expressed my agreement with Nuttall that the church is constituted by the call of Christ by the Spirit, and by the presence of the risen Lord within it; though I should myself couch the claim in trinitarian-*cum*-soteriological terms by saying that the Father constitutes the church by the Spirit through the Word on the ground of the Son's once-for-all saving work at the cross. I noted Nuttall's abhorrence of the Anglican-Reformed dialogue report, *God's Reign and Our Unity*, in which connection an autobiographical observation may not be inappropriate. The beginning of my period of service as Theological Secretary of the World Alliance of Reformed Churches coincided with the concluding session of this dialogue, whose co-secretary I thus became. By that time the final report, largely written by Lesslie Newbigin, was in draft form and, try as I might, I could not persuade Newbigin to say that the church is

---

Theology, ch. 9.

202. HSPFE, 171.

203. Ibid., 21; cf. 25.

constituted by God's gracious call in the Gospel to which the sacraments bear witness. I remain convinced not only that it is incorrect to speak of the sacraments as constituting the Church, but also that it is ill-advised to use such language in the presence of Roman Catholics and of those Anglicans who are tempted to wander down sacerdotalist paths. Those paths lead to the situation in which the church as such no longer keeps the sacraments; rather, religion is "done to" the people by members of a priestly caste, and a sectarian boulder is hurled into the ecumenical stream. [204]

The negative implication of the above position, namely, that since the church is constituted by the call of the Christ and by his presence through the Spirit in its midst the sacraments as such are not constitutive of the church, is of some ecumenical importance, as Nuttall knew full well; but I think that his Congregational heroes tempt him into making his point in a problematic way by conflating the marks, or notes, of the Church with its constituting factor. With regard to the Congregational view of the church's constitution he wrote, "It should be evident . . . that we are in another universe of discourse from the church whose marks are the preaching of the word and the administration of the sacraments. John Robinson explicitly states that these are not its marks. John Cook . . . also argues that they are not its constitution."[205] My point is that it is possible to hold that the Church is constituted as Nuttall says it is, whilst at the same time holding that the marks of the Church are the Word rightly preached and the sacraments rightly administered and (as some Reformed confessions add) discipline rightly exercised; for by "mark" or "note" is not meant the constituting factor or, for that matter, the formal definition of "church," but the ostensive definition of the term: that is, where you see these two (or three) phenomena, there you see the church. Thus, for example, in the Scottish Confession of Faith of 1560, "The notes by which the true Kirk shall be determined from the false . . ." are "first the true preaching of the Word of God . . . secondly, the right administration of the sacraments of Jesus Christ . . . and lastly, ecclesiastical discipline uprightly administered."[206]

Thirdly, we recall that Nuttall roundly declared that in the Congregational tradition "it is a church without a covenant which is the monstrosity,

---

204. See further Sell, *A Reformed, Evangelical, Catholic Theology*, 142.

205. Nuttall, "The Early Congregational Conception of the Church," 200, citing Robinson, *Works*, III, 428, and Cook, *What the Independents would have*, 4–5.

206. Cochrane, *Reformed Confession of the 16th Century*, 176–77. Cf. John Craig's *Catechism* of 1581, in Torrance, *The School of Faith*, 160.

The Theological Education of the Ministry

not a church without a minister."[207] At the same time, however, he was generous to the Trevecca evangelists who roamed far and wide in pursuit of souls. How are these positions to be reconciled? There can be no doubt that once the Evangelical Revival took hold, conversion rather than baptism followed by nurture within the covenant family became for many the way into the Church: "the birthday of a Christian was ... shifted from his baptism to his conversion";[208] and, moreover, from about 1830 onwards the number of new local covenants declined dramatically,[209] despite denominational growth, and Congregationalists established mission halls in many parts—the status of these in Congregational polity being somewhat less than crystal clear. It is, of course, preferable that people hear and respond to the gospel than that they do not; but it cannot be denied that with the changing attitude towards membership the church meeting, that credal assembly related to worship in which the Lordship of Christ is confessed and his will sought, declined, and sacramental discipline became lax, until today laxity is sometimes blessed in the name of the god Inclusivity.[210] The underlying question is, Do we still believe in the called, covenanted, separated, visible, saints of God (to Nuttall's adjectives I should add the term "catholic," since it is the Church catholic in heaven and on earth into which we are called, of which the local church is a manifestation)? Of the Separatist tradition Nuttall wrote that it is "a strand in our heritage which the United Reformed Church may not value but cannot discard."[211] It seems to me that if the United Reformed Church were to discard the biblical idea of the calling out of the saints into covenant fellowship its entire polity would be undermined, as would its necessary witness over against the Anglican establishment in the interests of the sole Lordship of Christ over his Church.[212] If it were to recover the idea of the saints as a people separated unto the Lord, we might hear more than we currently do about the obligation to seek after holiness (and not just justice, peace and ecological propriety—important though these are).

207. Nuttall, *Congregationalists and Creeds*, 11.

208. VS, 118, quoting Stoughton's quotation from an unnamed source in his *History of Religion*, VI, 136. Not, indeed, that regeneration is necessarily contemporary with the former.

209. See Sell, *Dissenting Thought*, ch. 1.

210. See further Sell, *Saints: Visible, Orderly and Catholic*; Sell, *Enlightenment, Ecumenism, Evangel*, 238–42, 325–75;

211. Nuttall, "The Speldhurst Church Book," 557.

212. See further Sell, *Testimony and Tradition*, ch. 11.

Is Geoffrey also among the Theologians?

Fourthly, it was only to be expected that one who devoted the larger part of his life to the training of ministers should have had some pertinent thoughts on that vocation. In the first place he took it for granted that it was a vocation, and talk of "ministerial job-hunting," "career patterns" and "hours per week worked" wounded him as much as it wounds me. Secondly, he knew that ministry was the concern of "gifted brethren [and now sisters]," and that without the gift of the Spirit no ministry would be effective (no matter how much technology surrounded it). God calls, and the congregation (presumably he had the "congregation of the saints" in mind here) ordains. Finally, at ordination the candidate makes his or her confession of faith, something which used to be required but in the most recent service books of the United Reformed Church is, sadly, optional. Whereas answers to formal questions may be sincere, and may also inform those visiting from other communions of the general doctrinal soundness of The United Reformed Church, the ordinand's own confession of faith is of great importance to the calling pastorate as announcing in personal terms the convictions on which the new ministry will be built.

Fifthly, Nuttall's ethical reflections stimulate thought. His remarks on the quest of one's rights are of particular interest. He exhorts us not to seek rights for ourselves, but for others. On occasion, however, the rights of others coincide with our own. When the Separatists claimed the right to worship according to their consciences they were claiming it for themselves as well as for others. Again, there is the question of the analysis of "right" in relation to "responsibility," and this in a culture which in some of its parts is characterized by an individualistic "I do as I please" mentality. Yet again, sometimes what are claimed as rights are really, according to Christians, for example, gifts. Thus if a woman says that she has a right to bear a child *via* AID whilst having no personal relationship with a man, a Christian may wish to retort, "But nobody has a right to a child—a child is always a gift." Then the discussion might well veer off into the distinction between moral rights and legal rights. So one could go on. The point is that with his remarks upon rights Nuttall started a hare of some practical theologico-ethical significance.

The pacifist witness, it is clear, was deemed by Nuttall to be a clear implicate of the Gospel, and he was a convinced pacifist from teenage years onwards. More generally, as we saw, he lamented the almost complete evaporation of the Nonconformist Conscience—a clutch of concerns which, temptations to a hard legalism notwithstanding—are by no means remote from the call to holy living. One traditional aspect of the conscientious platform was the advocacy of temperance and even of teetotalism. Nuttall was as lifelong a teetotaller as he was a pacifist, but whereas he wrote much on the latter, I do not find that he published a case for the former, and I find this surprising. Was this silence owing to the fact that the culture in New Testament times no more thought of repudiating alcohol than it did of repudiating slavery, and hence Jesus did not pronounce upon these matters, whereas he did enjoin pacific attitudes and was himself the Prince of Peace? We shall never know. But since many of the ethical issues which today confront us were not within the purview of first century people it would be a strangely restorationist ethical position which restricted its attention to the specific ethical content of New Testament texts. It occurs to me that a strong, cumulative case might be made in favour of teetotalism, which would turn upon appropriate answers to such questions as these: How consonant with holy living is it to introduce non-medically prescribed drugs of addiction into the temple of the Holy Spirit? How does drinking alcohol assist our witness, especially to the "weaker brethren"? Might there not be less crime, fewer accidents on the roads and at work, fewer days lost at work—with all the attendant costs involved—if the consumption of alcohol became as socially unacceptable as the imbibing of nicotine has become in many quarters? To the restorationist, selectively fundamentalist, retort that in 1 Timothy 5:23 Timothy is exhorted to "use a little wine for thy stomach's sake" it would be necessary only to issue the challenge: "I shall take your argument more seriously if you forgo the ministrations of the National Health Service in favour of all the other aspects of first century medicine." A footnote: in the back of Nuttall's copy of Charles Stanford's book, *Philip Doddridge*, which is now in my possession, there is a pamphlet by Stanford published under the auspices of the Pledge-Signing Crusade, entitled, *Total Abstinence—A Privilege*. "God helping me," Stanford concludes, "I will not drink wine while the world stands."[213] Exactly Nuttall's attitude!

Finally, to Nuttall, ethics implied, even demanded, heaven, as a sphere in which justice may be realized as it is not realized on earth. This, though not an argument for heaven capable of convincing a sceptic, is the hope and conviction of many a saint, and one for which there is much encouragement in the New Testament, as its words are brought home to saints by the Spirit.

---

213. For the Baptist minister, Charles Stanford (1823–1886) see ODNB.

VIII

There I might have left it, but there is one thing more. We have considered Nuttall's historical and devotional writings, and it will have become apparent that one who was famous for stringent criticism and reviews ranging from the generous to the devastating (he could have made the words of Baxter his own: "I have a strong natural inclination to speak of every Subject just *as it* is, and to call a Spade a Spade"[214]) could also exude tender affection. But in addition to the historical and devotional, he also ventured into at least one other literary territory: fantasy. In December 1965 *The Methodist Magazine* published "The keeper of the gate: a Christmas fantasy." The story is told in the first person. Nuttall says that he had been reading 1 Corinthians 13, when he dropped asleep. He dreamed that he had come to the gates of a palace where a crowd had gathered. Members of the crowd told him that the King's son had been born that day, and they had all come in the hope of seeing the new baby. Nuttall commented on the fine gates, and a man told him that they were the gates of heaven. At midnight the Lord Chamberlain appeared and began to select those who could go in to see the baby. A grand-looking lady rushed up to him, scolded him for keeping her waiting, and demanded to be let in first. He replied, "Love vaunteth not itself, is not puffed up," and barred her. At this a poor woman crowed over the fate of the excluded one and denigrated her. She was told, "Love thinketh no evil," and was likewise barred. Then a man came forward, but as he did so another ran up and the two began to fight for a place. The Lord Chamberlain barred both. To the first he said, "Love doth not behave itself unseemly"; to the second, "Love is not easily provoked." Then a poor woman with a child came up. She did not ask to go in herself, but said that her boy had so hoped to see the baby prince. They were both admitted: the boy because "love hopeth all things," the mother because "love seeketh not her own." Another boy protested his right to enter too, and was told, "Love envieth not," and barred. Then a donkey came along, obviously eager to pass through the gates, and an old hard-working man volunteered to take the animal in. They were let in on the ground that "love beareth all things," and "love suffereth long and is kind." By now Nuttall was wondering what response he would receive to a request to enter the palace. He began, "I'm only a stranger, sir," but the Chamberlain said, "Then certainly you may go in. Him that is a stranger,

---

214. Nuttall, *Richard Baxter and Philip Doddridge*, 13, quoting *Reliquiae Baxterianae*, i.213.40, p.137.

love asks in." Inside the gates was quite a small house, and in there was the new baby prince, together with those from the crowd who had been granted access. As Nuttall stood there he mused on the excluded ones and wondered whether there was really a place for him there: "Have I never been proud or spiteful or angry or irritable or envious? . . . I'm glad they're so kind to strangers here. But then love is."

> As I mused the scene began to grow dim . . . I was waking up; yet before I woke, I could hear what they were singing, for their voices were very distinct; and this is what I heard—or I think it was:
>
> God from on high hath heard! let sighs and sorrow cease;
> The skies unfold, and lo! descends the gift of peace.
> Fill us with heavenly love, heal Thou our earthly pride;
> Be born within our hearts; and ever there abide.[215]

It is fantasy (denuded of its poetry by compression); but it is fantasy of the most theological sort—and intensely practical too.

BIBLIOGRAPHY

(a) Manuscripts

Dr. Williams's Library, London, MSS. 1:11.
Swarthmore MSS, 3.66. At Friends House, London.

(b) Published Works

Anonymous. *God's Reign and Our Unity: The Report of the Anglican-Reformed International Commission 1981-1984*. London: SPCK and Edinburgh: The Saint Andrew Press, 1984.
Bartlet, William. Ἰχνογραφια: *or, a Model of the Primitive Congregational Way*. London, 1647.
Bates, William. *A Funeral-Sermon for the Reverend, Holy and Excellent Divine, Mr. Richard Baxter, Who deceased Decemb. 8. 1691. With some Account of His Life*. London: Brab. Aylmer, 1692.
Baxter, Richard. *A Christian Directory*. London: Robert White for Nevill Simmons, 1673.
———. *Church-History of the Government of Bishops and Their Councils Abbreviated*. London: B. Griffin for Thomas Simmons, 1680.
———. *The Divine Appointment of the Lord's Day*. London: Nevil Simmons, 1761.

---

215. Nuttall, "The Keeper of the Gate: A Christmas Fantasy," 463–65. This story is not recorded in the bibliographies of Nuttall's writings.

———. *Dying Thoughts on Phil. 1:23*. London: Tho. Snowden for B. Simmons, 1683.
———. *Plain Scripture Proof of Infants Church-Membership and Baptism*. London, 1653.
———. *The Practical Works of the Rev. Richard Baxter, with a life of the Author and a Critical Examination of His Writings by W. Orme*. 23 vols. London: John Duncan, 1830.
———. *The Quaker's Catechism*. London: A. M. for Thomas Underhill, 1655.
———. *The Reasons of the Christian Religion*. London, 1667.
———. *Reliquiae Baxterianae*, edited by Matthew Sylvester. London: Parkhurst et al., 1696.
———. *The Saint's Everlasting Rest*. London: Thomas Underhill and Francis Tyton, 1652.
Binfield, Clyde. "Profile: The Formation of an Independent Historian." *Epworth Review* 25 (1998) 79–106.
Bocking, Ronald. "Geoffrey Nuttall: Librarian." *The Journal of The United Reformed History Society* 9 (1996) 525–29.
Brooks, Peter Newman. *Reformation Principle and Practice: Essays in Honour of Arthur Geoffrey Dickens*. London: Scolar Press, 1980.
Brown, Raymond. "'With a Well-Tuned Heart': A Birthday Tribute from Friends." *The Journal of The United Reformed History Society* 9 (1996) 513–25.
Browne, John. *History of Congregationalism and Memorials of the Churches in Norfolk and Suffolk*. London: Jarrold, 1877.
Bunyan, John. *Grace Abounding to the Chief of Sinners*. London: George Larkin, 1666.
———. *Works*. Edited by Henry Stebbing. 4 vols. London, 1859–60.
Burton, Henry. *The Protestation Protested*. London, 1641.
Cadoux, C. J. *Catholicism and Christianity*. London: Allen & Unwin, 1928.
———. *The Early Church and the World*. Edinburgh: T. & T. Clark, 1925.
Calvin, John. *Institutes*. Translated by Ford Lewis Battles. Edited by John T. McNeil. 2 vols. Philadelphia: Westminster, 1960.
Carlson, Leland H. *The Writings of Henry Barrow*. London: Allen & Unwin, 1962.
Cochrane, Arthur C. *Reformed Confessions of the 16th Century*. Philadelphia: Westminster Press, 1966.
Coleridge, S. T. *Confessions of an Inquiring Spirit*. London: William Pickering, 1840.
Collinson, Patrick. "Geoffrey Nuttall: Early Modern Historian." *Journal of The United Reformed Church History Society* 9 (1996) 510–12.
Cook, John. *What the Independents Would Have*. London: Giles Calvert, 1647.
Cradock, Walter. *Divine Drops Distilled from the Fountain of Holy Scripture*. London: R. W. for George Whittington, 1650.
———. *Glad Tydings from Heaven to the Worst of Sinners on Earth*. London: Walter Simmons, 1648.
Creasey, John. "Geoffrey Nuttall and Three Libraries." *The Journal of The United Reformed Church History Society* 9 (1996) 529–32.
Croese, Gerardus. *General History of the Quakers*. London: John Dutton, 1696.
Cromwell, Oliver. *Letters and Speeches*. 3 vols. London: Dent, 1926–34.
Dale, R. W. *History of English Congregationalism*. London: Hodder & Stoughton, 1907.
Grieve, A. J., and W. Marshall Jones. *These Three Hundred Years: Congregational Work and Witness in Bury St. Edmunds 1646–1946*. London: Independent Press, 1946.

Hooker, Thomas. *A Survey of the Summe of Church Discipline.* London: A[braham] M[iller] for John Bellamy, 1648.
Howe, John. *Works.* Edited by Henry Rogers. 5 vols. London, 1862–63.
Howgill, Francis. *The Dawnings of the Gospel Day.* London (?), 1676.
Johnson, Francis and Henry Ainsworth. *Apologie or Defence of such True Christians as are Commonly (but Unjustly) called Brownists.* Amsterdam (?), 1604.
Lindsay, A. D. *The Modern Democratic State.* London: Oxford University Press, 1943.
Liu, Tai. "Scholar and Humanist: Reminiscences of a Chinese Student." *The Journal of The United Reformed Church History Society* 9 (1996) 532–34.
Llwyd, Morgan. *Gweithiau,* edited by T. E. Ellis and J. H. Davies. 2 vols. Bangor, 1899 and 1908.
Matthews, A. G. *The Savoy Declaration of Faith and Order.* London: Independent Press, 1959.
Nuttall, Geoffrey F. "Assembly and Association in Dissent 1689–1831." In *Councils and Assemblies,* edited by G. J. Cuming and Derek Baker, 289–309. Studies in Church History VII. Cambridge: Cambridge University Press, 1971.
———. *Better Than Life: The Lovingkindness of God.* London: Independent Press, 1962.
———. "Bishop Pecock and the Lollard Movement." *Congregational Historical Society Transactions* 13 (1938) 82–86.
———. "Calvinism in Free Church History." *The Baptist Quarterly* 23 (1968) 418–28.
———. "Chandler, Doddridge and the Archbishop." *The Journal of The United Reformed Church History Society* 1 (1973) 42–45.
———. "Charles Gore and the Solidarity of the Faith." *The Church Quarterly* 1 (1968) 52–64.
———. *Christian Love Manifested in History.* London: Fellowship of Reconciliation, 1960.
———. *Christian Pacifism in History.* Oxford: Blackwell, 1946.
———. "The Concept of the Chosen People in Chrisianity." *Common Ground* 22 (1968) 6–13.
———. *Congregationalists and Creeds.* London: Epworth, 1966.
———. "Cromwell's Toleration." *Congregational Historical Society Transactions* 11 (1932) 280–85.
———. "The Early Congregational Conception of the Church." *Congregational Historical Society Transactions* 14 (1944) 197–204.
———. "The First Quakers." *History of the English-Speaking Peoples* 51 (1970) 1634–39.
———. *The General Body of the Three Denominations: A Historical Sketch.* Privately printed for the General Body, London, 1955.
———. *Good Heavens!* London: *Provincial Papers* [Thames North Province of The United Reformed Church] 8 [1978]
———. "The Heart of *The Pilgrim's Progress.*" In *Reformation Principle and Practice: Essays in Honour of Arthur Geoffrey Dickens,* 229–39. London: Scholar Press, 1980.
———. "The Heirs of Heaven." *The Congregational Quarterly* 35 (1957) 9–20.
———. *The Holy Spirit and Ourselves.* London: Epworth, 1947.
———. *The Holy Spirit in Puritan Faith and Experience.* Oxford: Blackwell, 1946.
———. "The Keeper of the Gate: A Christmas Fantasy." *The Methodist Magazine* (1965) 463–65.
———. "Law and Liberty in Puritanism." *The Congregational Quarterly* 29 (1951) 18–28.

———. "The Logic of Discipleship." *The Friends' Quarterly* (1969) 294–300.
———. "The Lollard Movement after 1384: Its Characteristics and Continuity." *Congregational Historical Society Transactions* 12 (1935) 243–50.
———. "The Lord Protector: Reflections on Dr. Paul's Life of Cromwell." *The Congregational Quarterly* 33 (1955) 247–55.
———. "Methodism and the Older Dissent: Some Perspectives." *Journal of The United Reformed Church History Society* 2 (1981) 259–74.
———. *New College, London and Its Library: Two Lectures.* London: Dr. Williams's Trust, 1977.
———. "Nothing Else Would Do: Early Friends and the Bible." *The Friends' Quarterly* 22 (1982) 651–59.
———. "Our Freedom as Christians: Its Grounds and Limits." *Reconciliation Quarterly* 122 (1963) 367–73.
———. "Puritan and Quaker Mysticism." *Theology* 78 (1975) 518–31.
———. *The Puritan Spirit: Essays and Addresses.* London: Epworth, 1967.
———. "A Reading of the *Paradiso*." *The Congregational Quarterly* 34 (1956) 47–52.
———. *The Reality of Heaven.* London: Independent Press, 1951.
———. "Reflections on Books Reviewed." *The Congregational Quarterly* 34 (1956) 74–75.
———. "Reflections on William Penn's Preface to Fox's Journal." *The Journal of the Friends Historical Society* 57 (1995) 113–17.
———. Review of G. K. A. Bell, *Christian Unity: The Anglican Position*; and T. W. Manson, *The Church's Ministry*. *The Congregational Quarterly* 26 (1948) 361–62.
———. *Richard Baxter.* London: Nelson, 1965.
———. *Richard Baxter and Philip Doddridge: A Study in a Tradition.* London: Oxford University Press, 1951.
———. "The St. Andrews Conference: Impressions, II." *The Congregational Quarterly* 31 (1953) 325–28.
———. "St. Bernard of Clairvaux and His Ideal." *The Congregational Quarterly* 31 (1953) 221–26.
———. *The Significance of Trevecca College 1768–1791.* London: Epworth, 1968.
———. "The Speldhurst Church Book." *The Journal of The United Reformed Church History Society* 6 (2001) 557–67.
———. "The Theological Conference." *The Congregational Quarterly* 15 (1937) 503–5.
———. *To the Refreshing of the Children of Light.* Wallingford, PA: Pendle Hill, 1959.
———. *Visible Saints: The Congregational Way 1640–1660.* Oxford: Blackwell, 1957.
Nuttall, Geoffrey F., and Owen Chadwick. *From Uniformity to Unity 1662–1962.* London: SPCK, 1962.
Owen, John. *Eschol: . . . Or, Rules of Direction, for the Walking of the Saints in Fellowship, According to the Order of the Gospel.* London: Philemon Stephens, 1648.
———. Πνευματολογία: *or, a Discourse concerning the Holy Spirit.* London, 1674.
Penington, Isaac. *Works.* London: Benjamin Clark, 1681.
Penn, William. *Works.* 2 vols. London, 1726.
Richards, Colin: *Geoffrey Fillingham Nuttall (1911–2007), Puritan Scholar: Addresses, Sermons and Tributes from the Funeral and Memorial Services.* Prestatyn: Churchprint, 2008.
Rippon, John. *The Baptist Annual Register* 1 (1794).
Robinson, John. *Works*, edited by R. Ashton. 3 vols. London: John Snow, 1851.

Selbie, W. B. *Schleiermacher: A Critical and Historical Study*. London: Chapman & Hall, 1913.

Sell, Alan P. F. *Dissenting Thought and the Life of the Churches: Studies in an English Tradition*. Lewiston, NY: Mellen, 1990.

———. *Enlightenment, Ecumenism, Evangel: Theological Themes and Thinkers 1550–2000*. Milton Keynes, UK: Paternoster, 2005.

———. *Hinterland Theology: A Stimulus to Theological Construction*. Milton Keynes, UK: Paternoster, 2008. Reprinted Eugene, OR: Wipf & Stock, 2009.

———. *Nonconformist Theology in the Twentieth Century*. 2006. Reprinted Eugene, OR: Wipf & Stock, 2012.

———. *A Reformed, Evangelical, Catholic Theology: The Contribution of the World Alliance of Reformed Churches 1875–1982*. 1990. Reprinted, Eugene, OR: Wipf & Stock, 1998.

———. *Robert Mackintosh: Theologian of Integrity*. 1977. Reprinted Eugene, OR: Wipf & Stock, 2012.

———. *Saints: Visible, Orderly and Catholic; the Congregational Idea of the Church*. Princeton Theological Monograph Series 7. Allison Park, PA: Pickwick Publications, 1986.

———. *Testimony and Tradition: Studies in Reformed and Dissenting Thought*. 2005. Reprinted Eugene, OR: Wipf & Stock, 2012.

Stoughton, John. *History of Religion in England from the Opening of the Long Parliament to 1850*. 8 vols. London: Hodder & Stoughton.

Strong, William. *XXXI Select Sermons, Preached on Special Occasions*. London: R. W. for Francis Tyton, 1656.

Torrance, Thomas F. *The School of Faith: The Catechisms of the Reformed Church*. London: James Clarke, 1959.

Vaughan, Robert. *English Nonconformity*. London: Walford & Hodder, 1862.

Waddington, John. *Congregational History 1700–1800*. London: Longmans Green, 1876.

Winthrop, John. *History of New England from 1630 to 1649*. Boston: Little, Brown, 1853.

8

A Valued Inheritance of New Testament Scholarship

I AM HONOURED TO have been invited to contribute to this *Festschrift* for my good friend, Professor Zsolt Geréb. He was not the first scholar from Cluj that I met, for early in 1984 Professor Arpád Péntek, the then Rector of the Protestant Institute in Cluj, visited me at my office in Geneva, where I was Theological Secretary of the World Alliance of Reformed Churches (Presbyterian and Congregational). We had a good conversation, and I was invited to visit Cluj at the earliest opportunity. So it was that on 4 October 1984 I saw Cluj for the first time. Professor János Pásztor had driven me from Debrecen to Oradea—a journey made longer by a delay of two-and-a-half hours at the border—and from there Professor Péntek took me to Cluj. It was a memorable visit in political circumstances very different from those of today. I gave a lecture to all the students and professors, and on that occasion I met Zsolt Geréb for the first time. I also visited the widow of Professor Juhász. On 6 October I enjoyed a conversation with all the professors, at the end of which the Rector said that we were in such accord that it was as if I were one of their own! Later that day I was taken to the home of the renowned artist, Béla Szabo, who gave me a book about his work, and a signed print of his etching of the crucifixion, which hangs on the wall in front of me as I write. On Sunday 7 October I had the great privilege of preaching to the students, professors and guests. I was told that this was the first time that someone from the West had preached there since 1978. After a farewell lunch the Rector presented me with a copy of *An Analytical Concordance to the Revised Standard Version of the New Testament*. I often consult it to this day.

The Theological Education of the Ministry

In the years following I visited Cluj whenever I was able to do so, though there was an unavoidable gap during my sojourn in Canada. My wife and I kept in touch with Zsolt and Elisabeth by letter, and we were delighted when they were able to visit us in our home. My most staggering memory of Cluj concerns 8 November 2003. To my very great surprise I had been invited to accept the Honorary Doctorate of the Protestant Institute, and on that day the ceremony took place. Among others honoured were Professors Ferenc Szűcs of Budapest and Frank Sawyer of Sárospatak, both of whom I had known for a number of years. Our wives also had kindly been invited to attend this most memorable occasion, with students in traditional Transylvanian dress, wonderful choral singing, and appropriate speeches. I received my certificate from the Rector, Professor Tamás Juhász, and who should read a most gracious citation regarding myself but Zsolt Geréb!

How, then, could I refuse to contribute to this book? But what can a mere philosopher-theologian write that will be of interest to a New Testament scholar? Just as many scholars and ministers have benefited greatly from Zsolt Geréb's teaching and writing, so I am deeply indebted to those whose New Testament classes I attended in Manchester. I have therefore decided to devote the rest of this paper to a recollection of T. W. Manson, Owen E. Evans, W. Gordon Robinson and J. H. Eric Hull.

I

In 1836 Harry Longueville Jones published *A Plan for a University of Manchester*, but the time was not ripe for its implementation. The seed had been sown, however, and in 1851 Owens College, named in memory of its principal benefactor, John Owens (1790–1846), was founded, the idea being that students would read for external degrees of London University.[1] Similar colleges were established in Liverpool and Leeds, and from 1880 to 1903 the three colleges comprised The Victoria University, a federal body. Thus far Theology was not included in the curriculum, and some were determined to hold it at bay either because it was deemed to foment sectarian strife (to which Liverpool was no stranger), or because it was not respectably "scientific" (a view advanced in hostile manner by some in Leeds and elsewhere[2]). There was a more favourable reception to the

---

1. See Thompson, *The Owens College: Its Foundation and Growth*; Fiddes. *Chapters in the History of Owens College and of the Manchester University*.

2. Robert Mackintosh later recalled the late Professor Wilkins' remarking that

idea in Manchester, partly because the Trustees of Owens College were all members of one church or another, and partly because of the good reputation of the eight theological colleges that had already gathered in the town,³ of which the oldest were Didsbury Wesleyan College (1834) and Lancashire Independent [Congregational] College (1843). They were joined by the Unitarian College (1854), Victoria Park United Methodist Free Church College (1871), the Moravian Theological College (1877), Hartley Primitive Methodist College (1881), Manchester Baptist College, which transferred from Bury to the city in 1887, and the Anglican Clergy Training College established at Ordsall Hall in 1889, whence it removed in 1908 to Egerton Hall as Manchester Theological College. It closed in 1944.

In 1903 the federal university was dissolved and the Victoria University of Manchester was constituted. Those advocating the introduction of Theology into the University curriculum wasted no time, and in December 2003 the decision was taken to establish the Faculty. Its first session was held from 1904–1905.⁴ From the outset the professors and lecturers in the theological colleges were involved in the work of the Faculty, and some of them served terms as Dean and/or Secretary. The founding of the Faculty was marked by the publication of a series of twelve *Theological Lectures* edited by A. S. Peake. It is noteworthy that of the twelve lectures, seven were delivered by staff of the theological colleges: Principals J. T. Marshall (Baptist), L. Hasse (Moravian), and Alexander Gordon (Unitarian); Principal W. F. Adeney and Professor Robert Mackintosh of Lancashire Independent College (Congregationalists); H. D. Lockett (Anglican), and J. H. Moulton of Didsbury Wesleyan College.

Among the distinguished biblical scholars contributed by the colleges to the Faculty in its early years were J. H. Moulton (Wesleyan), Walter F. Adeney and W. H. Bennett (Congregationalists), and Arthur Samuel Peake (Primitive Methodist).⁵ Of these the last, while continuing

---

the "'brewers and dyers of Yorkshire' used to come and vote down Manchester opinion. One gain from the dissolution of the federal University was immediate hope for a theological faculty"—and of that Faculty Mackintosh became a founder-member. He refers to the classicist Augustus Samuel Wilkins. See Mackintosh, "Nonconformity in the Universities," 92.

3. Manchester became the world's first industrial city in 1853.

4. For the history of the Faculty see Burkitt, *Twenty-Five Years of Theological Study*; Anonymous, *Theological Essays in Commemoration of the Jubilee*; Pailin, *University of Manchester Faculty of Theology Seventy-Fifth Anniversary Papers*. .

5. For Moulton (1863–1917), Bennett (1855–1920) and Peake (1865–1929) see *The Oxford Dictionary of National Biography* (hereinafter ODNB). For Adeney (1849–1920) see Sell, ch. 9 and *passim*. Bennett was an alumnus of Lancashire Independent

to teach at Hartley College, became the first Dean of the Faculty and the first holder of the Rylands Chair of Biblical Criticism and Exegesis—an endowment by the Congregationalist Mrs. Enriqueta Rylands,[6] who also founded the Rylands Library in memory of her husband, John. In addition to Peake's Chair, the University contributed Chairs of Semitic Languages and Comparative Religion—a subject pioneered at Manchester—to the new Faculty. Thus opened the first free-standing, non-sectarian, theological faculty in the country. Lectures were given on the University campus and also in the colleges—notably the History of Christian Doctrine in the latter; but all recognized lectures, wheresoever held, were open to all students registered in the Faculty. A further pioneering decision taken at the outset was that all theological degrees should be open to women as well as to men, although it was not until 1931 that Dorothy Murray became Manchester's first female Bachelor of Divinity.

In his article of 1924 Robert Mackintosh, provides an insight into the curriculum objectives pursued by those who devised the programme of instruction:

> There was, and is, a large and distinguished Advisory Committee, with the function of helping the Senate and the Faculty in shaping or remodelling the University's regulations for theological study. [The Anglican scholar] Dr. [William] Sanday was one noted member at the outset; but perhaps even more weight was given to the views of Dr. Fairbairn [the Congregationalist Principal of Mansfield College, Oxford]. He it was who strongly urged that, as in Scotland or in Wales, but in contrast with London, the B.D. degree should presuppose an Arts degree. This became the standard Manchester policy. It is true that theoretic provision was made for an alternative method, by which the candidate might enter on a preliminary syllabus of theological and allied subjects immediately after passing the intermediate [first year] examination in Arts. But strait was that gate of entrance, and narrow was the way leading from it to successful graduation. I know of one student who, years after leaving college, gained

---

College, of which he later became Principal. He also studied at St. John's College, Cambridge, and was the first Nonconformist to be elected Fellow of a Cambridge College. He was a LittD of Cambridge, and the first President of the Society for Old Testament Study (1917–1920). As if this were not enough, he had earlier graduated MA in Mathematics in the University of London. For Mackintosh (1858–1933) see ODNB; Sell, *Robert Mackintosh*.

6. For whom see ODNB.

B.D. upon these lines, and I am told there has been one other instance of success.[7]

The Manchester Degree of Bachelor of Divinity was thus regarded as a degree of Master's status. It was awarded on the successful completion of fifteen examined year-long courses, together with a paper on the English Bible, and one essay on an unseen subject written within three hours under examination conditions. The subjects were divided into three divisions: Philosophy and Doctrine, Comparative Religion and Ecclesiastical History, and Old and New Testaments. Candidates were required to choose one division and take all of the subjects within it; and to select some subjects from the other two divisions, with the proviso that Comparative Religion and biblical texts in Hebrew and Greek were compulsory. Context questions in Greek, Latin, French, German and English were introduced into historical and doctrinal examination papers as appropriate. Candidates were required to pass a minimum of three papers at one examination session. Failed papers had to be re-taken the following year. All papers had to be successfully completed within seven years. It was a tough regime.

Much higher still was the standard required for the Degree of Doctor of Divinity, the University's senior theological doctorate, earned by published works deemed to be of originality and distinction. There have been fewer than ten successful supplicants since 1904. The degree was first awarded to Herbert McLachlan of the Unitarian College, in 1920. More than twenty years later the New Testament scholar, H. G. Meecham became the second person to earn the prestigious degree. In due course the New Testament scholars H. G. Marsh and A. J. B. Higgins were similarly successful.

A. S. Peake was succeeded in the Rylands Chair by the distinguished Congregational scholar, Charles Harold Dodd (1884-1973), who served from 1930 to 1935, when he removed to Cambridge. He was followed by the Presbyterian, Thomas Walter Manson (1893-1958), my senior New Testament teacher.[8]

---

7. Mackintosh, "Nonconformity in the Universities," 94.

8. For all of the Rylands professors to date see the volume celebratory of the centenary of the Faculty of Theology: Larsen, ed., *Biblical Scholarship in the Twentieth Century*. Larsen writes on Peake, James G. D. Dunn on Dodd, and Morna D. Hooker on Manson. For further assessments of the work of Peake, Dodd and Manson by New Testament specialists see McKim, *Dictionary of Major Biblical Interpreters*.

II

T. W. Manson was born in North Shields, Northumberland. He graduated with honours in logic and moral philosophy in the University of Glasgow, notwithstanding that his course had been interrupted by service in the Royal Field Artillery during World War I. He trained for the ministry of the Presbyterian Church of England at Westminster College, Cambridge, and concurrently studied at Christ's College. He won prizes and scholarships, and graduated with first class honours in Hebrew and Aramaic. He subsequently mastered Coptic. Following a three-year period as tutor at Westminster College, he was ordained in 1925 and, after a year with the Jewish Mission Institute in Bethnal Green, London, he became minister of the church at Falstone, Northumberland. Whilst there he published his first book, *The Teaching of Jesus* (1931), which earned him the degree of Doctor of Letters of Glasgow University. In 1932, on his appointment to the Rylands Chair at Manchester, C. H. Dodd vacated the Yates Chair of New Testament Greek at Mansfield (Congregational) College, Oxford, and Manson took his place. Then in 1936, when Dodd removed from Manchester to Cambridge, Manson again replaced him. Manson was the recipient of six honorary doctorates, and was elected a Fellow of the British Academy.

Armed with my Bachelor of Arts degree, I entered Manson's class in 1957, by which time his health was already causing concern, though from the cheerfulness of his disposition and the liveliness of his kindly wit, one would hardly have suspected this. His lectures were orderly, he breathed life into exegesis, and his expositions not only engaged the attention, but provided food for many a sermon thereafter. Above all, his were the lectures of one whose research instinct was undimmed, and who took delight in sharing his latest discoveries with his students. All of which is to say that far from reading the same lectures year after year, Manson's motivation in University teaching was "Come and see what I have found!" In this way he modelled the rigorous yet joyful life of scholarship to us, and this is what I have always sought to do in my own teaching. Manson certainly would not have understood the concept of "the text book for the course"; nor did he feel under any obligation to scamper through the set syllabus because of our forthcoming examination. The set New Testament Texts in my year were Luke, Romans and 1 John in Greek. Manson gave his lectures; we were examined on the syllabus! His manner was not dogmatic: he was not in the business of creating clones of himself, and he wanted us to reach our own conclusions. Thus, when discussing knotty problems of interpretation he would often present a variety of alternative views with great care and without bias, and then say, "You pay your money and you take your choice." Sadly, his illness progressed, he became more regularly absent from class, and he died, greatly mourned, on 1 May 1958, before the academic year was over.

Those who never had the privilege of sitting under him, should find no difficulty in detecting his enthusiasm for the subject, the depth of his scholarship, and the warmth of his humanity, from his writings, some of which contain material that he presented to us in class. The following are among the many themes that have remained with me from Manson's teaching and writings.

Given his thorough grasp of oriental languages, it is not surprising that Manson emphasised the importance of exploring the Jewish background to the New Testament. We must, he thought, "use every resource we possess of knowledge, of historical imagination, and of religious insight to the one end of transporting ourselves back into the centre of the greatest crisis of the world's history, to look as it were through the eyes of Jesus and to see God and man, heaven and earth, life and death, as he saw them..."[9] He was persuaded that while the gospels do not give us material for a full biography of Jesus—the objective of the evangelists is, after all, to tell good news—we can nevertheless reconstruct a sufficiently reliable account of his life, ministry and teaching. Indeed, with an enthusiasm that some subsequent scholars have questioned, he contended for the priority of Mark's gospel, and believed that it gave a reliable historical chronology of Jesus' ministry, the focal point of which was Peter's confession at Caesarea Philippi. He maintained this position in face of those form critics who emphasized the use of the history by the early church: "It is not higher criticism," he declared, "but the higher credulity that boggles at a verse of Mark and swallows without a qualm pages of pure conjecture about the primitive Christians' psychology and its workings on the pre-literary tradition."[10] Not the least important aspect of Manson's teaching regarding the Jewish context of Jesus' life, teaching and work, was his demonstration that, notwithstanding the "bad press" given to the scribes and Pharisees, there were in fact some good Jewish rabbis: a revelation indeed to any students who had been reared on sermons of the more undiscriminating type.

---

9. Manson, *The Teaching of Jesus*, 5.
10. Manson, "Is it Possible to Write a Life of Christ?" 249.

Manson devoted much thought to the question of the Son of Man, and especially to the relation of that term to the idea of the kingdom of God. He understood the kingdom in terms of God's reign, and of the faithful remnant who acknowledge it. The "Son of Man is, like the Servant of Jehovah, an ideal figure and stands for the manifestation of the Kingdom of God on earth in a people wholly devoted to their heavenly King."[11] That is to say, there is a collective dimension to the term. However, as a result of Jesus's prophetic ministry, "Son of Man" comes to designate Jesus himself: "His mission is to create the Son of Man, the Kingdom of the saints of the Most High, to realise in Israel the ideal contained in the term."[12] But "when it becomes apparent that not even the disciples are ready to rise to the demands of the ideal, he stands alone, embodying in his own person the perfect response to the regal claims of God."[13] It will be noted that the running theme in all of this is the way in which Jesus understood his mission; Manson was not given to speculative musings on the Messianic consciousness of Jesus. He was a "feet on the ground" kind of scholar.

Manson's enquiry into the ministry of John the Baptist is of particular interest. He argues that John's "very sharp and stinging point . . . is that he deliberately invites the children of Abraham to submit to a rite which had been devised for the benefit of pagans. He says in effect . . . You have only one chance. You must begin where the unclean Gentile begins—at the bottom. You must rediscover, and re-learn your Judaism from the beginning. Only so can you hope to have any part in the good time coming."[14] John is presented as a stern, uncompromising prophet in the mould of Amos. His baptism is not "the preliminary to something better, . . . it is the last chance of escaping something very much worse, namely, the coming judgement. John's positive teaching serves to mitigate the worst evils of an evil system; but it does not and cannot transform the system. It could relieve the sickness of society; but it was not the radical cure."[15] "In reality," as Manson put it elsewhere, "it was the last effort of the traditional Jewish legal religion to vindicate itself by producing changed lives. It failed, and where it had failed the gospel succeeded and took its place."[16]

---

11. Manson, *The Teaching of Jesus*, 227.
12. Ibid.
13. Ibid., 228.
14. Manson, *The Servant Messiah*, 44–45.
15. Manson, *The Sayings of Jesus*, 41, 254.
16. Manson, *The Servant Messiah*, 49.

A Valued Inheritance of New Testament Scholarship

In his scholarly enquiries into the sayings of Jesus, Manson delighted to bring out the heart of the Christian gospel. I give two examples. The first concerns the parable of the Good Samaritan (Luke 10:29-37), in which Jesus responds to a lawyer's question, What must I do to inherit eternal life? The response is part of what Manson calls Luke's "Gospel of the Outcast." He first notes that some have objected that Jesus fails to provide a definition of "neighbour." To Manson this is a "shallow criticism": "The question is unanswerable, and ought not to be asked. For love does not begin by defining its objects: it discovers them."[17] The priest and the Levite represent the national aristocracy, and they pass by the wounded man: "Their callousness stands in sharp contrast to the ideal of which they were the official guardians [Leviticus 19:18]."[18] The Samaritan helps the victim, leaves the equivalent of two days' wages with the owner of the caravanserai, and promises to make good any deficit on his return. On the supposition that the victim was a Jew, he was, technically, a neighbour of the priest and the Levite, but not of the Samaritan; yet it was the last who acted in love: "Love created neighbourliness" and "it is 'love' that is fundamental, not neighbourhood."[19] When the lawyer correctly specifies the true neighbour, Jesus's injunction, "Go, and do thou likewise," is the answer to the original question he asked.

For the second example I turn to the parable of the Labourers in the Vineyard (Matthew 20:1-18). In my mind this story functions as a standing rebuke to "Pelagians" in whatsoever guise they come, who think that their many years of good Christian works will earn them extra favour over any "Johnny-come-lately" who makes a death-bed repentance. In a nutshell, those who came to work last, and worked for one hour only, were paid twelve denarii—the same as those who had worked for twelve hours through the heat of the day. At the end of the day (= the end of the age) comes the reckoning. Those who worked all day long are aggrieved, and protest on grounds of human justice. The householder appeals to his generosity and implicitly rebukes the workers' covetousness: they have received what was agreed. Manson comments: "it is fortunate for most of us that God does not deal with us on the basis of strict justice and sound economics.... [T]he rewards of such poor service as men can give to the Kingdom are not an exact *quid pro quo*. They are an expression of love towards His servant.... There is such a thing as a twelfth part of a denar.

---

17. Manson, *The Sayings of Jesus*, 261.
18. Ibid., 262.
19. Ibid., 263.

It was called a *pondion*. But there is no such thing as a twelfth part of the love of God."[20]

Already we begin to detect the strong ethical thrust in Manson's expositions. Did he not say of Jesus's words, "why call ye me Lord, Lord, and do not the things which I say," that "There are few sadder words in the New Testament than Luke 6:46"?[21] Not, indeed, that he regarded Jesus as prescribing a collection of ethical prescriptions to be read straight off the page and obeyed. On the contrary, to identify one's will with God's will is to move towards a goal, and "for the purposes of that pilgrimage the teaching of Jesus is a compass rather than an ordnance map. He who grasps it in its wholeness and simplicity is sure of his direction: he must pick his own steps."[22] Thus, "In place of a rule of conduct to obey," the lawyer who was answered by the parable of the Good Samaritan "is given a type of character to imitate . . . [Jesus] refuses to legislate, because he is concerned with the springs of conduct rather than with the outward acts."[23] In my opinion, Manson's convictions on this matter are nowhere more clearly expressed than when, in a posthumous work, *Ethics and the Gospel* (1960), he contrasts the quintessence of the Jewish ethic with that of the Christian. He reflects upon Mark 12:28–34, where a scribe asks Jesus which is the first commandment, to which Jesus replies that the first is love God, the second is love your neighbour as yourself. This, Manson declares, is the quintessence of Jewish ethics. The quintessence of Christian ethics is to be found in John 14:12, "This is my commandment, that you love one another as I have loved you." This, Manson insists, is not an ideal, it is an act and deed; it does not abrogate the old law, but fulfils it: "Jesus shows what is really involved in love of neighbour; and shows it in thought, word and deed . . . To love as Christ loves means to put so high a valuation on your neighbour that it will be as impossible for you to harbour evil thoughts about him as to do him a physical injury."[24] Such love may be a matter of action rather

---

20. Ibid., 220. The last sentence here calls to mind the remark of the Congregational Cambridge historian, Bernard Lord Manning, who rebuked those who thought in terms of degrees of sacramental "validity" thus: "We do not deal in percentages with the grace of God." See *Essays in Orthodox Dissent*, 116.

21. Manson, *The Sayings of Jesus*, 60.

22. Ibid., 37.

23. Manson, *The Teaching of Jesus*, 301.

24. Manson, *Ethics and the Gospel*, 63, 64. The lectures in this book were assembled and seen through the press by Manson's colleague, Ronald Preston (1913–2001), who pioneered the teaching of Christian Ethics at Manchester. For Preston see ODNB.

than an ideal, but Manson is not unaware of the challenge involved. We are therefore relieved when he adds,

> The living Christ is there to lead the way for all who are prepared to follow him.
>
> More than that, the strength to follow is there too. The living Christ still has two hands, one to point the way, and the other held out to help us along. So the Christian ideal lies before us, not as a remote and austere mountain peak, an ethical Everest which we must scale by our own skill and endurance; but as a road on which we may walk with Christ as guide and friend. And we are assured, as we set out on the journey, that he is with us always, 'even unto the end of the world' (Matthew 28:20).[25]

There speaks Manson the preacher and pastor; and we should not forget that he fulfilled both of those roles with conspicuous success. As he well knew, "Historic Christianity is first and foremost a Gospel, the proclamation to the world of Jesus Christ and Him crucified. For the primitive Church the central thing is the Cross on the Hill rather than the Sermon on the Mount. . . . [Hence] the chief motive for the preservation and collection of the sayings of Jesus: they were needed in the pastoral work, which followed necessarily on any successful missionary effort."[26]

If Manson's major way of ministering was through his scholarship, he by no means neglected the life of the church around him. During World War II he assumed pastoral charge of St. Aidan's Presbyterian Church, Withington, Manchester; he was faithful at Presbytery meetings, served his church on numerous committees, and was called to be Moderator of the General Assembly of the Presbyterian Church of England in 1953. He was a leader in the Manchester Free Church Council, and in the Manchester and Salford Council of Churches, and when he died the Anglican Bishop of Manchester, William D. L. Greer, delivered the address at a memorial service in Manchester Cathedral.

Manson did not merely practise ministry, he wrote about it too. The heart of his position emerges in a discussion of the views of the Anglo-Catholic Bishop Kenneth Kirk, in which he demolishes Kirk's argument that, like the *shaliach*, the apostles were charged with transmitting their office and authority to their successors. Again, "When Dr. Kirk says that 'our Lord endowed his Church with two great gifts: the means of grace (the word and sacraments), and the ministry of grace (the apostles and

---

25. Ibid., 68.
26. Manson, *The Sayings of Jesus*, 9.

their fellow-labourers),'[27] my complaint is not that this doctrine is too high, but that it is not high enough. Our Lord did better than that: He gave the Church Himself. His real and abiding presence in the Church is the supreme 'means of grace' and the supreme 'ministry of grace.'"[28] More succinctly: "There is only one 'essential ministry' in the Church, the perpetual ministry of the Risen and Ever-Present Lord Himself."[29] This ministry has the power "to create and comprehend in itself a true priesthood of believers, whose priestly service is taken up into and made part of his supreme sacrifice'"[30] Where the Lord's Supper is concerned,

> The function of the minister who celebrates is to be the representative and spokesman of God through Christ to the congregation and of the congregation to God through Christ . . . A worthy minister is one who is so far identified with Christ by his calling and by his constantly renewed dedication of himself to God in Christ that the love of God is not only offered to the faithful but is also seen to be offered. A worthy minister is one who is so far identified with his people by sympathy and understanding that they can truly participate in the thanksgiving and self-oblation which he makes on their behalf as on his own.[31]

Thomas Walter Manson was such a minister.

III

During Professor Manson's absences through illness, the Reverend (now Doctor) Owen Ellis Evans, Lecturer in New Testament at Hartley Victoria College,[32] was drafted in to teach in his place. It was no easy task to pick up the threads of the course on more than one occasion. Indeed, Dr. Evans, who at the age of ninety is my sole surviving New Testament teacher, has referred in conversation to the experience as his "baptism of fire." It was not exactly plain-sailing for the students either, for Manson had set an un-

---

27. Manson quotes from Kirk's paper in *The Apostolic Ministry*, 8.

28. Manson, *The Church's Ministry*, 21. In Geoffrey Nuttall's opinion Manson justifiably "drove a coach and horses" through Kirk's argument. See his review of *The Church's Ministry*, 360.

29. Ibid., 100.

30. Manson, *Ministry and Priesthood: Christ's and Ours*, 63.

31. Ibid., 71.

32. Victoria and Hartley Colleges were united in 1934, consequent upon the Methodist union of 1932.

usually stiff examination paper on New Testament Texts, the contents of which were unknown to Evans. The entire class failed! We were required to take the course again, albeit with the texts prescribed for the following academic session, 1958-1959: John, 1 Corinthians, and 1 Peter. They were taught by Evans, whose health, mercifully, remained intact throughout. The upshot was that I, who specialized in the Philosophy and Doctrine set of courses, in the end was examined on as many New Testament texts in Greek as those students who had opted for the Old and New Testament group of subjects. I do not regret this uncovenanted mercy, though at the time it was something of an imposition, not least because, for a reason to be given shortly, I was bent on completing the Bachelor of Divinity course in two years, the minimum time permitted.

Owen Evans was born at Barmouth, Wales, in 1920. From 1945 to 1946 he served as a probationary minister in the Llanfair Caereinion circuit of the Methodist Church, and then trained for the ministry at Wesley College, Headingley, Leeds, where the distinguished New Testament scholar, Vincent Taylor, was Principal.[33] In 1949 he graduated Bachelor of Divinity (London) with First Class Honours. He was immediately appointed Assistant Tutor at Headingly, and in 1951 he was awarded the degree of Master of Arts (Leeds) with Distinction. He was ordained in the same year, and appointed to the Pwllheli circuit of the Methodist Church. From 1953 to 1969 he was Tutor in New Testament Language and Literature at Hartley Victoria College, combining this post from 1955 with that of Lecturer in New Testament at Manchester University. It was here that he worked initially under the direction of T. W. Manson, and he later published an account of this experience in the context of a comparison of Taylor, who had taught him, with Manson, whose lecturing apprentice he became.[34]

From 1969 until his retirement in 1988 Evans taught at the University of Wales Bangor, where he became Senior Lecturer, and served as Dean of the Faculty of Theology from 1983 to 1986. Before he left Manchester in 1969 he was already involved in the new Welsh translation of the Bible. From 1963 to 1988 he chaired the New Testament and Apocrypha Translation Panel, and in 1974 he became Director of the project as a whole. After the new version of the Bible, complete with Apocrypha, appeared in

---

33. For Taylor (1887-1968) see ODNB; McKim, *Dictionary of Major Biblical Interpreters*; Evans, "Theologians of Our Time: Vincent Taylor."

34. Evans, "On Serving Two Masters"; cf. 16. Evans was uniquely qualified to write this paper, for no other New Testament scholar both studied under Taylor and worked under Manson.

1988 as part of the celebration of the 400th Anniversary of the publication of the original Welsh Bible (the work of Bishop William Morgan) in 1588, Evans, who in 1986 had been appointed Eilian Owen Fellow at the National Library of Wales with such a project in view, spent the first ten years of his "retirement" preparing a comprehensive Concordance—a massive volume of 1180 pages—of the whole of the *New Welsh Bible*.[35] Without question Evans's work on the Welsh Bible will be his lasting memorial, and it is entirely fitting that, in recognition of his scholarly work, he was awarded the Honorary Degree of Doctor of Divinity (Wales) in 1989, and that in 2011 he was elected to the Fellowship of the Learned Society of Wales.

Evans has published a number of books and articles in Welsh. His English works include *The Gospel according to St. John* (1965) in the Epworth Preacher's Commentaries series, and the A. S. Peake Memorial Lecture for 1975, entitled *On Translating the Bible*—a lecture that he was very well placed to give. He edited Vincent Taylor's posthumous work, *The Passion Narrative of St. Luke: A Critical and Historical Investigation* (1972), and delivered a lecture at Wrexham on the occasion of the centenary of C. H. Dodd's birth in that town.[36]

It is the expanded version of his 1970 Pantyfedwen Trust Lecture that best shows Evans utilizing his linguistic skill and scholarly discrimination in order to develop an argument which has implications for Christian living. The book is entitled, *Saints in Christ Jesus* (1975). He sets out from an account of the Jewish background to the usage of "saints" as applied to Christians. We learn that lying behind the Christian use of the term is the Old Testament idea of Israel as God's holy, or separated, people; and that in this status both religious and ethical obligations are involved. He finds that from the final recension of Daniel 7, through the Similitudes of Enoch, the apocalyptic seventeenth Psalm of Solomon, and the Qumran writings, a development can be traced "in which the designation 'the holy ones', originally applied to heavenly beings close to God, came to be applied to the faithful, righteous remnant of Israel, the elect who were to inherit the eschatological Kingdom when the Messiah came."[37]

Turning to the New Testament, Evans shows that "the saints" is used of Christians on sixty occasions, "those who are sanctified" on eight occasions; and that of the former, thirty-nine occurrences are in the Pauline

---

35. *Mynegair I'r Beibl Cymraeg Newydd*, 1998.
36. See *The C. H. Dodd Centenary Lectures*, 1984.
37. Evans, *Saints in Christ Jesus*, 27.

epistles, thirteen in Revelation and two in Hebrews. He finds it most surprising that "the saints" is used on four occasions only in the Book of Acts, and "the sanctified" twice; moreover, "it is Palestinian Christians in and around Jerusalem that are designated 'saints' in each of the occurrences of *hoi hagioi*"[38] in Acts.

In Paul's letters the predominant idea is that Christians are already saints by calling—sainthood is not a future status to be aspired to—and their status has not been earned by them; it is God's free, unmerited, gift. Instead of being slaves to sin, Christians are now slaves of God. They are possessed by the Holy Spirit, who aids them in all aspects of their Christian life, not least in their prayers. While individual Christians are challenged to be holy, the overriding idea is that Christians belong to a fellowship of saints; indeed "almost invariably . . . this designation for Christians is used in the plural."[39] Their worship is not a matter of outward ritual but of inward disposition. Membership of this corporate body has ethical implications, especially *vis à vis* those who belong to the household of faith. Furthermore, "There is . . . an intimate connection between the concept of Christians as *hoi hagioi* and the Pauline concept of *en Christo*,"[40] for the saints "are incorporated 'in Christ' through baptism . . . What God effects in the believer at baptism . . . is grounded in what he did for him in the life and death and resurrection of Christ to be baptized means to be united with Christ in his death and resurrection."[41] Mutual familial duties and ministry in the sense of service to those of the community and beyond are reviewed; the fact is recognized that the saints are also sinners; and the cautionary word is noted, namely, that the believer's "consecration is not an irrevocable and automatic guarantee of his final salvation (cf. I Cor. 3. 7) . . . [it] depends upon his perseverance in faith."[42]

In his concluding chapter Evans draws out the implications of his analysis for Christian living. He reminds us that we are concerned with a community of saints; "the Christian life is not a private affair of the individual believer."[43] People become saints as Christ unites them with himself and imparts to them his life and character. Saints have been chosen and

---

38. Ibid., 41.

39. Ibid., 84.

40. Ibid., 57.

41. Ibid., 58–59.

42. Ibid., 103. Presumably this is an enabled perseverance of the "I, yet not I but Christ" variety.

43. Ibid., 125.

called by God—chosen (predestined) from the beginning, yet the call is not irrevocable. The saints "form the eschatological community to which belongs the inheritance of the Kingdom of God,"[44] and they are endowed with the gift of the Holy Spirit. They are a separated community, in the world, but not of it. While they have "a special degree of loyalty and of obligation to one another," they also have a relationship to non-Christians "which also involves love and obligation."[45] They are a universal and a witnessing community; they are also a militant community in the sense that although Christ has won the decisive battle in the cosmic war between God and his enemies, the struggle continues for the time being. Again, the saints are a worshipping community distinguished by moral purity and goodness. At this point Evans adds the important proviso: "Moral purity and goodness are not the *precondition* of sainthood in the New Testament sense; a person does not become a saint in virtue of the proved moral excellence of his character. But moral purity and goodness are the proper and necessary *consequence* of sainthood in the New Testament sense; a person who is a saint by virtue of God's call . . . and incorporation in Christ . . . is expected henceforth to display in his character the highest moral excellence. And to the fulfilment of this obligation the New Testament constantly calls him."[46] By the power of the Holy Spirit those who are saints by calling may become what they are.

I said that this fine study has implications for Christian living; its implications for ecclesiology and ecumenical theology are no less significant.

IV

As a candidate for the Congregational ministry,[47] I was able to live in Lancashire Independent College for six years. The idea was that I should spend three years on my BA and a further three on the BD. However, I fell foul of Manchester's matriculation regulations, owing to the policy at my school, which was that students who were destined to take advanced level examinations in particular subjects could skip the ordinary level papers

---

44. Ibid., 130.
45. Ibid., 135.
46. Ibid., 143.
47. Together with the majority of the English and English-speaking Welsh Congregationalists I (like Gordon Robinson and Eric Hull) went into the 1972 union of the Congregational Church in England and Wales with the Presbyterian Church of England which yielded the United Reformed Church.

in those subjects. Among my advanced level subjects was English Language and Literature, and the examining board used by my school was the University of London Matriculation Board. I successfully matriculated in that University. Manchester University, however, could not accept this, because the Northern Joint Matriculation Board required a pass in English Language at the ordinary level. Thus although I had passed English at the advanced level, I was required to delay my start on the BA degree until the following academic year so that I could, in late November, sit the Northern Board examination paper at the ordinary level. In this I succeeded, and I vowed that I would win back my "lost" year in due course by completing the formidable BD in the minimum period of two years—which I did.

Not all was lost, however, because I spent the bulk of the academic year 1953–1954 studying for the University's Certificate in Biblical Knowledge, the courses for which I found enjoyable and beneficial. The New Testament papers were taught by my College Principal, William Gordon Robinson (1903–1977).[48] He was born in Liverpool, graduated in philosophy at the University there, and won the Edward Rathbone Philosophy prize. He proceeded to Lancashire Independent College with a view to the Congregational ministry, and gained his BD at Manchester University. He then went, armed with scholarships, to Mansfield College Oxford, where he graduated in theology again. He later earned Manchester's degree of Doctor of Philosophy for a thesis on the history of Dissent in the North of England. At once we see that he was a man of parts: philosopher, New Testament scholar, historian. He was also a very lucid and orderly teacher, a thoughtful preacher, and a master of the art and craft of free, or conceived, prayer;[49] a writer and broadcaster able to engage with a variety of audiences from the scholarly to the youthful; and a diligent administrator who liked to reply to correspondence before the first lecture of the day.[50] He was possessed of a keen sense of humour, and more than competent in carrying on the College's tradition in those days of puncturing preten-

---

48. For whom see ODNB.

49. He published, anonymously, *Our Heritage of Free Prayer*.

50. I possess a letter of Robinson's written to a Mr. and Mrs. Doman on 15 June 1964. It reveals his graciousness, his administrative punctuality and his generosity (my italics): "I want to write this brief but very cordial note, *first thing on Monday morning*, to say how happy a time I had in your home yesterday and how grateful I am to you for all your kindness to me. It was a real pleasure to spend the day with you and to be made so welcome by you both Thank you very much indeed. *I hope you will accept the enclosed book as a little memento of my visit*. Warmest good wishes and regards, Yours sincerely, Gordon Robinson."

tiousness (especially of the ecclesiastical sort) with teasing witticisms. He believed in having things done decently and in order, as students who attended College prayers in carpet slippers swiftly discovered. Failure in such matters was more than a failure in etiquette, it was a poor witness. But any peevishness was more than compensated for by his kindness: quietly passing his preaching fee to the wife of the manse in which he had spent the weekend; travelling the length of the country to offer a prayer at the Valedictory Service held at my small home church prior to my ordination; and later conducting the Church Anniversary Services at Sedbergh, one of the two churches in my first pastorate. For reasons incomprehensible to some, he was a keen supporter of Manchester City Football Club.

Ordained in 1929, Robinson served the churches at Gatley (1929-1932) and Union Street, Oldham (1932-1941), and was then Principal until his retirement in 1968. He lectured in the University in New Testament from 1943 to 1951, and in the history of Dissent from 1951 to 1970.[51] He was secretary to the Faculty of Theology from 1948 to 1958. He was twice called to the chair of the Lancashire Congregational Union (1946, 1956); and, having been installed as Chairman of the Congregational Union of England and Wales (1955-1956), he returned to the College to be greeted by jubilant students, who had suspended across the entrance hall a large banner bearing the text 'Of sinners I am chief.' The College jazz band treated him and his wife to a boisterous rendering of "Home of the Range" (the College being situated in the Whalley Range district of the city),[52] following which the College hymn, "Jesus, Lover of my soul" was sung—always to "Aberystwyth."[53]

Robinson taught courses in New Testament Introduction, Mark and 1 Corinthians. He published *An Introduction to the New Testament*

---

51. Students who took the Reformation option in Ecclesiastical History, as I did, were well served by Gordon Rupp (the continental Reformation), C. W. Dugmore (the English Reformation: Church of England), and Gordon Robinson (the English Reformation: Dissent). Although they are outside the purview of this paper, we should note that in the field of Dissenting history Robinson published *William Roby (1766-1830) and the Revival of Independency in the North*—a work derived from his doctoral thesis; *A History of the Lancashire Congregational Union*, 1955; brief biographies of *Benjamin Waugh* and *Jonathan Scott* (1961); and articles in the *Transactions of the Congregational Historical Society* and *The Congregational Quarterly*.

52. I bury in a footnote the information that I was on banjo!

53. Given the (usually friendly) rivalry between Lancashire College and Hartley Victoria Methodist College (the "Jam Factory"—a reference to the business of William P. Hartley, its benefactor), I have no explanation of the choice by the Congregationalists of Charles Welsey's hymn.

A Valued Inheritance of New Testament Scholarship

(1949) which was twice reprinted within a year. This book was for the use of pupils and teachers in secondary schools. It is engagingly written and suitably stretching. It includes some illustrations, a table of dates, guidance on the pronunciation of difficult names, and questions and subjects for discussion. The themes include the world into which Jesus came, the life and teaching of Jesus, the early missions and letters, and the life of the early Christians. In a chapter entitled "How the gospels were written" he does not hesitate to introduce the children to the synoptic problem, providing a diagram for good measure; and when introducing 1 and 2 Corinthians he elucidates the four letters embedded within the latter. Robinson contributed *The Literature of the New Testament* (1971) to a series entitled *Understanding the Bible*, which was edited by his Old Testament colleague and successor as Principal, Edgar Jones.[54] The envisaged readership is senior school students and junior students in higher education. The kinds of literature are introduced: historical, theological, practical, gospels, general letters, and apocalyptic; the forming of the New Testament canon is discussed, and the apocryphal writings are introduced. Lest it be thought that Robinson was reluctant to stray from the New Testament, mention may be made of his lucid and thorough study of the *Historians of Israel (I) 1 and 2 Samuel, 1 and 2 Kings* (1962), which appeared in the series of *Bible Guides* edited by William Barclay of Glasgow University, and F. F. Bruce (Manson's successor in the Rylands Chair).

Robinson's most substantial study of a single New Testament book is found in *The Gospel and the Church in a Pagan World. A Study in I Corinthians* (1958). The basic material echoes his class lectures on the book, but here, with a wider adult readership in mind, it is illuminated by paraphrases of sections of the letter(s), and enlivened with exposition. The material is treated under the following headings: The Gospel for Corinth and the world; The Church and its fellowship; The Church and its problems; The Church and its worship; and Life in the setting of eternity. Each theme is appropriately sub-divided: the second, for example, concerns "The nature of the fellowship; The enemies of the fellowship; and Recall to fellowship." Robinson's approach may be illustrated by his introduction to the section headed, "The nature of the fellowship":

> It is said that there was once a Member of Parliament who in a speech in the House of Commons defined the Christian Church as "a voluntary association for providing religious services on

---

54. For Jones (1912–1991) see *Year Book* of the United Reformed Church, 1991–1992, 229.

> Sunday for that section of the population which chooses to take advantage of them." Apart from the glaringly false presuppositions that the Church works only on Sundays and is concerned only with "religious services" it is difficult to imagine anything further removed from the truth . . . At the very beginning of his letter, Paul stresses three phrases which are fundamental to his thinking. They are: "The Church of God," "sanctified," and "called saints" (*i.e.* saints who are called').[55]

It will be appreciated that Robinson the historian was no less interested in the "saints," for the concept of visible sainthood is at the heart of Congregational ecclesiology and polity.[56]

Gordon Robinson's writings were by no means directed to students only. He had a strong conception of the ministry of all the saints. Indeed, his address from the Chair of the Congregational Union is entitled, *Let us Give Ourselves to our Ministry*.[57] He took every opportunity of communicating with people of all kinds, mostly by writing, sometimes by broadcasting. Whether or not he learned the importance of deadlines from his father Frederick, who was chief reporter and assistant editor of the *Widnes Weekly News*, I do not know; but Robinson could certainly maintain the pace of the regular columnist. His weekly contributions to *The Christian World* were gathered in *New Testament Treasure* (1954), and for ten years he wrote articles for the wide readership of *The Daily Dispatch*, which achieved more permanent form in *Catchwords, Character and the Calendar* (1957). In the first section of the latter he found his point of departure in such catchwords as "I couldn't care less" and "Which way is the wind blowing?" He dealt with moral issues under "Character," and with the Christian year under "Calendar." His investigation of numerous by-ways in the New Testament which illuminate the text appeared under the title, *New Testament Detection* (1964). *Living Words and their Meaning* (1968) is a most useful glossary of biblical terms concisely defined, while *Deliverance, Challenge Victory* (1954) drives to the heart of the gospel message. Among his broadcast talks are *Perplexing Parables* (1955), and *You're the Man I'm Getting at* (1956)—David and Nathan, and others. I refer finally to Robinson's short book in the series, *Basics of the Christian*

---

55. Robinson, *The Gospel and the Church*, 41–42.
56. See Sell, *Saints: Visible, Orderly and Catholic*.
57. For the first epigraph in this book I have chosen the motto on the crest of Lancashire Independent College: εἰς ἔργον διακονίας (Ephesians 4:12), which the Principal would sometimes intentionally mistranslate, "Leave the work to the deacons!"

Faith (1975). Entitled, *Jesus, Lord and Saviour*,[58] it is a masterly account of Christ's person and work, with reference to Jesus's life, miracles, creeds and atonement theories, and more—all in just fifty-five pages. It ends thus: "Salvation comes 'by faith alone', not by man's striving to 'get right' with God but by his response to the love of God who first loved us . . . Because our deepest feelings are reflected in the exultant hymns of the Church our final thoughts about who Christ is and what he does can be looked for in the hymnaries of Christendom. Meditate then on these and let questing end in wonder and in praise."[59]

V

John Howarth Eric Hull (1923–1977), known as Eric, was my fourth teacher of New Testament: in particular, of New Testament Greek.[60] In my day he was a part-time tutor, who cycled to the College weekly to take his classes. A Lancastrian through and through, he was born at Penwortham, Preston, and was himself an alumnus of Lancashire Independent College. He graduated BA and BD of the University of Manchester, and was awarded the Bishop Lee Prize in New Testament Greek. He was ordained at Oakvale, Liverpool, where he served from 1946 to 1951. He removed to Timperley, where he remained until 1958, when he accepted the call to Chorlton-cum-Hardy, Manchester. His work in the churches was characterized by biblically-based preaching, energetic service, and assiduous pastoral care. He had something of the north-country directness about him (some 'soft' southerners like myself might be tempted on occasion to think it bluntness) as when, on his own account, he asked the deacons on his arrival at Timperley, "What night is [Masonic] Lodge night—there's no point planning church activities then!" But he was of the "salt of the earth," and very kind to me, not least when, in 1963, he accepted the invitation to preach at Sedbergh at the Church Anniversary, and baptized our second daughter during one of the services. His kindness did not in any way inhibit his slave-driving zeal in demanding a considerable number of Greek-English and English-Greek translations per week, or his determination to demolish us at table tennis after class.

---

58. Robinson's favourite way of concluding prayers was, "through Jesus Christ, our Lord and Saviour."

59. Robinson, *Jesus, Lord and Saviour*, 59.

60. See the *Year Book* of the United Reformed Church in England and Wales, 1979, 260.

In 1961 Hull was appointed to the Chair of New Testament Studies in the College, and from that time onwards he was able to devote himself more consistently to scholarly work. In 1967 his first, well-received, book, *The Holy Spirit in the Acts of the Apostles* was published. This was based on the thesis he successfully submitted for Manchester's degree of Master of Arts.[61] While not endorsing the sharp distinction that some scholars drew between history and theology, Hull argued that the theology of Acts is a developing theology, but theology is there. He grants that the relation of the Spirit to Christ is not consistently defined; he observes that although the work of the Spirit is diverse, little is said of the Spirit's work "in producing repentance and faith in Jesus; though, clearly, when men are led to Christ through preaching, for instance, the prior operation of the Spirit is envisaged."[62] He concludes that while the theology in Acts is by no means unimportant, Luke's primary objective was to show how the mission of the Church grew out of the labours of previously disillusioned disciples of Jesus, and how the Gospel spread far and wide. Indeed, "Perhaps [Luke's] greatest theological contribution was his understanding of why the Church is here, what its purpose is and how that purpose can be achieved. The Church is here to allow Christ to continue His ministry through it."[63]

In 1969 Hull was appointed part-time Lecturer in the University, and two years later he published *The Message of the New Testament*—a contribution to the series *Understanding the Bible*, edited by his colleague, Edgar Jones. He discusses the living God who rules, cares, judges and saves; the ministry, teaching and risen life of the Son of God; the person, work and gift of the Holy Spirit; and the Christian community, its nature, worship and sacraments. It is an admirable conspectus of great themes, which does not shirk the difficult textual and theological issues. Nothing but good would come if it were to be reprinted for the benefit of those church members who still engage in Bible *study*.

Who can say what more might have flowed from Eric Hull's pen? To great rejoicing he was installed as Principal of Lancashire Independent

---

61. In those days the MA was a research degree, the product of which was expected to be publishable in whole or in part. Entry to it was on the basis of the combination BA, BD, or BA with first or upper second class honours. In more recent time MAs in many universities have been achievable by course work which may, or may not, build upon work done in the first degree, and the M.Phil. has, in a number of universities, become the first research degree.

62. Hull, *The Holy Spirit*, 176.

63. Ibid., 178.

College, in succession to Edgar Jones, in July 1977. To the deep sorrow of many, and to the great loss of the church below, he died before his first term as Principal was ended, on 29 November 1977.

VI

In addition to the University courses, students at Lancashire College were required to attend courses on Pastoral Theology, Worship, and other topics; they were despatched to conduct services far and wide on most Sundays; the life of the College was sustained by morning and evening prayers; and on the first and last Saturday morning of every term they had to sit an examination on the English Bible. The scheme of these examinations had been devised by Gordon Robinson's predecessor, Principal A. J. Grieve.[64] The idea was that a student who completed the full six years of training would have been examined on the English text of every book in the Bible, and would therefore not enter the ministry having studied only the set texts in Hebrew and Greek required for University examinations. At the time it sometimes seemed to be a chore (and it is hard to see how it could be replicated today, when fewer ministerial candidates are in residence); but it was an invaluable discipline and I am grateful for it. When to this is added the benefits received from the teaching and writings of Manson, Evans, Robinson and Hull, I cannot but conclude that my inheritance of New Testament scholarship is a valuable one indeed, and that I was privileged to be a student in the University of Manchester's Faculty of Theology during a vintage period in its life.

BIBLIOGRAPHY

(a) Manuscript Letter

W. Gordon Robinson to Mr. and Mrs. Doman, 15 June 1964.

(b) Published Works

Anonymous. *Theological Essays in Commemoration of the Jubilee*. Manchester: John Rylands Library and Manchester University Press, 1954.
———. *Year Book of The United Reformed Church*. London, 1991–92; 1979.

---

64. For Grieve see Charles E. Surman, *Alexander James Grieve, 1874–1952*. Manchester: Lancashire Independent College, 1954.

Burkitt, F. C. *Twenty-Five Years of Theological Study*. Manchester: John Rylands Library and Manchester University Press, 1929.

Evans, Owen E. "C. H. Dodd: The Bible Translator." In *C. H. Dodd, 1884–1973: The Centenary Lectures*, edited by W. Eifion Powell, 14–28. Mold, UK: Gwasanaeth Lly-frgelloedd ac Amgneddfeydd, 1984.

———. *The Gospel according to St. John*. London: Epworth, 1965.

———. *Mynegair I'r Beibl Cymraeg Newydd*. Cardiff: University of Wales Press, 1998.

———. "On Serving Two Masters." In *The Bible in Church, Academy and Culture: Essays in Honour of the Reverend Dr. John Tudno Williams*, edited by Alan P. F. Sell, 124–41. Eugene, OR: Pickwick Publications, 2011.

———. *On Translating the Bible*. London: Epworth, 1976.

———. *Saints in Christ Jesus: A Study of the Christian Life in the New Testament*. Swansea: John Penry Press, 1975.

———. "Theologians of Our Time: Vincent Taylor." *The Expository Times* 75 (1964–65) 164–68.

Fiddes, Edward. *Chapters in the History of Owens College and of the Manchester University 1851–1914*. Manchester: Manchester University Press, 1937.

Hull, J. H. Eric. *The Holy Spirit in the Acts of the Apostles*. London: Lutterworth, 1967.

———. *The Message of the New Testament*. Oxford: Religious Education Press, 1971.

Kirk, Kenneth E. *The Apostolic Ministry: Essays on the History and Doctrine of Episcopacy*. London: Hodder & Stoughton, 1946.

Larsen, Timothy, editor. *Biblical Scholarship in the Twentieth Century: The Rylands Chair of Biblical Criticism and Exegesis at the University of Manchester 1904–2004; being the Bulletin of the John Rylands University Library of Manchester* 86/3 (2004).

McKim, Donald K. *Dictionary of Major Biblical Interpreters*. Downers Grove, IL: InterVarsity Press, 2007.

Mackintosh, Robert. "Nonconformity in the Universities. V. Manchester." *The Congregational Quarterly* 2 (1924) 90–96.

Manning, Bernard Lord. *Essays in Orthodox Dissent* (1939). London: Independent Press, 1953.

Manson, T. W. *The Church's Ministry*. London: Hodder & Stoughton, 1948.

———. *Ethics and the Gospel*. London: SCM, 1960.

———. "Is it Possible to Write a Life of Christ?" *The Expository Times* 53 (1942) 248–51.

———. *Ministry and Priesthood: Christ's and Ours*. London: Epworth, 1958.

———. *The Sayings of Jesus*. London: SCM, 1949.

———. *The Servant Messiah: A Study in the Public Ministry of Jesus*. Cambridge: Cambridge University Press, 1953.

———. *The Teaching of Jesus: Studies in Its Form and Content*. 2nd ed. Cambridge: Cambridge University Press, 1955.

Nuttall, Geoffrey F. Review of T. W. Manson, *The Church's Ministry*. In *The Congregational Quarterly* 26 (1948) 360–61.

Pailin, David A. *University of Manchester Faculty of Theology Seventy-Fifth Anniversary Papers*. Published by the Faculty, Manchester, 1980.

Robinson, W. Gordon. *A History of the Lancashire Congregational Union 1806–1956*. Manchester: Lancashire Congregational Union, 1955.

———. *Benjamin Waugh*. London: Independent Press, 1961.

———. *Catchwords, Character and the Calendar*. London: Independent Press, 1957.

———. *Deliverance, Challenge, Victory: A Biblical Study*. London: Independent Press, 1954.
———. *The Gospel and the Church in a Pagan World: A Study in 1 Corinthians*. London: Independent Press, 1958.
———. *Historians of Israel I: 1 and 2 Samuel, 1 and 2 Kings*. London: Lutterworth, 1962.
———. *An Introduction to the New Testament*. London: Edward Arnold, 1949.
———. *Jesus, Lord and Saviour*. Nutfield, UK: Denholm House Press, 1975.
———. *Jonathan Scott*. London: Independent Press, 1961.
———. *Let Us Give Ourselves to Our Ministry*. London:
———. *The Literature of the New Testament*. Oxford: Religious Education Press, 1971.
———. *Living Words and Their Meaning*. Nutfield, UK: Denholm House Press, 1968.
———. *New Testament Detection*. London: Lutterworth, 1964.
———. *New Testament Treasure*. London: Independent Press, 1954.
———. *Our Heritage of Free Prayer*. London: Independent Press, n.d., but 1950s.
———. *Perplexing Parables*. London: Independent Press, 1955.
———. *William Roby (1766–1830) and the Revival of Independency in the North*. London: Independent Press, 1954.
———. *You're the Man I'm Getting At*. London: Independent Press, 1956.
Sell, Alan P. F. *Hinterland Theology: A Stimulus to Theological Construction*. Milton Keynes, UK: Paternoster, 2008. Reprinted Eugene, OR: Wipf & Stock, 2009.
———. *Robert Mackintosh: Theologian of Integrity*. 1977. Reprinted Eugene, OR: Wipf & Stock, 2012.
———. *Saints: Visible, Orderly and Catholic: The Congregational Idea of the Church*. Princeton Theological Monograph Series 7. Allison Park, PA: Pickwick Publications, 1986.
Surman, Charles E. *Alexander James Grieve 1874–1952*. Manchester: Lancashire Independent College, 1954.
Taylor, *The Passion Narrative of St. Luke: A Critical and Historical Investigation*. Cambridge: Cambridge University Press, 1972.
Thompson, Joseph. *The Owens College: Its Foundation and Growth; and Its Connection with the Victoria University of Manchester*. Manchester: Cornish, 1886.

Bibliographical Appendix

OVER THE YEARS I have arranged 'mini-resurrections' for a number of divines who have taught in the academies and theological colleges of English and Welsh Dissent and Nonconformity, as well as studies of two colleagues who, happily, are still alive and well. Those interested may consult the following sources, a number of which represent the only modern studies of their subjects.

For numerous divines who taught philosophy (often among many other things) see *Philosophy, Dissent and Nonconformity, 1689–1920*, Cambridge: James Clarke, 2004; reprinted Eugene, OR: Wipf & Stock, 2009. For numerous twentieth-century theologians see *Nonconformist Theology in the Twentieth Century*. 2006. Reprinted Eugene, OR: Wipf & Stock, 2009.

For studies of individuals see the following list. Persons are listed in chronological order with their principal sphere of service indicated.[65]

ABBREVIATIONS

DECBP: *Dictionary of Eighteenth-Century British Philosophers*, eds. J. W. Yolton, J. Valdimir Price and John Stephens

DNCBP: *Dictionary of Nineteenth-Century British Philosophers*, eds. W. J. Mander and Alan P. F. Sell

DSCBP: *Dictionary of Seventeenth Century British Philosophers*, ed. Andrew Pyle

---

65. Lest I be suspected of undue bias, I might mention that I have treated the Church of England philosophers, T. H. Green, J. R. Illingworth, A. E. Taylor and C. C. J. Webb in *Philosophical Idealism and Christian Belief*, Cardiff: University of Wales Press and New York: St. Martin's Press, 1995; reprinted Eugene, OR: Wipf & Stock, 2006; and four more in *Four Philosophical Anglicans: W. G. de Burgh, W. R. Matthews, O. C. Quick and H. A. Hodges*, Farnham, UK: Ashgate, 2010. For some Scots see *Defending and Declaring the Faith: Some Scottish Examples, 1860–1920*. 1987. Reprinted, Eugene, OR: Wipf & Stock, 2012; Commemorations, ch. 10 (A. Campbell Fraser); and TEM, chs. 3–5. For the Irishman, Robert Watts, see DTLC, ch. 19.

DTCBP: *Dictionary of Twentieth-Century British Philosophers*, ed. Stuart Brown

The above volumes: Bristol: Thoemmes, 2000, 1999, 2002 and 2005 respectively.

BDTCP: *Biographical Dictionary of Twentieth-Century Philosophers*, ed. Stuart Brown, *et al.*, London: Routledge, 1996.
Comm.: *Commemorations: Studies in Christian Thought and History*, Cardiff: University of Wales Press and Calgary: University of Calgary Press, 1993; reprinted Eugene, OR: Wipf & Stock, 1998.
DBH: *Dictionary of Biblical Interpretation*, ed. John H. Hayes, Nashville: Abingdon, 1999.
DHT: *Dictionary of Historical Theology*, ed. Trevor Hart, Carlisle, UK: Paternoster, 2000.
DSCHT: *Dictionary of Scottish Church History and Theology*, ed. N. M. deS. Cameron, Edinburgh: T. & T. Clark, 1993.
DTLC: *Dissenting Thought and the Life of the Churches. Studies in an English* Tradition, Lewiston, NY: Mellen, 1990.
ERF: *Encyclopedia of the Reformed Faith*, ed. Donald K. McKim, Louisville: Westminster John Knox, 1992.
HT: *Hinterland Theology: A Stimulus to Theological Construction*, Milton Keynes, UK: Paternoster, 2008; Eugene, OR: Wipf & Stock, 2009.
ODNB: *The Oxford Dictionary of National Biography*
PTF: Ed., *P. T. Forsyth: Theologian for a New Millennium*, London: The United Reformed Church, 2000.
TEM: *The Theological Education of the Ministry. Soundings in the British Reformed and Dissenting Traditions*, Eugene, OR: Wipf & Stock, 2013.
TT: *Testimony and Tradition: Studies in Reformed and Dissenting Thought*, Aldershot, UK: Ashgate, 2005.

Warren, Matthew (c.1642–1706); Taunton Academy. DSCBP.
Rowe, Thomas (c.1657–1705); Newington Green/Clapham Academy, London. DSCBP.
Ridgley, Thomas (1667–1734); Moorfields Academy, London. HT, ch. 2.
Grove, Henry (1684–1738); Taunton Academy. DTLC, ch. 6; TT, ch. 5; DECBP.

Bibliographical Appendix

Taylor, John (1694–1761); Warrington Academy. DTLC, chs 5, 7; ODNB.

Taylor, Abraham (fl. 1721–1740); Deptford (King's Head Society), London. HT, ch. 3.

Ashworth, Caleb (1722–1775); Daventry Academy. TEM, ch. 2.

Rooker, James (1728/9–1780); Bridport Academy. DTLC. ch. 11.

Priestley, Joseph (1733–1804); Warrington Academy. DTLC, ch. 15.

Parry, William (1754–1819); Wymondley Academy. DNCBP.

Bennett, James (1774–1866); Rotherham Independent Academy. DNCBP.

Payne, George (1781–1848); Western Academy. Exeter/Plymouth. HT, ch. 5. DNCBP.

Vaughan, Robert (1795–1868); Lancashire Independent College. DNCBP.

Wardlaw, Gilbert (1798–1873); Blackburn Independent Academy. DNCBP.

Alliott, Richard (1804–1863); Spring Hill College, Birmingham. HT, ch. 6. DNCBP.

Martineau, James (1805–1900); Manchester New College, Manchester/London. Comm, chs. 1, 10.

Rogers, Henry (1806–1877); Lancashire Independent College, Manchester; DTLC, chs. 17, 18. DNCBP.

McAll, Samuel (1807–1888); Hackney College, London. DNCBP.

Stoughton, John (1807–1897); New College, London. DNCBP.

Godwin, John Hensley (1809–1889); Highbury/New College, London. DNCBP.

Gray, Joshua Taylor (1809–1854); Stepney Baptist College, London. DNCBP.

Pope, William Burt (1822–1903); Didsbury Wesleyan College. DTLC, ch. 19.

Simon, David Worthington (1830–1909); Yorkshire United Independent College, Bradford. HT, ch. 7.

Thomson, John Radford (/ –1918); New College, London. DNCBP.

Fairbairn, Andrew Martin (1838–1912); Mansfield College, Oxford. DTLC, ch. 19; DNCBP; ERF; ODNB (rev.).

Hodgson, James Muscutt (1841–1923); Congregational Theological Hall, Edinburgh. DNCBP.

Tymms, Thomas Vincent (1842–1921); Rawdon Baptist College, Leeds. HT, ch. 8.

Armitage, Elkanah (1844–1929); Yorkshire United Independent College. DNCBP.

Forsyth, Peter Taylor (1848–1921); Hackney College, London. DBI; DTLC, ch. 20; PTF, ch. 9; TT, chs. 7, 8.

Adeney, Frederic Walter (1849–1920); Lancashire Independent College, Manchester. HT, ch. 9.

Bennett, William Henry (1855–1920); Lancashire Independent College. ODNB.

Mackintosh, Robert (1858–1933); Lancashire Independent College. *Robert Mackintosh: Theologian of Integrity*. 1977. Reprinted Eugene, OR: Wipf & Stock, 2012; DNCBP; DSCHT; DTCBP; ODNB.

Oman, John Wood (1860–1939); Westminster College, Cambridge. TEM, ch. 3; BDTCP; ERF.

Peake, Arthur Samuel (1865–1929); University of Manchester; DBI.

Franks, Robert Sleightholme (1871–1964); Western College, Bristol. HT, ch. 10; DHT.

Cave, Sydney (1883–1953); New College, London. DHT.

Cocks, Harry Francis Lovell (1893–1984); Western College, Bristol. Comm, ch. 13; ODNB.

Manson, Thomas Walter (1893–1958); University of Manchester. TEM, ch. 8.

Whale, John Seldon (1896–1997); Cheshunt College, Cambridge. ODNB.

Robinson, William Gordon (1903–1977); Lancashire Independent College, Manchester. ODNB; TEM, ch. 8.

Duthie, Charles Sim (1911–1981); New College, London. HT, ch. 11.

Nuttall, Geoffrey Fillingham (1911–2007); New College, London. TEM, chs. 6, 7.

Huxtable, William John Fairchild (1912–1990); New College, London. ODNB.

Evans, Owen Ellis (1920–); Bangor University. TEM, ch. 8.

Hull, John Howarth Eric (1923–1977); Lancashire Independent/Northern College. TEM, ch. 8.

Owen, Huw Parri (1926–1996); King's College, London. *Convinced, Concise, and Christian: The Thought of Huw Parri Owen*, Eugene, OR: Pickwick Publications, 2012. DTCBP.

Williams, John Tudno (1938–); United Theological College, Aberystwyth. Ed., *The Bible in Church, Academy, and Culture. Essays in Honour of Dr. John Tudno Williams*, Eugene, OR: Pickwick Publications, 2011, ch. 1.

Index of Persons

Abelard, 114
Abbott, E. S., 195, 197
Abney, Elizabeth, 42
Abney, Mary, 13
Ackroyd, Peter, 198
Adams, G. W., 59
Adeney, W. F., 3, 253, 267, 294
Aikin, John, 11, 43
Ainsworth, Henry, 239
Alexander, A. B. D., 167
Alexander, George, 88, 107, 109
Alexander, Samuel, 117
Alexander, W. L., 73, 74
Allard, W., 42
Allen, Eric S., 203
Anderson, Peter D., 89
Andrews, Hope, 202
Andrews, Stanley, 202
Anselm, 65, 114
Antrobus, Alfred, 191
ap Thomas, Dafydd, 188, 190
Argent, Alan, 189
Aristotle, 187
Arnold, Raymond, 182, 183, 203
Arnold, Thomas, 13, 14
Artingstall, Leslie, 193
Ashton, R., 223
Ashworth, Caleb, ix, 2, 4, chapter 2, 293
   and church music, 31–35
   his death and memorial, 49–52
   his early years, 31–35
   his funeral sermons, 22–29
   his property dealings, 14–16, 30
   his students, 35–46
   his tutorship assessed, 46–49
   his work load, 29–30
Ashworth, James, 32

Ashworth, John (brother of Caleb), 5, 8, 9–10
Ashworth, John (son of Caleb)
Ashworth, John, of Lumb, 9
Ashworth, John, of Newchurch, 9
Ashworth, Miss H., 49, 52
Ashworth, Mrs., 5
Ashworth, Philip, 36
Ashworth, Richard, 5, 6–7, 8, 10, 32
Ashworth, Robert, 32
Ashworth, Thomas, 5, 7, 8
Atchison, John, 38–9
Aubrey, M. E., 110
Augustine, 138, 185
Axon, Ernest, 16, 94, 95
Ayer, A. J., 119–20, 157

Bacon, Francis, 60, 75
Baillie, Donald M., 155
Bain, Alexander, 59
Bainton, Roland, 199
Balfour, Alison, 89
Ballard, Frank, 202
Barclay, Robert, 19, 220
Barclay, William, 283
Bardgett, F. D., 84, 88
Barlee, William, 51
Barnes, E. W., 190
Barnes, Thomas, 42
Barr, James, 94
Barraclough, 202–3
Barrow, Henry, 234
Barth, Karl, 115–16, 155, 156, 157–59, 162, 164–66, 213, 214
Bartlet, J. Vernon, 188
Bartlet, William, 236, 238
Bates, William, 252

Index of Persons

Baxter, Richard, 19, 55, 203, 207, 222, 225–26, 229, 231, 233, 234, 237, 243, 249, 252, 259
Bazlee, William, 15
Bealey, Joseph, 41–42
Beattie, James, 60, 62
Bell, G. K. A., 242
Bellenden, Patrick, 88
Belsham, Thomas, 19, 35, 37, 40, 41, 43, 44–45, 46–47, 48, 49, 51–52, 138
Bennett, W. H., 3, 267, 294
Bentham, Jeremy, 156
Berg, Jan van den, 202, 219
Berkeley, George, 60, 65, 67–68, 75, 119
Bernard of Clairvaux, 192, 227
Berry, Sidney M., 110
Bevans, Stephen, 101, 116, 202
Bewley, William, 186
Bezzant, J. S., 145
Biggs, Wilfrid, 201, 203
Binfield, Clyde, 8, 182, 211, 215, 216, 231, 239, 241
Birkett, John, 94
Black, Matthew, 154, 155, 156
Blackman, E. Cyril, 197
Blair, Hunter, 102
Blair, Tony, 173
Bocking, Ronald, 197, 212
Bonhoeffer, Dietrich, 156
Bosanquet, Bernard, 118
Boston, Thomas, 93, 95, 96, 97
Boston, Thomas, Jr., 97
Bourne, Arthur A., 185, 191
Bourne, S. A. H. 185
Bowman, A. A., 154, 168
Boyle, Robert, 19
Bradley, F. H., 118, 161
Brainerd, David, 31
Brayshaw, A. Neave, 186, 246
Brooke, Christopher, 201
Broad, C. D., 119
Broadfoot, William, 91
Broadie, Alexander, 58
Brown, James, 101
Brown, John, of Haddington, 101
Brown, Raymond, 203, 212
Brown, Stuart, 154, 155, 187, 202
Browne, John, 39, 235

Browne, Simon, 31
Bruce, A. B., 76–77
Bruce, F. F., 283
Brunner, Emil, 155, 156, 157, 164–65
Bryce, James, 192
Buber, Martin, 119, 162, 172
Buchanan, James, 73
Buckley, William, 38
Buddell, J. L., 191
Bull, Joseph, 29
Bull, William, 46, 48, 51
Bultmann, Rudolf, 156, 190
Bunyan, John, 19, 191, 229, 237
Burder, George, 8
Burke, Edmund, 22
Burkitt, F. C., 267
Burroughes, Jeremiah, 235, 236, 237, 245
Burton, Henry, 238
Butler, David M., 194
Butler, Joseph, 19, 72, 73, 77, 148
Butterworth, Henry, 8
Butterworth, James, 8
Butterworth, John, 8
Butterworth, Lawrence, 8

Cadoux, C. J., 189, 199, 226, 227, 246
Caird, Edward, 59, 64, 69, 71, 79, 103
Caird, John, 59, 64, 103
Cairns, John (Principal), 58, 79, 98, 105, 106, 132, 145
Cairns, John, 98, 105, 132
Calamy, Edmund, 19
Calderwood, Henry, 59, 62, 68, 71, 78, 103
Calvin, John, 19, 106, 141, 213, 217, 221, 223, 253, 254
Camfield, F. W., 212
Campbell, C. A., 113
Carpenter, Benjamin, 40, 45
Carpenter, E. F., 195
Caston, M., 8
Cave, Sydney, 195–97, 198, 200, 206, 294
Chadwick, Owen, 229, 234
Chalmers, John, 95
Chalmers, Robert, 90
Chalmers, Thomas, 58, 61, 63, 73

Index of Persons

Chandler, J. H. 190
Chandler, Samuel, 15, 19
Chapman, A., 115
Charlton, Norman, 195
Chauncy, Isaac, 12
Chave, Peter, 203
Chillingworth, William, 19
Christian I, 84
Church, R. W., 192
Clark, James B., 194
Clark, Samuel (of Aylesbury), 28
Clark, Samuel (church historian), 28
Clark, Samuel (St. Albans), 10. 11, 28
Clark, Samuel (Daventry), 13, 14, 16, 18, 26–29, 38, 42, 48
Clarke, Samuel, 13, 19
Class, G., 107
Clement of Rome, 19
Clifford, Alan, 47
Clogg, F. Bertram, 197
Clouston, Mr., 86
Cochrane, Arthur C., 134, 255
Cocks, H. F. Lovell, 2, 200, 294
Cohen, Henry, 193
Coleman, Thomas, 10, 13, 44
Coleridge, S. T., 63, 226
Coles, John, 29
Colier/Collier, Thomas, 93, 94, 95, 96
Collins, Anthony, 72, 73
Collinson, Patrick, 201, 212
Colville, Harry, 89
Conder, John, 17
Cook, John, 230, 255
Cooke, Joseph, 9
Cooke, Leslie, 200
Cooper, A. S., 109
Cooper, Anthony Ashley, 156
Cooper, J. J., 13, 14
Cottle, J. L., 109
Cotton, John, 239
Coward, William, 15
Cowgill, Rachel, 32
Cox, Harvey, 156
Cradock, Walter, 224, 239
Craig, John, 134, 255
Craven, James B., 89
Cromwell, Oliver, 222, 230, 232, 242, 245

Crosley, David, 8
Cudworth, Ralph, 19
Culbertson, Robert, 90
Cunliffe-Jones, Hubert, 200, 212–13
Curry, George, ix, x–xi
Cyprian of Carthage, 19

Dale, R. W., 179, 239
Dante Alighieri, 204, 218, 229
Darwin, Charles, 78
Davidson, A. B., 108
Davidson, Hilary, 32
Davie, Donald, 203
Davie, G. E., 59, 63, 77
Davies, J. Trevor, 197
Davies, Madoc, 196
Davies, Rupert, 9, 201
Davies, W. A., 196
Davies, W. T. Pennar, 201, 202
Dawson, Joseph, 37–38, 48
Deacon, Malcolm, 14, 36
Demosthenes, 22
Denney, James, 69
Denny, William, 37
Densham, William, 41
Descartes, R., 64–66, 122
Dewhurst, Thomas, 7–8
Dewsbury, William, 247
Dibelius, Martin, 112
Dick, Alexander, 88
Dickens, A. G., 201
Dickie, E. P., 155
Dickie, John, 146
Dickinson, J. C., 199
Dodd, C. H., 269, 270, 278
Doddridge, Mercy, 13, 31, 36
Doddridge, Philip, 2, 10–12, 13–14, 15, 18, 19, 21, 28, 31, 36, 37, 42, 43, 47–48, 50 94, 191, 202, 203, 231, 252
Dodwell, Henry, 19
Doman, Mr. and Mrs., 281
Donaldson, Barbara, 185
Doncaster, Hugh, 193, 195
Donne, John, 192
Drage, Sally, 31, 32, 34
Dugmore, C. W., 199, 282
Duncan, George M., 67

Index of Persons

Dunn, James G. D., 269
Duthie, Charles S., 2, 142, 199, 200, 294
Dykes, James Oswald, 107

E. W. P., 147
Eames, John, 12, 17
Einstein, Albert, 190
Elliot, Ernest, 46
Elmslie, W. A. L., 109, 125, 146–47
Elmslie, W. G., 108, 109
Enfield, William, 45–46
Erasmus, D., 192, 193
Erskine, Ebenezer, 92, 97
Erskine, Ralph, 92
Eusebius of Caesarea, 19
Evans, Christopher, 198
Evans, E. D. Priestley, 9
Evans, George Eyre, 9, 13, 45, 46
Evans, Glyn, 195
Evans, Owen E., 3, 4, 276–80, 287, 294
   his life and work, 277–78
   at Manchester, 276–77
   on the saints, 278–80
Evans, R. J., 202
Evans, Sydney, 198

Fairbairn, A. M., 107, 268, 293
Falding, F. J., 181
Farmer, H. H., 109, 119, 120, 130–31, 146, 147, 162, 162, 172, 251
Fawcett, Benjamin, 31, 40–41, 49, 137
Fawcett, Samuel, 40–41
Fell, Margaret, 193
Fenton, Alexander, 85
Ferré, Nels F. S., 156
Ferriar, John, 37
Ferrier, J. F., 58, 61–63, 68, 76
Fichte, J. G., 65
Fiddes, Edward, 266
Fillingham family, 185
Fisher, Daniel, 201
Fisher, James, 92
Fleming, William, 59, 74
Flew, R. Newton, 195
Flint, Robert, 57, 58, 59, 70–71, 74, 77, 79, 80, 106
Floyd, James, 12, 25–26, 51
Floyd, Mrs., 12, 29

Forsyth, P. T., 2, 107, 120, 146, 200, 216, 294
Foster, James, 8, 9–10
Fox, George, 218, 222, 229, 247
Francis, Benjamin, 240
Frank, F. H., 107
Frankland, Richard, 1
Franks, Oliver, 154
Franks, Robert S., 108, 112, 141, 146, 212, 214, 217, 294
Fraser, A. Campbell, 58, 59, 63–64, 67–68, 74–76, 103
Frend, W. H. C., 199
Furneaux, Philip 44

Gale, John, 9
Gale, Theophilus, 19
Garvie, A. E., 107
Gentleman, Robert, 46
George, A. Raymond, 9
Geréb, Elisabeth, 266
Geréb, Zsolt, 265–66
Gibson, Margaret Dunlop, 107
Gill, John, 19, 48
Gillespie, Thomas, 93, 94, 95 96, 97
Gillespie, William Honeyman, 74
Gillie, R. C., 108
Gillies, J. R., 108
Glasson, T. F., 197
Goodall, Norman, 183, 203
Goodrich, Albert, 186
Gordon, Alexander, 3, 5, 11, 18, 47, 224, 267
Gore, Charles, 234, 249, 252
Goudge, H. L., 189
Graham, William, 90, 93
Grant, Cyril H., 195
Gray, George Buchanan, 187
Gray, Mrs. Buchanan, 187
Grebel, Conrad, 248
Green, Alan, 196, 202
Green, T. H., 58, 71
Greer, William D. L., 275
Grieve, A. J., 110, 182, 235, 287
Grotius, Hugo, 19
Guppy, Paul, 31
Guyse, John, 15

Index of Persons

Halcro, Magnus, 88
Haldane, Alexander, 90
Haldane, James, 90
Hall, Basil, 199
Hall, Robert, 47
Halley, Robert, 46
Halliday, Thomas, 43
Hamilton, Gavin, 90
Hamilton, William, 58, 61, 62, 76, 103
Hampton, John D., 42
Hardman, James S., 5
Harrison, Jonathan, 119
Harrison, Kenneth, 186
Hart, Rachel, 154
Hart, Trevor, 195, 202
Hartley, William P., 282
Hasse, L., 267
Hastings, James, 87
Hausrath, Adolph, 107
Haywood, John, 36
Healey, F. G., 101–3, 120, 146, 202
Hegel, G. W. F., 62, 65, 68, 69, 71, 79, 106, 118, 123
Heginbotham, Ottiwell, 39
Henderson, A., 97
Henderson, Henry F., 92
Henley, Samuel, 37
Hennings, Miss, 12
Henry, Matthew, 44
Hepburn, Ronald W., 119, 172
Herford, R. Tarvers, 9
Heywood Thomas, John, 200
Hick, John, 119, 120, 146
Higgins, A. J. B., 196, 269
Hill, Noah, 43
Hill, Thomas Wright, 137
Hoadly, Benjamin, 19
Hobbes, Thomas, 19, 156, 161–62
Hodgkinson, John, 39
Hodgson, Emily (neé Williams), 182, 187
Hodgson, James Muscutt, 179, 180, 182, 195, 204, 293
Hodgson, John, 182
Hodgson, Leonard, 195
Hodgson, Robert, 202
Holman, Paul, 31, 32, 34
Hood, Adam, 202

Hooker, Morna, 269
Hooker, Thomas, 19, 241
Horne, C. Silvester, 190
Horsey, John, 45
Horton, R. F., 185
Horton, W. M., 116
Hosken, T. J., 39
Howe, John, 231
Howgill, Francis, 220
Hughes, E. R., 193
Hughes, George, 228
Hull, J. H. Eric, 3, 4, 266, 280, 285–87, 294
  his life, 286–87
  on biblical introduction, 286
  on the Holy Spirit, 286
Hume, David, 60–61, 66, 67, 68, 69, 72, 119
Hunsworth, George, 41, 137
Hunt, Jeremiah, 9
Hunter, Jessie E., 95
Hutcheson, Francis, 59, 156
Huxtable, [W] John [F], 108, 197, 198–99, 200, 206, 294

Ince, Peter, 231
Iverach, James, 64–67, 71, 78–79

Jackson, Alvery, 7, 8, 10
James III, 84
James, E. O., 198
James, John, 38
Jasper, R. D. C., 198
Jenkins, Claude, 189, 195
Jenkins, Daniel T., 159, 206
Jennings, David, 11–12, 17, 19
Jennings, John, Sr., 11
Jennings, John, 11, 19, 48
Jeremy, Walter D., 16, 44
Jessop, T. E., 67
Joachim, H. A., 187
Joachim, Joseph, 187, 205
Johnson, Francis, 239
Johnston, Catherine, 155
Johnston, Christopher, 155
Johnstone, Edward, 36, 48
Johnstone, James, Sr., 36
Johnstone, James, 36, 48

Index of Persons

Jollie, Jane, 11
Jollie, Timothy, 11
Jones, Edgar, 283, 286, 287
Jones, Harry Longueville, 266
Jones, Henry, 59, 64, 69, 117–18
Jones, Noah, 43
Jones, R. Tudur, 201, 202
Jones, Rufus, 190
Jones, W. Marshall, 235
Joseph, H. W. B., 156, 205
Juhász, István, 265
Juhász, Tamás, 266
Justin Martyr, 19

Kant, I., 61, 65, 68, 69, 75, 80, 123, 161–62, 164, 171, 216
Kaye, Elaine, 179, 180, 186, 189, 196, 200
Keeble, N. H., 215
Kemp, J., 170
Kenrick, Timothy, 45
Kent, John, 145
Ker, John, 101–2, 105
King, Martin Luther, 200
Kirk, Kenneth E., 275, 276
Kirkwood, Thomas, 91, 101
Knight, William A., 59
Knowles, David, 199, 201
Knox, R. Buick, 146, 212
Knox, T. M., 146

Lachman, David, 92
Langford, Thomas A., 140
Langley, Arthur S., 8
Lardner, Nathaniel, 19, 73
Larsen, Timothy, 269
Leckie, J. H., 94, 96, 105
Lee, Thomas, 36
Leechman, William, 59, 73
Lehmann, 156
Leibniz, G. W., 65
Leland, John, 19
Lewis, Agnes Smith, 107
Lewis, Annie Edith, 184
Lewis, H. H., 156, 158, 172, 173–74, 198
Lidgett, J. Scott, 110
Limont, William, 102

Lindsay, A. D., 126, 187, 245
Lindsay, James, 59, 76
Llwyd, Morgan, 244
Locke, John, 19, 60, 65
Lockett, H. D., 267
Lovett, Richard, 182
Lowman, Moses, 19
Lucian, 19
Luther, Martin, 114, 125

McCosh, James, 61
McCrie, C. G., 92
MacEwen, Alexander R., 58, 59, 98, 105, 145
MacKelvie, William, 91, 93
M'Kerrow, John, 91, 92, 93
McKim, Donald K., 189, 269, 277
Mackintosh, H. R., 102, 114–15, 143, 144
Mackintosh, Robert, 3, 57, 59–60, 69–70, 72, 73, 80, 107, 180, 253, 266, 267, 268, 294
M'Intyre, John, 119
McLachlan, Herbert, 9, 11, 12, 13, 18, 19, 42, 46, 269
Macmillan, Donald, 74, 77
Macmurray, John, 155
McNaughton, William D., 95, 186, 194
Magee, John, 95
Mair, Thomas, 92
Malebranche, Nicholas, 220
Mander, William, 57, 103, 179
Manning, Bernard Lord, 274
Manning, James, 41, 137
Manson, T. W., 3, 4, 126, 147, 189, 195, 196, 242, 266, 269, 270–76, 277, 283, 287, 294
  on the gospels, 271
  on the gospel and ethics, 274–75
  on John the Baptist, 272
  as minister, 275
  on the ministry, 275–76
  on the Son of Man, 272
  on two parables
Margaret of Denmark, 84
Marriott, J. A. R., 185
Marryatt, Zephaniah, 17, 201
Marsh, H. G., 269

Index of Persons

Marshall, J. T., 3, 267
Marsh, John, 200, 206
Marshall, John, 101
Martin, C. B., 119
Mascall, E. L., 198
Mather, John, 37
Matthews, A. G., 11
Matthews, W. R., 198
Maurice, F. D., 63
Meecham, H. G., 269
Mein, B. R., 107
Merx, Adalbert, 107
Mesney, Mary (née Hayes), 185
Micklem, Nathaniel, 88, 188, 189, 191
Micklem, Romilly, 206
Mill, John Stuart, 57, 61, 67, 106
Milligan, Edward, 193
Milnes, J. Harrison, 188
Moncrieff, Alexander, 92
Montague, W. P., 59
Moore, G. E., 119, 156
Moorman, J. R. H., 199
Morgan, D. Densil, 202
Morgan, William, 278
Morris, John S., 129-30
Mott, N. F., 185
Moule, C. F. D., 146
Moulton, J. H., 3, 267
Mozley, J. K., 145
Murch, Jerom, 37, 38, 41, 45
Murray, Dorothy, 268
Murray, Gilbert, 187
Muscutt, James, 95, 179
Musson, A. E., 38
Mylne, James, 74

Nayler, James, 224, 244, 247
Needham, N. R., 93
Newbigin, J. E. Lesslie, 102, 147, 206, 254
Newbigin, J. L., 102
Newton, Isaac, 60
Newton, John, 46
Niblett, Roy, 188
Nicholson, Francis, 16, 94, 95
Niebuhr, Reinhold, 156
Nightingale, Benjamin, 38, 39, 45
Nineham, Dennis, 198

Nisbet, James S., 91
Norris, John, 220
Nuttall family, 178, 181
Nuttall, Evelyn, 183-84, 185
Nuttall, Geoffrey F., 2, 4, 10, 11, 12, 13, 94, chapter 6, chapter 7, 276, 294
    assessment of, 252-58
    on authority, 231-32
    on the church, 232-42
    on church discipline, 238
    on church meeting, 241
    on creeds and catechisms, 230-31
    on Jesus Christ, 216-20
    his assessment of others, 201-3
    his central theme, 216
    his eschatology, 248-52
    his practical theology, 243-48
    his self-assessment, 203-4
    on the Holy Spirit, 221-25
    on ministers, 241-42
    at New College, London, 195-201
    personal recollections of, 204-7
    on reason and the will, 225-32
    as story-teller, 259
    on theological trends, 212-14
    at Warminster, 190-93
    at Woodbrooke, 193-95
Nuttall, Harold, 182, 183, 191
Nuttall, J. K., 181
Nuttall, Mary (formerly Powley, née Preston), 184, 193-95, 199, 221
Nuttall Muriel (née Fillingham), 183, 185
Nuttall, Violet Mary (née Webb), 183, 191
Nygren, Anders, 236

Ogle, Joseph, 41
Oman, John, 2, 4, chapter 4, 202, 294
    at Alnwick, 101-2
    assessments of Oman, 145-48
    on Christianity's central message, 139-45

Index of Persons

his ecclesiastical context, 88–102
his ecclesiology, 98–99, 132–39
his family context, 84–86
his intellectual context, 103–9
his intellectual stance, 120–26
his wider activities, 109–10
the root of his theology, 126–32
on the thought of others, 110–20
Oman, Mary (née Blair), 102, 147
Oman, Simon Rust, 85
Orme, W., 223
Orr, James, 57, 69, 79–80, 97
Orton, Job, 13, 14, 19, 20, 21, 39, 49, 52, 94, 224
Osborn, G. F. A., 185
Oswald, James, 60, 62
Otto, Rudolf, 102, 112, 113, 115, 190, 214
Overend, Frederick, 5, 7, 8
Owen, H. P., 198, 294
Owen, John, 19, 222, 224, 225, 236, 237, 245
Owens, John, 266

Pailin, David A., 267
Paley, William, 73, 77
Palmer, Samuel, 5, 6, 8, 10–13, 16, 18, 20–23, 25, 30–32, 39, 48, 49–51
Paplay, Thomas, 89
Parrinder, E. Geoffrey, 198
Parry, Abel Jones, 5–7, 32
Parry, William, 18, 293
Parsons, R. G., 3, 4
Pascal, B., 122, 148
Pásztor, János, 265
Paterson, W. P., 188
Paton, H. J., 154
Peake, Arthur Samuel, 3, 267, 269, 294
Pecock, Reginald, 227
Peel, Albert, 185, 189, 191
Peel, David R., 206
Penington, Isaac, 246
Penn, William, 220, 247
Péntek, Arpád, 265
Pirie, William Robinson, 74

Plato, 19, 186, 187
Pliny, 19
Pollard, F. E., 186
Pope, Robert, 202
Potter, Beatrix, 194
Powicke, F. J., 101, 203
Powley, George Philip, 194
Preston, Ronald H., 274
Price, J. V., 57
Price, Richard, 35, 156
Prichard, H. A., 156
Priestley, Joseph, 16, 17–18, 19–20, 35, 38, 40, 45–48, 137–38, 293
Pringle-Pattison; see Seth, A.
Pufendorf, Samuel, 19

Rail, Tony, 16
Ramsey, Ian, 156
Ramsey, Paul, 156
Rashdall, Hastings, 114, 125, 126
Raven, Charles, 190
Rawlins, Mary, 29
Reid, H. M. B., 73
Reid, Thomas, 60–62, 63, 67, 68, 75, 76, 103, 170
Reith, George M., 102, 110
Rendall, Isabella Irvine, 85
Reynell, John, 38
Reynolds, Henry Roberts, 101
Richards, Colin, 215
Richards, Leyton, 190
Richmond, James, 119
Ridgley, Thomas, 12, 292
Rippon, John, 241
Ritchie, Anna, 84
Ritchie, James, 95
Ritschl, Albrecht, 80, 111
Rivière, Hugh, 109, 147
Rix, Wilton, 191
Roberts, Harold, 199
Robins, Thomas, 43–44, 49, 51, 101
Robinson, Barbara (née Fraser), 154
Robinson, Catherine, 155
Robinson, E., 38
Robinson, Frazer, 154, 155
Robinson, Frederick, 284
Robinson, George, 154
Robinson, Gordon, 155

Index of Persons

Robinson, H. Wheeler, 189, 190
Robinson, J. A. T., 156, 160
Robinson, John, 223, 232, 233, 255
Robinson, Mary Elizabeth
   (née Johnston), 155, 175
Robinson, Maureen, 155
Robinson, N. H. G., 2, 4, chapter 5.
   assessment of his work, 169–75
   on Barth, 158–59, 165–66
   on ethics, 163–66
   his life, 154–6
   his writings, 256–57
   on Jesus Christ, the norm of
      theology and ethics, 165–69
   on the personal, 161–63, 172
   on religious language, 160–61
Robinson, Robert, 231
Robinson, W. Gordon, 3, 4, 266, 280, 281–85, 287, 294
   on 1 Corinthians, 283–84
   on biblical introduction, 283
   his life and character, 281–82
   as historian of Dissent, 282
   as popular communicator, 284–85
Robson, R. S., 109
Rogers, Henry, 101, 179, 293
Ross, Isabel MacGregor, 193, 194
Ross, W. D., 137, 156
Rotheram, Caleb, 16–17
Rotheram, Caleb, Jr., 17
Routley, Erik, 199
Rowntree, Arthur, 186
Rupp, E. Gordon, 9, 199, 282
Rusland/Russell, John, 90, 93
Russell, Bertrand, 119, 161, 162, 190
Rutt, J. T., 17
Rylands, Enriqueta, 268
Ryle, Gilbert, 57, 62

Salt, Thomas, 185
Salt, Thomas, Jr., 185
Salt, William, 185
Sanday, William, 268
Sangster, W. E., 185
Sawyer, Frank, 266
Schelling, F. W. J. von, 65

Schleiermacher, F. D. E., 102, 114
Scholefield, Radcliffe, 38
Schomer, Howard, 200
Schopenhauer, A., 65
Schweitzer, A., 111
Scopes, Roger, 197
Scorgie, G. G., 79
Scott, C. A. A., 108, 109, 190
Scott, Caleb, 180
Scott, Walter, 180
Scougal, Henry, 19
Selbie, W. B., 186–90, 215
Sell, Alan P. F., 8, 11, 12, 15, 17, 35, 39, 42, 43, 57, 59, 61, 63, 64, 67, 70–72, 76, 79, 92, 94, 99, 101, 103, 104, 106, 112, 118–20, 135, 138, 139, 141, 145, 156, 157, 160, 172, 173, 179, 181, 189, 195, 197, 198–200, 203, 205–7, 214, 217, 220, 253–56, chapter 8
Sell, Karen E., 101, 204–5, 206
Selina, Countess of Huntingdon, 235
Seth, Andrew (afterwards Pringle-Pattison), 61, 76, 104, 156
Seth, James, 59, 62
Seymour, Jane, 32
Shaftesbury; see Cooper, Anthony Ashley
Sibree, John, 8
Simons, Menno, 248
Simpson, Patrick Carnegie, 107, 108, 117, 120, 143
Simpson, W. C. E., 202
Simson, John, 59
Sinclair, Hugh, 137
Sippell, Theodore, 190
Skepp, John, 8
Skinner, John, 107–8, 190
Small, David, 89, 91, 95
Smart, J. R., 202
Smeeton family, 182, 184, 191
Smeeton, Mary, 250
Smith, George Adam, 108
Smith, Pam, 30
Smith, William, 89
Smith, William Robertson, 104–5, 106, 108, 123
Smithson, Isaac, 17

303

Index of Persons

Sorley, W. T., 59
Southern, Richard, 188
Spalding, Anthony, 188, 191
Spears, Robert, 24
Spencer, Herbert, 65, 78, 106
Spilsbury, Francis, 40
Spinoza, B., 62, 66–67, 69
Staines, E. N., 42
Staker, Jane, 102
Stanford, Charles, 258
Stanley, Howard S., 189, 197, 200
Stell, Christopher, 15, 190
Stephens, John, 57
Sterry, Peter, 252
Stevenson, Thomas, 89
Stewart, Dugald, 62
Stewart, John, 89
Stewart, Patrick, 89
Stillingfleet, Edward, 19
Stirling, J. H., 59
Stobbs, William, 91
Stone, C. G., 187
Stoughton, John, 256, 293
Strange, Thomas, 44
Streeter, B. H., 252
Strong, William, 241
Struthers, Gavin, 95, 96
Stuart, John, 91
Surman, Charles E., 182, 287
Sykes, Norman, 199
Szabo Béla, 265
Szűcs, Ferenc, 266

Tai Liu, 212
Tatlow, Tissington, 182
Tattersall, William, 36–37
Tayler, Thomas, 42–43, 49
Taylor, A. E., 59
Taylor, Abraham, 11
Taylor, George (pseud.), 107
Taylor, John, 45
Taylor, John H., 182, 201
Taylor, Thomas, 10, 44, 49
Taylor, Vincent, 277, 278
Temple, William, 190
Tennant, F. R., 117, 127–29, 141–42, 145, 156
Terry, W. N., 5, 47

Thomas Aquinas, 188
Thomas, Beryl, 16
Thomas, Thomas, 13, 20–22, 49
Thompson, John Handby, 14, 15
Thompson, Joseph, 180, 266
Thompson, Margaret, 85
Thompson, W. P. L., 85, 88
Thomson, Andrew, 91, 95
Thomson, Arthur, 59
[Thornton, Alfred], 30
Thornton, Betty, 30
Thornton, John, 46
Tillich, Paul, 156
Tillotson, John, 19
Tindal, Matthew, 19
Todd, James, 206
Toller, Thomas, 47
Tomes, Roger F., 197
Torrance, T. F., 134, 159, 255
Towgood, Micaijah, 19, 35, 41, 45, 137
Troeltsch, E., 190
Trotman, Nathaniel, 219
Tulloch, Jerome, 89
Turner, J. H., 38
Tyndale, William, 110

Ullmann, Walter, 199, 202
Upcott, E. A., 187
Urwick, William, 31, 45

Vaughan, Robert, 225, 293
Veitch, John, 59, 63
Vickers, John A., 185
Vine, Aubrey, 199

Waddington, John, 231
Wadsworth, Kenneth W., 181, 195, 200
Wainwright, Geoffrey, 206
Walker, (Captain), 192
Walsh, W. H., 161
Warburton, William, 19
Ward, Keith, 156
Ward, Ronald, 203
Ward, W. Reginald, 201
Wardlaw, Gilbert, 107, 293
Wardlaw, Ralph, 63
Warren, Max, 195
Waterhouse, E. S., 197

Index of Persons

Watson, George, 44
Watts, Isaac, 13, 19, 23–25, 34–35, 203
Webb, C. C. J., 189
Webb, Francis, 37
Webb, Ronald, 206
Webber, Edward, 15
Wellhausen, Julius, 104
Wenley, R. M., 59, 74
Wernle, P., 221
Wesley, Charles, 282
Wesley, John, 8
Whiston, William, 19
Whitby, Daniel, 19
Whitehead, A. N., 118–19
Whitehead, Thomas (Daventry student), 17
Whitehead, Thomas (author), 94, 95
Whitehorn, R. D., 147–8
Whitehouse, W. A., 200
Whitley, W. T., 7, 11
Wicken, Joan C., 193
Wigley, Thomas, 212
Wilkins, A. S., 266, 267
Wilkinson, John T., 9
William and Mary, 89
Williams, Charles, 182, 228–29

Williams, Charles, Jr., 182
Williams, Florence, 183
Williams, John, 43–45, 49
Wilson, Joshua, 13
Wilson, Walter, 8, 9, 17, 31, 37, 40, 42
Wilson, William, 92
Wilson, Woodrow, 108
Winthrop, John, 239
Witsius, Hermann, 19
Wittgenstein, L., 119, 156, 160, 162
Wood, John, 86
Wood, John, Jr., 86
Woodger, Phyllis L., 95
Woolf, Virginia, 192
Woolston, Thomas, 72
Worthington, Hugh, 39–40, 41, 48–49
Worthington, William, 19
Wundt, W. M., 65
Wylie, Robert J. V., 6, 9
Woodhouse, John, 1

Yolton, John W., 57
Yule, George, 201

Zahn, F. T. R. von, 107

Index of Educational Establishments

Dissenting Academies

Blackburn Independent Academy, 23, 293
Carmarthen Academy, 46
Daventry Academy, 2, chapter 2, 101, 138, 293
Exeter Academy (3rd), 45
Hackney Academy (Unitarian), 138
Homerton Academy (College from 1824), 201
Hoxton Academy, 18
Kendal Academy, 16
Kibworth Academy, 11
Manchester Academy, 42
Market Harborough Academy, 11
Mile End Academy, 17
Moorfields Academy, 12, 17, 44, 292
Newport Pagnell Academy, 46
Northampton Academy, 10, 11, 12, 14, 16, 17, 28, 38, 43, 45, 47–48, 94
Rathmell Academy, 1
Rotherham Academy/College, 18, 181, 293
Sheriffhales Academy, 1
Taunton Academy, 1, 292
Warrington Academy, 11, 45, 46, 293
Wymondley Academy, 18, 293

Schools

Baswich House School, 185
Bootham School, 186
Clark's School, 194
Clifton College, 183, 186
Daventry Charity School, 51
Dawson's School, 37
Gentleman's School, 46
Hodgkinson's School, 39
Palmer's School, 39
St. Albans Charity School, 31
Silcoates School, 180
Tatop Farm School, 8
Taylor's School, 45
Wentworth College, 183
Women's Christian College, 183

Theological Colleges and Seminaries

Airedale College, 180, 181
Anglican Clergy Training College, 267
Auburn Theological Seminary, 102
Chicago Theological Seminary, 200
Cheshunt College, 101
Coward College, 2
Didsbury Wesleyan College, 267
Free/United Free Church College, Aberdeen, 64, 104

Index of Educational Establishments

Free/United Free Church College, Glasgow, 76, 79, 108
Hackney College (Congregational), 44, 179, 186
Hartley Primitive Methodist College, 267, 268
Hartley Victoria College, 276, 272, 282
Highbury College, 2
Homerton College, 2, 45
Lancashire Independent College, 3, 69, 179, 180, 182, 196, 267, 268, 277, 281, 282, 284, 285, 286, 287
Manchester Baptist College, 267
Mansfield College, 186, 188, 190, 192, 197, 199, 268, 270, 281
Moravian Theological College, 267
New College, Edinburgh, 58, 73, 102
New College, London, 2, 185, 195–201, 202, 204, 206, 228–29
Presbyterian Theological College, 2, 100
Richmond College, 197, 199
St. Boniface Missionary College, 192
Scottish Congregational College, 179
Spring Hill College, 101
Trevecca College, 235
Unitarian College Manchester, 267, 269
Unitarian Home Missionary College, 9
United Presbyterian Theological Hall, 98, 101, 105
Victoria Park United Methodist Free Churches College, 267
Wesley College Headingley, Leeds, Westminster College, Cambridge, 2, 85, 102, 107, 108, 116, 117, 120, 146, 148, 202, 270
Western College, Bristol, 108
Yorkshire United Independent College, 181

Universities and Other Colleges

Aberdeen University, 44, 74, 201
  Marischal College, 31
Anstey Training College, 193
Cambridge University, 1, 12, 87, 104, 108, 109, 185, 199, 268, 270, 274
  Christ's College, 1, 270
  Jesus College, 109
  King's College, 186
  St. John's College, 268
  Trinity College, 1
College of William and Mary, 37
East India Company's College, 37
Edinburgh University, 36, 46, 58, 59, 63, 103, 104, 107, 154, 155, 179, 182, 183
Erlangen University, 107
Glasgow University, 37, 58, 59, 64, 69, 73, 74, 79, 95, 103, 106, 154, 155, 179, 181, 199, 270, 283
Harvard University, 200
Leeds University, 277
Liverpool University, 281
London University, 2, 180, 188, 197, 198, 266, 268, 277, 281
  King's College, 197, 197, 199
Manchester University, 3, 199, 266, 267, 268, 277, 281, 282, 285, 286, 287
Nottingham University, 119
Owens College, 266, 267
Oxford University, 1, 12, 108, 109, 119, 154, 155, 187, 205, 220
  Balliol College, 187, 201, 244
  The Queen's College, 154
  St. John's College, 1

Index of Educational Establishments

Protestant Theological Institute, Cluj, 266
Rhodes University, 155, 161
St. Andrews University, 2, 58, 59, 154, 155, 180
Syracuse University, 102
University of Wales, 179, 277
Woodbrooke College, 193

Index of Subjects

absolute idealism, 62 69–72, 78, 103
Alnwick, 100–102
Anglicans, 100, 155, 183, 184, 190, 192, 196, 198, 206, 234, 254, 256, 267, 268, 275; see also Church of England
antinomianism, 7, 92, 219
apologetics, 64, 69, 72, 74–80, 102, 106, 107, 108, 116, 159
Arianism, 15, 18, 35, 37, 38, 40–42, 44–46, 94, 95, 135, 137–38
Arminianism, 11, 17, 35, 41,137, 219
authority, 26, 27, 89, 95, 96, 120, 122, 136, 137, 158, 166–67, 214, 221–22, 227, 231–32, 275

baptism, 11, 44, 138, 234, 239, 256, 272, 279
Baptists, 5, 7, 11, 31, 32, 36, 37, 47, 110, 191, 203, 206, 218, 239, 240, 247, 258, 267
Bible, 8, 11, 20, 27, 28, 35, 36, 42, 46, 125, 135, 139, 165, 186, 221–24, 248, 250, 253, 269, 277–78, 283, 286, 287
British and Foreign Bible Society, 110

Calvinism, 8, 11, 17, 35, 40, 41, 46, 59, 63, 69, 73, 90–92, 98, 116, 135, 137, 202, 219, 223, 239–40

Castle Hill Church, 11, 13–14, 45, 94, 231
Christology, 131, 139, 143, 216–17, 237, 285
church discipline, 238
church meeting, 135, 238–41, 256
church music, 31–35
Church of England, 37, 206, 235, 237, 282, 291; see also Anglicans
Church of Scotland, 58, 59, 63, 89, 92, 93, 95, 99, 100, 102, 155, 202
Cluj, 265–66
collective responsibility, 173–75
common sense philosophy, 60–61, 62, 63, 67, 75, 103, 170
confessions/declarations of faith, 6, 7, 92, 95, 125, 134, 135, 185, 191, 200, 214, 215, 230, 231, 238, 242, 255, 257, 271
Congregational Church in England and Wales, 280
Congregational Fund, 42, 201
Congregationalism, 3, 32, 41, 69, 107, 110, 135, 191, 200, 204, 206, 215, 230, 237, 238, 239, 243, 253, 256, 265, 267, 269, 274, 280–82, 284
Congregational Union of England and Wales, 282, 284
conscience, 17, 50, 69, 80, 95, 120, 121, 123, 142, 192, 193, 220, 226, 227–28, 235, 241, 244, 246–47, 257

Index of Subjects

Corinthians (1st letter to), 283–84
Coward Trust, 15, 16
creation, 78, 122, 148, 214
creeds and catechisms, 230–31

Daventry alumni, 35–46
Daventry curriculum, 18–20
Declaration of Faith (1967), 200, 238
dialogues, 155, 156, 206, 234, 254
Disruption, 58, 100, 107
Dissenters, 1–2, chapter 2, 93, 95, 138, 203, 224, 282

ecclesiology, 132–39, 232–42
empiricism, 64, 69, 115, 127, 129, 158, 161
eschatology, 248–52
ethics, 163–75, 274–75
evidences, 20, 71–74, 122, 129
evolution, 76–77, 97, 106, 127
experience, 17, 60, 61, 64, 65, 68, 70, 98, 118, 123, 128–32, 163, 165, 172, 203, 204, 214–16, 218, 219, 220, 221, 226, 233, 242, 250–54

faith, 27, 68, 76–80, 96, 118, 124, 126, 127, 129, 131, 137, 147, 158, 159, 161–63, 164–65, 168, 169, 171, 172, 174, 191, 212, 124, 215, 217–18, 227, 232, 235, 238, 239, 242, 248–51, 254, 279, 285, 286
Free Church of Scotland, 58, 69, 103
freedom, 11, 18, 22, 46, 60, 66, 71, 75, 93, 98, 123–27, 131, 133–37, 140, 142, 161, 163, 213, 222, 224–25, 227–30, 234, 241, 245, 248
funeral sermons, 22–29, 49–51

gospels, 271
Great Ejectment, 1, 228

Holy Spirit, 40, 134, 167, 173, 189, 214, 220, 221–25, 226–27, 243, 253–54, 258, 279–80, 286

intuitionism, 62, 69, 70, 73

John the Baptist, 272

King's Head Society, 17, 201
knowledge, 60–62, 64, 66, 70, 76, 77, 79, 80, 99, 103, 104, 108, 111, 116, 119, 123, 125–27, 129, 130, 161, 164, 212–13, 226–27, 254, 271

Lancashire Congregational Union, 282
logical positivism, 119, 157, 158, 160
Lord's Supper, 7, 44, 90, 95, 138, 196, 239–40, 276
Lutherans, 155

Manchester, theology in, 266–69
Methodism, x, 3, 8, 50, 74, 110, 192, 195, 197, 199, 233, 259, 267, 276, 277
Methodist Unitarians, 9
ministers, 241–42, 275–76
Moderates, 59, 63, 89
moral sense, 76, 173

New Light Antiburghers, 93
New Testament scholarship, chapter 8

Orkney, 84–86

parables, 273–74
personal, the, 161–63

philosophico-theological relations, 157–59
practical theology, 243–48
Presbyterian Fund, 16, 17
Presbyterianism, 2, 9, 16, 17, 32, 36, 38, 39, 42, 46, 47, 59, 89, 94–101, 103, 107, 108, 110, 135, 137, 190, 197, 224, 238, 247, 265, 269, 270, 275, 280
Presbyterian Church in England, 100
Presbyterian Church of England, 100, 101, 108, 110, 270, 275, 280

Quakers, 45, 182, 190, 193, 194, 199, 218, 220–22, 224, 226, 229, 233, 244, 246, 247, 248

rationalism, 58, 62, 64, 68, 121–23, 125, 135, 227, 231
reason, 24, 65, 68, 75, 77, 79, 106, 111, 120, 123, 125, 142, 157–58, 164, 203, 212, 219, 220, 222, 225–27, 235
reason and will, 225–32
Reformed, 90, 206, 231, 254, 255
Relief Church, 93–96
religious language, 160–61, 163, 172
Rossendale, 5–8, 10, 31–32

saints, 278–80
Savoy Declaration of Faith and Order, 135, 231
scepticism, 60, 68, 69
Scots Confession, 134
Scottish nonconforming traditions, 88–102
Scottish philosophy, chapter 3
Second London Confession, 7
Son of Man, 272
soteriology, 115, 131, 140–41, 143–44, 216, 217–18, 244, 248, 254, 275

theistic arguments, 65, 75, 77, 79, 80, 129, 158, 172
theology, 126–45, chapter 7, 266–67
toleration, 2, 89, 135, 245
Toleration Act, 1–2
Trinity, 8, 24, 138, 139, 166, 190, 214, 215, 246, 254

Unitarians, 3, 24, 35, 36, 37, 38, 39, 40, 41, 42, 44, 47, 100, 138, 206, 267, 269
United Presbyterian Church, 97, 98, 100, 101, 103, 107, 110
United Reformed Church, 256, 257, 280
United Secession Church, 94

Warminster, 190–93
Welsh Bible, 277–78
Westminster Confession, 95, 134
World Alliance of Reformed Churches, 156, 254, 265
World Council of Churches, 155, 246

www.ingramcontent.com/pod-product-compliance
Lightning Source LLC
Chambersburg PA
CBHW050619300426
44112CB00012B/1572